Hands-On GPU Computing with Python

Explore the capabilities of GPUs for solving high performance computational problems

Avimanyu Bandyopadhyay

BIRMINGHAM - MUMBAI

Hands-On GPU Computing with Python

Commissioning Editor: Pavan Ramchandani
Acquisition Editor: Heramb Bhavsar
Content Development Editor: Shubham Bhattacharya
Technical Editor: Rudolph Almeida
Copy Editor: Safis Editing
Project Coordinator: Nusaiba Ansari
Proofreader: Safis Editing
Indexer: Pratik Shirodkar
Graphics: Jisha Chirayil
Production Coordinator: Arvindkumar Gupta

First published: May 2019

Production reference: 1130519

Published by Packt Publishing Ltd.
Livery Place
35 Livery Street
Birmingham
B3 2PB, UK.

ISBN 978-1-78934-107-2

www.packtpub.com

I dedicate this book to my late maternal grandfather, Shri Sudhir Kumar Halder.

He was a great human being at heart and an amazing trigonometrician. I wouldn't have been able to write this book without his constant encouragement in the early days of my life, especially in mathematics, which is the foundation of computing.

I extend my love and thanks to my mother, Smt Uma Bandyopadhyay, who has been so constantly supportive throughout my journey of life, and also now as a researcher. I also extend my love and thanks to my father, Shri Amitava Bandyopadhyay, for being so supportive while I was writing this book, and for my new lab, which was very helpful during the book's development. I'm forever indebted to my alma mater, PVP Siddhartha Institute of Technology.

I would especially like to thank Christel Pilz, a loving grandma who has always been by my side to encourage and support me so selflessly during all my creative endeavors, especially when deploying the AMD Radeon VII GPU at my lab, which contributed to the book.

I would also like to thank my fellow tech enthusiasts, Siddhant Pati and Amlan Madhab Panigrahi, for being so supportive throughout my journey in PhD research. I would also like to thank my researcher friend from Peru, Antony Brayan Campos Salazar.

Finally, I extend my sincere gratitude and thanks to my PhD mentor and advisor, Professor Dr. Dipankar Chaudhuri, for being so continuously supportive throughout the development of this book and all of my research endeavors. I'm really very grateful to him for providing a flexible framework for writing this book while pursuing my PhD.

`mapt.io`

Mapt is an online digital library that gives you full access to over 5,000 books and videos, as well as industry leading tools to help you plan your personal development and advance your career. For more information, please visit our website.

Why subscribe?

- Spend less time learning and more time coding with practical eBooks and Videos from over 4,000 industry professionals

- Improve your learning with Skill Plans built especially for you

- Get a free eBook or video every month

- Mapt is fully searchable

- Copy and paste, print, and bookmark content

Packt.com

Did you know that Packt offers eBook versions of every book published, with PDF and ePub files available? You can upgrade to the eBook version at `www.packt.com` and as a print book customer, you are entitled to a discount on the eBook copy. Get in touch with us at `customercare@packtpub.com` for more details.

At `www.packt.com`, you can also read a collection of free technical articles, sign up for a range of free newsletters, and receive exclusive discounts and offers on Packt books and eBooks.

Contributors

About the author

Avimanyu Bandyopadhyay is currently pursuing a PhD degree in Bioinformatics based on applied GPU computing in Computational Biology at Heritage Institute of Technology, Kolkata, India. Since 2014, he developed a keen interest in GPU computing, and used CUDA for his master's thesis. He has experience as a systems administrator as well, particularly on the Linux platform.

Avimanyu is also a scientific writer, technology communicator, and a passionate gamer. He has published technical writing on open source computing and has actively participated in NVIDIA's GPU computing conferences since 2016. A big-time Linux fan, he strongly believes in the significance of Linux and an open source approach in scientific research. Deep learning with GPUs is his new passion!

I'm very thankful to Professor Rumpa Hazra, Teacher and Master's thesis mentor for her kind guidance, Mainak Bhattacharjee, Technical Assistant at my academic laboratory for his creative microbiology inputs and Argha Mandal, my co-researcher. Thank you Jithu Nair, Yumlembam Rupert Anand, Nilanjan Mukherjee, and Rakhi Chatterjee, for your constant support while I was building my own GPU Computing Laboratory. I would also like to thank Shubham Bhattacharya, my content editor, and the entire team at Packt, for providing the opportunity to create this book and bring the author out of me.

About the reviewer

Amlan Madhab Panigrahi is a BTech graduate who has just recently ventured into the IT industry. An experienced gaming/tech blogger by heart, he also happens to be a GPU computing and machine learning enthusiast. He loves and promotes community-driven learning by organizing technical events and workshops. Cosplaying as popular gaming characters also happens to be one of his interests.

When not gaming or developing something, you will find him sampling wonderful delicacies or traveling. This technical nerd is currently working at Accenture as an Application Development Associate.

> *I am thankful for Mr. Avimanyu's innovative and authentic work in educating the community about GPU computing and its advantages. The author has put a lot of effort and care into making the content simple and understandable. It was purely due to him that I was able to delve into the world of GPU computing. I would like to thank both him and Packt for making me a part of such an amazing project.*

Packt is searching for authors like you

If you're interested in becoming an author for Packt, please visit `authors.packtpub.com` and apply today. We have worked with thousands of developers and tech professionals, just like you, to help them share their insight with the global tech community. You can make a general application, apply for a specific hot topic that we are recruiting an author for, or submit your own idea.

Table of Contents

Section 2: Hands-On Development with GPU Programming

Preface

This book aims to be your guide to getting started with GPU computing. It will start by introducing GPU computing and explaining the architecture and programming models for GPUs. You will also be briefed about the minimum system requirements to get ready for some hands-on experience with GPU computing.

You will learn to how to set up an IDE and learn GPU programming with Python, along with its integrations, including PyCUDA, PyOpenCL, and Anaconda, for performing machine learning for data mining tasks. You will also learn how to port NVIDIA CUDA code to AMD ROCm HIP code that has been tested on the all-new AMD Radeon VII GPU with Linux!

Going further, the book will explain GPU workflows, management, and deployment. You will learn how to use the Anaconda platform to conveniently enhance your existing CPU-based applications with GPU code through CuPy and Numba. Steps to set up container platforms, such as Docker and Kubernetes, have been included. You will also learn to deploy your GPU code on Google Colaboratory (featuring a free-to-use AI inference accelerator – the NVIDIA Tesla T4!) and introduce AI principles to your normal GPU workflow.

During the course of the book, you will learn the principles behind GPU-supported machine learning platforms, such as TensorFlow and PyTorch, to help you bring efficiency and performance to your AI applications.

Toward the end of the book, you will learn about efficiently deploying GPU-supported deep learning libraries by setting up and using the Python-based DeepChem scientific library as a hands-on example in medicinal drug design. To enable easier understanding, a comprehensive illustration of various scientific concepts for DeepChem has been included.

Who this book is for

This book is aimed at data scientists, machine learning enthusiasts and professionals, application scientists, and computer science students who want to get started with GPU computation and perform complex tasks with low latency. Intermediate knowledge of Python and basic knowledge of C/C++ programming is assumed.

What this book covers

Chapter 1, *Introduction to GPU Computing*, covers the diverse impact of GPUs beyond the gaming industry. Conventional CPU models and accelerated GPU models are compared. A brief history and some fundamental concepts are discussed.

Chapter 2, *Designing a GPU Computing Strategy*, focuses on computer hardware-related discussions. You will gain knowledge on how to get started with GPU computing-friendly hardware. The impact on GPU performance will also be discussed, with a comparison of air and liquid cooling.

Chapter 3, *Setting Up a GPU Computing Platform with NVIDIA and AMD*, focuses on leading GPU manufacturers NVIDIA and AMD, with a comparison of their readily available programmable models. The differences in computing on both platforms will be highlighted.

Chapter 4, *Fundamentals of GPU Programming*, introduces GPU programming and three different platforms, namely CUDA, ROCm, and Anaconda. NVIDIA and AMD GPUs will be revisited here to explore the practical usage of GPUs with a selection of computer hardware platforms.

Chapter 5, *Setting Up Your Environment for GPU Programming*, offers a brief guide on choosing the most suitable IDE for GPU computing with Python. PyCharm will be discussed in detail, and its effectiveness as a GPU-programmable platform will also be illustrated.

Chapter 6, *Working with CUDA and PyCUDA*, teaches you how to install and configure the PyCharm IDE with PyCUDA. You will be able to develop your own code through Python after learning about how to make use of NVIDIA's CUDA API within Python code.

Chapter 7, *Working with ROCm and PyOpenCL*, introduces you to the open source world of GPU computing! You will learn about ROCm, and a CUDA converter called HIPify, to easily port GPU code for both NVIDIA and AMD GPUs. With PyOpenCL, you will be able to develop your own code through Python, after learning about how to make use of the OpenCL API within Python code.

Chapter 8, *Working with Anaconda, CuPy, and Numba for GPUs*, teaches you how to use Anaconda specifically with GPUs. This chapter will introduce you to writing pure Python code with CuPy, a GPU implementation such as NumPy, and another library called Numba for CUDA and ROCm.

Chapter 9, *Containerization on GPU-Enabled Platforms*, introduces you to the concept of containerization and shows you how open and closed environments work as local or cloud containers. You will learn about Virtualenv and Google Colab with hands-on exercises.

Chapter 10, *Accelerated Machine Learning on GPUs*, is a hands-on guide to installing, configuring, and testing your first GPU-accelerated machine learning program. Besides Tensorflow and PyTorch, we will explore nueral networks to get understand GPU-enabled deep learning better.

Chapter 11, *GPU Acceleration for Scientific Applications Using DeepChem*, is where a Python-based and GPU-enabled deep learning library known as DeepChem will be discussed in detail, with a comprehensive but simple introduction to the various scientific concepts behind it.

Appendix A, discusses various use cases wherein machine learning and Python work in tandem to enhance the data processing and analysis procedures.

To get the most out of this book

While I have tried my best to be as simple as possible in explaining the concepts in this book, knowledge of the basics of programming paradigms will be a big help to you.

This book uses the Ubuntu 18.04 LTS Linux operating system for the hands-on examples. Running the code on an Ubuntu system would, thus, be an ideal choice.

Download the example code files

You can download the example code files for this book from your account at www.packt.com. If you purchased this book elsewhere, you can visit www.packt.com/support and register to have the files emailed directly to you.

You can download the code files by following these steps:

1. Log in or register at www.packt.com.
2. Select the **SUPPORT** tab.
3. Click on **Code Downloads & Errata**.
4. Enter the name of the book in the **Search** box and follow the onscreen instructions.

Once the file is downloaded, please make sure that you unzip or extract the folder using the latest version of:

- WinRAR/7-Zip for Windows
- Zipeg/iZip/UnRarX for Mac
- 7-Zip/PeaZip for Linux

The code bundle for the book is also hosted on GitHub at `https://github.com/PacktPublishing/Hands-On-GPU-Computing-with-Python`. In case there's an update to the code, it will be updated on the existing GitHub repository.

We also have other code bundles from our rich catalog of books and videos available at `https://github.com/PacktPublishing/`. Check them out!

Download the color images

We also provide a PDF file that has color images of the screenshots/diagrams used in this book. You can download it here: `https://www.packtpub.com/sites/default/files/downloads/9781789341072_ColorImages.pdf`.

Code in Action

Visit the following link to check out videos of the code being run: `http://bit.ly/2Jb0liA`

Conventions used

There are a number of text conventions used throughout this book.

`CodeInText`: Indicates code words in text, database table names, folder names, filenames, file extensions, pathnames, dummy URLs, user input, and Twitter handles. Here is an example: "All the elements of the p and q arrays are set to 24 and 12 respectively"

A block of code is set as follows:

```
// Run function on 500 Million elements on the CPU
begin = clock();
multiply(N, p, q);
end = clock();
cpu_time_used = ((double) (end - begin)) / CLOCKS_PER_SEC;
```

Any command-line input or output is written as follows:

```
$ g++ cpu_multiply.cpp -o cpu_multiply
$ ./cpu_multiply
```

Bold: Indicates a new term, an important word, or words that you see onscreen. For example, words in menus or dialog boxes appear in the text like this. Here is an example: "Choose **New Project** from the PyCharm main menu."

 Warnings or important notes appear like this.

 Tips and tricks appear like this.

Get in touch

Feedback from our readers is always welcome.

General feedback: If you have questions about any aspect of this book, mention the book title in the subject of your message and email us at customercare@packtpub.com.

Errata: Although we have taken every care to ensure the accuracy of our content, mistakes do happen. If you have found a mistake in this book, we would be grateful if you would report this to us. Please visit www.packt.com/submit-errata, selecting your book, clicking on the Errata Submission Form link, and entering the details.

Piracy: If you come across any illegal copies of our works in any form on the Internet, we would be grateful if you would provide us with the location address or website name. Please contact us at copyright@packt.com with a link to the material.

If you are interested in becoming an author: If there is a topic that you have expertise in and you are interested in either writing or contributing to a book, please visit authors.packtpub.com.

Reviews

Please leave a review. Once you have read and used this book, why not leave a review on the site that you purchased it from? Potential readers can then see and use your unbiased opinion to make purchase decisions, we at Packt can understand what you think about our products, and our authors can see your feedback on their book. Thank you!

For more information about Packt, please visit packt.com.

Section 1: Computing with GPUs Introduction, Fundamental Concepts, and Hardware

In this section, you will be introduced to the world of GPUs by looking at the subject from a scientific, an industrial, and also a social perspective.

The following chapters are included in this section:

Introducing GPU Computing

Many years ago, I used to think that a **graphics processing unit** (**GPU**), more commonly known as a graphics card, was just a device dedicated to playing video games on a computer at their maximum potential. But, one day, while going through a textbook (*Advanced Computer Architecture* by Kai Hwang), I realized that I was unaware of a world that goes way beyond PC gaming.

Without a doubt, most consumer GPUs are manufactured to achieve those amazing graphics and visuals to enable some spell-binding gameplay. But there's a world that explores its application a whole lot further, and that is the world of GPU computing.

In this chapter, we are going to learn the basic ideas behind GPU computing, a historical recap on computing, and the rise of GPU computing. We will also read about the simplicity of Python and the power of GPUs, and learn about the scope of applying GPUs in science and AI. Summarized research work by scientists working in different fields through GPUs will help you in following the same.

In the final part of this chapter, we will be able to understand the social impact of GPUs by learning about more research work in fields beyond science. By the end of this chapter, you will have developed a general idea about implementing your own GPU-enabled applications, regardless of your field of study.

This chapter is divided into the following sections to facilitate the learning process:

- The world of GPU computing beyond PC gaming
- Conventional CPU computing – before the advent of GPUs
- How the gaming industry made GPU computing affordable for individuals
- The emergence of full-fledged GPU computing
- The simplicity of Python code and the power of GPUs – a dual advantage
- How GPUs empower science and AI in current times
- The social impact of GPUs

The world of GPU computing beyond PC gaming

If you are a PC gamer, you must be very familiar with the world of graphics cards. Depending on their specifications, you might also be familiar with how each of them would affect your gaming experience. Let's explore extensively what lies beyond that domain through the subsequent sections in this chapter.

What is a GPU?

A GPU, as the initialism suggests, is an electronic circuit that serves as a processor for handling graphical information to output on a display. The scope of this book is to go beyond just handling graphical information and stepping into the **general purpose computing with GPUs** (**GPGPU**) arena. GPGPU is all about the use of what is typically performed with **central processing units** (**CPUs**), which we are going to discuss in detail in the next section. The terms *GPU* and *graphics card* are used interchangeably very frequently. But both are in fact quite different. The graphics card is a platform that serves as an interface to the GPU. Just like a CPU is seated over a motherboard socket, a GPU is seated over a socket on the graphics card (comparably to a motherboard, we may think of it as a mini-motherboard but only to facilitate the GPU and its cooling).

What about computing? The word *computing* is most obviously derived from the word *compute*. To compute is simply to harness your own hardware to deploy applications with the help of your own programmable processes. Programmable processes are a set of rules defined by you that are always ready to operate at your disposal. They are, of course, based on your own algorithms, which allow you to address your own specific requirements, depending on the application at hand.

If you look at computing on a universal scale, you'd find that the specific requirement that we speak of in the previous paragraph isn't just limited to computer science. Computing can be inferred as a technique to calculate any measurable entity that can belong to any field, be it the field of science or even art. Now that we have described the terms *GPU* and *computing* individually, let's go ahead with an introduction to our primary topic: **GPU computing**.

As we can comprehend by now, GPU computing is all about the use of a GPGPU with program code that executes on GPUs. When a GPU programmer writes a GPU program, the primary motive is to handover a certain workload that is computationally much more intensive for a CPU to handle.

Within the code, the CPU is instructed to hand over those particular operations to the GPU, which are then computed by the GPU. When these computations are done, the GPU sends back all of this information to the CPU and shows that output to you. Since the results are computed many times faster, such work can also be called **GPU-accelerated computing**.

Conventional CPU computing – before the advent of GPUs

Before GPUs arrived, general-purpose computing, as we know it, was only possible with CPUs, which were the first mainstream processors manufactured for both consumers as well as advanced computing enthusiasts.

Both computational and graphical processing were handled only by them. This meant that both the tasks of processing and handling computation of input and showing its corresponding computed output on a display were all handled by a CPU.

The history of general-purpose computing goes way back to the 1950s, before GPUs arrived and revolutionized the concept. The 1970s witnessed the rise of a new era, when the first commercial CPU, the Intel 4004, was released by Intel in 1971. The first AMD CPU was also launched in the 70s with the launch of AM2900 in 1975. There was no looking back, and a new cycle of CPU manufacturing came into effect, bringing up a new range of microprocessors for every generation.

Though Intel and AMD are the popular competitors in the CPU sector, there are other manufacturers as well, such as Motorola, IBM, and many others. Qualcomm and MediaTek, in particular, dominate the mobile industry.

Since this book is going to be about GPU computing with Python, let's briefly look back at how CPU computing evolved, before Python had any GPU implementations developed. If we want to learn about the computing power of CPUs, we have to look into how modern CPUs evolved before GPU computing wasn't heard of or deployed.

Since the inception of the third generation of **Integrated Circuits (ICs)** and microprocessors, the thinking has always been about how much power you can put into a single chip to get the maximum performance out of it. In the early 60s, a chip used to contain just tens of transistors, but that number rose to tens of *thousands* during the 70s. In the 80s, it became hundreds of thousands, while today's chips contain billions. So, how much power can you put into a single chip to get the maximum performance out of it?

This is why CPUs are evolving continuously. During this time, both Intel and AMD invented new technologies to improve CPU design. Being in the same field, they entered into a 10-year agreement in 1981 to enable mutual technology exchange. Dual core, Core 2 Duo, and many other technologies became popular.

But, eventually, a time arrived when the need for a device to accelerate general-purpose CPU computing was acknowledged. That's when GPGPUs entered the arena and the processing power of general CPUs increased tenfold.

How the gaming industry made GPU computing affordable for individuals

Gaming is over a $100 billion USD industry. But way back in the 1950s, video games were purely made for academic purposes. Video games were a medium to demonstrate the capabilities of a newly invented technology. They were also a good application to test AI applications through tic-tac-toe or chess. But access to such platforms was still limited to computer lab environments.

 Spacewar became the first purpose-built computer game in 1962.

By the 1970s, the area of gaming started to change. Arcade gaming became very popular. The PC gaming landscape took proper shape in the 80s with programmable computers in almost every household equipped with popular games such as *Super Mario Bros*, *Donkey Kong*, *Prince of Persia*, and more.

The 90s saw the emergence of legendary games such as *Doom* and *Quake*, which radically changed the PC gaming scenario. Many PC enthusiasts and gamers developed an immense interest in understanding the benefit of PC hardware customization. Such options to customize PC hardware grabbed the attention of many to enable smooth gameplay and the best possible visuals at that time.

During this time, the console market also started to hit the roof, which continued through the 00s, with branded hardware shipped as a single unit. Later, many became curious about the specifications of these devices to learn about their full potential, and even today when a new console arrives on the market, it is a very common to debate about the GPU that lies inside the new console.

By 2016, there were over 2 billion gamers, and half of them lived in the Asia-Pacific region. As we can see, the rise of the gaming industry is known to many, and a graphics card is a necessary requirement to get the most out of games that can deliver some amazing visual experiences.

Integrated graphics, as seen in many Intel systems, could not keep up with the game developers' or players' requirements. So, a time came when the gaming industry took off massively and GPUs began to get much cheaper, enabling an affordable market of GPGPUs. Previously, they used to be very expensive when the PC gaming industry wasn't so popular. Computer scientists began to tap into this fantastic resource and so began an incredible adventure in the field of accelerated science.

 The NVIDIA GeForce 3 Ti 200 was the first ever programmable GPU.

One of the early significant breakthroughs with GPGPUs that were applied for scientific computing was the use of 3,000 Tesla GPUs for finding the chemical structure of the HIV protein in order to create better drugs for battling the virus, which affects millions. On a CPU computing model, the same effort would have required to be five times larger to pursue the same objective.

Due to the huge demand for PC gaming hardware and the GPU being a prime component for amazing visuals, the graphics card became a quintessential element of every PC used for video games.

Also, many individuals in the community of technology enthusiasts were not just gamers. Many of them included quite a number of programmers as well. So, that's when the magic happened, creating a new community for GPU programming.

The emergence of full-fledged GPU computing

From the first GPUs to the most powerful GPUs seen today, GPUs continue to make a noticeable mark upon society with limitless applications, as we are going to see in the *The social impact of GPUs* section of this chapter. For now, let's look into how GPU specifications evolved since they became available at much reduced costs, since the rise of the gaming industry.

GPU computing has massively grown in the last two decades with the creation of GPU **application programmable interfaces** (**APIs**) such as **Compute Unified Device Architecture** (**CUDA**) and OpenCL. These APIs allow the programmer to harness the parallel computational elements within the GPU.

Let's compare these two APIs:

CUDA	OpenCL
CUDA has been specifically written for NVIDIA GPU architecture.	OpenCL is not architecture-specific and is more commonly known as a computing standard. You can write OpenCL code for both NVIDIA and AMD GPUs.
CUDA is a proprietary API from NVIDIA available specifically for their GPUs.	OpenCL is an **open computing language** as the abbreviation suggests and is not limited to any particular platform. In other words, OpenCL is cross platform in nature.
CUDA programs can only be developed with NVIDIA GPUs.	You can develop programs on OpenCL, regardless of the manufacturer's brand, be it NVIDIA, AMD, or any other.
CUDA was first released in 2007, starting with version 1.0.	OpenCL 1.0 was originally released by Apple in 2009 and subsequent development was carried out by the Khronos group.
Over the years, there have been several releases of the API, with version 10.0 being the most recent release, on September 19, 2018.	The most recent version of OpenCL is 2.2-8, which was released on October 8 2018.

As we can see from the comparison, CUDA is now a leading API in the field of GPU programming. Some of the libraries available with CUDA are useful for linear algebra, fast fourier transforms, random number generation, and many other computational implementations.

The basic idea of a CUDA or OpenCL operation works with three steps:

1. Transfer data (meant for intensive computation) from the main memory to the GPU
2. Use the CPU to invoke the GPU kernel for computing on that data
3. After the results are computed, they are transferred back to the main memory from the GPU memory

Since its inception, CUDA has received great academic support and is backed by NVIDIA. As GPUs become better and better every year, new technologies and libraries also keep evolving to maximize the productivity of the previous process at minimum latency. NVIDIA GPUs are classified into different groups based on their compute capabilities. Starting from 1.0, the most recent compute capability number is 7.5, if we consider the recent GPUs based on the Turing architecture at the time of writing this book.

The different architectures of NVIDIA GPUs in chronological order are **Tesla**, **Fermi**, **Kepler**, **Maxwell**, **Pascal**, **Volta**, and the most recent one, **Turing**, which was released over the years. The different architectures of AMD GPUs (previously ATI), again in chronological order, are the R series of cards starting from **R100-R600**, **R670**, and **R700**, followed by the Islands series, **Northern**, **Southern**, **Sea**, **Volcanic**, and **Artic** GPUs. Since 2017, the most recent architecture is called **Vega**.

In 2016, AMD released a software suite called **GPUOpen** that can be used to create GPU computing applications for general-purpose usage. GPUOpen is not proprietary but entirely open source.

The rise of AI and the need for GPUs

CUDA paved the way to the development of libraries such as **cuDNN** for deep neural networks, which are essential in the field of deep learning as a new approach within machine learning and as a part of AI programming through GPUs. The cuDNN library can be installed and invoked within your developmental code.

AI studies began in the 1950s and led to the creation of machine learning. Machine learning has now evolved toward deep learning, which uses neural networks implementations to train AI algorithms on large datasets. Over the years, several machine learning and deep learning libraries have been created and are under active development, such as **TensorFlow**, **Keras**, **Theano**, and many others.

Going a step further as a subset of such machine learning libraries, new libraries dedicated toward specific scientific studies have also been developed. **Deepchem** is an excellent example of the same, developed with machine learning libraries, which we will study in Chapter 12, *GPU Acceleration for Scientific Applications using Deepchem*.

The creation of such dedicated libraries have made it easier for scientists to think more about developing useful applications rather than the creation of libraries from scratch. These efforts are more significant for scientists coming from backgrounds such as biology who want to deploy these applications as quickly as possible with a simplified understanding of code. Such applications also make collaborations between computer scientists and bioinformaticians much more convenient and easier.

So, why are GPUs needed for deep learning, machine learning, or AI? Before we try to understand the reason, it is important to know in brief what **big data** is. Big data, as the term suggests, involve the process of data mining and data warehousing on enormous amounts of data. As an example, let's take the study of genomics. In the field of modern genomics, the average size of data in a simple run of DNA sequencing generates can be up to 1 TB per run.

Computational data is not restricted in any particular field, but can belong not only to scientific but also geographical data. Think of the datasets the world map can generate. Historical studies based on archaeological datasets can also be quite large. Consider the example of the digital restoration of a priceless painting or artifact. The imagery data can be huge but perfect for use with GPUs, which have huge amounts of memory. Recent NVIDIA GPUs have up to 32 GB of video memory!

GPU computing can speed up the ability of a system to read such big data. When AI algorithms train on datasets (as is the regular process in deep learning), bringing in GPUs can reduce the training time by a huge timescale, and this is why the use of GPUs in machine learning can be so crucial.

Today's GPUs have thousands of cores, thus enabling a significant performance boost many times faster than CPUs. For the same reason, many machine learning developers now have separate GPU versions for their libraries.

As AI acceleration is now a new computing model and the era of AI has just arrived, GPUs are the perfect choice for students, professionals, and scientists to learn or implement AI for their research.

The Volta architecture, which we just mentioned, is an AI-focused architecture from NVIDIA. The GPUs belonging to the Volta micro-architecture from NVIDIA contain tensor cores, which are designed especially for deep learning. The introduction of these tensor cores enables a huge increase in the throughput and efficiency of deep learning applications. This new technology makes Volta GPUs perform training and inference tasks three times faster than the Pascal architecture GPUs. The **NVIDIA Tesla V100**, for example, is a Volta GPU and contains 640 tensor cores, hundreds of which can operate in parallel. *Tesla* is also the name of an earlier micro-architecture from NVIDIA, but it is no longer used to make GPUs. NVIDIA still uses it as a brand name, as a tribute to Nikola Tesla, a legend in the world of science.

Google is also quite ahead in the AI race with its own line of **tensor processing units** (**TPUs**). These TPUs are specifically built as **application-specific integrated circuits** (**ASICs**) to accelerate neural network-based machine learning. As these TPUs are extremely powerful, liquid cooling became a necessary step to get the best and optimum performance out of these AI accelerators. There have been three generations of TPUs to the present day. The most recent and third-generation TPU (3.0) can perform machine learning computations of up to 100 petaflops.

The simplicity of Python code and the power of GPUs – a dual advantage

Python is a programming language with syntax that is very easy to grasp and understand, especially for computational analysts from backgrounds other than computer science. Due to this reason, it is adopted quite whole-heartedly throughout the entire research community in the world. When we also consider the powerful computational capabilities of GPUs, a dual advantage is clearly noticeable, when combined with the simplistic nature of Python syntax.

The C language – a short prologue

The **C** language was created as a procedural and structured programming language, developed between 1969 and 1973 at AT&T Bell Labs by Dennis M. Ritchie. As the legendary programming language gave birth to many well-known and popular programming languages, software, and operating systems, we can never forget the contributions of the C language to the developer community.

The heart of the Linux-based OSes, the Linux kernel, was originally designed in C in 1991 by Linus Torvalds. This universal platform is found in almost every device, big or small. Without C, perhaps Linux would never had come into existence. There wouldn't be any Android phones either, as Android is completely Linux-based. There wouldn't be any C++ as well, without C, and the contribution of these two languages in the development world will always hold paramount importance.

From C to Python

Python is one of the greatest programming languages ever built. It was developed by Guido van Rossum in 1990. Today, Python is exhaustively used in numerous fields. **CPython** is the most popularly used interpreter and reference implementation of Python. C and Python's programming syntax are very similar. So, if you are migrating from programming in C to Python, you can do the transition quite quickly.

Even if Python is not your first programming language to begin with, it's a great way to get introduced to the programming world. Python can also be an ideal language for someone who is learning programming for the first time and choosing Python for the same.

Python comes installed by default whenever you install a Linux-based distribution. The present community of AI developers prefer Python over others for machine learning. **TensorFlow**, **scikit-learn**, **Theano**, and **Keras** are some good examples.

The simplicity of Python as a programming language – why many researchers and scientists prefer it

Python is loved by many to develop an application or utility due to its simple and easy-to-understand syntax. A novice user will not take long to get a brief idea on what a few lines of Python code are meant to deliver. For example, in C, we import other header files with the `#include` prefix, whereas in Python, we can simply use the `import` prefix. The latter clearly makes it easier to understand. Furthermore, the following example to print a simple text via both clearly explains the same:

The following is a program to print `Hello Reader!` in C:

```
#include <stdio.h>
int main() {
    printf("Hello Reader!");
    return 0;
}
```

The following is the equivalent program in Python 3:

```
print('Hello Reader!')
```

We can see an example in C for displaying `Hello Reader!` as an output. The same can be done with just a single line in Python.

Due to the extreme simplicity of Python syntax, many researchers and scientists who come from a non-CS background find it much easier to get started with programming in Python.

You can also use Python to develop your own programming language.

The power of GPUs

GPUs have come a long way from when they were used just for graphics applications. For decades now, their significance continues to gain attention in limitless fields of applications due to their unique advantages over traditional CPUs.

Empowered with thousands of cores, today's GPUs continue to be tapped into by both academia and industry in order to achieve amazing levels of parallelism in their research-focused applications. Massive CPU clusters can now be replaced with a few or, in some cases, just a single GPU server to deliver the same level of productivity.

GPUs have made it possible to create the next level of supercomputers to accelerate research on diverse fields. Big data can now be efficiently computed upon with the use of GPU parallelism. The latest NVIDIA GPU architecture is Turing, as we mentioned earlier. Some of its noteworthy facts and features are mentioned in the following sections.

With the advent of the era of AI, GPUs now are needed more than ever to handle the training of enormous datasets with various deep learning techniques. And looking at the progress in this landscape so far, it is evident that we are on the right track.

Ray tracing

In simple terms, **ray tracing,** as the term suggests, is the process of how the pathways of light (rays) sources are computed (traced) to simulate their behavior on different objects within an environment. So, ray tracing allows the differentiation between lightning and shadow scenarios to be much more efficient while simulating a 3D environment with a graphics engine.

NVIDIA's latest Turing GPUs have introduced this feature with their RTX series of cards, which, when enabled, allow a virtual simulation in modern video games and graphics to become many times more realistic. There are many older technologies being employed through graphics engines such as **HairWorks, PhysX**, and **Tress FX**, the last of the three being from AMD. The RTX GPUs have 72 Turing RT Cores, and can deliver up to 11 gigarays per second of real-time ray tracing performance.

Artificial intelligence (AI)

Simply put, AI is the process of mimicking human intelligence and behavior. An AI system is said to have passed the **Turing test** when it convinces a human that it itself is not AI but just another human. There are a plethora of fields where AI is used and applied. Some of these fields are science, health, commerce, and transport. All of these fields and more use AI for effective precision in carrying out computational operations on datasets involving loads of data.

NVIDIA's new RTX line of GPUs are also focused on accelerated AI.

With 576 multi-precision Turing tensor cores, they can provide up to 130 Teraflops of deep learning performance and 24 GB of high-speed GDDR6 memory with 672 GB/s of bandwidth—twice the memory of previous generation Titan GPUs, which are ideal for larger models and datasets.

Programmable shading

Shading is the process of varying darkness at different levels to perceive the depth of the shadow on a 3D object based on the intensity of light falling on it. **Programmable shading** is the method of using algorithms to compute such shading to simulate shadows of objects in a 3D environment at realistic levels.

NVIDIA's new RTX GPUs enable advanced programmable shading by taking it further ahead with variable-rate shading, texture-space shading, and multi-view rendering.

RTX-OPS

RTX-OPS is a new performance metric from NVIDIA to calculate the compute power of each of the RTX lines of GPUs. It is based on the following formula:

$$
\begin{aligned}
&\textit{Peak FP32 performance (in TFLOPS) x 80\%} \\
&+ \\
&\textit{Peak INT32 performance (in TFLOPS) x 28\%} \\
&+ \\
&\textit{Peak Ray Tracing performance (in Tera-OPS) x 40\%} \\
&+ \\
&\textit{Tensor Core performance (in TFLOPS) x 20\%} \\
&= \\
&\textit{Tera RTX-OPS}
\end{aligned}
$$

Latest GPUs at the time of writing this book (can be subject to change)

Founders Editions are manufactured by NVIDIA themselves: the card body, **Printed Circuit Board** (PCB), cooling technology, and, of course, the GPU itself. **Non-Founders Editions** have only the GPUs manufactured by NVIDIA. The card body, PCB, and cooling technology are all manufactured by aftermarket partners.

The latest NVIDIA GeForce RTX GPUs and their specifications in brief are as follows.

NVIDIA GeForce RTX 2070

This is the entry-level GPU in the RTX series with 42 T RTX-OPS, 1,620 Mhz boost clock speed, 8 GB GDDR6 frame buffer, and 14 Gbps of memory speed. Its Founders Edition comes factory overclocked at 1,710 Mhz and 45 T RTX-OPS.

NVIDIA GeForce RTX 2080

This is the mid-range GPU in the RTX series with 57 T RTX-OPS, 1710 Mhz boost clock speed, 8 GB GDDR6 frame buffer, and 14 Gbps of memory speed. Its Founders Edition comes factory overclocked at 1,800 Mhz and 60 T RTX-OPS.

NVIDIA GeForce RTX 2080 Ti

This is the high-end GPU in the RTX series with 76 T RTX-OPS, 1,545 Mhz boost clock speed, 11 GB GDDR6 frame buffer, and 14 Gbps of memory speed. Its Founders Edition comes factory overclocked at 1,635 Mhz and 78 T RTX-OPS.

NVIDIA Titan RTX

This is the most recent Titan GPU launched through the RTX series with 84 T RTX-OPS, 1,770 Mhz boost clock speed, 24 GB GDDR6 frame buffer, and 14 Gbps of memory speed.

The latest AMD Radeon RX Vega GPUs and their specifications in brief are as follows.

Radeon RX Vega 56

The Radeon™ RX Vega 56 GPU has 1,471 Mhz boost clock speed, 8 GB HBM2 frame buffer, and 1.6 Gbps of memory speed.

Radeon RX Vega 64

The Radeon™ RX Vega 64 GPU has 1,546 Mhz boost clock speed, 8 GB HBM2 frame buffer, and 1.89 Gbps of memory speed.

Radeon VII

The Radeon™ VII GPU has up to 1,750 Mhz boost clock speed, 16 GB HBM2 frame buffer, and 4 Gbps of memory speed.

Significance of FP64 in GPU computing

FP32 is a single precision floating-point format requiring 32 bits of memory allocation. Similarly, FP64 is a double precision floating-point format requiring 64 bits of memory allocation. FP64 allows high precision computing theoretically at 1:2 FP32.

It involves computing with double the number of bits as FP32, and hence many computer scientists prefer GPUs with the best 1:2 FP32 performance. Applications that require the modeling and simulation of physical environments with extreme precision and high accuracy computations will always need double precision accuracy at a high performance.

Therefore, FP64 GPUs become quite significant and absolutely needed for such purposes. But in the case of the non-computational processing of imagery or statistical data, FP32 would be sufficient. The RTX line of cards do not have FP64 support. The NVIDIA Titan V based on the Volta architecture is the latest NVIDIA GPU to support FP64.

The dual advantage – Python and GPUs, a powerful combination

The simplicity of Python code syntax enables the user to develop GPU applications with ease. The user might not be from a computer science background, but that does not stop them from contributing to research and development effectively and efficiently.

An important thing to note here is the use of an open source approach while developing Python-based GPU applications because only such a model would build transparency among the developer/researcher community and bring trust among users to use such applications to benefit humanity through any field.

How GPUs empower science and AI in current times

NVIDIA RAPIDS is a very recent example of using an open source system to carry out research related to science, AI, and other fields. There are numerous examples of research work in science that has been empowered by GPU acceleration. Let's understand its significance through some of these amazing research examples.

Bioinformatics workflow management

The following research paper is discussed in this section: *Managing Complex Workflows in Bioinformatics: An Interactive Toolkit With GPU Acceleration, A* Welivita, I Perera, D Meedeniya, A Wickramarachchi, V Mallawaarachchi (2018), IEEE Transactions on NanoBioscience, 17(3), 199-208, doi:10.1109/tnb.2018.2837122.

BioWorkflow is a GPU-accelerated workflow management system based on the Amazon cloud. The application uses three levels of parallelism:

- Parallel execution inside workflow nodes
- Parallel execution among workflow nodes
- Concurrent execution of different instances of the workflow with different user inputs

The Amazon cloud-enabled GPU-accelerated computing allowed achieving the preceding three levels of parallelism, which helped to reduce workflow execution times and enable high speedups by approximately two to three times.

Magnetic Resonance Imaging (MRI) reconstruction techniques

The following research paper is discussed in this section: *A survey of GPU-based acceleration techniques in MRI reconstructions,* H Wang, H Peng, Y Chang, D Liang (2018), *Quantitative Imaging in Medicine and Surgery,* 8(2), 196-208, doi:10.21037/qims.2018.03.07.

GPU programming enables the provision of more easy-to-use libraries and frameworks for programmers. The remarkable role of GPUs has been noted in medical imaging, image reconstruction, and image analysis in clinical applications. But, despite the same, there are still many challenges ahead.

GPU parallel architectures require the pipeline re design of reconstruction algorithms. Pre-optimization of algorithms for GPU computing would bring huge improvements, even over GPU-based libraries that people use to deploy GPUs with.

Digital-signal processing for communication receivers

The following research paper is discussed in this section: *GPU Acceleration of DSP for Communication Receivers,* Gunther J, Gunther H, Moon T, Proceedings of the GNU Radio Conference, 2(1), 2017, Pmc: pmc5695887.

In this project, digital-signalling algorithms were implemented in NVIDIA's CUDA API to harness the computational power of GPUs to accelerate digital-signal processing of huge amounts of bandwidth in real time. With Ubuntu 16.04 and a GTX 1080 Ti, 20 MHz of bandwidth was consumed.

Their ultimate goal was to implement the interference, cancellation, and demodulation functions on GPU hardware and achieve faster-than-real-time execution. They mentioned the demand for higher data rates, driving the need for acceleration even further.

Specifically, in separate sections of their research papers, they clearly describe how traditional CPUs are composed of a small number of cores (four to eight), surrounded by large cache memories and compare them to a GPU, composed of hundreds of cores (100-1,000, or more) and can support thousands of threads simultaneously. They highlight the limitations of CPUs as only being able to support a few software threads at a time.

The advantage of GPUs over **field programmable gate arrays** (**FPGAs**) is also highlighted. They are often used to accelerate digital-signal processing, by stating how GPUs can be programmed using well-known extensions of the C language, such as CUDA and OpenCL.

Studies on the brain – neuroscience research

The following research paper is discussed in this section: *BrainFrame: A node-level heterogeneous accelerator platform for neuron simulations*, G Smaragdos, G Chatzikonstantis, R Kukreja, H Sidiropoulos, D Rodopoulos, I Sourdis, C Strydis (2017), Journal of Neural Engineering, 14(6), 066008, doi:10.1088/1741-2552/aa7fc5.

BrainFrame is a heterogeneous acceleration platform to serve computational neuroscience studies in conducting numerous experimentation, which is often required for understanding how the brain works.

The scientists analyzed biophysically accurate neuron models, as such models are considered essential for the deeper understanding of biological brain networks. The BrainFrame system addresses the need for convenient programming and the computational requirements of the field. They made use of a **high performance computing** (**HPC**) platform that integrates three accelerator technologies, namely the following:

- An Intel Xeon-Phi CPU
- A NVIDIA GPGPU
- A Maxeler dataflow Engine

A Python package for the simulator-independent specification of neuronal network models called **PyNN** has been used in this project. The PyNN frontend allows the heterogeneous platform to be immediately accessible to a multitude of prior modeling works, which is essential for the wide adoption of complex HPC platforms in the neuroscientific community.

Large-scale molecular dynamics simulations

The following research paper is discussed in this section: *Graphics Processing Unit Acceleration and Parallelization of GENESIS for Large-Scale Molecular Dynamics Simulations*, J Jung, A Naurse, C Kobayashi, Y Sugita (2016), *Journal of Chemical Theory and Computation*, 12(10), 4947-4958, doi:10.1021/acs.jctc.6b00241.

Molecular dynamics (**MD**) in the scientific community can play an exceptional role in the discovery of new drugs to address a challenging disease. GPUs can accelerate molecular dynamics simulations to enable better productivity in drug discovery research. This paper is one of the many examples of GPU-accelerated molecular dynamics.

The researchers developed a parallelization scheme of all-atom MD simulations suitable for hybrid (CPU+GPU) processors in multiple nodes. Time-consuming real-space non-bonded interaction is calculated on GPUs, while other parts are done on CPUs. Acceleration of GPU calculations allows you to utilize the total simulation time for reciprocal-space (other) calculations on CPUs.

The two NVIDIA Tesla K40 GPUs accelerated the overall speed of MD simulations, while keeping good parallel efficiency. This development could be helpful for long MD simulations of large systems on massively parallel computers that are equipped with GPUs.

GPU-powered AI and self-driving cars

Self-driving cars have now become quite a buzz phrase. GPUs are now used extensively to power AI to take crucial decisions during travel. But there is a need for greater accuracy and reliability in this sector. Faster training on huge datasets for efficient deep learning can be heavily influenced by GPUs.

Research work posited by AI scientists

Artificial intelligence has been the talk of the town and has garnered immense attention in recent years. As a result, there has been much research encircling AI that has redefined the way we perceive technology. Lets talk about such examples from recent research in AI where GPUs have been extensively used.

Deep learning on commodity Android devices

The following research paper is discussed in this section: *RSTensorFlow: GPU Enabled TensorFlow for Deep Learning on Commodity Android Devices,* M Alzantot, Y Wang, Z Ren, M B Srivastava (2017), Proceedings of the First International Workshop on Deep Learning for Mobile Systems and Applications, EMDL 17, doi:10.1145/3089801.3089805.

This is an interesting project that was done by AI scientists on mobile GPUs who integrated an acceleration framework tightly into TensorFlow (as we mentioned earlier) to make good use of heterogeneous computing resources on mobile devices without the need for any extra tools. They evaluated their system on different Android phone models to study the trade-offs of running different neural network operations on the GPU.

They also compared the performance of running different models architectures such as convolutional and recurrent neural networks on the CPU only versus using heterogeneous computing resources (CPU and GPU). Their results reveal that the GPUs on the phones are capable of offering substantial performance gain in matrix multiplication on mobile devices. Therefore, models that involve the multiplication of large matrices can run approximately three times faster due to GPU support.

Motif discovery with deep learning

The following is the research paper discussed in this section: *YAMDA: thousandfold speedup of EM-based motif discovery using deep learning libraries and GPU*, D Quang, Y Guan, S C Parker (2018), Bioinformatics, 34(20), 3578-3580, doi:10.1093/bioinformatics/bty396.

A **motif** is a genetic sequence/structure that can be of biological significance, and thereby a path toward understanding genetics one step further.

YAMDA is a Python-based and GPU-enabled deep learning tool that can be used for motif discovery in large biopolymer sequence datasets that can be computationally demanding, presenting significant challenges for discovery in **omics** research. Omics relates to the study of genomics, proteomics, and metabolomics.

The challenges of one the most popular motif discovery software tools named **MEME** was addressed, highlighting its excessively long runtimes for large datasets. YAMDA takes care of this challenge as a highly scalable motif discovery software package built on **Pytorch**, a tensor computation deep learning library with strong GPU acceleration, highly optimized for tensor operations that are also useful for motifs.

YAMDA accurately does the same job as MEME but completes execution in seconds or minutes, which translates to speedups of over a thousandfold! Notice the connection between two different fields (science and AI) here!

Structural biology meets data science

The following is the research paper discussed in this section: *Structural biology meets data science: Does anything change?*, C Mura, E J Draizen, P E Bourne, (2018) Current Opinion in Structural Biology, 52, 95-102, doi:10.1016/j.sbi.2018.09.003.

Data science has a lot to do with datasets, and with datasets, you need some efficient machine learning tools to handle them conveniently. Machine learning tools, on the other hand, can rely on powerful GPUs for managing enormous datasets.

This research paper discusses the significance of both GPU computing and data science in the advancement of the field of structural biology. The researchers particularly mentions the use of deep learning libraries in drug discovery while also not leaving out the significance of the exceptional computational performance of modern GPU-equipped clusters.

Heart-rate estimation on modern wearable devices

The following is the research paper discussed in this section: *Unsupervised heart-rate estimation in wearables with liquid states and a probabilistic readout,* A Das, P Pradhapan, W Groenendaal, P Adiraju, R T Rajan, F Catthoor, C V Hoof (2018), Neural Networks, 99, 134-147, doi:10.1016/j.neunet.2017.12.015.

Heart-rate monitoring can be crucial, especially for diabetic and cardiac patients. **CARLsim**, a GPU-accelerated library for simulating spiking neural network models with a high degree of biological detail, has been used by the scientists to create novel learning techniques. This enables an end-to-end approach to estimate heart-rate in wearable devices with embedded neuromorphic hardware. Thus, it sets a benchmark for the neuromorphic community.

Neuromorphic computing is basically an engineering approach to studying the activity of the biological brain, in this case, the translation of ECG signals into a meaningful form.

Drug target discovery

The following is the research paper discussed in this section: *DeepSite: Protein-binding site predictor using 3D-convolutional neural networks*, J Jiménez, S Doerr, G Martínez-Rosell, A S Rose, G D Fabritiis (2017), Bioinformatics, 33(19), 3036-3042, doi:10.1093/bioinformatics/btx350.

Drug target discovery is the method of finding a potential site or pocket on a target protein where a small molecule can dock on to. This method has the larger goal of addressing a particular disease that the target protein is related to.

DeepSite is a protein-binding site predictor that uses 3D convolutional neural networks. The novel knowledge-based approach uses state-of-the-art convolutional neural networks. The algorithm learns by examples from 7,622 proteins from the scPDB database of binding sites using both a distance and a volumetric overlap approach.

The machine learning-based method that was developed by the scientists demonstrates superior performance compared to two other competitive algorithmic strategies. Users can submit a protein structure file for pocket detection to their NVIDIA GPU-equipped servers through a WebGL graphical interface to study and find new sites on proteins for potential docking.

Deep learning for computational chemistry

The following research paper is discussed in this section: *Deep learning for computational chemistry*, G B Goh, N O Hodas, A Vishnu (2017), Journal of Computational Chemistry, 38(16), 1291-1307, doi:10.1002/jcc.24764.

Computational chemistry is a branch of chemistry that uses computer simulations to address a chemical problem. It is very crucial in the field of medicinal studies. The researchers highlight specifically that the availability of big data coupled with technological advances in GPU hardware, which were both absent in the last century, have created a revolution. This has facilitated the advent of **deep neural networks (DNNs)**, which are completely different compared to the **artificial neural networks (ANNs)** of the last century.

The paper stresses on the effect of GPU-accelerated computing on computational chemistry and also discusses the difference between machine learning and deep learning models. One important point we cannot leave out is how this paper highlights the significance of an open source approach (both code and documentation) for training neural networks on GPUs as a strong reason for the rapid growth of deep learning in recent years and also its impact on academic research, which was revealed by the growing amount of deep learning-related publications since 2010.

The social impact of GPUs

Big data is everywhere and so datasets are also everywhere, meaning that GPUs and AI can be applied to any other computational field. Since we have already discussed how GPUs can contribute in science and AI, let's read about some more examples in other fields that reveal more about how GPUs can contribute to our society.

We are going to discuss some diverse fields here, but, of course, there are no limits!

Archaeological restoration/reconstruction

The following research paper is discussed in this section: *Automated GPU-Based Surface Morphology Reconstruction of Volume Data for Archaeology*, D Jungblut, S Karl, H Mara, S Krömker, G Wittum (2012), Contributions in Mathematical and Computational Sciences Scientific Computing and Cultural Heritage, 41-49, doi:10.1007/978-3-642-28021-4_5.

GPUs can be used to reconstruct archaeological data that could be of historical significance and value. A team of researchers used a highly parallelized implementation for NVIDIA Tesla GPUs using the CUDA programming library to reconstruct archaeological datasets of several hundreds of megabytes within a few minutes of time, thanks to GPU speedup.

Rendering the generated triangular meshes in real time allows you to view ceramics in an interactive manner. Automated segmentation of density allows you to isolate different areas of interest, which are used as features for archaeological classification. This revealed ancient applications of bronze scales, a characteristic technique of Este pottery from the 7th-6th century BC.

So, these techniques can be crucial in the accurate restoration of ancient artifacts that can tell us a lot about lost cultures. One great example where such techniques can be of significant value is the preservation of the Kailash temple at the Ellora Caves in India, which is a heritage site of ancient value, holding the key to lost values of a great time in humanity. GPUs can contribute a lot in the 3D reconstruction of such a priceless heritage site.

Numerical weather prediction

The following research paper is discussed in this section: *GPU acceleration of numerical weather prediction,* J Michalakes and M Vachharajani (2008), Parallel Processing Letters, 18(04), 531-548. doi:10.1142/s0129626408003557.

This paper highlights the emerging need of increased parallelism rather than increased processor speed for the prediction of weather and the climate. The use of large-scale parallelism is described to be ineffective for many scenarios, where strong scaling is required.

The GPU computing approach with fine-grained parallelism reveals an increase in speeds of nearly 10 times for a computationally intensive portion of the **Weather Research and Forecast** (**WRF**) model on a variety of NVIDIA GPUs.

Composing music

The following research paper is discussed in this section: *Machine Learning Research that Matters for Music Creation: A Case Study*, B L Sturm, O Ben-Tal, U Monaghan, N Collins, D Herremans, E Chew, F Pachet (2018), Journal of New Music Research, 48(1), 36-55, doi:10.1080/09298215.2018.1515233.

Artificial Intelligence Virtual Artist (**AIVA**) is a revolutionary AI creation that can compose beautiful music. The deep neural network has been taught to understand the art of music composition by reading through a large database of classical partitions written by the most famous composers (Bach, Beethoven, Mozart, and others). Just by acquiring existing musical compositions, AIVA can capture concepts of music theory and create new compositions.

AIVA is powered by CUDA, NVIDIA, Titan X, Pascal, GPUs, and cuDNN, which is a GPU-accelerated CUDA library for deep neural networks.

Real-time segmentation of sports players

The following research paper is discussed in this section: *Real-time GPU color-based segmentation of football players*, M A Laborda, E F Moreno, J M Rincón, and J E Jaraba (2011), Journal of Real-Time Image Processing, 7(4), 267-279, doi:10.1007/s11554-011-0194-9.

GPUs can be used in different kinds of sports. Here, we are sharing an example for the game of football. Please note we aren't talking about the popular EA FIFA video game here, but actual football players!

The objective of this project was to work in real time under an uncontrolled environment of a sport event, such as a live football match. A **Gaussian mixture model** (**GMM**) was applied as a segmentation paradigm to identify football players composed of diverse and complex color patterns by analyzing football-related live images and video. An image that demonstrates the use of segmentation in real-time is available in the included reference paper (*Figure 5*).

Time-consuming tasks were accelerated with NVIDIA's CUDA platform, and later restructured and enhanced, significantly speeding up the whole process. The code was around 4–11 times faster on a low-cost GPU than on a highly optimized C++ version on a CPU over the same data, which was being processed at 64 frames per second in real time. An important conclusion that was derived from the study is the scalability of the application to the number of cores on the GPU.

Creating art

GPU-powered deep learning can also create some amazing works of art that could be even compared to man-made masterpieces such as Munch's *The Scream*. Undoubtedly, the restoration of old and damaged paintings back to their original state is also quite feasible with GPU-powered AI.

Neural algorithms enable the understanding of how humans create and perceive artistic imagery. A Titan X GPU-powered AI can be about three times faster than naive per-frame processing while providing temporally consistent output.

The following research papers can be read to learn more about this particular topic:

- *A Neural Algorithm of Artistic Style,* Leon Gatys, Alexander Ecker, Matthias Bethge, Journal of Vision 2016;16(12):326. doi: 10.1167/16.12.326.
- *Artistic style transfer for videos,* M Ruder, A Dosovitskiy, T Brox (2016), Lecture Notes in Computer Science Pattern Recognition, 26-36. doi:10.1007/978-3-319-45886-1_3.

Security

The following research paper is discussed in this section: *Real-time multi-camera video analytics system on GPU,* P Guler, D Emeksiz, A Temizel, M Teke, T T Temizel (2013), Journal of Real-Time Image Processing, 11(3), 457-472. doi:10.1007/s11554-013-0337-2.

Parallel implementation of a real-time intelligent video surveillance system on GPUs is described here. The system is based on background subtraction and composed of the following:

- Motion detection
- Camera sabotage detection (the camera could be moved, out of focus, or covered)
- Abandoned object detection
- Object-tracking algorithms

As the algorithms have different characteristics, their GPU implementations have different speed up rates. When all the algorithms run at the same time, parallelization in a GPU makes the system up to 21.88 times faster than its CPU counterpart, enabling real-time analysis of a higher number of cameras.

Agriculture

The following research paper is discussed in this section: *DeepAnomaly: Combining Background Subtraction and Deep Learning for Detecting Obstacles and Anomalies in an Agricultural Field*, P Christiansen, L Nielsen, K Steen, R Jørgensen, H Karstoft (2016), Sensors, 16(11), 1904. doi:10.3390/s16111904.

This paper highlights the visual characteristics of a farmer's crop field where obstacles, such as people, animals, and others, occur rarely. Particularly, these obstacles are of distinct appearance compared to an empty field (which is the most usual scenario). With an algorithm called **DeepAnomaly**, deep learning and anomaly detection are used to exploit the homogeneous characteristics of the field to perform anomaly detection.

In a human-detector test case, it has been demonstrated that DeepAnomaly detects humans at longer ranges (45–90 m) than RCNN (a previously existent convolutional neural network with real-time object detection with region proposal networks). RCNN has a similar performance at a short range (0–30 m). However, DeepAnomaly has much fewer model parameters and a (182 ms/25 ms) 7.28 times faster processing time per image. Unlike most CNN-based methods, it allows high accuracy, low computation time, and has a low memory footprint, making it ideal for a real-time system running on an embedded GPU.

Automated drones are also being used in agriculture to water plants. Their implementation requires the use of deep learning, and hence GPUs are being used to accelerate such complex computations, with the help of NVIDIA Jetson-TX.

Economics

The computational benefits of GPU computing in economics is discussed in the following paper. A general equilibrium model with heterogeneous beliefs about the evolution of aggregate uncertainty is highlighted.

The following research paper is discussed in this section: *GPU Computing in Economics*, E M Aldrich (2014), Handbook of Computational Economics Vol. 3, Handbook of Computational Economics, 557-598, doi:10.1016/b978-0-444-52980-0.00010-4.

Toronto-based Triumph Asset Management (reorganized as Amadeus Investment Partners) is using GPUs for financial analysis. They explore tens of thousands of news articles every day to predict stock market situations and to enable better investment decisions.

Summary

In this chapter, we learned about the basic concepts behind GPU computing, the history behind its evolution, and its scope of use in diverse fields. We also learned about the simplicity of Python syntax and why this simplicity can be of great significance when harnessing GPUs for computational work. In the final section, we looked at the uses of GPU applications beyond just science and AI, and we looked at various fields, such as archaeology, weather, music, sports, art, security, agriculture, and economics.

If you are a gamer and/or a computing enthusiast, from now on, you will be able to better understand the computational aspect of GPUs and Python code. The various fields of applications that were discussed in the later sections of this chapter will now allow you to have a general idea about the limitless areas in which you can create your own GPU applications. GPU application users can come from any field of work or study; they do not necessarily come from a scientific background.

In the next chapter, we will read about the significance of the system components that center around the use of graphics cards to ensure their optimized usage.

Further reading

You can read the following research papers and articles to gain more knowledge about the topics that were discussed in this chapter:

- *How video games became a $100-billion industry*, J Desjardins (2017), (online) Business Insider: `https://www.businessinsider.com/the-history-and-evolution-of-the-video-games-market-2017-1`
- *Global Games Market Revenues 2018 | Per Region and Segment*, T Wijman (2018), (online) Newzoo: `https://newzoo.com/insights/articles/global-games-market-reaches-137-9-billion-in-2018-mobile-games-take-half/`
- *INFOGRAPHIC: A History Of Gaming*, PC Tech Magazine (2018) (online): `https://pctechmag.com/2018/03/infographic-a-history-of-gaming/`
- BMW and NVIDIA DRIVE partnership (online): `https://www.nvidia.com/en-us/self-driving-cars/partners/bmw/`
- *Nvidia Jetson TK1 vs TX1 for autonomous road sign recognition*, Antmicro.com (2016) (online): `https://antmicro.com/blog/2016/02/tx1-vs-tk1/`
- *NVIDIA Announces Jetson Nano: NVIDIA CUDA-X AI Computer That Runs All AI Models*, NVIDIA Developer News Center (2019) (online): `https://news.developer.nvidia.com/%ef%bb%bfnvidia-announces-jetson-nano/`

- *Real-Time GPU Color-Based Segmentation of Football Players*, M A Laborda, E F Moreno, J M Rincón, J E Jaraba (2011), Journal of Real-Time Image Processing, 7(4), 267-279, doi:10.1007/s11554-011-0194-9 (online): `http://webdiis.unizar.es/gaz/biblio/pdfs/Torres2010b_provisional.pdf`
- *How AI Can Accelerate Analytics in Financial Markets*, A Dave (2017), (online) The Official NVIDIA Blog: `https://blogs.nvidia.com/blog/2017/08/30/qualitative-financial-analysis/`

2
Designing a GPU Computing Strategy

The aim of this chapter is to introduce computer hardware with a GPU perspective and how to get started with GPU computing-friendly hardware. Though the GPU is the most important component in our complete read-through, knowledge of gathering all the other essential components to make the most out of the GPU is also quite necessary.

Therefore, the significance of such compatible computer components will be discussed to show their significance while configuring any GPU to derive maximum performance out of it.

An impact in the GPU health-to-performance ratio will also be discussed with a comparison of air and liquid cooling. Both types of cooling techniques will be discussed in detail by exploring different scenarios of usage and applicability. If you are looking to use GPUs for extended computations that can last for days, you can opt for custom liquid cooling to ensure a smooth lifespan of the GPU and operation at optimum temperatures on full load. This chapter discusses this subject in detail.

Branded PCs equipped with GPUs that are ready for deployment will be discussed, followed by a complete DIY guide on building a custom GPU computing setup based on three different proficiency levels, namely entry-level, mid-range, and high-end. If you don't want to build a custom GPU-enabled PC, you can directly skip this chapter and move on to Chapter 3, *Setting Up a GPU Computing Platform with NVIDIA and AMD*, after reading about ready-to-deploy GPU systems in the branded market.

The DIY walkthrough will guide you on how to build a GPU-enabled PC for hands-on GPU computing. The entry-level guide is focused on novice users and beginners who want to learn GPU computing on a basic build. The mid-range guide is meant for intermediate users who would like to use GPU-enabled hardware for learning and developmental purposes on a mid-range configuration.

In order to make the learning seamless, this chapter is divided into the following sections:

- Getting started with the hardware
- Building your first GPU-enabled parallel computer – minimum system requirements
- Liquid cooling – should you consider it?
- Branded GPU-enabled PCs
- Why not DIY?
- Entry-level budget
- Mid-range budget
- High-end budget

Getting started with the hardware

In this section, we will focus on the importance of GPU computing hardware as an essential part of setting up a GPU computing platform. We'll enlist all the hardware components required for building such a system. We know that this book is related to GPU computing. But, apart from the GPU, why are the other hardware components also important? Let's read on.

The significance of compatible hardware for your GPU

As per the scope of this book, the graphics card is, of course, our primary hardware component. But a careful assessment of the system configuration that it would be a part of is also extremely crucial. A self-assessment of the graphics card would make it possible to achieve the maximum performance from your GPU.

Why are you willing to carry out GPU acceleration? It is essential to answer this question to address your specific hardware requirements and also to plan an economic budget. Building a PC on your own allows you to maximize your price-to-performance ratio.

Beginners

Hardware requirements for beginners can be assumed to be a set of minimum requirements to get started with the basics of GPU computing. In the upcoming sections of this chapter, we will discuss them in detail by exploring different budget options you can opt for.

Intermediate users

Intermediate users are most likely to learn as well as carry out qualitative testing of their GPU applications on their systems. We will explore a range of mid-range budget configurations to fulfill those objectives.

Advanced users

High-end configurations are undoubtedly the preference of advanced and expert users. So, in this final section, we will look into the best options in hardware by considering best performance at reasonable costs.

So, let's discuss the following components individually with respect to a GPU performance perspective.

Motherboard

The motherboard is one of the most essential components you must consider. Also known as the main board, this is the interface that will interconnect all of your peripherals and components to work together in unison. Motherboard specifications play a crucial role in deciding whether your CPU and GPU are compatible enough to achieve maximized productivity. Whenever you purchase a CPU and GPU, there are a lot of factors you might consider. These factors are related to the latest technological offerings in the two processors and whether the motherboard would support them in order to deliver the same. We will discuss them in detail further throughout this chapter.

In general, motherboards are available in ATX, microATX (**ATX** stands for **Advanced Technology eXtended**), and Mini ITX (**ITX** stands for **Information Technology eXtended**) form factors. **ATX** specification was developed by Intel in 1995 to improve IBM's existing AT form factor in classifying different motherboard configurations. For general-purpose computing, the regular norm is to prefer either of the first two (ATX and microATX) for developmental work. Mini ITX is preferable for minimal configurations for home and office PCs:

Form Factor	Size in inches
Standard ATX	12 × 9.6
microATX	9.6 × 9.6
Mini ITX	6.7 × 6.7

Let's continue with the remaining hardware essentials that would all be connected to the motherboard.

Case

The PC case, chassis, or cabinet is where you build your system configuration. This unit is what would house your motherboard and its interconnected components that can dictate the size of the case you want, depending on the requirements of your internal hardware that would have to be accommodated within the case. PC cases are available on the market in different forms corresponding to standard ATX, Mini ITX size, and microATX.

A microATX motherboard is always compatible with a standard ATX case. But a standard-ATX motherboard will definitely never fit inside a microATX case. Hence, when purchasing a PC case and considering future upgrades, going for a standard-ATX model can be your preferred choice if you get a microATX board but later require an upgrade that requires a standard-ATX form factor.

While choosing a PC case, optimum cooling (air or liquid) options can also be an important factor to consider if you want your system to remain well-ventilated and cooled at all times, be it in an idle state or while on full load.

Power supply unit (PSU)

This is a very important specification you have to consider to ensure all your systems are adequately powered. Many people prefer using an online power-supply calculator to estimate the complete wattage required for their custom PCs. But in addition to just knowing the wattage requirements, a complete understanding of rails, voltage, and amperage can play a vital role in choosing the best PSU for your system. We will discuss them in detail in the *Do it yourself (DIY) desktops* section of this chapter.

CPU

When you develop your code and invoke the GPU for delivering intense computational tasks, the CPU will still be responsible for fetching the computed results back and reporting them on your display. The operating system and applications instances would all be running because of the CPU, which is why it should be good at multitasking. Hence, choosing an equally compatible CPU is also very essential in order to get the most out of your GPU computing programs. Choosing an unevenly matched CPU paired with a high-end GPU can lead to **bottlenecking**, which can restrict GPU performance, thereby not allowing you to get the most out of it.

RAM

Depending on your line of work, a basic GPU computing setup for minimal learning purposes can be sufficient with 8-12 GB of RAM. But if you are looking to perform some heavy-duty experiments, you may want to populate your system with more RAM. If you prefer to use **virtual machines** (**VMs**), you have to have adequate RAM to support them. We'll discuss more as we move on to the next sections.

Hard-disk drive (HDD)

When working with GPU computing systems, big-data storage is a primary thing to consider, since a huge amount of data is involved. High-storage HDDs fulfill this need when GPUs handle data in large amounts for computing or in the form of datasets for machine learning.

Solid-state drive (SSD)

Popular mostly because of its fast boot speeds, SSDs are also preferred for their ability to launch applications quite quickly compared to HDDs, which is a big plus for GPU-computing enthusiasts.

Monitor

A good monitor ensures you can visualize your 3D structures with greater accuracy and precision. So, such a monitor complements a good GPU very well. For experimental work, it is always preferable to work at least on a 1080p display.

Building your first GPU-enabled parallel computer – minimum system requirements

In the previous section, we discussed the main components of the required configuration in brief. Since this configuration is primarily focused on GPU computing, it calls for a minimum set of requirements, in addition to your GPU. Thorough research on these is very essential, regardless of opting for a branded pre-assembled desktop or an assembled version you built yourself.

Scope of hardware scalability

Minimum system requirements set the scope of your computing needs to a bare minimum. That means with such a configuration at minimum expenditure, you should at least be able to carry out specific types of operation you intend to do on that hardware. It is always good practice to opt for a hardware configuration that is slightly higher than your minimum set of system requirements to ensure better stability.

Depending on the nature of your work, you can broaden your expenditure focus on that particular component. After finalizing this, you can go ahead with planning the expenses on the remaining components accordingly. Through this practice, you can maximize the most out of your budget, as you are focusing on the most important component for your PC.

Let's look at it with an example application. Suppose you want to develop an application that involves handling a minimum range of 1-2 GB of data. In that case, you might want to consider a GPU with at least 3 GB of video memory. In addition to this, you would also want to have adequate amounts of storage if you plan store such output at regular intervals. In such a case, you can opt for a hard drive with 1-2 TB of storage space. So, apart from the GPU, a 5,400 rpm HDD would be sufficient with at least 1 TB of storage.

If we consider a different example, you might want to opt for an SSD or a 7,200 rpm HDD if faster loading speeds are your primary concern rather than storage when computing with your GPU.

As per your computing needs, we recommend that you have at least 8-12 GB of RAM for smooth operation, in addition to a current or recent generation CPU. This step will allow you to maximize your computing productivity. If we carefully manipulate our system components according to our computing requirements, achieving the best performance at the best price would become much easier.

Branded desktops

Currently, many leading brands are offering **high-performance computing** (HPC) workstations and GPU-enabled PCs ready for deployment. They range from low-end to mid-end to high-end specifications with their respective budgets. Depending on your requirement and application usage, you can opt for the specification you want. While assessing the prices of such ready-to-deploy systems, a careful assessment of price-to-performance is necessary. Some good precautionary steps to take are as follows:

- Compare the prices of the components present in a branded specification of your choice and compare them individually to the current market price listings
- It is also important to assess a particular configuration and its price to determine whether you are paying more than what you actually need to pay

These two steps will help you cut down costs at the time of purchasing a branded GPU computing system. We will discuss branded GPU-enabled configurations in a separate section later in this chapter.

Do it yourself (DIY) desktops

As the heading suggests, DIY is all about building your system from scratch, starting from the smallest component to the largest. To do this successfully, a thorough review of each of them is quintessential to coming up with the best possible configuration.

Let's go back to comparing individual components to those of branded PCs. We might come across many cases when opting for assembling a PC on par with the branded counterpart could cost much less in the long run. The savings you incur can be invested in making your PC even better than the branded model.

A DIY methodology gives you more freedom and flexibility in choosing your target system configuration. Since you assemble the system yourself, it becomes much easier in the future to diagnose any hardware issues you might come across. The reason behind this would be your familiarity with each and every component and their location within the case. In the case of a branded system, you might void its warranty whereas with an assembled system if you are sure of an issue you can troubleshoot it yourself or even upgrade your system with ease.

The **NVIDIA corporation**, as we mentioned in the previous chapter, provides great support to the academic community. So, let's begin by exploring the minimum system requirements to set up a GPU computing platform based on the three aforementioned levels of usage, and consumer NVIDIA cards.

This minimum set of requirements will be different for all three levels and is based on usage requirements. Here are three examples.

Beginner range

For a novice user who wants to learn the basics of GPU computing, a very low-cost PC that is compatible with a GPU such as an NVIDIA GeForce GT 730 4 GB should suffice for basic computing needs and learning programming on CUDA. This card belongs to the **Kepler** architecture.

Mid range

An experienced user already acquainted with professional work with GPUs would require at least a mid-range PC with a GPU such as an NVIDIA GeForce GTX 1060 6 GB. This card from the **Pascal** architecture would generally suffice for work that usually requires the testing and calibration of professional GPU applications.

High-end range

The high-end range of systems required by advanced users, preferably for scientific research, would require GPUs with higher amounts of video memory with at least 8 GB of VRAM. A GeForce GTX 1070 8GB card would meet such a requirement. But if the experimental data demands more, 11 GB is available on the 1080 Ti. Higher amounts of VRAM are also available in 12, 24, and 32 GB variants.

We will read more about such cards with their respective configurations later in this chapter. We will also learn how to use free online tools to plan our hardware accordingly, along with compatibility checks and individual pricing.

Liquid cooling – should you consider it?

Liquid cooling involves the passing of liquid through CPU or GPU blocks within a loop in order to reduce temperatures by a huge extent. Achieving such drastic reductions in temperature levels (up to 30°C) is not so feasible when implemented with conventional air-cooling methods. The following image shows a liquid-cooled system:

The temperature factor

When processors are busy at work, they obviously generate heat continuously as they compute. Depending on variable loads, the temperatures are also affected. The main goal behind cooling is always to keep such temperatures down, especially when the processors are operating under a full load. It is always good practice to also keep a check on idle temperatures.

Airflow management

Managing airflow in any cooling system involves a fan that may be attached to one of the following:

- A heat sink, in the case of air cooling
- A radiator, in the case of liquid cooling
- The front, side, or rear portions of the PC case

Considering the preceding three scenarios, these are the different ways you can configure a fan:

- A **push** configuration involves pushing air in through the attachment
- A **pull** configuration involves pulling air out of the attachment
- A **push-pull** configuration involves pushing air in through one side of the attachment and pulling air out of the other side
- A **pull-push** configuration involves pulling air out of one side of the attachment and pushing air in from the other side

It all really depends on how you set up your entire system to decide the configurations and also the kind of fan you use. We'll read more about heat sinks, radiators, and more in the *Do it yourself (DIY) desktops* section of this chapter.

Thermal paste

Thermal paste is a thermal compound that is applied to the surface of the processor before attaching the heat sink or block. This paste allows for the efficient distribution and dissipation of heat through the cooling unit. Some users prefer spreading the paste uniformly over the surface of the processor, while some prefer creating a pea shape in the center before mounting the heat sink or block over it.

Conventional air cooling

Before we dive deep into liquid cooling, it is essential to discuss regular air cooling. Conventional air cooling generally involves a heat sink and a fan attached to the processor with its board designed to lower the temperatures on the processor during its operation. When you buy a CPU, you are also supplied with an air cooler along with a heat sink within the same package. When you buy a graphics card, the GPU is shipped mounted with a heat sink and a fan on the card as a single unit, ready to connect to the motherboard.

Stock coolers

Both of these CPU and GPU coolers can be more specifically referred to as stock air coolers on a technical basis, where the term *stock* relates to their factory-shipped state. In the case of a CPU, you have to assemble the cooler yourself, but you need not do so for your GPU, as it already comes within a single unit as a graphics card. So, bundled coolers are referred to as stock coolers.

Overclocking

Overclocking is the process of increasing the factory-shipped parameters such as the clock speed of hardware components usually with the objective to boost its performance. These hardware components can be a CPU, GPU, or even a RAM module.

The basic idea regarding overclocking a component is to change its operational parameters in baby steps and check for stability. When a stable state is achieved by tuning voltage, clock speeds and/or other related parameters, we achieve an overclocked state for that component at an operational level.

So, what are custom/aftermarket coolers?

Custom coolers are those coolers that are separately available for purchase in the PC hardware market. Custom coolers are more popularly known as **aftermarket coolers**. With the help of these aftermarket coolers, overclocking becomes much easier, because when you manually change the operational parameters of a hardware component, operational temperatures can be greatly affected, and that is when customized cooling options can be extremely important. So, monitoring temperatures on overclocked components can be a lot more crucial.

Overclocking on stock coolers is not usually recommended. Preferring an aftermarket cooler is always a better choice and more suitable, as it is designed for such a purpose. In air cooling as well as liquid cooling, aftermarket coolers are available for both CPUs and graphics cards.

Air cooling is obviously not just limited to the CPU or the GPU; it is also used to keep the ambient temperature of your entire system main board and case.

Liquid cooling

Liquid cooling is the process of using liquid as a circulatory cooling agent for the processor under operating loads. Rather than using a heat sink attached to a fan, a cooling agent or coolant is used for the same purpose. This coolant is circulated through a block that is mounted and attached to the processor. A fan, or fans, connected to the radiator is part of this circulatory loop. Cooling loops are available as branded **all-in-one** (**AIO**) units, as well as custom assemblies.

Liquid cooling reduces temperatures by a huge extent and is great for executing lengthy operations that could last for days. Since liquid cooling keeps the temperatures really low, it is really good for the health and lifespan of the processor. So, it's preferred by many researchers, scientists, and professionals to empower scientific and professional applications that can take many days to complete execution. The most recent **tensor processing unit** (**TPU**) from Google requires liquid cooling for optimal performance that we mentioned in our previous chapter.

One point to debate here is that air cooling might require less maintenance compared to liquid cooling, but maintaining the latter is well worth it.

The specific heat capacity of cooling agents

The **specific heat capacity** is the amount of heat required to raise the temperature of a substance by 1°C. This factor is considered by many liquid-cooling enthusiasts when they are researching and looking for the best coolants.

Why is water the best liquid coolant?

Water has the highest specific heat capacity (4.18 J/g/°C) under normal conditions and is also readily available. As it is so easily accessible, water is the best form of coolant available for many overclockers who prefer liquid cooling. In water-cooling systems, distilled water is mostly used as a coolant. Some people also use raw **reverse osmosis** (**RO**) water. You might be surprised to know that you can temporarily bypass the filtration process of a home RO water filter and collect raw RO water (without the minerals) for your coolant requirements.

Branded GPU-enabled PCs

If you are not currently looking to build a PC yourself but want to get started with GPU programming straightaway, this section will help you decide the branded system that's best for you.

Leading PC brands offer HPC workstations and GPU-enabled PCs ready for deployment. Such systems are equipped with GPUs that range from low-end to mid-range to high-end specifications and have their respective budgets. **Jetson Nano**, from NVIDIA, is a cost-effective **System on a Chip** (**SoC**) like Raspberry Pi, built especially for AI-based GPU computing. The price is just $99 USD, apparently, as unveiled at the GTC in 2019. It is a great gizmo for beginners getting started with AI computing.

While comparing different brands, your best way to explore is to look into each and every specification of such systems in detail. Depending on your requirements and application usage, you can go for the branded system of your choice. Since our primary intention is GPU computing, the first component we should review in the system is the GPU. After a careful assessment of this, we should check the CPU it is packaged with to study the overall compatibility.

Let's look deeper into some factors that will help us in the long run.

Purpose

The purpose behind buying your branded PC can again be broken down into novice, mid-range, and advanced levels. All three purposes will be different and serve different goals. Beginner level is focused on learning, mid-range on professional tasks that might require referring to advanced concepts at work, while advanced users are more experienced and maximize the most out of their systems for their computational tasks.

Feasibility

It is important to study how feasible the system really is that you intend to use. A carefully prepared feasibility report will help you assess this in great detail. Some points worth noting are the following:

- How long do you intend to use the system?
- How long do you plan to carry out the operations for which you purchased the branded system?
- Do you plan some other nature of work on the system at a later stage in time? Will the system be able to meet such requirements in the future?

Upgradeability

The ability of the system to replace its parts with better ones is its upgradeability. The third feasibility point we discussed in the previous list will help you decide which system is the most upgradable. Some examples to explain this can be as follows:

- Suppose you plan to upgrade your graphics card after, say, a year. To address this requirement, you would have to keep a track of the dimensions of the branded PC case. Will it be able to accommodate space if the new graphics card is larger than the current one?
- If you plan to increase your storage space by adding a new HDD, will the current choice suffice?
- Is the motherboard in the branded PC compatible enough for better CPUs in the future?

Refining an effective budget

Earlier, we talked about the prices of the components that are present in a branded specification of your choice and comparing them individually to the current market price listings. When you add up the total cost of the individual components (including the PC case) that's used for every brand, you will be able to decide which of them offers the best price. This will help you a lot to get the same performance but at an effective price.

Warranty

It is a good step to evaluate the nature of the warranty that's applicable to your new PC. The most common type of warranty is for manufacturing defects, which are usually offered for one year from the date of purchase. Additional warranty options can be accidental damage protection and onsite services.

Accidental damage protection can save you a lot of money for unexpected incidents, such as liquid spills or unintended damage. Onsite services are one step ahead of the regular depot services. This means you don't need to worry about going to the service center to get your system repaired. Instead, a serviceman will be sent to your location to repair it.

One thing to be cautious about before upgrading your system when it is under warranty is to know whether you can do it yourself. There have been many instances where a warranty goes void when someone tried to upgrade a component in the system on their own. Usually, the upgrade process in branded systems under warranty is to first inform the manufacturer directly. So, you will not have to worry about the warranty going void.

Bundled monitors

Many systems are shipped with bundled monitors. In such a case, you might want to consider the price of the actual system and purchase a monitor separately to reduce the overall cost. Many systems are sold only as the PC case.

Ready-to-deploy GPU systems

There are many GPU systems specifically designed and fine-tuned for GPU-based computational work. They are available in different forms with both air-cooling and liquid-cooling options. The advantages of such systems are that they can be deployed very easily after purchase.

You only need to set up your GPU applications and henceforth you are ready to work on them right away. Some brands also come pre-installed with a set of GPU applications to enable better productivity for professionals and scientists. In such a case, all you would require is your set of parameters or programs to start running on them.

Some noted brands in this sector are **Microway**, **Advanced HPC**, and **Velocity Micro**. These brands are more suitable for institutions and firms than individuals.

GPU solutions for individuals

An effective way of searching GPU-enabled PCs that are shipped pre-assembled is to look for gaming PCs at different budgets and enlisting the GPUs in them. A comparison of their compute capabilities will help you decide which GPU would be most suitable for your experimental or professional work. It is a cheaper way for individuals to purchase a GPU computing system.

Branded solutions in liquid cooling

Many systems provide liquid-cooling solutions with AIO units both for CPUs and GPUs. This is a good option if you aren't going for a custom DIY loop. AIO units for CPUs have to be installed manually, but GPU AIOs come shipped as a single unit.

Why not DIY?

Here, we will revisit all the points of the previous section. But, this time, DIY options will make it more flexible and offer you a greater freedom of choice. Flexibility and freedom come from choosing each and every component that you are going to assemble yourself. It is recommended that you dedicate at least a month to researching different PC components on the market to build the best system possible on your estimated budget.

So, to build your system from scratch, let's start our DIY walkthrough with the most important component.

GPU

Without a doubt, this is our most important component, and is directly related to our subject of study in this book. If you are looking toward GPU computing applications that would also involve deep learning, it is highly recommended that you go for a NVIDIA GPU because of widespread support for such devices.

A GPU with good memory bandwidth and adequate memory is great for beginning computational work on your new system with a faster access rate to handle huge amounts of data.

CPU

As we have previously discussed, even though you will carry out the intense computational tasks on the GPU, the CPU will still be responsible for processing the informative results that are computed. So, it is good practice to choose a CPU with a good number of cores with efficient threading per core. For multi-GPU setups, the more **Peripheral Component Interconnect Express (PCIe)** lanes a CPU supports, the better it is for the GPU to handle data. An AMD Ryzen CPU can be an ideal choice for your first build.

Motherboard

Go for a motherboard that has enough features so that it can support your requirements for at least three to five years. Look for motherboards that allow you to upgrade other components of your build. Explore their features and upgradeability options in detail.

You may want to opt for a second GPU in the future. In that case, check whether you have extra PCIe slots on the motherboard beforehand. The PCIe is where you connect your GPU. Try to opt for a PCIe 3.0 motherboard if you can.

Similarly, look for expansion options for all types of components, such as RAM or other storage.

RAM

Considering you will be working with huge datasets, go for at least 16 GB of RAM. 32 GB would be great! Many consumer motherboards also have support for 64-128 GB RAM.

Storage

For your OS and the data, with which you will be working in real-time, using an SSD can be very ideal to enable faster boots and less loading time. To manage high amounts of data, HDDs would be more preferable for the storage of computed data.

PSU

Use a power supply calculator online to calculate the estimated wattage of your PC. Previously, we read that a complete understanding of rails, voltage, and amps in a PSU can play a vital role in choosing the best **PSU** for your system. Just going through the wattage specifications might not be enough.

A **rail** is an electrical wire in a PSU. If a PSU has three rails offering a voltage of 12V, that means it has three individual wires with a 12V supply on each of them. A 750 W PSU may be advertised, so even if it offers an amperage (current) of 50 A, the actual wattage would be as follows:

$$Power = Voltage\ X\ Current = 12V\ X\ 50\ A = 600\ W$$

So, the reason behind advertising the PSU as 750 W instead of 600 W would be the availability of other rails at lower voltages. There might be another rail offering 150 W, say, as 5V x 30 A.

So, please check such specifications in detail and know the maximum true wattage when you purchase your PSU. This can be extremely crucial because high-end GPUs can demand a lot of power.

It is always recommended to go for at least a bronze-rated PSU if not a gold one. Opting for a modular cable system will also make your job easier during cable management.

Uninterrupted power supply (UPS)

Choosing a good UPS can be a wise choice, especially when you plan to run long simulations or computations on your GPU computing system. To estimate the capacity required, you can use the following formula:

$$Minimum\ Volt\ Amperes = Power\ Load\ in\ Watts\ X\ 1.6$$

So, for a power load of 650 W, you would require a UPS with a capacity of *650 W x 1.6 = 1,040 VA*.

The battery backup would also be calculated with the following formula:

$$UPS\ Backup = Battery\ Ah\ X\ (volts/load)\ X\ (1/Power\ factor)$$

On average, the value of the power factor is *1.4*.

Alternatively, now, there are many UPS capacity calculators online where you feed your PC specifications and find out the right kind of UPS you would require.

Thermal paste

It is always good to have a sufficient amount of thermal compound available at all times. **Cooler Master Nano** is one of the best **thermal paste** brands. Usually, these are required for CPUs, but they are also required for GPUs if you go for a custom water-cooling loop.

Heat sink

Heat sinks are relevant in air-cooling systems that continuously absorb heat from the processor for distribution and dissipation through itself.

Radiator

Radiators are important in water-cooling systems because they help cool down hot water that's circulating through a cooling loop.

Types of cooling fans

Cooling fans come in different sizes, ranging from 40, 80, 120, 140, 200, and also 240 mm.

Mainly, there are two types of fans:

- **High airflow**: We are already familiar with such fan designs, as they are quite conventional and common in use. Airflow fans are connected to processor heat sinks and PC cabinet walls where there is less resistance and more airflow is required.
- **High static pressure**: These fans have their fins designed in the best way to manage air moving through radiators at high-static pressure. They have to be built differently considering the amount of resistance experienced when mounted with radiators.

So, for air-cooling systems, high airflow fans would be the first choice. But in liquid-cooling systems, high-static pressure fans would be the ideal preference.

Bottlenecking

This is a concept you must keep in mind to ensure you are able to use all your PC components at their maximum potential. When one component holds back the entire system from delivering its maximum potential as per capability, that component is said to be creating a bottleneck.

An example of a CPU bottleneck would be using an older-generation CPU with a current-generation GPU. However powerful the GPU may be, you cannot perform your GPU computing operations productively because the old CPU will hold it back, as it is not capable of facilitating the GPU with the necessary operations.

Similarly, an example of a GPU bottleneck would be using an older-generation GPU with a current-generation CPU.

Therefore, always remember this point when purchasing the CPU and GPU together and also when upgrading any one of them.

Estimating the build and performing compatibility checks

Sites such as `pcpartpicker.com` can greatly reduce your time and effort while you plan your target build. Not only does it help you plan the build, it also gives many more options such as saving your configuration, compatibility checks, and price estimation.

Let's also look into the same points we considered earlier for branded options and discuss them again from a DIY perspective.

Purpose

The purpose behind buying your DIY PC is again to be targeted down for novice, mid-range, and advanced users. All three purposes will be different and serve different goals. Beginner level is focused on learning, mid-range on professional tasks that might require referring to advanced concepts at work, while advanced users are more experienced and maximize the most out of their systems for their computational tasks.

Feasibility

In the previous section, we read about how a feasibility study can be so important for your system. But when you consider a DIY approach instead of a branded choice, it is very apparent how the same questions can be addressed again with more freedom and flexibility:

- For how long do you intend to use the system?
- For how long do you plan to carry out the operations for which you purchased the branded system?
- Do you plan some other nature of work on the system at a later stage in time? Will the system be able to meet such requirements in the future?

Upgradeability

Building the complete system from scratch gives you complete control over any minor or major upgrade.

Refining an effective budget

Online tools such as **PC Part Picker** can help you a lot in estimating a price for your complete system. You also have the option to manually add prices for components that aren't available on their database at that time.

Warranty for individual components

It is a good step to evaluate the nature of the warranty that's applicable to your new PC build. In contrast to a branded PC, you are eligible for the warranty on your individual components in your DIY PC. DIY gives you the freedom to upgrade your PC any time you want, without worrying about the warranty going void.

DIY solutions in liquid cooling

While you can also go for an AIO for your CPU when you water-cool your GPU, the general practice is to use a single custom water loop to circulate it through both the CPU and the GPU.

Assembling your system

Before going ahead with the assembly, it is essential to have all the manuals packaged with your major components. The documents bundled with your PC case and your motherboard include a lot of useful information. Usually, they have a quick-start guide with the detailed manual:

1. First, it is recommended to wear anti-static gloves or bands before you start assembling your system. A multi-purpose magnetic screwdriver is highly recommended during the installation.

2. Place the motherboard on an anti-static surface and raise the latch on the CPU socket to make way for the CPU.

3. Carefully mount the CPU on the socket by noting the correct orientation. The correct orientation can be understood by matching the design on the empty socket to the CPU pins. Bring down the latch and the CPU will attach firmly into its place.

4. If you want to use the stock cooler, it would already have the thermal paste applied. If you chose an aftermarket cooler (highly recommended), you will have to manually apply the thermal paste over the surface of the mounted CPU lying on the motherboard CPU socket. Choose the correct mounting plate for your CPU. The cooler manual will help you decide the same. Intel and AMD may require different plates for mounting the cooler.

5. After the CPU assembly is over, we can go ahead and fix the PSU (modular preferred) inside the case.

6. Carefully place the motherboard inside the PC case. Match the screws on the case to the motherboard's mounting points and fix them.

As we placed the PSU inside the case early on, cable management will be easier to follow. You can keep all the cables on the rear end of the motherboard so that you can get a nice look at all the parts of the motherboard.

Connecting all the power and case cables in place

Connect the RAM sticks to the motherboard. Slide them inside the slots gently until the two latches at both ends lock in firmly. If you find it inconvenient to do the next step because of lack of space to work, install the storage first before installing the RAM.

Now, we can install the SSD and the **hard disk drive** (**HDD**) on the case compartments. Connect their data and power cables too. You might want to refer to the case manual while setting up storage. Some cabinets may require the removal of additional HDD compartments to make space for graphics cards that are quite lengthy in size. Finally, install the GPU on the PCIe slot of the motherboard and connect the power cable carefully.

So, that should be it. You have just completed assembling your first GPU computing system!

Installing CUDA on a fresh Ubuntu installation

If all goes well, the system will boot up and you can go ahead and install Linux from a bootable USB stick. You can use a tool such as Rufus for this. For beginners, Ubuntu 18.04 is a great choice, as it has long-term support until 2028. After you are done installing Ubuntu 18.04, you can go ahead with the following simple steps to install CUDA on your system:

1. From the main menu, navigate to **Additional Drivers**. In this example, Ubuntu MATE 18.04 was used:

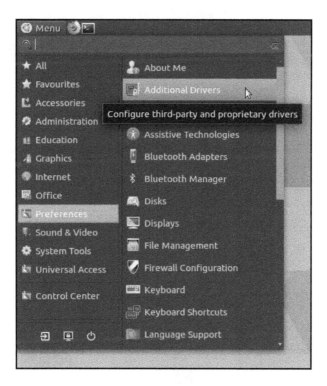

2. By default, Ubuntu doesn't use the proprietary driver but an open source alternative called **Nouveau display driver** by default. For CUDA, we would require installing the proprietary NVIDIA driver. So, select it and apply those changes. Here, it has already been done.
   Reboot the system after the installation is complete and you will see the effective changes if you open it once again:

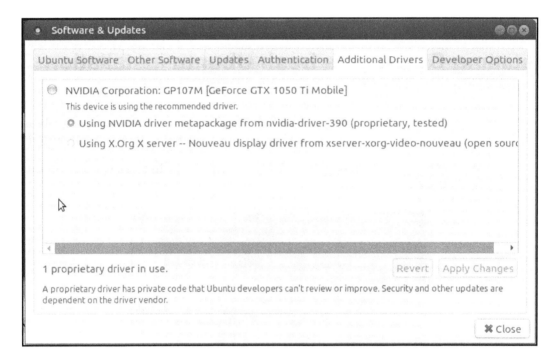

3. Now, open a **Terminal**:

4. Run the following two commands. The first one updates your downloadable package lists from repositories to their newest versions:

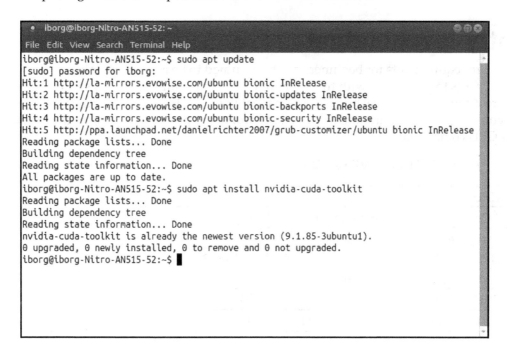

5. After the second command completes the installation of CUDA on your system, reboot it. In the previous screenshot, you can see that the NVIDIA CUDA toolkit is already installed.

Now, you can start writing your own CUDA programs on your system:

```
●  iborg@iborg-Nitro-AN515-52: ~
File  Edit  View  Search  Terminal  Help
iborg@iborg-Nitro-AN515-52:~$ nvcc
nvcc fatal   : No input files specified; use option --help for more information
iborg@iborg-Nitro-AN515-52:~$ █
```

As you can see, just entering the nvcc command gives you an error because **NVCC** (**NVIDIA CUDA Compiler**) couldn't find a file with a .cu for compilation.

In our forthcoming chapters, we'll also learn how to install more programs related to GPU applications.

In the following sections, we'll read about different configurations compiled according to three budgets: entry-level, mid-range, and high-end.

Entry-level budget

Hardware requirements for beginners can be assumed to be a set of the minimum requirements to get started with the basics of GPU computing. So, in this section, we will explore different entry-level budget options that you can also access on PC Part Picker. So, let's enlist the PC configurations with their approximate prices, according to the following CPU-GPU combinations:

- Intel CPU and NVIDIA GPU:

CPU	Intel Core i3-8100	$118.89
CPU Cooler	Cooler Master – Hyper 212 EVO	$24.99
Motherboard	Gigabyte H310M A	$55.14
GPU	Asus NVIDIA GeForce GTX 1050Ti 4GB	$201.12
RAM	Corsair Vengeance 2x8GB	$119.99
SSD	ADATA – Ultimate SU800 128 GB	$28.99
HDD	Western Digital – Caviar Green 1 TB	$44.89

Case	Cooler Master – MasterBox Lite 5 ATX Mid Tower	$55.98
PSU	SeaSonic – FOCUS Plus Gold 650 W 80+ Gold Certified Fully-Modular ATX	$89.99
Monitor	Acer – G226HQL 21.5 1920x1080	$89.99
Keyboard	Logitech – K120	$8.99
Mouse	Logitech – M100	$4.29

PC Part Picker Link: `https://pcpartpicker.com/user/avimanyu786/saved/pfzr6h`

- AMD CPU and NVIDIA GPU:

CPU	AMD – Ryzen 3 2200G	$93.99
CPU Cooler	Cooler Master – Hyper T2 54.8 CFM	$16.99
Motherboard	ASRock – B450M-HDV microATX AM4	$63.98
GPU	Asus NVIDIA GeForce GTX 1050Ti 4GB	$201.12
RAM	Corsair Vengeance 2x8GB	$119.99
SSD	ADATA – Ultimate SU800 128 GB	$28.99
HDD	Western Digital – Caviar Green 1 TB	$44.89
Case	Cooler Master – MasterBox Lite 5 ATX Mid Tower	$55.98
PSU	SeaSonic – FOCUS Plus Gold 650 W 80+ Gold Certified Fully-Modular ATX	$89.99
Monitor	Acer – G226HQL 21.5 1920x1080	$89.99
Keyboard	Logitech – K120	$8.99
Mouse	Logitech – M100	$4.29

PC Part Picker Link: `https://pcpartpicker.com/user/avimanyu786/saved/D6t299`

- Intel CPU and AMD GPU:

CPU	Intel Core i3-8100	$118.89
CPU Cooler	Cooler Master – Hyper 212 EVO	$24.99
Motherboard	Gigabyte H310M A	$55.14
GPU	Gigabyte AMD Radeon RX 570 4 GB	$149.99
RAM	Corsair Vengeance 2x8GB	$119.99
SSD	ADATA – Ultimate SU800 128 GB	$28.99
HDD	Western Digital – Caviar Green 1 TB	$44.89

Case	Cooler Master – MasterBox Lite 5 ATX Mid Tower	$55.98
PSU	SeaSonic – FOCUS Plus Gold 650 W 80+ Gold Certified Fully-Modular ATX	$89.99
Monitor	Acer – G226HQL 21.5 1920x1080	$89.99
Keyboard	Logitech – K120	$8.99
Mouse	Logitech – M100	$4.29

PC Part Picker Link: `https://pcpartpicker.com/user/avimanyu786/saved/pjV8YJ`

- AMD CPU and AMD GPU:

CPU	AMD – Ryzen 3 2200G	$93.99
CPU Cooler	Cooler Master – Hyper 212 EVO	$24.99
Motherboard	Gigabyte H310M A	$55.14
GPU	Gigabyte AMD Radeon RX 570 4 GB	$149.99
RAM	Corsair Vengeance 2x8GB	$119.99
SSD	ADATA – Ultimate SU800 128 GB	$28.99
HDD	Western Digital – Caviar Green 1 TB	$44.89
Case	Cooler Master – MasterBox Lite 5 ATX Mid Tower	$55.98
PSU	SeaSonic – FOCUS Plus Gold 650 W 80+ Gold Certified Fully-Modular ATX	$89.99
Monitor	Acer – G226HQL 21.5 1920x1080	$89.99
Keyboard	Logitech – K120	$8.99
Mouse	Logitech – M100	$4.29

PC Part Picker Link: `https://pcpartpicker.com/user/avimanyu786/saved/nTkZRB`

Mid-range budget

Intermediate users are most likely to learn as well as carry out qualitative testing of their GPU applications on their systems. Let's explore the four combinations with a mid-range goal.

- Intel CPU and NVIDIA GPU:

CPU	Intel – Core i5-8400	$399.79
CPU Cooler	Corsair – H60 (2018) 57.2 CFM	$69.98
Motherboard	Gigabyte – B360M DS3H microATX LGA1151	$69.99
GPU	Asus – NVIDIA GeForce GTX 1070 Ti 8 GB	$399.99
RAM	Corsair Vengeance LPX 2x16GB	$200.00
SSD	ADATA – Ultimate SU800 256 GB	$44.99
HDD	Western Digital – Caviar Green 2 TB	$89.89
Case	Cooler Master – MasterBox Lite 5 ATX Mid Tower	$55.98
PSU	SeaSonic – FOCUS Plus Gold 850W 80+ Gold Certified Fully-Modular ATX	$119.89
Monitor	Acer – G226HQL 21.5 1920x1080	$89.99
Keyboard	Logitech – K120	$8.99
Mouse	Logitech – M100	$4.29

PC Part Picker Link: `https://pcpartpicker.com/user/avimanyu786/saved/C6WsZL`

- AMD CPU and NVIDIA GPU:

CPU	AMD – Ryzen 5 2600	$150.98
CPU Cooler	Corsair – H60 (2018) 57.2 CFM	$69.98
Motherboard	Gigabyte – B450M DS3H microATX AM4	$73.98
GPU	Asus – NVIDIA GeForce GTX 1070 Ti 8 GB	$399.99
RAM	Corsair Vengeance LPX 2x16GB	$200.00
SSD	ADATA – Ultimate SU800 256 GB	$44.99
HDD	Western Digital – Caviar Green 2 TB	$89.89
Case	Cooler Master – MasterBox Lite 5 ATX Mid Tower	$55.98
PSU	SeaSonic – FOCUS Plus Gold 850W 80+ Gold Certified Fully-Modular ATX	$119.89

Monitor	Acer – G226HQL 21.5 1920x1080	$89.99
Keyboard	Logitech – K120	$8.99
Mouse	Logitech – M100	$4.29

PC Part Picker Link: `https://pcpartpicker.com/user/avimanyu786/saved/XbPkdC`

- Intel CPU and AMD GPU:

CPU	Intel – Core i5-8400	$193.99
CPU Cooler	Corsair – H60 (2018) 57.2 CFM	$69.98
Motherboard	Gigabyte – B360M DS3H microATX LGA1151	$69.99
GPU	XFX AMD Radeon RX 580 8 GB	$189.99
RAM	Corsair Vengeance LPX 2x16GB	$200.00
SSD	ADATA – Ultimate SU800 256 GB	$44.99
HDD	Western Digital – Caviar Green 2 TB	$89.89
Case	Cooler Master – MasterBox Lite 5 ATX Mid Tower	$55.98
PSU	SeaSonic – FOCUS Plus Gold 850W 80+ Gold Certified Fully-Modular ATX	$119.89
Monitor	Acer – G226HQL 21.5 1920x1080	$89.99
Keyboard	Logitech – K120	$8.99
Mouse	Logitech – M100	$4.29

PC Part Picker Link: `https://pcpartpicker.com/user/avimanyu786/saved/GPpvnQ`

- AMD CPU and AMD GPU:

CPU	AMD – Ryzen 5 2600	$150.98
CPU Cooler	Corsair – H60 (2018) 57.2 CFM	$69.98
Motherboard	Gigabyte – B450M DS3H microATX AM4	$73.98
GPU	XFX AMD Radeon RX 580 8 GB	$189.99
RAM	Corsair Vengeance LPX 2x16GB	$200.00
SSD	ADATA – Ultimate SU800 256 GB	$44.99
HDD	Western Digital – Caviar Green 2 TB	$89.89
Case	Cooler Master – MasterBox Lite 5 ATX Mid Tower	$55.98
PSU	SeaSonic – FOCUS Plus Gold 850W 80+ Gold Certified Fully-Modular ATX	$119.89

Monitor	Acer – G226HQL 21.5 1920x1080	$89.99
Keyboard	Logitech – K120	$8.99
Mouse	Logitech – M100	$4.29

PC Part Picker Link: `https://pcpartpicker.com/user/avimanyu786/saved/KXwbXL`

High-end budget

High-end configurations are undoubtedly the preference of advanced and expert users who are already experienced in the field. So, in this final section, we will look into the best options in hardware, considering the best performance. Feel free to tweak or modify the respective configurations, the links to which have been provided for each:

- Intel CPU and NVIDIA GPU:

CPU	Intel – Core i7-9700K	$193.99
CPU Cooler	Corsair – H60 (2018) 57.2 CFM	$69.98
Motherboard	Asus – ROG STRIX Z390-E ATX LGA1151	$238.89
GPU	Gigabyte NVIDIA GeForce GTX 1080 Ti 11 GB	$754.98
RAM	Corsair Vengeance LPX 2x16GB	$200.00
SSD	ADATA – Ultimate SU800 256 GB	$44.99
HDD	Western Digital – Caviar Green 2 TB	$89.89
Case	Cooler Master – MasterBox Lite 5 ATX Mid Tower	$55.98
PSU	SeaSonic – FOCUS Plus Gold 850W 80+ Gold Certified Fully-Modular ATX	$119.89
Monitor	Acer – G226HQL 21.5 1920x1080	$89.99
Keyboard	Logitech – K120	$8.99
Mouse	Logitech – M100	$4.29

PC Part Picker Link: `https://pcpartpicker.com/user/avimanyu786/saved/kDRtgs`

- AMD CPU and NVIDIA GPU:

CPU	AMD – Ryzen 5 2600	$150.98
CPU Cooler	Corsair – H60 (2018) 57.2 CFM	$69.98
Motherboard	Gigabyte – B450M DS3H microATX AM4	$73.98

GPU	Asus – NVIDIA GeForce GTX 1070 Ti 8 GB	$399.99
RAM	Corsair Vengeance LPX 2x16GB	$200.00
SSD	ADATA – Ultimate SU800 256 GB	$44.99
HDD	Western Digital – Caviar Green 2 TB	$89.89
Case	Cooler Master – MasterBox Lite 5 ATX Mid Tower	$55.98
PSU	SeaSonic – FOCUS Plus Gold 850W 80+ Gold Certified Fully-Modular ATX	$119.89
Monitor	Acer – G226HQL 21.5 1920x1080	$89.99
Keyboard	Logitech – K120	$8.99
Mouse	Logitech – M100	$4.29

PC Part Picker Link: `https://pcpartpicker.com/user/avimanyu786/saved/fhzr6h`

- Intel CPU and AMD GPU:

CPU	Intel – Core i7-9700K	$193.99
CPU Cooler	Corsair – H60 (2018) 57.2 CFM	$69.98
Motherboard	Asus – ROG STRIX Z390-E ATX LGA1151	$238.89
GPU	PowerColor – Radeon RX VEGA 64 8 GB	$399.99
RAM	Corsair Vengeance LPX 2x16GB	$200.00
SSD	ADATA – Ultimate SU800 256 GB	$44.99
HDD	Western Digital – Caviar Green 2 TB	$89.89
Case	Cooler Master – MasterBox Lite 5 ATX Mid Tower	$55.98
PSU	SeaSonic – FOCUS Plus Gold 850W 80+ Gold Certified Fully-Modular ATX	$119.89
Monitor	Acer – G226HQL 21.5 1920x1080	$89.99
Keyboard	Logitech – K120	$8.99
Mouse	Logitech – M100	$4.29

PC Part Picker Link: `https://pcpartpicker.com/user/avimanyu786/saved/YWQQZL`

- AMD CPU and AMD GPU:

CPU	AMD – Ryzen 7 2700X	$304.97
CPU Cooler	Corsair – H60 (2018) 57.2 CFM	$69.98
Motherboard	Gigabyte – B450M DS3H microATX AM4	$73.98

GPU	PowerColor – Radeon RX VEGA 64 8 GB	$399.99
RAM	Corsair Vengeance LPX 2x16GB	$200.00
SSD	ADATA – Ultimate SU800 256 GB	$44.99
HDD	Western Digital – Caviar Green 2 TB	$89.89
Case	Cooler Master – MasterBox Lite 5 ATX Mid Tower	$55.98
PSU	SeaSonic – FOCUS Plus Gold 850W 80+ Gold Certified Fully-Modular ATX	$119.89
Monitor	Acer – G226HQL 21.5 1920x1080	$89.99
Keyboard	Logitech – K120	$8.99
Mouse	Logitech – M100	$4.29

PC Part Picker Link: `https://pcpartpicker.com/user/avimanyu786/saved/X2s7WZ`

 Note that for all AMD GPU configurations, you can explore AMD's new platform called **Radeon Open Compute Platform** (**ROCm**). GPU computing on AMD GPUs is now possible through an open source initiative from AMD known as **GPUOpen**.
CUDA (proprietary) is to NVIDIA, what ROCm (open source) is to AMD.

Summary

In this chapter, we learned about the basic concepts behind PC hardware, the different components of a PC, and ideas so that you can build your first GPU computing system. Then, we focused on various PC-cooling techniques, particularly focusing on liquid cooling. After discussing options regarding branded hardware for GPU computing solutions, we discussed different PC components and looked at a step-by-step procedure on how to assemble them into a single unit. Finally, we listed four different CPU-GPU configurations for each level of hardware requirement with links for you to tweak or modify.

Now that we're at the end of this chapter, you should now be able to distinguish between different PC hardware components and also how to assemble them to set up a GPU computing system on your own. You are now acquainted with how liquid cooling works and you can now think of ways to apply such techniques to cool a CPU or a GPU in a computer system.

In the next chapter, we will read about different computing models on both NVIDIA and AMD. We will also learn about building systems based on the three listed configuration levels at the end of this chapter. We will revisit them again in the next chapter and discuss different ways to set them up in detail.

Further reading

You can read the following articles to learn more about the topics we discussed in this chapter:

- *NVIDIA Jetson Nano is a $99 Computer Built for AI, Powered by Ubuntu*, J Sneddon (2019), OMG! Ubuntu! (online). Available at `https://www.omgubuntu.co.uk/2019/03/nvidia-jetson-nano-99-computer-for-ai`.

3
Setting Up a GPU Computing Platform with NVIDIA and AMD

This chapter's objective is to introduce you to the world of GPU manufacturers and the leaders in the same field—AMD and NVIDIA. We will start with a history of various GPU makers from their inception, up to today. In the subsequent sections, we'll explore the scenario on computing on NVIDIA and AMD separately. After that, we will compare both of them before discussing the most recent GPU models from each of the brands.

The entry-level guide will be about a DIY walkthrough based on a basic approach targeted toward individuals who are looking into learning GPU computing for the first time. Four different CPU-GPU combinations that were highlighted in the previous chapter will be detailed on a step-by-step basis so that you can build them easily.

The mid-range guide will be focused on intermediate users who are already familiar with GPU computing and who are looking to gain more knowledge in the field. The four different CPU-GPU combinations that were highlighted in the previous chapter for intermediate users will be explored with an intermediate approach.

The high-end guide will focus on advanced users who use GPU computing for industrial and scientific applications, and it will explore different ways to maximize performance at optimum temperatures.

Different cooling options will be looked into while building such high-end configurations. The four different CPU-GPU combinations that were highlighted in the previous chapter for advanced users will be explored in detail with that approach.

The list of each of the entry-level, mid-range, and high-end components will be recompiled, and more of these configurations will be explored.

GPU manufacturers

Before we go ahead with the different computing platforms and modules on AMD/NVIDIA, let's first look into how the first GPU came into being.

Though the term *GPU* was first coined by NVIDIA, the IBM **Professional Graphics Controller** (**PGA**) was one of the first 2D/3D video cards that was released for the PC in 1984. It used an onboard Intel 8088 microprocessor to handle the processing of all video-related tasks instead of the CPU for video processing (such as the drawing and coloring of filled polygons).

Due to a high price tag of around $5,500 and incompatibility with many programs and non-IBM systems during that time, it could not gain a significant hold on the industry. But, even then, the PGA did establish a standardized model for hardware 2D/3D acceleration as a separate on-board processor, marking an important step in GPU evolution to improve the framework of separately using a processor for graphics computation.

Silicon Graphics Inc. (**SGI**) released OpenGL in 1989; it was widely used and supported as a cross-platform 2D/3D **Application Programming Interface** (**API**). So, through OpenCL support, SGI was also a significant contributor to the design evolution of modern graphics hardware.

In 1993, SGI released its **RealityEngine** board for graphics-processing with distinct boards and logic chips. The CPU handled the graphics pipeline for the first half. For its second half, the RealityEngine board took over to handle the various later stages of the graphics pipeline with fixed data flow through each stage. SGI cards were used mostly on workstations in the 90s.

Leading 3D graphics hardware makers in the 90s, such as 3DFX, NVIDIA, ATI, and Matrox, started offering 3D graphics boards for consumers. 3DFX launched its **Voodoo** lineup, and NVIDIA released **Riva TNT**. ATI (which at this point had been acquired by AMD) launched **Rage**, and Matrox released their **Millennium** series of cards. Games such as *Quake* and *Doom* became really popular on these platforms, pushing the gaming industry to greater heights while encouraging GPU adoption as we know today.

First generation

The 3DFX Voodoo was extremely popular during its time (1996). It was considered one of the first true 3D game cards. It offered only 3D acceleration and depended on a separate 2D accelerator.

It had the following specifications:

- It operated over the PCI bus
- It had a million transistors
- It had 4 MB of 64-bit DRAM
- It had a 50 MHz core clock speed

Voodoo provided texture mapping, z-buffering, and rasterization, but it still depended on the CPU for vertex transformations.

Second generation

The first GPU was released by NVIDIA on August 31, 1999, known as **GeForce 256**. Capable of billions of calculations per second and processing 10 million polygons per second, it had 23 million transistors, 32 MB of 128-bit DRAM, 120 MHz core clock speed, and four 64-bit pipelines for rendering.

The **accelerated graphics port (AGP)** was first used by this generation of cards instead of the PCI bus, and the new graphics features they offered in hardware were multi-texturing, bump maps, light maps, and hardware geometry transform and lighting.

On this generation of cards, once the programmer sent graphics data into the GPU's pipeline, it could not be modified. So, such pipelines came to be known as **fixed function pipelines**. This was a disadvantage because it resulted in inflexible graphical effects. Such hardware could not utilize the up-to-date standards defined by OpenGL and DirectX APIs, and hence were left behind in that aspect, even though they were much faster.

Third generation

NVIDIA released GeForce 3 in 2001, and that gave programmers the ability to program on parts of the previously non-programmable pipeline we spoke of in the previous section. They could now send data along shaders with the ability to operate on it while being in the pipeline. The shader programs were small kernels, written in assembly-like shader languages. For the first time, a limited amount of programmability in the vertex-processing stage of the pipeline became possible. NVIDIA's competitor, ATI, also had its Radeon 8500 card available for consumers at the same time.

The GeForce 3 GPU had 57 million transistors, 64 MB of 128-bit DDR DRAM, with a 200 MHz core clock speed.

The Radeon 8500 GPU had 60 million transistors, 64 MB of 128-bit DDR DRAM, a 275 MHz core clock speed, and it also had a 128 MB variant available.

Fourth generation

The first fully programmable GPUs arrived at the launch of the **NVIDIA GeForce FX** and **ATI Radeon 9700**.

These cards allowed per-pixel operations with programmable vertex and pixel shaders. They allowed limited user-specified mapping of input-output data operations and served as separate, dedicated hardware that was allocated for pixel shader and vertex shader processing.

The ATI Radeon 9700 released in 2002 had 110 million transistors, 128 MB of 256-bit DDR DRAM, and a 275 MHz core clock speed.

There was another 9500 Pro that budget buyers were extremely fond of due to its 8-pixel pipelines and resulting fast performance. Some PC enthusiasts were able to modify it into a 9700 non-Pro!

The first GeForce FX (FX 5200) was released in 2003 with 45 million transistors, 128 MB of 128-bit DDR DRAM, and a 250 MHz core clock speed.

With the introduction of DirectX 9 in 2003, the era of GPU computing had just arrived! GPU hardware became fully programmable for non-graphics accessibility (general-purpose computing). Full floating-point support and advanced texture processing started to show up in cards.

Fifth generation

According to Moore's law, the number of transistors in a dense integrated circuit doubles about every two years. But from 2003 through 2004, the rate of GPU hardware technology was accelerating at a rate much faster than Moore's law. **NVIDIA GeForce 6** and **ATI Radeon X800** were some of the first cards to use the PCI-express bus in 2004. Early high-level GPU languages such as Brook and Sh had been developed for GPU programming. They offered greater control through true conditionals, loops, and dynamic flow control in shader programs. On the hardware side, some new features that were being introduced were higher precision (64-bit double support), multiple rendering buffers, increased GPU memory, and texture access.

The NVIDIA GeForce 6800 Ultra Extreme had 222 million transistors, 256 MB of 256-bit GDDR3 DRAM with a 450 MHz core clock speed.

The ATI Radeon X800 XT Platinum had 160 million transistors, 256 MB of 256-bit GDDR3 DRAM with a 520 MHz core clock speed.

A new trend started to take shape toward GPU programmability. A GPU started to be seen as a great harness as an alternative processor for non-graphics applications. It began to be realized that a GPU can serve as a large amount of programmable floating-point horsepower and memory bandwidth that can be exploited purely for computationally intensive calculations! En route to the sixth generation!

Sixth generation

NVIDIA released their GeForce 8 series of GPUs as massively parallel processors in 2006. It was also the same year in July when AMD acquired ATI for $5.4 billion.

In 2007, CUDA was released as a freely available proprietary API by NVIDIA, only for NVIDIA GPUs. Through the years, CUDA became very popular in academia and industry for GPU computing. C/C++ programmers began their journey with the NVCC compiler from CUDA:

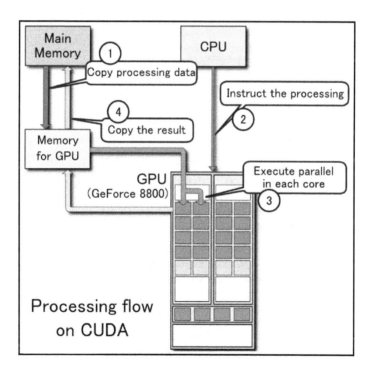

The preceding diagram describes in a simple manner how intense computations are accelerated on a GPU with CUDA.

Seventh generation and beyond

In early 2010, NVIDIA's **Fermi** architecture was introduced for GPGPU computing. The new features it brought were the following:

- True HW cache hierarchy
- **Error-correcting Code** (**ECC**)
- Unified memory address space
- Concurrent kernel execution
- Better double-precision performance
- Dual warp schedulers

The GTX 480 was launched with 480 CUDA cores: 15 streaming multiprocessors, each with 32 CUDA cores.

An AMD equivalent card to the GTX 480 was the Radeon HD 5870. The HD 5000, 6000, and 7000 families were launched between 2010 and 2012. AMD's Radeon HD 5000 family had a particular advantage over NVIDIA's products at that time.

AMD announced the first generation **accelerated processing units** (**APUs**), **Llano** for high-performance and **Brazos** for low-power devices, in January 2011. These 64-bit microprocessors were designed to function as a CPU and GPU on a single die. Thus, APUs were deemed to be more powerful than Intel's integrated graphics.

NVIDIA grew dominant in the HPC and self-driving car industry with its GPUs. From 2010-2017, it launched the GTX 500, 600, 700, 800, 900, and 10 series of GPUs.

In 2016, AMD launched a new open source initiative called **GPUOpen**. Within this initiative, **ROCm (Radeon Open Compute Platform)** was introduced. This was a fresh new start for AMD. For the first time, an open source alternative to CUDA had arrived! Like CUDA's NVCC compiler driver, ROCm released the open source HCC compiler. During its launch, AMD highlighted the open source advantage in one of its early presentations:

> *"Through GPUOpen, we can notice the significance of an open source model, making the compiler much more programmer friendly to allow better debugging!"*

In addition to HCC, ROCm also includes HIP, which can be very useful for converting CUDA code into portable C++. HIP can be used for GPU computing on both NVIDIA and AMD GPUs. OpenCL is also a part of the ROCm stack.

In 2017, AMD launched its **Vega** series of GPUs. In 2018, NVIDIA launched its new RTX line of GPUs with tensor cores specialized for deep learning (a subset of machine learning).

In 2019, AMD announced its new Vega 20 GPU, namely the **Radeon VII**.

So, we can note how the competition between NVIDIA and ATI continues to evolve; it now continues between NVIDIA and AMD, since the latter acquired ATI in 2006.

Let's now look deeper into NVIDIA's computing platforms in the next section.

Computing on NVIDIA GPUs

NVIDIA has three notable GPU platforms, namely **GeForce**, **Quadro**, and **Tesla,** that support general- purpose computation. At the higher end of the GeForce series are the consumer-level GPUs that GPU computing enthusiasts are usually interested in for running GPU-accelerated applications at a lower budget range (with the exception of the Titan series). On the higher budget perspective, the Quadro and Tesla lineup are specifically targeted toward GPU-accelerated computational applications. A lot of features for such applications are available only on Quadro and Tesla GPUs. All GPUs belonging to these three platforms differ in performance and features. They have transitioned to different micro-architectures through the years since their inception.

GeForce platforms

Launched in 1999 (as we mentioned earlier) and also quite popular as the gamer's GPU lineup from NVIDIA, affordable GeForce GPUs is what makes it possible to start learning CUDA or test your GPU- programmable applications. This is great for individuals who also happen to be HPC enthusiasts, in addition to being passionate gamers. With a higher price, the GeForce Titan series is what specifically addresses this requirement.

The Titan V belongs to the NVIDIA Volta architecture. It has 12 GB of HBM2 memory, a 1,455 Mhz boost clock speed, 640 tensor cores, and 5,120 CUDA cores.

Quadro platforms

The Quadro product lineup is primarily focused toward professional-level graphical rendering for **computer-aided design (CAD)**, **computer-generated imagery (CGI)**, and **digital content creation (DCC)** on developer workstations. The first Quadro GPU was launched in 2004.

One factor that makes Quadro GPUs ahead of GeForce GPUs in scientific calculations and machine learning is the highly optimized ECC memory and greater floating-point precision throughput. Among all three GPU product lines, the Quadro series is currently the one that offers 48 GB DDR6 memory!

The Quadro RTX 8000 belongs to the NVIDIA Turing architecture. It has a 48 GB GDDR6 memory with ECC at 1,770 MHz boost clock speed, 576 tensor cores, and 4,608 CUDA cores.

Tesla platforms

Built primarily for GPGPU and stream processing, **Tesla** GPUs were originally launched in 2007, based on the Tesla microarchitecture named after the legendary electrical engineer and scientist, Nikola Tesla. Though the Tesla C-class GPUs were released with dual-link DVI outputs, the general norm was not having any output ports.

The Tesla V100 belongs to the NVIDIA Volta architecture. It comes in 32 GB and 16 GB HBM2 memory versions with a 1,380 MHz boost clock speed, 640 tensor cores, and 5,120 CUDA cores.
As they are purely made with the purpose of accelerating computational applications, such GPUs are most suitable when displaying requirements are nil and computational tasks are the only priority. So, Tesla GPUs are specifically focused toward supercomputing.

They are very power efficient and generate less heat. This makes them ideal for industry-level deployment.

Currently, Tesla GPUs can immensely contribute to simulations and large-scale calculations (especially floating-point calculations—this is where double precision can be a huge advantage). Apart from pure computations, high-end image generation for applications in professional and scientific fields with CUDA or ROCm is also possible.

Tesla and Quadro GPUs have higher double-precision power when compared to consumer-level GeForce GPUs. Double precision makes mathematical computations much more accurate than single precision. GeForce's Titan GPUs also take care of this requirement when scientific computing and machine learning really matters a lot. But there are many other features that can be found only on the professional Quadro and Tesla series within NVIDIA.

To have a deeper understanding of the three, let's compare the specifications of the previous three GPU models.

First, let's see how the Titan V differs from the Quadro RTX 8000 and Tesla V100:

- Memory and features comparison:

	GeForce Titan V	Quadro RTX 8000	Tesla V100
Microarchitecture	Volta	Turing	Volta
Memory size	12 GB	48 GB	16 GB
Memory type	HBM2	GDDR6	HBM2
Memory bus	3,072-bit	384-bit	4,096-bit
Bandwidth	652.8 GB/s	672.0 GB/s	897.0 GB/s
NVLink support	No	Yes	Yes
GPUDirect support	Limited	Full	Full

- Performance comparison:

	GeForce Titan V	Quadro RTX 8000	Tesla V100
Pixel Rate	~139.7 GPixel/s	~169.9 GPixel/s	~176.6 GPixel/s
Texture rate	~465.6 GTexel/s	~509.8 GTexel/s	~441.6 GTexel/s
FP16 (half) performance	~27.5 TFLOPS	32.6 TFLOPS	~31.4 TFLOPS
FP32 (float) performance	~14.8 TFLOPS	~16.3 TFLOPs	~14.1 TFLOPS
FP64 (double) performance	Up to 6.875 TFLOPS	~0.5 TFLOPS	~7.8 TFLOPS

- Clock speeds:

	GeForce Titan V	Quadro RTX 8000	Tesla V100
GPU clock	1,200 Mhz	1,395 MHz	1,246 MHz
Boost clock	1,455 MHz	1,770 MHz	1,380 MHz
Memory clock	850 MHz	1750 MHz	876 MHz
Effective memory clock	1,700 MHz	14 GHz	1,752 MHz

- Deep learning performance comparison:

	GeForce Titan V	Quadro RTX 8000	Tesla V100
TensorTFLOPS	110	130.5	125

GPUs without tensor cores can equivalently compare with their conventional **floating-point operations per second** (**FLOPS**) to benchmark their maximum DL performance.

The Tesla V100 comes in four different variants:

	Double precision performance (FP64)	TensorTFLOPS
Tesla V100 PCI-E 16GB	7 TFLOPS	112
Tesla V100 PCI-E 32GB	4.7 TFLOPS	18.7
Tesla V100 SXM 16GB	7.8 TFLOPS	125
Tesla V100 SXM 32GB	5.3 TFLOPS	21.2

GPUDirect

GPUDirect is an NVIDIA technology that was made to lower latency by bypassing CPU workloads to enable greater transfer speeds between GPUs.

Direct memory access (DMA) is a feature that allows hardware components of a computer system to access system RAM without having to harness the CPU.

The **message passing interface (MPI)** is a portable standard for invoking executable code through a process and its resources to function on diverse parallel-computing architectures. The process is notified via an invoking program. So, it is referred to as **message-passing**. The MPI standard was designed by researchers from both academia and industry.

GPUDirect Peer-to-Peer enables high-speed DMA transfers to copy data between the memories of two GPUs attached on two PCIe buses on the same system's motherboard. So, this can be helpful for individuals who have multiple GPUs in their system.

GPUDirect **remote direct memory access (RDMA)** allows third-party devices such as **solid state drives (SSDs)**, **network interface cards (NICs)**, and **InfiniBand adapters** to directly access memory on multiple GPUs across remote systems, lowering the latency of MPI send-and-receive messages to/from GPU memory.

GeForce GPUs support only GPUDirect peer-to-peer, whereas Tesla and Quadro also support RDMA.

GPU Direct RDMA ASYNC allows the GPU to initiate RDMA transfers without any CPU interaction.

SXM and NVLink

SXM stands for **Sign extension mode**. **NVLink**, as stated by NVIDIA, is a high-bandwidth and energy-efficient interconnect that enables ultra-fast CPU to GPU and GPU to GPU communication.

A new SXM2 mezzanine connector was introduced by NVIDIA for NVLink in order to address the issues of **Peripheral Component Interconnect Express** (**PCIe**), such as overloads causing performance bottlenecks in high-end GPUs and multi-GPU systems.

Titan V does not support NVLink 2.0, but its CEO edition, a 32 GB version, does support it.

The three GPUs that we compared here are available at extremely high prices: thousands of dollars. On the affordability level, it can be considered feasible for academic institutions and industries, but not for individuals who are small, independent researchers.

NVIDIA CUDA

Compute Unified Device Architecture (**CUDA**) is a proprietary API that was released by NVIDIA for GPGPU programming in 2007. It allows you to harness the computational power of your NVIDIA GPU through CUDA-based C programming and predefined libraries. With exhaustive documentation on the API by NVIDIA, CUDA has grown extensively to be widely adopted in academia and industry, since its inception. Several implementations have been built using CUDA for GPGPU development. Since CUDA is not open source, cross-platform programmability isn't possible. To be able to use CUDA, owning an NVIDIA GPU is a mandatory requirement.

Computing on AMD APUs and GPUs

AMD-based GPU programmable platforms are centered around the **Heterogeneous System Architecture** (**HSA**). HSA is a cross-vendor set of specifications that allows the integration of CPUs and GPUs on the same bus, with shared memory and tasks. The HSA Foundation continues to be developed by AMD and many other members. AMD was one of the founding members of HSA.

HSA was developed with a programmer's perspective, to take care of the issue of prolonged data transfer between memories, especially when both CPUs and GPUs are involved (as is the norm when programming on CUDA or OpenCL).

Accelerated processing units (APUs)

Originally started as the **Fusion project** in 2006, **accelerated processing units** (**APUs**) that unify CPUs and GPUs on a single silicon die were released by AMD in 2011.

AMD APUs support the following HSA features.

The GPU in the APU – the significance of APU design

The prime advantage of the APU design is that the distance between the CPU and the GPU is reduced by a huge extent, as both processors are present on the same unit. Such a model leveraged by HSA allows CPU-GPU or intra-APU communication at a much faster rate than the conventional method: CPUs and GPUs being separately assembled on a motherboard. So, APU motherboards are specifically designed for this purpose.

Though APUs are marketed as an AMD product, Intel also manufactures such units according to the same standards.

AMD GPUs – programmable platforms

AMD has three notable GPU platforms, namely Radeon, Radeon Pro, and Instinct. Like NVIDIA, each of these product lines evolved into different Vega GCN microarchitectures through the years.

Radeon platforms

Actually launched by ATI in 2000, Radeon became an AMD brand in 2006 after AMD took over ATI. Radeon is the first choice for AMD gamers at the consumer level. Radeon developers, also at the consumer level, now also have access to the open source AMD ROCm that gives them an added advantage to start learning GPU programming or test their GPGPU applications. We can say this because of the Radeon VII, available at $699 USD, having a 1:4 FP64 performance at 3.46 TFLOPS!

Radeon VII belongs to the AMD Vega GCN 5.1 architecture. It has a 16 GB HBM2 memory at 1,750 MHz boost clock speed, 3,840 stream processors, 60 compute units, and 1 TB/s memory bandwidth.

Radeon Pro platforms

The **Radeon Pro** (successor to FirePro) series competes with NVIDIA's Quadro cards and also is primarily focused on professional-level graphical rendering for **computer-aided design** (**CAD**), **computer-generated imagery** (**CGI**), and **digital content creation** (**DCC**) on developer workstations. The first Radeon Pro GPU was launched as the **Radeon Pro Duo** in April 2016.

One factor that makes Radeon Pro GPUs ahead of Radeon GPUs in scientific calculations and machine learning is the high bandwidth HBM2 ECC memory and greater FP64 power.

The Vega Frontier Edition with 16 GB is marketed within the Radeon Pro series, but is not branded as a Pro card.

Vega Frontier belongs to the AMD Vega GCN 5.0 architecture. It has 16 GB HBM2 memory, a 1,600 MHz boost clock speed, 4,096 stream processors, 64 compute units, and 484 GB/s memory bandwidth.

Radeon Instinct platforms

Built primarily to accelerate deep learning, artificial neural networks, and HPC/GPGPU applications, Instinct GPUs were originally launched in December 2016 based on the GCN third- and fourth- generation microarchitectures.

The Instinct MI50 belongs to the AMD Vega 20 GCN 5.1 architecture. It has a 16 GB HBM2 memory, a 1,746 MHz boost clock speed, 3,840 stream processors, 60 compute units, and 1 TB/s memory bandwidth. It offers full FP64 performance at 6.7 TFLOPS (1:2).

AMD's Instinct GPUs are direct competitors to NVIDIA's Tesla GPUs and are also made with the purpose of accelerating computational tasks with unrestricted computing power.

Like NVIDIAs Tesla GPUs, the Instinct series can also immensely contribute to computations where floating-point calculations require double precision for greater accuracy. Apart from pure computations, high-end image generation for applications in professional and scientific fields is also possible with ROCm.

In general, Radeon Pro and Instinct GPUs have higher double-precision power compared to the consumer-level Radeon GPUs. Instinct GPUs cost around $10,000, while the Pro series are also available for mid-to-high range budgets, comparable to the Radeon series.

Reviewing all three GPU prices to performance ratios, a notable advantage for gamers who also happen to be equally passionate developers is the price point at which the new Radeon VII will be available at the time of writing this chapter. A margin of $699 USD really makes it easier for them to get involved with GPU computing, considering its 1:8 FP64 metric at 1.6 TFLOPS!

Let's compare the specifications of the three GPU models, which also includes all three FP64 metrics:

- Memory and features comparison:

	Radeon VII	Radeon Vega Frontier Edition	Radeon Instinct MI50
Microarchitecture	Vega second generation	Vega second Generation	Vega second generation
Memory size	16 GB	16 GB	16 GB
Memory type	HBM2	HBM2	HBM2
Memory bus	4,096-bit	2,048-bit	4,096-bit
Bandwidth	1 TB/s	484 GB/s	1 TB/s
xGMI connect support	No	No	No
DirectGMA support	No	Yes	No

- Performance comparison:

	Radeon VII	Radeon Vega Frontier Edition	Radeon Instinct MI50
Pixel rate	112.0 GPixel/s	102.4 GPixel/s	111.7 GPixel/s
Texture rate	420.0 GTexel/s	409.6 GTexel/s	419.0 GTexel/s
FP16 (half) performance	27.7 TFLOPS	26.2 TFLOPS	26.8 TFLOPS
FP32 (float) performance	13.8 TFLOPS	13.1 TFLOPS	13.4 TFLOPS
FP64 (double) performance	3.46 TFLOPS	0.8 TFLOPS	6.7 TFLOPS

- Clock speeds:

	Radeon VII	Radeon Vega Frontier Edition	Radeon Instinct MI50
GPU clock	1,400 MHz	1,382 MHz	1,200 MHz
Boost clock	1,750 MHz	1,600 MHz	1,746 MHz
Memory clock	1,000 MHz	945 MHz	1,000 MHz
Effective memory clock	2,000 MHz	1,890 MHz	2,000 MHz

For a **deep learning** (**DL**) performance comparison of GPUs without tensor cores, they can be equivalently compared to their conventional FLOPS to benchmark maximum DL performance (particularly FP16/FP32 mixed precision).

We can see that apart from the 1:4 FP64 metric, the Radeon VII is just a revised version of the Instinct MI50 card! The Vega Frontier edition has a much lower FP64 value!

If we revisit the affordability level that we spoke of in the *Computing on NVIDIA GPUs* section for NVIDIA, AMD GPU prices with the mentioned specifications can be considered a win-win situation both for organizations (academia/industry) and individuals who are independent researchers.

Just like NVIDIA has GPUDirect and NVLink, AMD has DirectGMA and xGMI Interconnect (upcoming). **GMA** stands for **Graphic Memory Access** and **xGMI** stands for **inter-chip Global Memory Interconnect**. DirectGMA is open source via AMD's GPUOpen initiative. **GCN** refers to AMD's **Graphic Core Next** architecture.

AMD ROCm

Contrary to NVIDIA's proprietary CUDA, ROCm is an open source platform that was released by AMD for open GPU computing in 2016. Since ROCm is open source, cross-platform programmability is very convenient through HIP, HC, and OpenCL. To be able to use ROCm, owning an AMD GPU is not a mandatory requirement, and GPGPU programming can be achieved through HIP on NVIDIA GPUs. AMD GPU owners can directly use HC for the same purpose.

Comparing GPU programmable platforms on NVIDIA and AMD

So far, we have explored the scope of computing on NVIDIA and AMD GPUs through two separate chapters. Now, let's specifically look into the comparisons between their respective APIs:

NVIDIA CUDA	AMD ROCm
The API is called **Compute Unified Device Architecture**	The API is called **Radeon Open Compute platform**
Proprietary	Open source
Released in 2007	Released in 2016
Wider support	Still under adoption and very actively catching up
Significant number of programmable libraries	Fewer libraries than CUDA but active ongoing development

Cannot be used with non-NVIDIA devices	Cross-platform independence due to open standards
CUDA-C language being used	HIP for cross-platform; HC for AMD GPUs
`.cu` extension used for files	`.cpp` extension used for files
Non-portable	CUDA code portability possible with HIP
OpenCL compatible	Also OpenCL compatible
Significant progress in machine learning	Steady progress in machine learning

It is interesting to note that C++ programmers learning GPU computing for the first time will still be using the `.cpp` extension with AMD ROCm. So, in terms of familiarity, ROCm looks like a better option. NVIDIA GPU owners can opt for HIPCC, whereas AMD GPU owners can go for HCC.

GPUOpen

GPUOpen is AMD's open initiative in the world of GPUs. It encourages open standards with the inclusion of the newly released open source ROCm 2.1 and much more!

The following are the laws of open science:

- **First law**: All data is open and all ideas are shared
- **Second law**: Anyone can take part at any level
- **Third law**: There will be no patents
- **Fourth law**: Suggestions are the best form of criticism
- **Fifth law**: Public discussion is much more valuable than private emails
- **Sixth law**: An open project is bigger than, and is not owned by, any given lab

So, considering the applicability of these laws, we can perceive that they are not only limited to just science, but a plethora of other areas! One multi-disciplinary example that unites both science and art is the field of computational archaeology! GPUOpen and ROCm are a lot more relatable to the six ideals because of their open source model.

Considering both GPU manufacturers in current times, AMD is more inclined toward HBM2 memory, whereas NVIDIA is more inclined toward DDR6.

AMD is the first company to have released a 7 nm GPU as the Radeon VII on February 7, 2019.

With the advent of the new Radeon VII and its affordability, it has been perceived as highly recommendable in the double-precision arena, as we can see from the following diagram, which shows benchmarks based on data from `anandtech.com`:

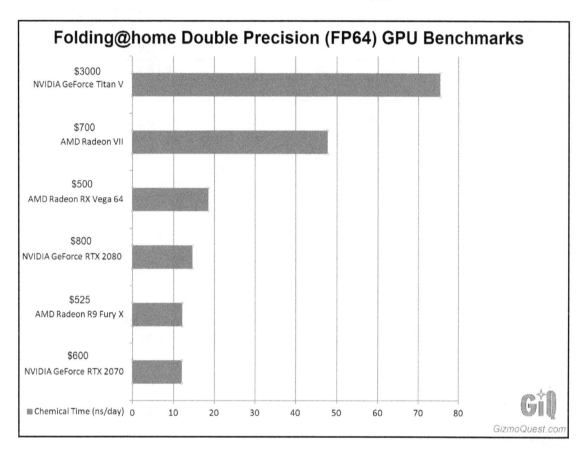

Folding@home (`foldingathome.org`) is a distributed computing project that simulates protein-folding, computational drug design, and molecular dynamics to research disease. GPUs significantly accelerate such initiatives.

As we can see from the preceding diagram, the AMD Radeon VII does pretty well on the price-to-performance ratio. At $1,400 USD, a dual Radeon VII setup could prove immensely beneficial compared to the Titan V, which is priced at $3,000 USD!

Here are some more statistics that compare the latest second-generation Vega GPU on the market to its competitors:

GPU	Titan V	Radeon VII
Double-precision performance	6.9 TFLOPS FP64	3.46 TFLOPS FP64
Memory	12 GB HBM2	16 GB HBM2
Bandwidth	652.8 GB/s	1 TB/s
Price	$3,000	$700

The following table shows how the card fares against NVIDIA's recent RTX line of GPUs, the GTX 1080Ti, AMD's Vega 64, and RX 570 GPU in terms of double precision:

GPU	Radeon VII	Titan RTX	RTX 2080 Ti	RTX 2080	GTX 1080Ti	Vega 64	RX 570
Double-precision performance in GFLOPS	3,456	510	420	315	354.4	786.4	318.5

Consumer-grade GPUs usually have much less FP64 performance. But the new budget-friendly Radeon VII GPU breaks that barrier for both gamers and enthusiasts. So, small, independent researchers can now also afford high-accuracy double-precision scientific computing. It is the cheapest card on the market so far in the NVIDIA versus AMD segment for high-performance GPU computing. On average, the new 7 nm Vega GPU is 30% faster than the previous 14 nm Vega. Through time and better drivers, this card could prove to be even better!

The significance of double precision in scientific computing from a GPU perspective

Though molecular dynamics is dominated by single precision, double precision is useful in force accumulation calculations in molecular dynamics.

Double precision accuracy is very important in the field of quantum chemistry.

Even when capped at a 1:4 ratio, a dual 2x AMD Radeon VII setup is still less than half price ($1,400 USD) compared to a single $3,000 USD Titan V; this will greatly motivate small independent researchers.

At $700 USD, single GPU (Radeon VII) owners can get another one and have access to 32 GB of video memory. Even 2x Titan Vs ($6,000 USD) would still be 24 GB. That extra 8 GB means a lot for managing simulation and modeling data!

Finally, let's look at the following FP64 chart by Rob Williams at `techgage.com`, which shows Radeon VII's superiority over some other cards:

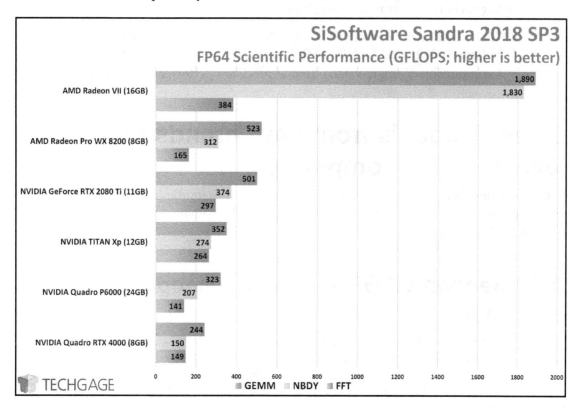

The benchmarks are as follows:

- **GEMM** implies **GEneral Matrix to Matrix multiplication**
- **NBDY** relates to **N-BoDY** simulation, which is a simulation of a dynamical system of particles under the influence of physical forces such as gravitational force
- **FFT** refers to **Fast Fourier Transforms**

That being observed, let's also not skip the prices of the previous GPUs:

GPU	Radeon Pro WX 8200 8 GB	RTX 2080Ti 11 GB	Titan Xp 12 GB	Quadro P6000 24 GB	Quadro RTX 4000
Price	$990 USD	$999 USD	$1,200 USD	$4,950 USD	$1,250 USD

The significance of double-precision accuracy in scientific computing with NVIDIA/AMD GPUs can be better understood through two examples cited at the end of this chapter in the *Further reading* section. The corresponding topics are as follows:

- GPU-based calculation of various gas flows with double-precision accuracy on Radeon R9 280X and Tesla M2090
- A comparison of single-versus double-precision performance for Tesla GPUs

Current models from both brands that are ideal for GPU computing

In the following comparative study, we will explore the capabilities of the best GPUs available from both AMD and NVIDIA to understand the scenarios for adopting a computing-based approach.

AMD Radeon VII GPU – the new people's champion

As a GPU that is affordable by both gamers and computing enthusiasts at $699 USD, the AMD Radeon VII GPU absolutely befits Radeon VII when compared to the Titan V. With superior FP64 performance compared to its competitors in a similar price bracket, this GPU is clearly a very preferable choice for scientific computing. We will explore it in more detail later, with a few benchmarks included through out this section.

NVIDIA Titan V GPU – raw compute power

Priced at $3,000 USD, the Titan V GPU is the leader in terms of FP64 performance.

The RTX lineup of NVIDIA GPUs is preferable if you are looking toward building a machine learning setup and tapping into their tensor cores.

The Vega series from AMD at the lower price bands are also preferable if you consider their superior half-precision performance for machine learning.

We will read more about the machine learning aspect later in this book.

Radeon VII absolutely dominates the RTX 2080 by offering 3.2x FP64 performance.

Now, let's also look into the encryption, financial, and single-precision benchmarks after the entry of the latest consumer-level GPU on the market. This will help you choose the best GPU according to your specific task-driven requirement.

The following statistics are based on benchmarks made by Jamie Fletcher and Rob Williams at techgage.com with the **SiSoftware Sandra** benchmark tool:

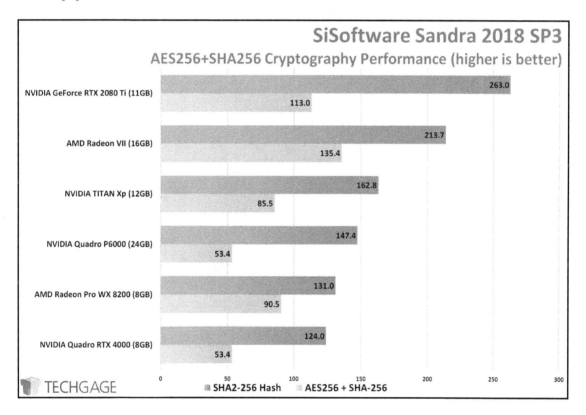

AES stands for **Advanced Encryption Standard**, whereas **SHA** stands for **Secure Hash Algorithm**. Both are cryptography algorithms or, in other words, ways to encrypt data.

With a block size of 128 bits, AES-256 uses a key length of 256 bits. SHA2-256 uses 32-bit words, whereas SHA2-512 uses 64-bit words:

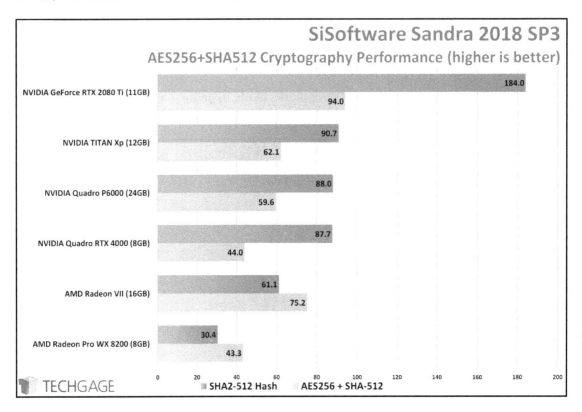

We can note that the RTX 2080Ti hugely dominates the Radeon VII, especially in terms of SHA2-512 hash performance.

In the financial performance benchmark, the RTX 2080 Ti again beats the Radeon VII in terms of **Aggregate Option Pricing Performance (kOPT/s)**:

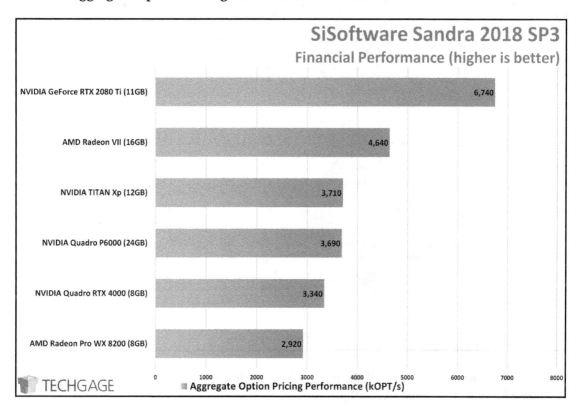

But when it comes to single-precision (FP32) scientific performance, Radeon VII takes its place at the top:

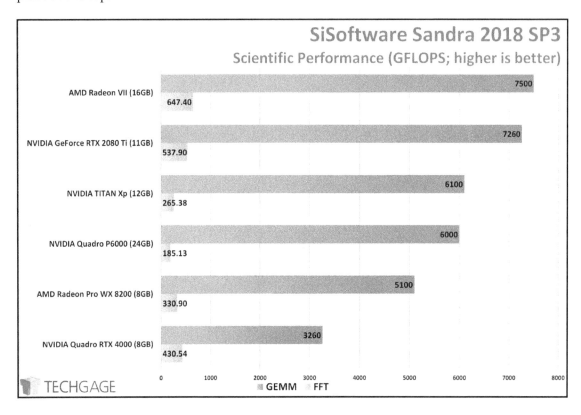

In the next section, we will revisit the previously enlisted system configurations and also include a Radeon VII-based PC configuration.

An enthusiast's guide to GPU computing hardware

In the previous chapter, we listed several configurations for building a GPU computing setup and also saw the basic steps for assembling the PC.

In this final section, let's revisit those configurations and explore how we can enhance them by opting for after-market or customized liquid-cooling options for CPUs and GPUs.

While it is incredibly adventurous to tweak and assemble such a system on your own, an extra pair of helping hands is a big plus!

Custom water cooling on GPUs involves removing the graphic card's air cooler and replacing it with a **waterblock**. The complete water-cooling unit also comes with a reservoir for storing the water, a radiator for constantly cooling the circulating water, and of course the pipes to transport the water through the waterblock, reservoir, and radiator.

The following is the **EKWB Advanced Anti-Virus Waterblock** for the NVIDIA GTX 1050Ti GPU:

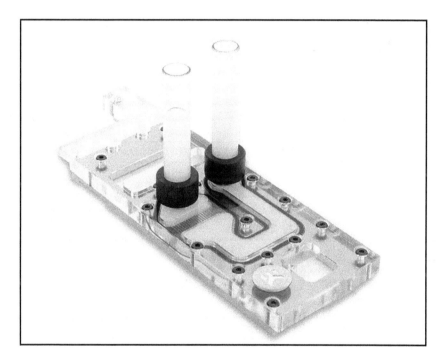

The following configurations have been revised again based on liquid cooling:

- A liquid-cooled Intel CPU with a custom water-cooled NVIDIA GPU configuration:

CPU	Intel Core i3-8100	$118.89
CPU Cooler	CORSAIR Hydro Series H80i v2 AIO Liquid CPU Cooler	$84.99
Motherboard	Gigabyte H310M A	$55.14

GPU	Asus NVIDIA GeForce GTX 1050Ti 4GB	$201.12
GPU Cooler	EKWB Advanced Anti-Virus Waterblock with pipes, reservoir and radiator	~$300
RAM	Corsair Vengeance 2x8GB	$119.99
SSD	ADATA - Ultimate SU800 128 GB	$28.99
HDD	Western Digital - Caviar Green 1 TB	$44.89
PSU	SeaSonic - FOCUS Plus Gold 650 W 80+ Gold Certified Fully-Modular ATX	$89.99
Monitor	Acer – G226HQL 21.5 1920x1080	$89.99
Keyboard	Logitech - K120	$8.99
Mouse	Logitech - M100	$4.29

- A liquid-cooled AMD CPU with a custom water cooled NVIDIA GPU configuration:

CPU	AMD - Ryzen 3 2200G	$93.99
CPU Cooler	Cooler Master MasterLiquid ML120L RGB AIO CPU Liquid Cooler 120 mm	$54.99
Motherboard	ASRock - B450M-HDV Micro ATX AM4	$63.98
GPU	Asus NVIDIA GeForce GTX 1050Ti 4GB	$201.12
GPU Cooler	EKWB Advanced Anti-Virus Waterblock with pipes, reservoir, and radiator	~$300
RAM	Corsair Vengeance 2x8GB	$119.99
SSD	ADATA - Ultimate SU800 128 GB	$28.99
HDD	Western Digital - Caviar Green 1 TB	$44.89
PSU	SeaSonic - FOCUS Plus Gold 650 W 80+ Gold Certified Fully-Modular ATX	$89.99
Monitor	Acer – G226HQL 21.5 1920x1080	$89.99
Keyboard	Logitech - K120	$8.99
Mouse	Logitech - M100	$4.29

The following is a Bykski A-SP57MI-X GPU Water Cooling Block for the AMD RX 570 GPU:

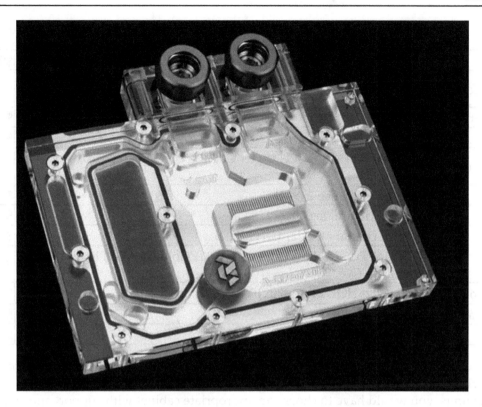

- A liquid-cooled Intel CPU with a custom water cooled AMD GPU configuration:

CPU	Intel Core i3-8100	$118.89
CPU Cooler	CORSAIR Hydro Series H80i v2 AIO Liquid CPU Cooler	$84.99
Motherboard	Gigabyte H310M A	$55.14
GPU	Sapphire AMD Radeon RX 570 4 GB	$149.99
GPU Cooler	Bykski A-SP57MI-X GPU Water Cooling Block with pipes, reservoir, and radiator	~$200
RAM	Corsair Vengeance 2x8GB	$119.99
SSD	ADATA - Ultimate SU800 128 GB	$28.99
HDD	Western Digital - Caviar Green 1 TB	$44.89
PSU	SeaSonic - FOCUS Plus Gold 650 W 80+ Gold Certified Fully-Modular ATX	$89.99
Monitor	Acer – G226HQL 21.5 1920x1080	$89.99
Keyboard	Logitech - K120	$8.99
Mouse	Logitech - M100	$4.29

- A liquid-cooled AMD CPU and a custom water-cooled AMD GPU configuration:

CPU	AMD - Ryzen 3 2200G	$93.99
CPU Cooler	Cooler Master MasterLiquid ML120L RGB AIO CPU Liquid Cooler 120 mm	$54.99
Motherboard	Gigabyte H310M A	$55.14
GPU	Sapphire AMD Radeon RX 570 4 GB	$149.99
GPU Cooler	Bykski A-SP57MI-X GPU Water Cooling Block with pipes, reservoir, and radiator	~$200
RAM	Corsair Vengeance 2x8GB	$119.99
SSD	ADATA - Ultimate SU800 128 GB	$28.99
HDD	Western Digital - Caviar Green 1 TB	$44.89
PSU	SeaSonic - FOCUS Plus Gold 650 W 80+ Gold Certified Fully-Modular ATX	$89.99
Monitor	Acer – G226HQL 21.5 1920x1080	$89.99
Keyboard	Logitech - K120	$8.99
Mouse	Logitech - M100	$4.29

We've revisited four configurations from Chapter 2, *Designing a GPU Computing Strategy*, and revised them with a liquid-based cooling perspective. Note that for each of these water-cooling units, you would have to choose an appropriate cabinet with support and space for the placement of the pipes, radiator, and reservoir with fans.

Here is an example of how a complete liquid-cooled system works (including the CPU) from Andrey Lebrov's clip at vimeo.com (zoomed in and cropped for better viewing):

Note how both the CPU and 4x GPUs are part of the same liquid-cooled custom loop.

In reference to each of the mid-range configurations enlisted in the previous chapter, if you're looking to build a deep learning box, you might consider using an NVIDIA RTX 2060 GPU instead of the GTX 1050 Ti, as it features 240 tensor cores with 52 teraflops of deep learning performance.

As for the high-end perspective, this RTX 2080 Ti-based configuration is ideal for cryptography enthusiasts and financial computing as per our observations of benchmarks in the previous section:

CPU	Intel - Core i7-9700K	$193.99
CPU Cooler	Corsair - H60 (2018) 57.2 CFM	$69.98
Motherboard	Asus - ROG STRIX Z390-E ATX LGA1151	$238.89
GPU	Gigabyte NVIDIA GeForce RTX 2080 Ti 11 GB	$999
RAM	Corsair - Vengeance LPX 2x16GB	$200.00
SSD	ADATA - Ultimate SU800 256 GB	$44.99
HDD	Western Digital - Caviar Green 2 TB	$89.89
Case	Cooler Master - MasterBox Lite 5 ATX Mid Tower	$55.98
PSU	SeaSonic - FOCUS Plus Gold 850W 80+ Gold Certified Fully-Modular ATX	$119.89
Monitor	Acer – G226HQL 21.5 1920x1080	$89.99
Keyboard	Logitech - K120	$8.99
Mouse	Logitech - M100	$4.29

Also, according to the detailed performance benchmarks we noted in the *The significance of double precision in scientific computing from a GPU perspective* and *An enthusiast's guide to GPU computing hardware* sections, this Radeon VII-based configuration is undoubtedly much more ideal for scientific computing:

CPU	AMD - Ryzen 7 2700X	$304.97
CPU Cooler	Corsair - H60 (2018) 57.2 CFM	$69.98
Motherboard	Gigabyte - B450M DS3H Micro ATX AM4	$73.98
GPU	Sapphire - Radeon VII 16 GB HBM2	$699
RAM	Corsair - Vengeance LPX 2x16GB	$200.00
SSD	ADATA - Ultimate SU800 256 GB	$44.99
HDD	Western Digital - Caviar Green 2 TB	$89.89
Case	Cooler Master - MasterBox Lite 5 ATX Mid Tower	$55.98
PSU	SeaSonic - FOCUS Plus Gold 850W 80+ Gold Certified Fully-Modular ATX	$119.89
Monitor	Acer – G226HQL 21.5 1920x1080	$89.99
Keyboard	Logitech - K120	$8.99
Mouse	Logitech - M100	$4.29

Based on the benchmarks we saw in the previous section, we modified the configurations we previously listed in the high-end side (Chapter 2, *Designing a GPU Computing Strategy*) with the RTX 2080Ti and the Radeon VII. The RTX 2080Ti system would interest cryptography enthusiasts and financial analysts, whereas the Radeon VII system would catch the attention of scientific computing enthusiasts.

The end result of replacing all the previously enlisted air-cooled configurations with their liquid-cooled counterparts will primarily extend the lifespan of those GPUs at significantly lower temperatures when operational at full load.

Finally, let's end this chapter with this newly built Radeon VII setup:

Note that we have used two separate power cables from the PSU to the GPU. This ensures better distribution of power to the unit and optimized thermal stability, especially when the recommended power requirement for the GPU is greater than 350 W.

Summary

In this chapter, we learned about different GPU manufacturers and computing on NVIDIA and AMD GPU platforms. We also compared these two leading GPU manufactures and explored their scope and applicability options through a CUDA versus ROCm comparison. We looked through different GPUs and saw which one to choose according to a specific requirement. Finally, we revisited configuration options from `Chapter 2`, *Designing a GPU Computing Strategy*, and saw how we can modify them toward a liquid-cooled setup. Considering the RTX 2080 Ti and the Radeon VII, we understood their applicability by modifying two of our previously listed configurations in the *High-end budget* section in `Chapter 2`, *Designing a GPU Computing Strategy*.

Now that you have come to the end of this chapter, you should now be able to distinguish between NVIDIA and AMD GPUs based on your set of computational requirements. You should also be able to decide whether to opt for CUDA or ROCm based on your project goals. You have now become much more acquainted with how customized liquid cooling works and you can now think of ways to apply them based on your computing field.

In the next chapter, we will learn about the fundamentals of GPU programming. These fundamental concepts will help you understand how GPUs can reduce the CPU's workload by handling intensive computational tasks. We will then introduce you to CUDA, ROCm, PyCUDA, PyOpenCL, OpenCL, Anaconda, CuPy, and Numba—all from a Python-programming perspective.

Further reading

You can refer to the following links to learn more about the topics discussed in this chapter:

- *The NVIDIA Titan V Preview - Titanomachy: War of the Titans*, page 5, R Smith, N Oh (2017)(online), `anandtech.com`. Available at `https://www.anandtech.com/show/12170/nvidia-titan-v-preview-titanomachy/5`.
- *The AMD Radeon VII Review: An Unexpected Shot at the High-End*, page 15, N Oh (2019) (online), `anandtech.com`. Available at `https://www.anandtech.com/show/13923/the-amd-radeon-vii-review/15`.
- *A Look At AMD's Radeon VII Workstation and Compute Performance*, page 4, R Williams (2019) (online), Techgage. Available at `https://techgage.com/article/amd-radeon-vii-workstation-performance/2/`.

- *Testing AMD Radeon VII Double-Precision Scientific And Financial Performance,* J Fletcher, R Williams (2019) (online), Techgage. Available at `https://techgage.com/article/testing-amd-radeon-vii-double-precision-scientific-and-financial-performance/`.

- *GPU implementation of algorithm SIMPLE-TS for calculation of unsteady, viscous, compressible, and heat-conductive gas flow,* K Shterev (2018), ArXiv (online). Available at `https://arxiv.org/abs/1802.04243`.

- *Comparison of Single and Double Floating Point Precision Performance for Tesla Architecture,* page 53 *GPUs,* L Itu, C Suciu, F Moldoveanu, A Postelnicu (2011), Engineering Sciences (online), 4(2). Available at `http://webbut.unitbv.ro/BU2011/Series%20I/BULETIN%20I/Itu_LM.pdf`.

- Pictures and price quotes of the Matrox **Programmable Graphics Controller (PGC)**: Clone of the original IBM PGC. Available at `https://threadreaderapp.com/thread/1024809967360995328.html`.

- *Exploiting Graphics Accelerators for Computational Biology,* Beyer, L. (2012), Diploma Thesis, Computational Engineering Sciences, RWTH Aachen University. Available at `http://lucasb.eyer.be/academic/gwas/lbeyer-thesis-gwas.pdf` (mentions an approximate price of $5,500 USD for the original IBM PGC).

- Intel is teasing its own GPU, to be released sometime in 2020. Available at `https://www.extremetech.com/computing/282303-intel-shows-off-new-gen11-graphics-teases-xe-discrete-gpu`.

Section 2: Hands-On Development with GPU Programming

This section discusses the fundamental concepts behind GPU computing. You will learn how to set up different development environments and will be introduced to GPU programming platforms.

The following chapters are included in this section:

4
Fundamentals of GPU Programming

In this chapter, we will be moving on from the hardware perspective of GPUs toward a computing perspective, as is the primary objective of this book. We will begin with an introduction to GPU programming and fundamental ways to set up three different platforms, namely **CUDA**, **ROCm**, and **Anaconda**. NVIDIA and AMD GPUs will be revisited here to explore the practical usage of GPUs with the three platforms.

The concept of Python programming integrated with GPU code invocation will be discussed. Anaconda users and Python programming enthusiasts will be motivated to invoke GPUs within their program code with **CuPy** and **Numba** (formerly Accelerate) via Anaconda. Additionally, we will learn about a few basics of hands-on GPU programming, GPU programmable platforms, CUDA, CUDA libraries, OpenCL, and ROCm.

Moving on, we will explore the Python programming aspect: PyCUDA, PyOpenCL, CuPy, and Numba, which are very convenient ways to accelerate Python code with GPUs. We will also learn how to set up Anaconda on your system. This knowledge will help us understand why it is so convenient to program on GPUs with Python (even with no or limited knowledge of C/C++).

To that end, the following topics will be covered in this chapter:

- GPU-programmable platforms
- Basic CUDA concepts
- Basic ROCm concepts
- The Anaconda Python distribution
- GPU-enabled Python programming

GPU-programmable platforms

Since our primary subject is GPU computing, it is essential that we learn the fundamentals of GPU programming from a computing perspective. GPU programming is the foundation of GPU computing. The question that should be pondered upon here, is why is it significant in GPU computing? To know the answer, let's first understand the basic differences between programming and computing. Here is a short comparison:

Programming	Computing
Involves developing programs.	Involves performing computations through programs.
Intends to solve multiple problems in a generalized manner.	Focused on solving a single problem that can be interdisciplinary in nature.
Programming is applied to broader scenarios.	Computing is applied to a single specific scenario that is based on and chosen from those broader scenarios.
Here is a simple example: when listing all the steps to buy a commodity irrespective of its brand, we are following a programming approach, say, the steps to buy computer component.	Here is a simple example: when listing the steps to buy a commodity very specific in nature belonging to a particular brand, we are following a computing approach, say, the steps to buy a Seasonic 850W gold series power supply for a computer.

As we can see, computing is a very crucial subset of programming that can be extremely important in the field of computational studies. A GPU-programmable platform provides you with an interface so that you can specifically solve a computational problem with GPUs step by step. Both GPU programming and GPU computing follow a general set of instructions but differ in their nature of specificity, the latter being highly focused on a specific computational task.

Developers entering a new world of GPU programming are already familiar with the following syntax code:

```
Header files
Declarations
Main program()
{
  Conventional CPU code
}
```

Here is a very basic way to understand how a GPU program differs from the previous code:

```
Header files
Declarations
GPU Function() // Can perform intensive computational tasks
// Referred to as a kernel in GPU terminology
Main program() // The one that we are already familiar with
{
 Conventional CPU code
 Call GPU Function() // Invoking execution of intensive computation on GPU
}
```

As we can see, the entire code is still present within a single program, but the set of tasks that are intensive in nature are handed over to the GPU for execution.

For a broader outlook on migrating from a CPU to GPU perspective, please refer to the *Further Reading: Conventional CPU Computing vs GPU Computing*, before we move on to the next section of this chapter. In the upcoming sections on CUDA, ROCm, and Python, we'll cover all the basics so that you can start working hands-on with GPU-powered Python programs in order to carry out different types of computational tasks. Throughout this book, we will pursue our hands-on approach with the recent 64-bit version of the Ubuntu 18.04.2 operating system.

Basic CUDA concepts

Since we have discussed various points of **Compute Unified Device Architecture (CUDA)** in our earlier chapters, let's now focus on its technical aspects and GPU programmability.

Apart from the installation procedure that's unique to CUDA, the remaining concepts that will be discussed here in brief will be useful for getting started with GPU programming on all platforms.

Installing and testing

Before we discuss some fundamental GPU programming concepts, it is essential that we revisit the CUDA installation and testing procedure that we covered earlier in Chapter 2, *Designing a GPU Computing Strategy*, while concluding the DIY section. Step-by-step screenshots of a fresh Ubuntu 18.04 Linux installation were illustrated. There were only two basic steps involved, as we discussed previously.

It requires performing the following sequential tasks:

1. **Driver installation:** The driver installation can be done by installing the most recent version of the NVIDIA graphics driver from the available Ubuntu repository via **Additional Drivers**.

2. **CUDA toolkit installation**: The toolkit package goes by the name of `nvidia-cuda-toolkit`, which will also set the path to the **NVIDIA CUDA Compiler** (**NVCC**) driver after installation. A reboot is recommended post installation, after which you will be able to compile a CUDA program source code files with the `nvcc` command from any Terminal. You can verify your new CUDA installation with the following code:

```
nvidia-smi
```

This is followed by checking the NVCC version:

```
nvcc -version
```

The syntax for `nvcc` compilation in simple form goes like this:

```
nvcc Your-CUDA-GPU-program.cu
```

As we can see here, the extension for CUDA source files is `.cu`. What we require next for hands-on computing is an IDE, which will be covered later in this book.

It's always good practice to choose the CUDA toolkit available on the Linux repository by default, as it makes it convenient while upgrading your Linux system. Manual installation of separately downloaded versions may lead to system instability if not properly configured. But should you choose to have more than one CUDA version in accordance to a specific application requirement, you can install and configure them from the following archive link. It also shows relevant documentation after selecting your CUDA version and operating system.

Follow this link to download the CUDA toolkit: `https://developer.nvidia.com/cuda-toolkit-archive`.

To retain system stability, after updating your repository based on the previous link, install only your specific toolkit version using the following format:

```
sudo apt install cuda-toolkit-x-x
```

x-x refers to the version number of your CUDA Toolkit. For example, `cuda-toolkit-9-0` would install CUDA 9.0.

Do not install the package `cuda` or `cuda-x-x` as either would also try to install a new NVIDIA driver along with CUDA, and thus could disrupt your existing NVIDIA graphics that were installed earlier from the default settings (**Additional Proprietary Drivers**).

Compute capability

Every NVIDIA GPU has its own general specifications and available features. These parameters can be understood better through **compute capability**, which is a standard set by NVIDIA to classify each GPU according to its hardware and software specifications/features. Through compute capability, NVIDIA GPUs can be compared easily based on such classifications. As the CUDA API evolves, so does the compute capability. The most recent CUDA SDK 10.1 support for compute capability is from 3.0 to 7.5 for NVIDIA GPUs belonging to Kepler, Maxwell, Pascal, Volta, and Turing architectures. More information on this can be found at the following link: `https://developer.nvidia.com/cuda-gpus`.

Threads, blocks, and grids

Efficiently manipulating the number of threads, blocks, and grids while addressing a GPU program kernel allows us to make the most of the GPU device's computational throughput. The following diagram demonstrates the components of a grid. We can see that it consists of blocks. A single block has also been zoomed into and illustrated to show what it contains as well.

The components of **Block (1, 1)** are 12 threads, each represented as arrows. Note that each block in the grid (shown in green) also include 12 such arrows to represent the individual threads. Every block in the grid is structured in this manner:

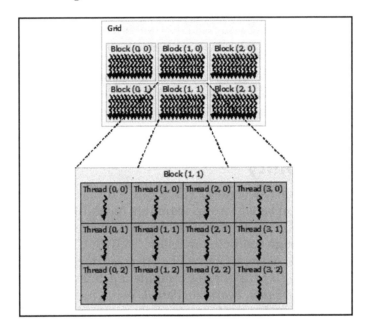

Figure 1: Grid of thread blocks, as illustrated in the official CUDA toolkit documentation

These three forms of CUDA code implementation will help you manage various ways of handling GPU device code execution according to your computational requirements. A CUDA program can be launched with many threads in a group of **thread blocks**. A group of thread blocks, in turn, forms a grid. When using many groups of thread blocks, we are then, in fact, using multiple grids and, therefore, making it possible to maximize the total number of threads to be used throughout CUDA code execution.

Threads

Threads are basic units that execute in parallel together to process single kernel jobs on the GPU. GPU threads are very similar to CPU threads, with the only difference being that the number of threads available can be much higher in the case of GPUs.

Blocks

Thread blocks, as we can see in the preceding diagram, are a collection of threads. The number of threads in each block is limited to the architecture of the GPU. For example, in an NVIDIA GeForce Titan X GPU belonging to the Maxwell architecture, the maximum number of threads in a block is 1,024. But in spite of this limitation, a GPU program can definitely make use of a huge number of blocks instead. This allows the program to maximize thread parallelization, especially on high-performance GPUs.

Grids

Going one level further, grids are a collection of blocks. Based on the compute capability of your NVIDIA GPU, you can set the maximum size of blocks with respect to the grid's maximum number of threads and blocks. In this manner, you'll be able to get the most out of the GPU's compute power with maximum occupancy. To make this easier, NVIDIA provides a **CUDA Occupancy Calculator** for estimation:

- Download the link for offline use by following this link: `https://developer.download.nvidia.com/compute/cuda/CUDA_Occupancy_calculator.xls`
- The online version of the same is also available at the following URL: `https://xmartlabs.github.io/cuda-calculator/`

Managing memory

Just as conventional C++ uses standard C functions to handle memory, CUDA also uses its own memory management functions in a similar fashion. CUDA does not use C functions for managing device (GPU) memory variables. It has its own functions for allocating memory for GPU device variables, but they are designed to be used through similar syntax as in C. On the other hand, variables with unified memory allocations through CUDA can be used on both a host and a device. C++ code is referred to as **host code**, while CUDA code is known as **device code**. The following functions are very frequently used when developing GPU programs and code execution through device kernels:

Conventional C/C++ functions	CUDA version of the same functions
malloc	cudaMalloc
memcpy	cudaMemcpy
free	cudaFree

`cudaMemcpyHostToDevice` and `cudaMemcpyDeviceToHost` are two functions in the CUDA API that are used interchangeably with both host and device variables. They are extremely significant and used to transfer data between the CPU and the GPU.

Unified Memory Access (UMA)

This feature allows data pointers to allocate memory on the GPU device that can be accessed by both the CPU and the GPU. With this shared memory access, the need for CPU allocation for host variables is eliminated. The following declaration example differentiates UMA from conventional memory allocation:

Conventional CPU memory allocation	Unified memory allocation
`char *data;` `data = (char *)malloc(N)`	`char *data` `cudaMallocManaged(&data, N)`

By using `cudaMallocManaged`, we can allocate memory on the GPU that can be migrated between both the CPU and the GPU. So, with unified memory access, we can pass that data pointer to a CPU function, as well as a GPU kernel!

Dynamic parallelism

GPU devices with a compute capability of 3.5 or higher can make use of a feature that is primarily about reducing CPU-GPU interaction and instead works directly from the GPU. With **dynamic parallelism**, during runtime execution, threads can decide to launch configurations on the GPU itself. So, the need to transfer execution control and data between CPU and GPU can be greatly minimized.

Predefined libraries

Predefined libraries are basically existing modules that are already available for you to implement within your code and eliminates the necessity to spend time developing them on your own. Each predefined library is focused toward computing a specific task. By using predefined libraries in your code, you can focus on your primary project objective without having to worry about the additional development of common core features.

For example, you can use the predefined CUDA Math library to accelerate your math functions without having to write one on your own. This helps you focus better on solving the actual computational problem at hand. NVIDIA also offers readily available libraries to use with CUDA for application-specific purposes. Some of these libraries are listed here:

- **cuDNN**: This is a library of primitives for deep neural networks that's widely used in deep learning frameworks, including **Caffe**, **Caffe2**, **Chainer**, **Keras**, **MATLAB**, **MxNet**, **TensorFlow**, and **PyTorch**
- **cuFFT**: **Fast Fourier Transform** implementations perform up to 10 times faster than CPU-only alternatives
- **cuBLAS**: Implementation of **Basic Linear Algebra Subroutines** for compute intensive operations
- **CUDA Math Library**: Accelerated standard mathematical function library
- **cuSPARSE**: Accelerated **BLAS** for sparse matrices
- **cuRAND**: Accelerated **Random Number Generation** (RNG)
- **cuSOLVER**: Dense and sparse direct solvers for computer vision, computational fluid dynamics, computational chemistry, and linear optimization applications
- **AmgX**: Accelerated linear solvers for simulations and implicit unstructured methods

We will learn more about programming in this model in Chapter 6, *Working with CUDA and PyCUDA*, through CUDA-C examples.

OpenCL

Apart from CUDA-C, CUDA toolkits also come with **OpenCL** support. The only extra step to take care of here is to install the OpenCL headers package:

```
sudo apt install opencl-headers
```

Following this, you will be able to compile a .c or .cpp file containing OpenCL code by running the gcc or g++ compiler with the –lOpenCL flag. The command to compile a .c file using gcc is as follows:

```
gcc openclprogram.c –lOpenCL
```

The corresponding command for a .cpp file using g++ is as follows:

```
g++ openclprogram.cpp –lOpenCL
```

As we discussed earlier, the basic difference between CUDA and OpenCL is cross-platform compatibility and code syntax. Their generic applicability remains the same. We will explore these similarities and differences through Chapter 6, *Working with CUDA and PyCUDA*, and Chapter 7, *Working with ROCm and PyOpenCL*.

Basic ROCm concepts

In Chapter 3, *Setting Up a GPU Computing Platform with NVIDIA and AMD*, we discussed AMD ROCm and also compared it with NVIDIA CUDA. Like we did in the previous section of this chapter, let's look into the **Radeon Open Compute Platform** in a similar manner.

AMD ROCm includes a set of fundamental ways to set up a GPU programming platform for Open Compute. The basic ROCm concepts you need to know to start programming on AMD or NVIDIA GPUs are as follows.

Installation procedure and testing

According to the official documentation, an ROCm installation requires performing the following Terminal-based tasks that are compatible with Ubuntu 18.04:

1. Update your system and install `libnuma-dev` using the following commands:

```
sudo apt update
sudo apt dist-upgrade
sudo apt install libnuma-dev
sudo reboot
```

2. Add the `apt` repository using the following commands:

```
wget -qO - http://repo.radeon.com/rocm/apt/debian/rocm.gpg.key |
sudo apt-key add -

echo 'deb [arch=amd64] http://repo.radeon.com/rocm/apt/debian/
xenial main' | sudo tee /etc/apt/sources.list.d/rocm.list
```

3. The ROCm package goes by the name of `rocm-dkms`, which can be installed after updating the system with the recently updated `apt` repository list using the following commands:

```
sudo apt update
sudo apt install rocm-dkms
```

4. After installing ROCm, you will have to make sure as a user that you are included in the `video` group. Only then will you have access to the GPU:

```
groups
```

5. The previous command will show whether you are already a member of the `video` group. If not, use the following command to do the same:

```
sudo usermod -a -G video $LOGNAME
```

After a reboot, using the `groups` command again should reveal that you are now a member of the `video` group on your Ubuntu Linux system.

6. You can verify your new ROCm installation with the following:

```
/opt/rocm/bin/rocminfo
/opt/rocm/opencl/bin/x86_64/clinfo
```

7. Set up the paths for easier access later on using the following commands:

```
echo 'export ROCm=/opt/rocm/bin' >> ~/.bashrc
echo 'export PATH=$PATH:$ROCm' >> ~/.bashrc
echo 'export ROCm_PROFILER=/opt/rocm/profiler/bin' >> ~/.bashrc
echo 'export PATH=$PATH:$ROCm_PROFILER' >> ~/.bashrc
echo 'export ROCm_OpenCL=/opt/rocm/opencl/bin/x86_64' >> ~/.bashrc
echo 'export PATH=$PATH:$ROCm_OpenCL' >> ~/.bashrc
```

8. You can reload the Bash shell for the changes to take effect immediately using the following command:

```
. ~/.bashrc
```

Now, you can use commands such as `rocminfo`, `clinfo`, and all other related ROCm commands from any Terminal. ROCm also offers the following command, which is similar in nature to `nvidia-smi`:

```
rocm-smi
```

The syntax for `hcc` (equivalent to `nvcc` on NVIDIA CUDA) for compilation on AMD GPUs in simple form goes like this:

```
hcc Your-ROCm-HC-GPU-program.cpp
```

As we can see here, the extension for HC source files is same as for C++, which is `.cpp`. The syntax for `hipcc` (compatible with both AMD and NVIDIA GPUs) in simple form goes like this:

```
hipcc Your-ROCm-HCC-GPU-program.cpp
```

HIP also uses a `.cpp` extension. It's a runtime library that layers on top of HC for AMD ROCm platforms and uses the NVCC compiler for NVIDIA CUDA platforms.

We know about the widespread use of CUDA in the research world and the large amount of CUDA code available on various hosting sites such as GitHub, GitLab, and others. If you do not own a NVIDIA GPU but an AMD GPU instead, you will still be able to easily test a variety of CUDA-converted code on low- cost AMD GPUs from now on!

Official deprecation notice for HCC from AMD

After June 2019, HCC will be deprecated. This is a very thoughtful decision considering the striking similarity of HIP syntax to that of CUDA. The official notice can be found on both of AMD's ROCm and HCC repositories at GitHub:

- ROCm: `https://github.com/RadeonOpenCompute/ROCm`
- HCC: `https://github.com/RadeonOpenCompute/HCC`

"AMD is deprecating HCC to put more focus on HIP development and on other languages supporting heterogeneous compute. We will no longer develop any new feature in HCC and we will stop maintaining HCC after its final release, which is planned for June 2019. If your application was developed with the hc C++ API, we would encourage you to transition it to other languages supported by AMD, such as HIP or OpenCL. HIP and hc language share the same compiler technology, so many hc kernel language features (including inline assembly) are also available through the HIP compilation path."

Generating chips

Every AMD GPU also has its own general specifications and available features. AMD GPUs can be classified based on their generations of chips. The most recent ROCm SDK, version 2.1, supports generations GFX7, GFX8, and GFX9 for select AMD GPUs, which belong to Hawaii, Fiji, Polaris, and Vega architectures. More information can be found via this link: `https://rocm.github.io/hardware.html`.

ROCm components (APIs), including OpenCL

Similar to CUDA, the three major components of ROCm have similar naming conventions:

- **HC**: Threads, tiles, and extents
- **HIP**: Threads, blocks, and grids (exactly the same as in CUDA)
- **OpenCL**: Work-items, work-groups, and NDRanges

CUDA-like memory management with HIP

Just as conventional C++ uses standard C functions to handle memory, HIP also has memory-management functions that it uses in a similar manner. C++ code is referred to as host code, while HIP code is known as device code. The following functions are frequently used with HIP when developing or porting AMD/NVIDIA GPU programs and during code execution through device kernels:

CUDA version	HIP version of the same functions
cudaMalloc	hipMalloc
cudaMemcpy	hipMemcpy
cudaFree	hipFree

Similar to CUDA, `hipMemcpyHostToDevice` and `hipMemcpyHostToDevice` on HIP correspond to what `cudaMemcpyHostToDevice` and `cudaMemcpyDeviceToHost` are meant to do on CUDA.

hipify

ROCm offers a unique tool to easily convert CUDA code into HIP. The following are the steps to install `hipify` on a Terminal:

1. First, install all dependencies to install and run `hipify`:

```
$ sudo apt install git cmake clang-6.0 libclang-6.0-dev libclang-
perl libclanlib-dev libclang-dev zlib1g-dev
$ git clone
https://github.com/GPUOpen-ProfessionalCompute-Tools/HIP HIP
$ cd HIP/hipify-clang/
$ mkdir build dist
```

```
$ cd build
$ cmake \
 -DCMAKE_INSTALL_PREFIX=../dist \
 -DCMAKE_BUILD_TYPE=Release \
 ..
```

The output will look similar to this:

```
-- The C compiler identification is GNU 7.3.0
-- The CXX compiler identification is GNU 7.3.0
-- Check for working C compiler: /usr/bin/cc
-- Check for working C compiler: /usr/bin/cc -- works
-- Detecting C compiler ABI info
...
-- Linker detection: GNU ld
-- Configuring done
-- Generating done
-- Build files have been written to: /home/iborg/HIP/hipify-
clang/build
```

2. Now, we will install `hipify` in the same build location:

```
make -j install
```

The preceding command will show output such as this:

```
Scanning dependencies of target hipify-clang
[ 7%] Building CXX object CMakeFiles/hipify-
clang.dir/src/CUDA2HIP.cpp.o
[ 11%] Building CXX object CMakeFiles/hipify-
clang.dir/src/CUDA2HIP_CAFFE2_API_types.cpp.o
...
[ 99%] Linking CXX executable hipify-clang
[100%] Built target hipify-clang
Install the project...
-- Install configuration: "Release"
-- Installing: /home/iborg/HIP/hipify-clang/dist/bin/hipify-clang
```

3. Now, to set up the `hipify` command, we can use the following command:

```
echo 'alias hipify=~/HIP/hipify-clang/dist/bin/./hipify-clang' >>
~/.bashrc
```

Reload the Bash shell:

```
. ~/.bashrc
```

Now, you can use the following command to easily convert CUDA code into HIP:

```
hipify CUDA-program.cu -o HIP-program.cpp
```

You can use any .cu file of your choice that's been developed with CUDA-C.

The usefulness of this feature is the ability to make cross-platform portability possible. We will learn more about this in Chapter 7, *Working with ROCm and PyOpenCL*.

Predefined libraries

AMD also offers readily available libraries to use with ROCm for application-specific purposes. Some of these libraries are listed here:

- **MIOpen**: Similar to cuDNN on NVIDIA CUDA, AMD ROCm has the MIOpen library for deep neural networks can be used for TensorFlow and PyTorch deep learning frameworks.
- **rocFFT**: A software library for computing FFT written in HIP. The library can be used with both NVIDIA and AMD GPU devices.
- **rocBLAS**: Implementation of basic linear algebra subroutines for compute intensive operations implemented in the HIP programming language and optimized for AMD's GPUs.
- **Open Compute Math Library (OCML)**: Contains 250+ optimized math functions for single, double, and half precision.
- **rocSPARSE**: Accelerated BLAS for sparse matrices provides basic linear algebra subroutines for sparse computation.
- **rocRAND**: Accelerated RNG similar to cuRAND provides functions that generate pseudo-random and quasi-random numbers.
- **rocSOLVER**: Similar to cuSOLVER, rocSOLVER is a work-in-progress implementation of a subset of LAPACK functionality on the ROCm platform that uses rocBLAS. LAPACK is a standard software library for numerical linear algebra.
- **Hardware Accelerated Cosmology Code (HACC)**: This framework uses N-body techniques to simulate the formation of structure in collisionless fluids under the influence of gravity in an expanding universe. HACCMK has been ported with the HCC compiler with C++ dialect.

We will learn more about programming in this model in Chapters 6, *Working with CUDA and PyCUDA*, and Chapter 7, *Working with ROCm and PyOpenCL*.

OpenCL

As we already know, ROCm comes with HC, HIP, and OpenCL. If you require only OpenCL, instead of using `sudo apt install rocm-dkms`, which we mentioned earlier in the ROCm installation steps, the alternative command would be this:

```
sudo apt install dkms rock-dkms rocm-opencl-dev
```

The Anaconda Python distribution for package management and deployment

Anaconda is a distribution for package management and deployment. It facilitates the development of scientific computing and machine learning through Python and R (a programming language focused on statistical computing). Anaconda simplifies the process of managing various packages and also their deployment. The Anaconda repository maintains more than 1,000 professionally built packages for data science.

It has a package management system called `conda` to install various scientific packages. It also provides a build feature for building your own Python packages and uploading them to Anaconda servers. `conda` can be used for installing, executing, and also updating packages, along with their dependencies. It can facilitate software for any language, even though it was made for Python packages.

The Anaconda distribution also includes a graphical user interface called **Anaconda Navigator** that simplifies `conda` usage without the use of commands. The main version of Python in Anaconda 2 is 2.x and for Anaconda 3, it is Python version 3.x.

Installing the Anaconda Python distribution on Ubuntu 18.04

The **Anaconda distribution** is used by over 12 million users with more than 1,400 packages on data science. It was written in Python and first released in 2012 by Continuum Analytics (now Anaconda Inc.). The Anaconda distribution is free and open source under the BSD license and is available for Linux, Windows, and macOS. The following are the steps you need to take to install the Anaconda Python distribution on Ubuntu 18.04:

1. On a Terminal on Ubuntu, use the following commands step by step:

```
cd /tmp
```

/tmp is a temporary location to download the installer. To keep the installer, you can skip this command. Then, use the following command to download the Anaconda installer:

```
wget
https://repo.anaconda.com/archive/Anaconda2-2018.12-Linux-x86_64.sh
```

2. To check whether the file is free of any corruption, you can verify the file's integrity with the sha256sum command:

```
sha256sum Anaconda2-2018.12-Linux-x86_64.sh
```

The output will look as follows:

```
1821d4b623ed449e0acb6df3ecbabd3944cffa98f96a5234b7a102a7c0853dc6
Anaconda2-2018.12-Linux-x86_64.sh
```

3. You can then visit the hash page for all Anaconda installers at http://docs. anaconda.com/anaconda/install/hashes/all/.

Here, you can verify the hash you saw on your Terminal against the hash shown on the page for the recently downloaded Anaconda version by using the find feature on your web browser.

The 1821d4b623ed449e0acb6df3ecbabd3944cffa98f96a5234b7a102a7c0853dc6 hash can be verified by copying and pasting it onto the find tool. Once you find the hash with that paste, you can confirm its integrity and go ahead with the installation:

```
$ bash Anaconda2-2018.12-Linux-x86_64.sh
```

When you enter the preceding command to launch the installer, you'll be asked to review the Anaconda license agreement:

```
Welcome to Anaconda2
In order to continue the installation process, please review the license
agreement.
Please, press ENTER to continue
```

Press *Enter*, scroll down through the license, and type in yes as an answer:

```
Do you accept the license terms? [yes|no]
[no] >>>
Please answer 'yes' or 'no':'
```

Now, you will see a prompt to accept the default Anaconda installation path or choose a different one:

```
Anaconda2 will now be installed into this location:
/home/iborg/anaconda2
- Press ENTER to confirm the location
- Press CTRL-C to abort the installation
- Or specify a different location below
```

Following the preceding code, the installer will ask you to add the Anaconda path to your system PATH via your ~/.bashrc file.

Let's proceed with the same:

```
Do you wish the installer to prepend the Anaconda2 install location
to PATH in your /home/iborg/.bashrc ? [yes|no]
Appending source /home/iborg/anaconda2/bin/activate to /home/iborg/.bashrc
A backup will be made to: /home/iborg/.bashrc-anaconda2.bak


For this change to become active, you have to open a new Terminal.

Thank you for installing Anaconda2!

===========================================================================

Anaconda is partnered with Microsoft! Microsoft VSCode is a streamlined
code editor with support for development operations like debugging, task
running and version control.

To install Visual Studio Code, you will need:
 - Administrator Privileges
 - Internet connectivity

Visual Studio Code License: https://code.visualstudio.com/license

Do you wish to proceed with the installation of Microsoft VSCode? [yes|no]
```

Since we will be using a different IDE called PyCharm for this book (this will be covered in Chapter 5, *Setting Up Your Environment for GPU Programming*), we can skip the Microsoft VSCode installation. Type no and press *Enter*.

The new Anaconda installation can be activated via, or by reloading, the ~/.bashrc file:

```
. ~/.bashrc
```

The Anaconda installation can now be verified and version checked:

```
conda --version
```

The output will display the conda version:

```
conda 4.5.12
```

To keep the conda utility up-to-date, you can use the following command on a regular basis:

```
conda update conda
```

After the preceding command has been successfully executed, you can proceed with updating Anaconda:

```
conda update anaconda
```

Application-specific usage

There is also another alternative distribution from Anaconda, which is called **Miniconda**. It is not as exhaustive as Anaconda and includes only conda and its dependencies for basic usage. You can opt for Miniconda if you need only conda and its dependencies for very specific and minimal requirements.

 For more information on Anaconda installers, the Anaconda repository, and Miniconda installers, you can refer to this link: https://repo. continuum.io/.

GPU-enabled Python programming

The fundamental concept behind Python programming on GPU devices is based on what we have learned so far about CUDA, ROCm, and Anaconda. It is all about using their integrations with Python developed as PyCUDA, PyOpenCL, CuPy, and Numba, respectively.

With PyCUDA, you can use Python with NVIDIA GPUs, while with PyOpenCL, you can use NVIDIA, AMD GPUs and other massively parallel compute devices. CuPy allows you to implement NumPy like features on an NVIDIA GPU. After installing Accelerate with Conda, you can import the `numba` package very easily within your code to leverage your GPU device. We will explore this in detail in `Chapter 8`, *Working with Anaconda, CuPy, and Numba for GPUs*.

The dual advantage

Python is a very simple and easy-to-understand language. To use the preceding GPU wrappers on Python, you needn't learn the languages of all those APIs (specifically CuPy and Numba). Like we do with Python code, you can directly harness the compute power of GPU devices. Let's explore this further by looking into the features of the API integrations we just mentioned for Python according to their official technical documentation.

PyCUDA

Programming on Python with **PyCUDA** requires you to have knowledge of basic CUDA-C programming skills in order to harness NVIDIA GPU devices. PyCUDA provides the following benefits:

- It is easier to write correct, leak, and crash-free code. PyCUDA knows about dependencies too, so (for example) it won't detach from a context before all memory allocated in it is also freed.
- Abstractions such as `pycuda.driver.SourceModule` and `pycuda.gpuarray.GPUArray` make CUDA programming even more convenient than with NVIDIA's C-based runtime.
- PyCUDA puts the full power of CUDA's driver API at your disposal, if you wish. This also includes code for interoperability with OpenGL.
- All CUDA errors are automatically translated into Python exceptions.
- PyCUDA's base layer is written in C++, so all the niceties mentioned are virtually free.

PyOpenCL

Programming on Python with **PyOpenCL** requires you to have knowledge of basic OpenCL-C programming skills across heterogeneous compute devices, including GPUs. PyOpenCL provides the following benefits:

- It is easier to write correct, leak, and crash-free code.
- PyOpenCL puts the full power of OpenCL's API at your disposal, if you wish. Every obscure `get_info()` query and all CL calls are accessible.
- All CL errors are automatically translated into Python exceptions.
- PyOpenCL's base layer is written in C++, so all the niceties that are mentioned are virtually free.
- PyOpenCL was tested and works with Apple's, AMD's, and NVIDIA's CL implementations.

CuPy

Programming on Python with **CuPy** does not necessarily involve the use of CUDA-C/C++ within your Python code in order to harness NVIDIA GPU devices. You can implement CuPy for NVIDIA GPUs in a way that looks very similar to a traditional NumPy implementation in Python. CuPy's features include the following:

- High performance with CUDA
- Highly compatible with NumPy
- Easy to install
- Easy to write a custom kernel
- Customizable memory allocator and memory pool
- cuDNN utilities

Numba (formerly Accelerate)

Programming in Python with **Numba**, or Accelerate, does not mandate the use of CUDA-C or OpenCL-C syntax within your Python code, though knowledge of those platforms is definitely an added advantage. With Numba on Anaconda, you can program across heterogeneous compute devices, including NVIDIA and AMD GPUs.

It comes with both CUDA (`cudatoolkit` Python package) and ROCm (`rocmtools` Python package) support, though Numba `rocmtools` is currently in an experimental stage. Numba provides the following features:

- On July 27, 2017, Numba was split into the Intel Distribution for Python and the open source Numba project's sub-projects, `pyculib`, `pyculib_sorting`, and `data_profiler`. Numba and all its sub-projects are now available under a BSD license.
- Accelerate provides bindings to the following CUDA libraries through Python code:
    - cuBLAS
    - cuFFT
    - cuSPARSE
    - cuRAND
    - CUDA-sorting algorithms from the CUB (a flexible library of cooperative threadblock primitives and other utilities for CUDA kernel programming) and modern GPU libraries
- Speed-boosted linear algebra operations in NumPy, SciPy, scikit-learn, and NumExpr libraries using Intel's **Math Kernel Library** (**MKL**).
- Accelerated variants of NumPy's built-in UFuncs (a universal function that takes a fixed number of specific inputs and produces a fixed number of specific outputs).

- Increased speed FFT in NumPy.

Summary

In this chapter, we learned about the basic differences between programming and computing. We learned about some of the fundamental concepts regarding how CUDA, ROCm, and Numba leverage GPUs. We also learned the many libraries facilitated by CUDA, ROCm, and Numba. The features of PyCUDA, PyOpenCL, and Numba were mentioned and highlighted.

Now that we're at the end of this chapter, you should be able to install CUDA, ROCm, and Anaconda on an Ubuntu-based system. You should also be able to set up the `hipify` tool and start porting existing CUDA code to its HIP version, especially if you are a research-code enthusiast. You are now familiar with the configurational differences between OpenCL with CUDA and OpenCL with ROCm. You have also learned the various reasons behind why Python is a great choice for GPU programming.

Before we start our hands-on experience with programming on CUDA, ROCm, PyCUDA, PyOpenCL, and Anaconda Accelerate, it is necessary to learn how to set up a platform on your operating system for source-code development in a convenient manner. So, in the next chapter, we will learn about how to set up an IDE to configure PyCUDA, PyOpenCL, and Anaconda Accelerate with the same in detail. Henceforth, we can go ahead with developing our GPU-accelerated Python programs with a hands-on approach.

Further reading

More information on PyCUDA, PyOpenCL, CuPy, and Numba with their features can be obtained from the following comprehensive resources:

- Official PyCUDA home page at `https://mathema.tician.de/software/pycuda/`
- Official PyOpenCL home page at `https://mathema.tician.de/software/pyopencl/`
- Official CuPy website at `https://cupy.chainer.org/`
- Official Numba website at `https://numba.pydata.org`
- Conventional CPU Computing vs GPU Computing: `http://www.mediafire.com/file/dv4llvwd9klnat2/Conventional_CPU_Computing_vs_GPU_Computing.pdf`

5
Setting Up Your Environment for GPU Programming

In this chapter, we will learn about the basic concepts behind using an **Integrated Development Environment** (**IDE**). We will look into choosing the most suitable IDE for GPU computing with Python by enlisting four IDEs. PyCharm will be discussed in detail and its effectiveness as a GPU programmable platform will be illustrated. Different editions of PyCharm will be compared and their features discussed. Every additional feature in the professional feature will be mentioned. Academic users and dedicated open source developers will learn how to apply for the professional edition free of charge.

We will learn how to install the educational version of PyCharm to get started with Python-oriented GPU computing so as to prepare you for the next chapter. In addition to setting up PyCharm, you will also read about PyDev, a Python programming IDE for Eclipse and Jupyter Lab, a web-based IDE that can run locally on your web browser. For PyDev, we will focus on LiClipse for installation, which offers lightweight editors, theming, and usability improvements for Eclipse. For Jupyter, we will use the Conda environment for installation that we learned about setting up in our previous chapter.

By the end of this chapter, you will be ready to configure PyCUDA, PyOpenCL, and Numba (Accelerate), and start programming within PyCharm itself (Chapter 6, *Working with CUDA and PyCUDA*). You will have the freedom to choose a system-wide interpreter or your existing Anaconda configuration in order to code within separate virtual environments. You will also be able to create your own virtual environments before proceeding with testing and learning how GPU computing programs work.

Choosing a suitable IDE for your Python code

An IDE is the digital home of every developer's workspace that seeks to serve as an intelligent source code development platform. A new-age IDE of this current era facilitates the creation of new tools for diversified application purposes. It primarily includes a source code editor, a debugger, and various automation tools in order to build new source code from scratch or improve existing code.

Choosing a suitable IDE that is most suitable for you as a programmer depends on your usage and programming preferences. Some of the most desirable features on an IDE are as follows:

- **Intelligent editor**: An IDE that can intelligently keep a watch over your code syntax while you write your programs can be extremely helpful in reducing errors in order to improve code productivity and in leading toward better quality assurance of the final release.
- **Integrated debugger**: When you compile your code successfully, line-by-line interpretation with a debugger integrated with your editor can help a lot in fine-tuning your program code. A quality debugger provides support for setting breakpoints and the visual rendering of steps within the editor.
- **Automated refactoring**: *Factoring* implies breaking up a complex problem or system into multiple portions that are easier to perceive, understand, program, and maintain. *Refactoring* is the process of restructuring the existing source code of a program and altering its internal structure without changing the external behavior of the program. An advanced IDE that automates this process is a definite advantage.
- **Version control integration:** When updating your source code within a repository, multiple versions of the same file are generated through multiple revisions. With efficient version control, tracking changes in code becomes very convenient. So, this feature is desired by many programmers and developers due to its significance in agile development. Version controlling is usually referenced via a revision number of the source file under review.

Some more desired features within an IDE would be code search, multiple language support, applied computing, AI assistance, and a web-integrated development environment. All of these requirements vary from programmer to programmer, depending on usage and applicability preferences.

There are numerous IDEs available for programming with Python. Let's explore some of them:

- **PyCharm**: PyCharm was developed by JetBrains and was first released in July 2010 specifically for the Python programming language. This is our IDE of choice for our hands-on development of Python-based GPU programs throughout this book. The following screenshot is an example from Numba's official CUDA documentation. Here, we have tested the `cuda.atomic.max` operation by setting up a CUDA toolkit with `numba` and executing the program. We will explore customized examples and more in `Chapter 8`, *Working with Anaconda, CuPy, and Numba for GPUs.*The following is a screenshot of the PyCharm editor:

In the next section, we will explore more on PyCharm and its various features in detail. For now, let's look into some other Python IDEs and their features:

- **PyDev, Python IDE for Eclipse**: PyDev is a plugin for Eclipse that can be used as a cross-platform Python IDE. It also supports **IronPython** and **Jython**. It was first released in July 2003 and was developed by Appcelerator. We will learn how to install this IDE in the *Installing the PyDev Python IDE for Eclipse* section of this chapter. Some of its features through its advanced type inference techniques are as follows:

  - Code completion
  - Code analysis
  - A debugger
  - An interactive console
  - Refactoring
  - Tokens browser
  - Django integration

  The following is a screenshot of PyDev in Eclipse:

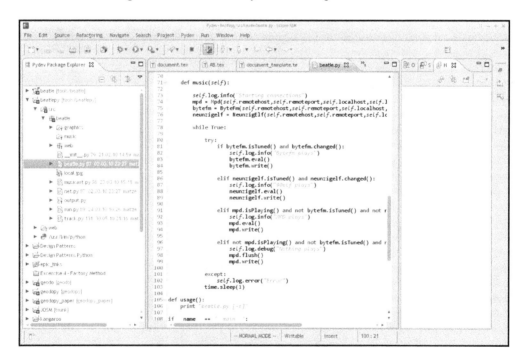

- **Jupyter Notebook and Jupyter Lab**: Jupyter Notebook and Jupyter Lab are both web-based implementations of IDEs. Jupyter Notebook allows web-based interaction and line-by-line implementation of Python code. On the other hand, Jupyter Lab is a full-fledged IDE with a source code editor that can be launched from a browser. We will learn how to use it in the *Installing Jupyter Notebook and Jupyter Lab* section of this chapter. Its features are as follows:

  - **JavaScript Object Notation** (**JSON**) document format
  - Markdown text
  - Versioned schema
  - Ordered list of input/output cells
  - Mathematical implementations
  - Plot generation
  - Version-control integration (available as an add-on for both Jupyter Notebook and Jupyter Lab)

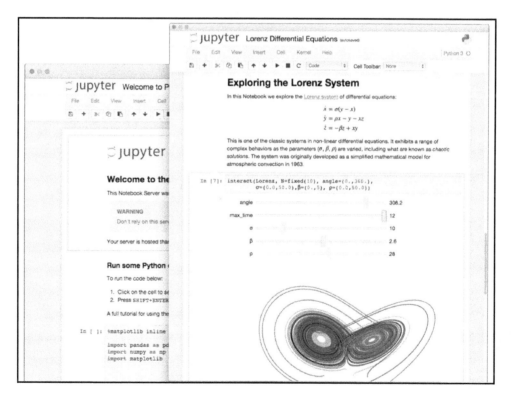

Screenshots of Jupyter Notebook (left) and Jupyter Lab (right) via the official Jupyter home page

- **Eric**: Eric is a fully-featured Python IDE and editor based on the cross-platform Qt UI toolkit. Developed in Python itself by Detlev Offenbach, Eric was first released in 2002. Some of its many features are as follows:
  - Unlimited number of editors
  - Configurable syntax highlighting
  - Content assist:
    - Source code auto-completion
    - Source code call tips
  - Brace matching
  - Error highlighting
  - Advanced search functionality including project-wide search-and-replace
  - Integrated class browser
  - Integrated version-control interface for Mercurial, Subversion, and Git repositories (as core plugins)

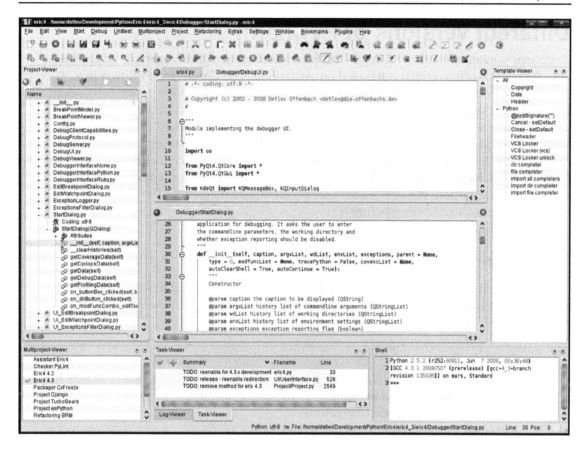

Screenshot of Eric 4, a free Python IDE uploaded by the development team: https://commons.wikimedia.org/wiki/
File:Screenshot_Eric_4.png

PyCharm – an IDE exclusively made for Python

PyCharm is a fully-featured IDE specifically focused on the Python programming language with unique code assistance and analysis, improved productivity, and web and scientific development. In this section, we will learn about the various editions of PyCharm, including the most recent one. Before moving on to its installation process walkthrough, we will learn about each of these editions in detail, including their different features.

Different versions of PyCharm

PyCharm is available in four different editions: **Community**, **Professional**, **Educational**, and the latest edition, which is focused on Anaconda. The Community edition is a lightweight version with limited features, but it is quite powerful for performing scientific tasks. The Professional edition includes each and every feature offered by PyCharm for professional usage in productivity-focused environments. The Educational version, or the Educational Edition, is focused toward learners and educators that includes courses to get started with Python programming even for novices. The most recent edition of PyCharm is known as **PyCharm for Anaconda**, which is specially designed for working with the Anaconda distribution. We will learn more about it after discussing the first three editions that have been available since before it.

The Community edition

The Community edition is a lightweight version of the PyCharm IDE for Python and scientific development. It is completely open source under the Apache 2 license and is freely available for download and deployment.

The following features are available in the Community edition:

- **Intelligent editor:** When editing Python code, the PyCharm editor makes the development process extremely convenient through the implementation of intelligent source code navigation.
- **Graphical debugger:** PyCharm's debugger GUI is more than just a debugger because it allows the visual confirmation of source code during debugging.
- Refactoring: PyCharm offers multiple refactoring abilities to track down affected source code references with automatic correction.
- **Code inspections:** Code inspection through a built analysis configuration is possible through PyCharm. It goes beyond just compiling errors by notifying you about different code inefficiencies. One example is this: reporting code statements that remain unused during execution.
- **Version control integration:** PyCharm provides version control not only at IDE level but also at project level. At IDE level, it is facilitated through bundled plugins, whereas at project level, it can implemented through project folder association with one or more version control systems.

Here is a list of support for frameworks and tools:

- Core Python language support
- Test runners
- reStructuredText support
- PyQt
- PyGTK
- Package management
- Virtualenv/Buildout
- Python console
- IPython notebook
- Anaconda

Here are some supported platforms:

- XML, HTML, YAML, JSON, RelaxNG
- Git, Mercurial, CVS, Subversion, GitHub
- IntelliLang
- Local Terminal
- Task management

The Professional edition

PyCharm Professional edition is a full-featured IDE for Python and web development. It is available under a paid subscription format for businesses, organizations, and individuals. But students, teachers, academic institutions, and open source project developers can apply for a free annual license.

If you are a student or a teacher with an academic email address, you are eligible to apply for a free license at `https://www.jetbrains.com/student/`.

If you work on an Apache Foundation project or a dedicated regular open source project, you can also apply for a free license by following this URL: `https://www.jetbrains.com/buy/opensource/`.

The Professional edition offers a host of additional features:

- Web development with JavaScript, CoffeeScript, TypeScript, HTML/CSS, and others
- Frameworks such as Django, Flask, Google App Engine, Pyramid, web2py
- Remote development capabilities, such as remote run/debug, VM support
- Database and SQL support
- UML and SQLAlchemy diagrams
- Scientific tools

Additional frameworks and tools are Cython, Django, AppEngine, Flask, Jinja2, Mako, web2py, Pyramid, Profiler, SQLAlchemy, diagrams, remote, interpreters, remote debugging, Vagrant, Docker, duplicate code detection, code coverage, `.po` files support, BDD support, profiler integration, and thread concurrency visualization.

The Professional edition can also support the following additional platforms. Using these differs from developer to developer, depending on diverse application preferences:

- CSS/HAML/SASS/LESS/Stylus
- Database/SQL
- JavaScript and JS debugger
- Perforce, TFS
- FTP/SFTP/FTPS remote host deployment
- TextMate bundles
- REST client
- Puppet
- File watchers

The Educational edition – PyCharm Edu

The PyCharm Edu IDE is a must-have for beginners who are new to the world of Python programming. This educational version is very comprehensive for both learners and educators. If you do not have prior experience with Python, you can opt for this edition for an easier way to get started with Python-based GPU computing. When you feel confident enough with the language's usage, you can simply switch to a pure development mode without having to install a separate edition all over again!

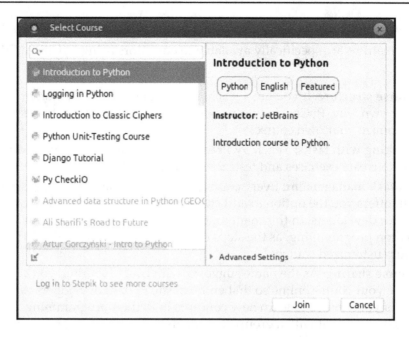

A screenshot of PyCharm Edu's inbuilt introductory courses on Python

Features for learners

The following featurs are available in PyCharm for learners who are using PyCharm Edu for learning Python:

- **Easy start:** With PyCharm Edu, you do not require any prior experience with the Python programming language, as it is bundled with a built-in introductory course so that you can get started learning the language. It also has many additional features.
- **Adaptive learning:** Adaptive learning is a very desirable feature because it allows you to adjust the difficulty level of a course according to the learner's skillset. As you keep learning more, the level will keep increasing in gradual steps.
- **Professional environment:** Even if it is an educational edition, PyCharm Edu includes all the primary professional features comprising of smart code completion, code inspections, and visual debugger.
- **Switching to development:** You always have the option to switch to the professional interface whenever you like (mostly, once you are comfortable with the language skillset and wish to switch over).

Features for educators

The following features are specifically available to educators using PyCharm Edu to teach Python:

- **Course structure:** If you are a teacher and want to teach Python programming in your own way, PyCharm Edu provides you with the option to create and customize your own courses.
- **Working with tasks: Teach by Practice** is a feature in PyCharm Edu that allows you to create exercises and tests for the learner, along with hints.
- **Subtask management:** Every course consists of certain tasks to pursue. PyCharm Edu offers you the option to add steps or subtasks to each of these tasks for novice developers. In this manner, they can gain further, in-depth knowledge in Python programming, as the steps or subtasks can increase the difficulty level of your customized courses.
- **Course sharing:** As the name suggests, with course sharing, you can publicly share your course online so that enthusiastic Python developers can make good use of your course to learn new concepts in Python programming. You can also privately share it with a group of students, co-workers, or anyone interested in learning the concepts you share throughout your course.

PyCharm for Anaconda

PyCharm for Anaconda is a special edition focused on Anaconda. JetBrains, the official developers of PyCharm, did a great thing by announcing its release. Previously, many developers and researchers had to configure PyCharm and Anaconda individually. But thanks to this latest edition, you can now make use of the built-in Anaconda support within PyCharm to create Conda environments and manage the installation of packages from the Anaconda repository. Most obviously, PyCharm for Anaconda also includes the same features we discussed previously for Professional and Community editions.

Installing PyCharm

As we are now familiar with PyCharm's basic functionalities, features, and its various editions, let's proceed with the steps that are required to install PyCharm on an Ubuntu-based Linux system. Since we are having a learning experience, we'll focus on installing the Educational edition of PyCharm, that is, PyCharm Edu:

1. Download PyCharm Edu. To download PyCharm Edu, you can directly visit the following page on your web browser: `https://www.jetbrains.com/pycharm-edu/download/`:

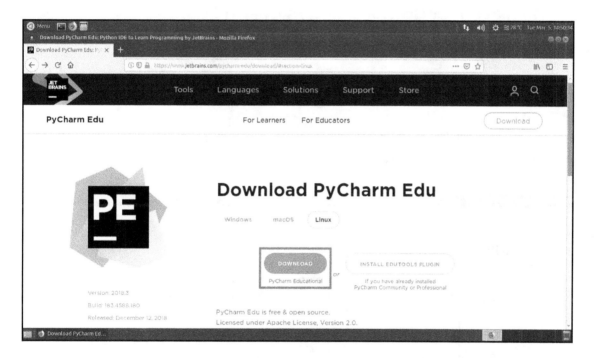

This link will automatically detect your operating system and provide the appropriate download link:

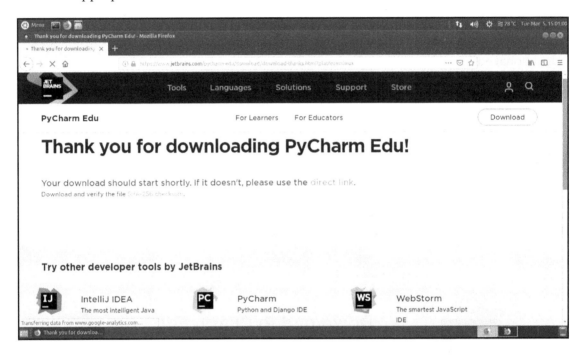

2. Note that you will have to ensure that **Save File** is selected before proceeding with the download:

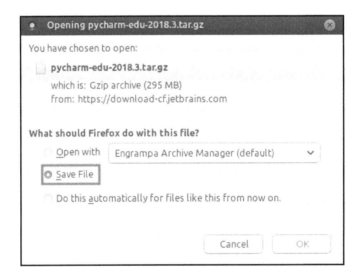

After downloading, the compressed file will be located at the `Downloads` directory, which is located at `/home/<user-name>/`:

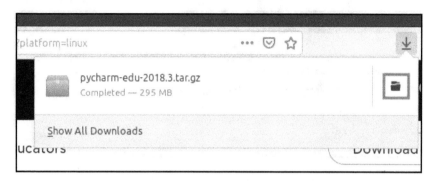

3. Now, from the `Downloads` directory, right-click beside the file and select **Open in Terminal** from the drop-down menu:

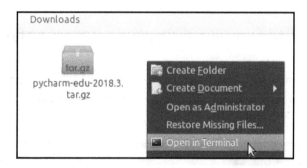

4. The Terminal will open within the same directory. Use the following commands to set up PyCharm:

```
$ tar -xvzf pycharm-edu-2018.3.tar.gz --directory /opt
$ echo 'export PYCHARM=/opt/pycharm-edu-2018.3' >> ~/.bashrc
$ echo 'export PATH=$PATH:$PYCHARM' >> ~/.bashrc
$ echo 'alias pycharm=$PYCHARM/bin/./pycharm.sh' >> ~/.bashrc
$ . ~/.bashrc
```

You can also add it to the system menu later via **PyCharm Menu** > **Tools** > **Create Desktop Entry...**:

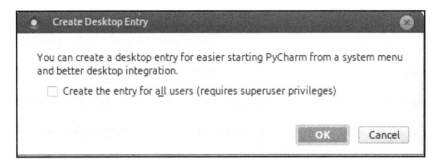

At this point, we have successfully completed our PyCharm installation.

First run

The following steps will take you through the process of setting up PyCharm the first time it is started:

1. Now, you can launch PyCharm from any Terminal with the `pycharm` command. Since this is a new installation, we do not need to import any older PyCharm settings and can select **OK**:

2. Accept the user agreement and click on **Continue**:

3. JetBrains will now ask you to opt for anonymous data sharing of usage information. Choose either of the two, according to your preference, and proceed:

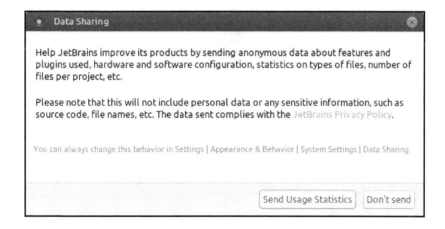

4. Let's select **Learner** and then **Start using EduTools**:

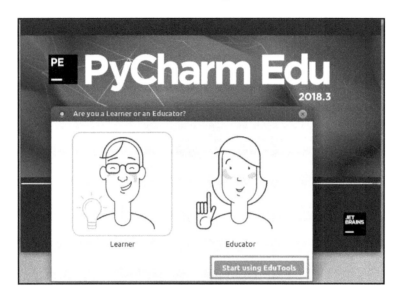

Welcome to PyCharm Edu! Now, you can starting learning Python with the inbuilt integrated courses or create a new project in addition to opening existing ones besides version control. We will learn more about setting up GPU implementations with Python and computing through them starting from the next chapter:

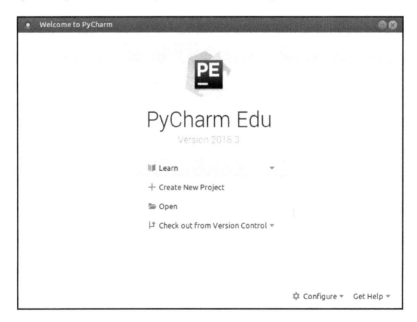

EduTools plugin for existing PyCharm users

If you have the Community or Professional edition of PyCharm already installed but still would like to have an educational experience, you need not install PyCharm Edu separately. EduTools can be additionally installed as a plugin, as shown in the first screenshot of the *Installing PyCharm* section.

Alternative IDEs for Python – PyDev and Jupyter

At the beginning of this chapter, we also mentioned two other IDEs and their features, namely PyDev for Eclipse IDE and Jupyter. Before discussing the steps to install both of them, let's read a bit more about them in this section, specifically from a Python programming perspective.

PyDev is available as a standalone IDE called **LiClipse**, and also as a plugin for the Eclipse IDE. We will focus on the standalone version, as it is the recommended way of using PyDev and also focus on Python only. LiClipse provides the option to start your work as a PyDev project after you have finished installing PyDev and have run it for the first time:

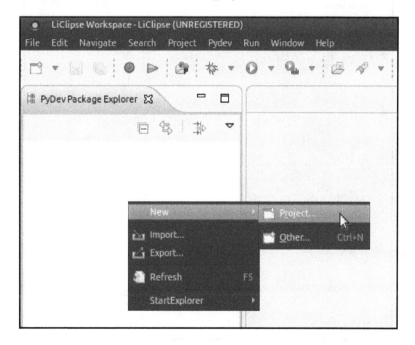

In the case of Jupyter, we focus more on Jupyter Lab, a computational environment that's a web-based IDE accessible from a web browser, along with Jupyter Notebook. This gives us the benefit of working on your Python source code right from your browser, preferably Mozilla Firefox. In the following screenshot, Jupyter Lab runs locally on port 8888 inside the Firefox browser.

Jupyter Lab provides access to four important interfaces all within a single user interface:

- **Notebook**
- The Python **Console**
- **Terminal**
- **Text File** (file names ending with .py are recognized by Jupyter Lab as Python files)

The following screenshot shows the Jupyter Lab components:

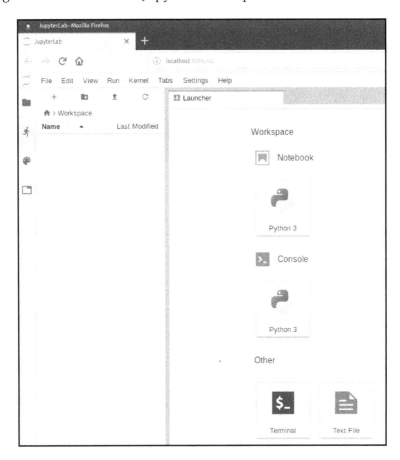

Installing the PyDev Python IDE for Eclipse

Installing and setting up PyDev is very similar to PyCharm. To install it, first download LiClipse, which is available as a compressed archive from `https://www.liclipse.com/download.html`:

Installing LiClipse

The recommended way of using LiClipse is by downloading the native installer for your platform, which provides a pre-configured standalone for Windows (32 bits or 64 bits), Mac OS (64 bits) or Linux (32 bits or 64 bits).

However, it's also possible to install it through the update site:
http://update.liclipse.com/latest
(note that you must have Java 8 installed in this case -- see details on the Update Site Install section).

The latest versions may be downloaded through the links below:

- LiClipse 5.1.3 Windows (64 bits)
- LiClipse 5.1.3 Windows (32 bits)
- LiClipse 5.1.3 Mac OS (64 bits)
- LiClipse 5.1.3 Linux (64 bits)
- LiClipse 5.1.3 Linux (32 bits)
- LiClipse 5.1.3 Local Update Site

Select the appropriate file for your platform and architecture:

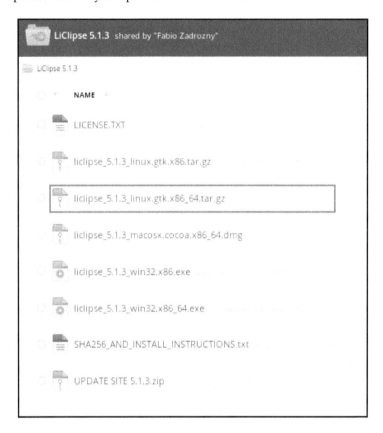

Once you have downloaded the file, you can use the following commands to set it up after opening the Terminal from the same location, as we saw for PyCharm earlier:

```
$ tar -xvzf liclipse_5.1.3_linux.gtk.x86_64.tar.gz --directory /opt
$ echo 'export LICLIPSE=/opt/liclipse' >> ~/.bashrc
$ echo 'export PATH=$PATH:$LICLIPSE' >> ~/.bashrc
$ echo 'alias liclipse=$LICLIPSE/bin/./LiClipse' >> ~/.bashrc
$ . ~/.bashrc
```

Note that in the fourth command, LiClipse is case-sensitive. So, ensure that L and C are in capital letters.

Now, you can launch LiClipse with the liclipse command from any Terminal.

Installing Jupyter Notebook and Jupyter Lab

The installation of Jupyter Notebook and Jupyter Lab is very simple, since we have already learned how to install Anaconda.

For a system-wide installation for both of them on Anaconda, open a Terminal and run the following command with `conda`:

```
$ conda install jupyter jupyterlab
```

For a separate installation, you can first create a virtual environment with `conda` and then use the preceding command. Here, we use `jupyterworld` as the name of the virtual environment. Enter `y` to proceed:

```
$ conda create --name jupyterworld
---
proceed ([y]/n)? y
$ conda activate jupyterworld
(jupyterworld)$ conda install jupyter jupyterlab
```

To run Jupyter Notebook, use the following command:

```
jupyter notebook
```

To run Jupyter Lab, use the following command:

```
jupyter lab
```

Your default web browser will launch it as soon as you enter the command.

Here is how the web-based IDE running on the localhost looks. The local URL is `localhost:8888/lab`:

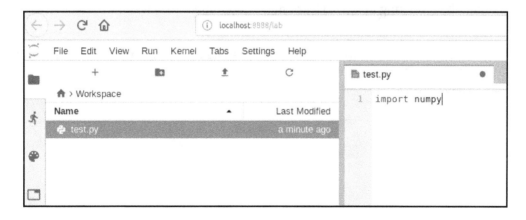

Summary

In this chapter, we learned about IDEs and their significance. We learned about different IDEs and also went through PyCharm, PyDev for Eclipse, and Jupyter Lab. We also mentioned another IDE named Eric, along with highlighting some of its many features. We discussed PyCharm in detail and learned the differences between the various editions of PyCharm and also how to apply for a free license as an academician or a dedicated open source developer. Installation steps for PyCharm, PyDev, and Jupyter Lab were covered in detail.

Once we were done setting up our IDE, we were able to dive deeper into the GPU-enabled Python programming perspective, hands-on. We customized and explored various programs through CUDA, PyCUDA-C, OpenCL, PyOpenCL, Anaconda, and Numba, making it more convenient for us to understand why PyCUDA, PyOpenCL, and Anaconda Accelerate were developed. We looked at the differences between CUDA-C and PyCUDA; OpenCL-C and PyOpenCL; and finally Anaconda, CuPy, and Numba (formerly Accelerate). You can also optionally use PyDev or Jupyter Notebook, as we discussed in this chapter, or any other IDE of your preference. Jupyter Lab in particular would prove helpful, as it's a computational environment within an existing Anaconda configuration.

In the next chapter, we will focus on PyCUDA. We will start with basic CUDA-C examples to understand how we can use C programming skills to leverage NVIDIA GPUs. This will be helpful for our PyCUDA computing experience that will follow. We will learn about the different ways to install it in a simple manner before we start our hands-on programming walkthrough with PyCUDA on PyCharm.

Further reading

You can read the following article to learn more about the topics we discussed in this chapter:

- Extensions such as **Hinterland** can be installed for content assist on Jupyter. It is available at `https://github.com/ipython-contrib/jupyter_contrib_nbextensions/tree/master/src/jupyter_contrib_nbextensions/nbextensions/hinterland`.

6
Working with CUDA and PyCUDA

With this chapter, we begin our hands-on Python-based experience with GPUs via a computing approach. From this perspective, it is important to understand that a computing approach primarily focuses on computational problem-solving as a series of steps: problem outline, problem solution, programming the underlying solution to the problem, and, finally, testing its effectiveness. We will follow this approach for all our computing problems in this book that we try to solve through GPU-accelerated programming.

C programming enthusiasts will be encouraged to invoke NVIDIA GPUs within their program code with CUDA-C, while Python programming enthusiasts will be motivated to use PyCUDA to invoke NVIDIA GPUs within their program code. We first start by understanding how a CUDA-C program works. The fundamental concepts behind a CUDA program and its components will be discussed with some basic examples that will help you to transition toward a PyCUDA environment. PyCUDA will be explained with a practical approach and also will be compared to CUDA. We focus on the applicability preference of PyCUDA over CUDA pertaining to the simplicity and power of Python's syntax.

This chapter is divided into the following sections to facilitate the learning process:

- Understanding how CUDA-C/C++ works via a simple example
- Installing PyCUDA for Python within an existing CUDA environment
- Configuring PyCUDA on your Python IDE
- How computing in PyCUDA works on Python
- Comparing PyCUDA to CUDA – an introductory perspective on reduction
- Writing your first PyCUDA programs to compute a general-purpose solution
- Useful exercise on computational problem solving

Technical requirements

Check out the following video to see the Code in Action:

```
http://bit.ly/2WAeVTy
```

Understanding how CUDA-C/C++ works via a simple example

By now, you must be aware of the computational advantages of CUDA C/C++ as per our earlier discussions. C/C++ coupled with CUDA allows you to modify parts of your source code to accelerate your computational results. The primary steps necessary for implementing CUDA code will be explored through a GPU program.

Please manually type in the code used in this book on your IDE from this point onward. Directly copying and pasting from the PDF will ruin the indentations in the code and make it unready to deploy.

First, let's look into the following conventional C++ program that multiplies two array elements using double precision. We'll run the kernel on 500 million elements on the CPU. All the elements of the p and q arrays are set to 24 and 12 respectively.

The following is the C++ program we've just described (cpu_multiply.cpp):

```cpp
#include <iostream> //Defining standard input/output stream objects
#include <math.h> //For using predefined math functions
#define N 500000000 //500 Million elements

clock_t begin, end;
float cpu_time_used;

// This is a function to multiply two array elements and also update the
results on the second array
void multiply(int n, double *p, double *q) {
  for (int i = 0; i < n; i++) q[i] = p[i] * q[i];
}

int main(void) {
  double *p = new double[N];
  double *q = new double[N];
```

Now we initialize the arrays:

```
// initialize arrays p and q on the host
for (int i = 0; i < N; i++) {
  p[i] = 24.0;
  q[i] = 12.0;
}

// Run function on 500 Million elements on the CPU
begin = clock();
multiply(N, p, q);
end = clock();
cpu_time_used = ((double) (end - begin)) / CLOCKS_PER_SEC;

// Verifying all values to be 288.0
// fabs(q[i]-288) (absolute value) should be 0
double maxError = 0.0;
for (int i = 0; i < N; i++){
    maxError = fmax(maxError, fabs(q[i]-288.0));
}
```

Now we verify the results and clear the memory:

```
std::cout << "Multiply function CPU execution time: " << cpu_time_used <<
" second(s)" << std::endl;
std::cout << "Max error: " << maxError << std::endl;
// Free memory
delete [] p;
delete [] q;
return 0;
}
```

Use the following commands to compile and run the preceding program:

```
$ g++ cpu_multiply.cpp -o cpu_multiply
$ ./cpu_multiply
Multiply function CPU execution time: 1.34016 second(s)
Max error: 0
```

As we can see from the preceding code, the CPU execution time for the multiply function is 1.34016 seconds. The CPU execution time can be variable.

Let's now look into the GPU version of the same program.

In `Chapter 4`, *Fundamentals of GPU Programming*, we briefly discussed the concepts of threads, blocks, and grids. Accordingly, to set the index on the GPU global function where we define the kernel, we use the following declaration:

```
index = threadIdx.x + blockIdx.x * blockDim.x
```

The variables we used are defined as:

- `threadIdx.x` is the thread index within the block
- `blockIdx.x` is the block index within the grid
- `blockDim.x` is the dimension of the block

Note that the preceding declarations for grids and blocks are both **1-dimensional** (**1D**).

1D grids and 2D blocks can be declared as follows:

```
index = threadIdx.x + blockDim.x*threadIdx.y +
blockDim.x*blockDim.y*blockIdx.x
```

For 1D grids and 3D blocks, we can use the following:

```
index = threadIdx.x + threadIdx.y* blockDim.x + threadIdx.z* blockDim.x*
blockDim.y
```

To ensure thread synchronization, we can also use `__syncthreads()` to make sure all the threads in the block go through the `if` statement defined within the kernel. If the `if` condition isn't met, none of the threads in the block will go through it.

In our main program, we use `cudaMalloc` to specifically allocate memory for GPU-only variables. In that case, we would have to specify transferring the variables from the CPU to the GPU and bring back the computed results to the CPU again. In the revised version, we also use unified memory allocation (`cudaMallocManaged`) to enable access to variables from both the CPU or the GPU. The revised code has also been included within comments inside the revised CUDA example included in this section.

When invoking the GPU kernel function, we use the following syntax:

```
multiply<<<Blocks_per_grid, Threads_per_block>>>(args)
```

The variables are defined as:

- `multiply` is the name of our kernel
- `Threads_per_block` is the number of threads inside each block, that is, the dimensions of each block

- `Blocks_per_grid`, on the other hand, is the number of blocks inside a grid or, in other words, the dimensions of the grid

Additionally, we can also opt to use a third parameter for shared memory when invoking the kernel.

`args` refers to the arguments we are passing to the GPU kernel function to be computed on the GPU for parallel computation with multiple threads.

`dim3` variables with integer vector data types can also be used to specify `Threads_per_block` or `Blocks_per_grid`. They can be declared as follows:

```
dim3 Threads_per_block(32,32)
dim3 Blocks_per_grid(N / Threads_per_block.x, N / Threads_per_block.y)
```

32 x 32 is 1,024 threads per block.

We calculate the number of blocks to get at least N threads in order to process N elements (500 million in this case) using 1,024 threads per block. We divide N by the number of threads per block (block size) and round it up if N is not a multiple of the number of threads per block.

Also note that we can use both `printf` or `cout` statements within the same program.

The following is the same program in CUDA (`gpu_multiply.cu`):

```
#include <iostream>

#define N 500000000 //500 Million Elements
#define THREADS_PER_BLOCK 1024

/* GPU kernel function to multiply two array elements and also update the
results on the second array
*/
__global__ void multiply(double *p, double *q, unsigned long n) {
  int index = threadIdx.x + blockIdx.x * blockDim.x;
  if (index < n) q[index] = p[index] * q[index];
}

int main(void) {
  double *p, *q; // host copies of p, q
  double *gpu_p, *gpu_q; // device copies of p, q

  // we need space for N unsigned long integers
  unsigned long size = N * sizeof(unsigned long);
  unsigned long i;
```

The following section of code shows the GPU device memory allocation with `cudaMalloc`:

```
// Allocate GPU/device copies of gpu_p, gpu_q
cudaMalloc((void**)&gpu_p, size);
cudaMalloc((void**)&gpu_q, size);

// Allocate CPU/host copies of p, q
p = (double *)malloc(size);
q = (double *)malloc(size);
```

After allocating memory for the CPU/host copies, let's now assign two values for both arrays. The `cudaMemcpyHostToDevice` function transfers host data to the device:

```
// Setup input values
for (i = 0; i < N - 1; ++i) {
  p[i] = 24.0;
  q[i] = 12.0;
}

// Copy inputs to device
cudaMemcpy(gpu_p, p, size, cudaMemcpyHostToDevice);
cudaMemcpy(gpu_q, q, size, cudaMemcpyHostToDevice);
//INITIALIZE CUDA EVENTS
cudaEvent_t start, stop;
float elapsedTime;
//CREATING EVENTS
cudaEventCreate(&start);
cudaEventCreate(&stop);
cudaEventRecord(start, 0);
```

Now we invoke the CUDA kernel and also pass the necessary arguments for computation on the GPU:

```
/*CUDA KERNEL STUFF HERE...
Launch multiply() kernel on GPU with N threads
*/
multiply << <(N + THREADS_PER_BLOCK - 1) / THREADS_PER_BLOCK,
THREADS_PER_BLOCK >> >(gpu_p, gpu_q, N);

//FINISH RECORDING
cudaEventRecord(stop, 0);
cudaEventSynchronize(stop);

//CALCULATE ELAPSED TIME
cudaEventElapsedTime(&elapsedTime, start, stop);

//DISPLAY COMPUTATION TIME
cudaDeviceProp prop;
```

```
int count;
cudaGetDeviceCount(&count);
for (int igtx = 0; igtx < count; igtx++) {
  cudaGetDeviceProperties(&prop, igtx);
```

You can also use GPUs to simultaneously compute an elementary multiplication table up to an enormous range. All you have to do is to add a third array, say, `r`, and pass it to the GPU to be used as `gpu_r`. n2 is a variable referring to the number for which you want to display the table, which you also must declare to be accepted as user input:

```
/*
printf("The GPU '%s' computed the multiplication table for %d in %f
milliseconds", prop.name, n2, elapsedTime);
printf("\n\nGPU Computation Time = %f ms",elapsedTime);
*/
```

The following code snippet displays the GPU device name and reports the computation time:

```
printf("\nGPU Device used for computation: %s\n", prop.name);
printf("\nMultiplication on GPU computed in: %f milliseconds",
elapsedTime);
}

// Copy device result back to host copy of q
cudaMemcpy(q, gpu_q, size, cudaMemcpyDeviceToHost);

// Verifying all values to be 288.0
// fabs(q[i]-288) (absolute value) should be 0
double maxError = 0.0;
for (int i = 0; i < N-1; ++i) maxError = fmax(maxError,
fabs(q[i]-288.0));
std::cout << "\nMax error: " << maxError << std::endl;
```

Finally, we clear up the CPU and GPU memory allocations:

```
// Clean CPU memory allocations
free(p); free(q);

// Clean GPU memory allocations
cudaFree(gpu_p);
cudaFree(gpu_q);
return 0;
}
```

Use the following commands to compile and run `gpu_multiply.cu`:

```
$ nvcc gpu_multiply.cu -o gpu_multiply
$ ./gpu_multiply
GPU Device used for computation: GeForce GTX TITAN X
Multiplication on GPU computed in: 46.440865 milliseconds
Max error: 0
```

Even though the GPU version shows itself to be about 28.8 times faster in the preceding example, the actual computation time depends on the entire operation, including the transfer of data between the CPU and the GPU. This Titan X version from NVIDIA belongs to the Maxwell architecture released in 2015. To get a complete estimate of the entire computation time, we can use the following Terminal-based profiling command, `nvprof`:

```
$ nvprof ./gpu_multiply
==23253== NVPROF is profiling process 23253, command: ./gpu_multiply

GPU Device used for computation: GeForce GTX TITAN X

Multiplication on GPU computed in: 45.111168 milliseconds
Max error: 0
==23253== Profiling application: ./gpu_multiply
==23253== Profiling result:
           Type  Time(%)      Time     Calls       Avg       Min       Max  Name
 GPU activities:   64.48%  863.43ms         2  431.71ms  429.96ms  433.47ms  [CUDA memcpy HtoD]
                   32.16%  430.61ms         1  430.61ms  430.61ms  430.61ms  [CUDA memcpy DtoH]
                    3.37%  45.061ms         1  45.061ms  45.061ms  45.061ms  multiply(double*, double*, unsigned long)
      API calls:   90.15%  1.29438s         3  431.46ms  430.04ms  433.56ms  cudaMemcpy
                    5.78%  83.029ms         2  41.515ms  3.3217ms  79.708ms  cudaMalloc
                    3.14%  45.126ms         1  45.126ms  45.126ms  45.126ms  cudaEventSynchronize
                    0.87%  12.533ms         2  6.2664ms  2.7815ms  9.7513ms  cudaFree
                    0.02%  263.33us        94  2.8010us     300ns  106.54us  cuDeviceGetAttribute
                    0.02%  261.07us         1  261.07us  261.07us  261.07us  cudaGetDeviceProperties
                    0.01%  145.22us         1  145.22us  145.22us  145.22us  cuDeviceTotalMem
                    0.00%  28.937us         1  28.937us  28.937us  28.937us  cudaLaunch
                    0.00%  27.919us         1  27.919us  27.919us  27.919us  cuDeviceGetName
                    0.00%  9.4900us         2  4.7450us  1.3550us  8.1350us  cudaEventCreate
                    0.00%  7.2200us         2  3.6100us  3.0590us  4.1610us  cudaEventRecord
                    0.00%  5.6390us         1  5.6390us  5.6390us  5.6390us  cudaEventElapsedTime
                    0.00%  1.8280us         3     609ns     329ns  1.1010us  cuDeviceGetCount
                    0.00%  1.0300us         3     343ns     122ns     490ns  cudaSetupArgument
                    0.00%     992ns         2     496ns     324ns     668ns  cuDeviceGet
                    0.00%     871ns         1     871ns     871ns     871ns  cudaConfigureCall
                    0.00%     207ns         1     207ns     207ns     207ns  cudaGetDeviceCount
```

You can see in the first row that the actual computation time for our GPU kernel named `multiply` is `45.061` milliseconds. The majority of the time is consumed by data transfers between the CPU and the GPU and the usage of `cudaMemcpy`, which facilitates these transfers.

Unified memory functionality has significantly improved since the launch of Pascal GPUs and later architectures. Even though we use a Titan X GPU that belongs to the Maxwell architecture preceding Pascal, we also modified and tested the preceding GPU code for unified memory:

```
#include <iostream>

#define N 500000000 //500 Million Elements
```

```
#define THREADS_PER_BLOCK 1024

// GPU kernel function to multiply two array elements and also update the
results on the second array
__global__ void multiply(double *p, double *q, unsigned long n) {
  int index = threadIdx.x + blockIdx.x * blockDim.x;
  if (index < n) q[index] = p[index] * q[index];
}

int main(void) {
  double *p, *q; // host copies of p, q
  // double *gpu_p, *gpu_q; // device copies of p, q
  // we need space for N unsigned long integers
  unsigned long size = N * sizeof(unsigned long);
  unsigned long i;
```

Comment out `cudaMalloc` allocations, as we are going to use unified memory:

```
/*
// Allocate GPU/device copies of gpu_p, gpu_q
cudaMalloc((void**)&gpu_p, size);
cudaMalloc((void**)&gpu_q, size);

// Allocate CPU/host copies of p, q
p = (double *)malloc(size);
q = (double *)malloc(size);
*/
```

Memory allocation of variables with `cudaMallocManaged` enables access from both the CPU and the GPU:

```
// Unified Memory Allocation for CPU and GPU
cudaMallocManaged((void**)&p, size);
cudaMallocManaged((void**)&q, size);

// Setup input values
for (i = 0; i < N - 1; ++i) {
  p[i] = 24.0;
  q[i] = 12.0;
}

/*
// Copy inputs to device
cudaMemcpy(gpu_p, p, size, cudaMemcpyHostToDevice);
cudaMemcpy(gpu_q, q, size, cudaMemcpyHostToDevice);
*/
```

After transferring the arrays to the GPU device, we now initialize events to record the computation time:

```
//INITIALIZE CUDA EVENTS
cudaEvent_t start, stop;
float elapsedTime;

//CREATING EVENTS
cudaEventCreate(&start);
cudaEventCreate(&stop);
cudaEventRecord(start, 0);
cudaMemPrefetchAsync(p, N * sizeof(double), 0);
cudaMemPrefetchAsync(q, N * sizeof(double), 0);
cudaDeviceSynchronize();

//CUDA KERNEL STUFF HERE...
// Launch multiply() kernel on GPU with N threads
multiply << <(N + THREADS_PER_BLOCK - 1) / THREADS_PER_BLOCK,
THREADS_PER_BLOCK >> >(p, q, N);
```

After invoking the kernel, we finish recording the computation time:

```
// FINISH RECORDING
cudaEventRecord(stop, 0);
cudaDeviceSynchronize();
cudaEventSynchronize(stop);

//CALCULATE ELAPSED TIME
cudaEventElapsedTime(&elapsedTime, start, stop);

//DISPLAY COMPUTATION TIME
cudaDeviceProp prop;
int count;
cudaGetDeviceCount(&count);
for (int igtx = 0; igtx < count; igtx++) {
  cudaGetDeviceProperties(&prop, igtx);
  printf("\nGPU Device used for computation: %s\n", prop.name);
  printf("\nMultiplication on GPU computed in: %f milliseconds",
elapsedTime);
  }
```

We do not need the following line that uses cudaMemcpyDeviceToHost (commented) because we are using unified memory:

```
/*
// Copy device result back to host copy of q
cudaMemcpy(q, gpu_q, size, cudaMemcpyDeviceToHost);
*/
```

```
    // Verifying all values to be 288.0
    // fabs(q[i]-288) (absolute value) should be 0
    double maxError = 0.0;
    for (int i = 0; i < N-1; ++i) maxError = fmax(maxError,
fabs(q[i]-288.0));
    std::cout << "\nMax error: " << maxError << std::endl;

    // Clean unified memory allocations
    cudaFree(p);
    cudaFree(q);
    return 0;
}
```

Once again, we run `nvprof` to check the output along with the profiling:

```
$ nvcc gpu_multiply_revised.cu -o gpu_multiply_revised
$ nvprof ./gpu_multiply_revised
==24085== NVPROF is profiling process 24085, command: ./gpu_multiply_revised

GPU Device used for computation: GeForce GTX TITAN X

Multiplication on GPU computed in: 707.247864 milliseconds
Max error: 0
==24085== Profiling application: ./gpu_multiply_revised
==24085== Profiling result:
            Type  Time(%)      Time     Calls       Avg       Min       Max  Name
 GPU activities:  100.00%  44.840ms         1  44.840ms  44.840ms  44.840ms  multiply(double*, double*, unsigned long)
      API calls:   35.14%  714.82ms         2  357.41ms  286.24ms  428.58ms  cudaMallocManaged
                   32.56%  662.39ms         1  662.39ms  662.39ms  662.39ms  cudaLaunch
                   30.04%  611.13ms         2  305.57ms  282.21ms  328.92ms  cudaFree
                    2.21%  44.925ms         2  22.462ms  47.642us  44.877ms  cudaDeviceSynchronize
                    0.03%  677.37us        94  7.2060us     374ns  304.22us  cuDeviceGetAttribute
                    0.01%  258.02us         1  258.02us  258.02us  258.02us  cudaGetDeviceProperties
                    0.01%  194.39us         1  194.39us  194.39us  194.39us  cuDeviceTotalMem
                    0.00%  45.546us         1  45.546us  45.546us  45.546us  cuDeviceGetName
                    0.00%  17.407us         2  8.7030us  8.3380us  9.0690us  cudaEventRecord
                    0.00%  16.356us         2  8.1780us  1.2330us  15.123us  cudaEventCreate
                    0.00%  4.2530us         2  2.1260us  1.1520us  3.1010us  cudaMemPrefetchAsync
                    0.00%  2.9140us         1  2.9140us  2.9140us  2.9140us  cudaEventElapsedTime
                    0.00%  2.8480us         1  2.8480us  2.8480us  2.8480us  cudaEventSynchronize
                    0.00%  2.5410us         3     847ns     411ns  1.4760us  cuDeviceGetCount
                    0.00%  1.4210us         2     710ns     489ns     932ns  cuDeviceGet
                    0.00%     763ns         3     254ns     123ns     327ns  cudaSetupArgument
                    0.00%     599ns         1     599ns     599ns     599ns  cudaConfigureCall
                    0.00%     153ns         1     153ns     153ns     153ns  cudaGetDeviceCount

==24085== Unified Memory profiling result:
Device "GeForce GTX TITAN X (0)"
   Count  Avg Size  Min Size  Max Size  Total Size  Total Time  Name
    3817  1.9988MB  256.00KB  2.0000MB  7.450584GB  662.1459ms  Host To Device
   68690  170.61KB  4.0000KB  0.9961MB  11.17603GB  983.5813ms  Device To Host
Total CPU Page faults: 34345
```

Optimizing GPU+CPU execution times greatly depends on the efficient use of parallel reduction, shared memory, and dynamic parallelism within the __global__ kernel. These measures ensure the efficient use of available hardware resources on the GPU to keep overall execution times as low as possible. This is extremely necessary for a professional environment.

Also, a good measure to take is to connect a secondary low-end GPU to your PC monitor to take readings during computations. This way, you can lift the burden off your primary GPU for the unnecessary sharing of resources (display) and dedicate its complete power to performing your computations.

In the next section, we start exploring how to make use of this CUDA API with the simplicity of Python code. When we begin computing with PyCUDA, we'll explore the scope of the functionalities and parallelism features cited previously, specifically in Python. While PyCUDA allows you to use both CUDA-C/C++ and Python code, our focus will be on making the most of a Python programming approach toward NVIDIA GPUs.

Installing PyCUDA for Python within an existing CUDA environment

Since we have already learned about CUDA's installation and implementation, it will now be easier for us to get started with our PyCUDA installation procedure for Python. You also do not need to install Python as it is already available (both 2.x and 3.x) with a freshly installed version of the Ubuntu 18.04 Linux operating system.

As we have also learned about Anaconda and its setup, we can also make use of Python 2.x or 3.x, which is readily available with an existing Anaconda configuration. Setting up PyCUDA will enable implementing CUDA kernels within your existing Python setup of choice and then computing with it on your NVIDIA GPU.

There are primarily two methods of installation.

Anaconda-based installation of PyCUDA

This is the recommended way to get started with PyCUDA for a productivity environment. By using a virtual environment, you can safely experiment with your programming skills without affecting the system-wide Python setup.

To set up PyCUDA within Anaconda, let's install `pycuda` with `conda` via the following commands on a Terminal. Proceed by entering `y`. The first command would be necessary depending upon the updated state of the Anaconda installation:

```
$ conda update -n base conda -c anaconda
Collecting package metadata: done
Solving environment: done
---
```

```
proceed ([y]/n)? y
---

$ conda install -c lukepfister pycuda
Collecting package metadata: done
Solving environment: done
The following NEW packages will be INSTALLED:
pycuda lukepfister/linux-64::pycuda-2017.1-py36_0
---
proceed ([y]/n)? y
```

pip – system-wide Python-based installation of PyCUDA

For a system-wide installation of PyCUDA tied to your existing Python base, we first have to install `pip`, which is a tool for installing Python packages.

To install Pip for Python 3.x, use the following command:

```
sudo apt install python3-pip
```

`pip` for Python 2.x can be installed via the following:

```
sudo apt install python-pip
```

Here is an important note from the developers of `pip`:

```
Python 2.7 will reach the end of its life on January 1st, 2020. Please
upgrade your Python as Python 2.7 won't be maintained after that date. A
future version of pip will drop support for Python 2.7.
```

It is recommended to use/transition to Python 3.x to work on Python-based packages or to develop new Python software to future-proof GPU support.

Coming back to our system-wide PyCUDA installation, the Python 3.x version can be installed with the following commands on a terminal:

```
$ pip3 install --upgrade pip
$ pip3 install --user pycuda
```

Note that `pip install --user pycuda` also performs the same operation as `pip3 install --user pycuda`.

The alternative commands for installing PyCUDA for Python 2.x would be this:

```
$ pip2 install --upgrade pip
$ pip2 install --user pycuda
```

Now you have a user-specified configuration ready for use system-wide on your Ubuntu Linux system. In the next section, we'll learn how to configure both Conda-based and user-specified system-wide configurations on the PyCharm IDE.

Configuring PyCUDA on your Python IDE

In this book, we use PyCharm as our preferred IDE because of its unique design focusing on the Python programming language alone. The next steps are specifically used in two scenarios, namely, using an already-existing Conda environment and a system-wide setting. If you prefer a different IDE, you can still use these steps as a reference because the procedure is very similar. To configure PyCUDA with PyCharm, we will revisit the two methods of installing packages as discussed in the previous chapter.

Conda-based virtual environment

Now let's create a virtual environment with conda as a new PyCharm pure Python project. Perform the following steps to create and configure the environment in PyCharm:

1. Launch PyCharm:

2. Choose **New Project** from the PyCharm main menu:

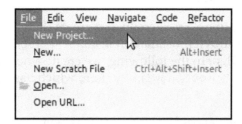

3. Now make sure the new environment is using Conda:

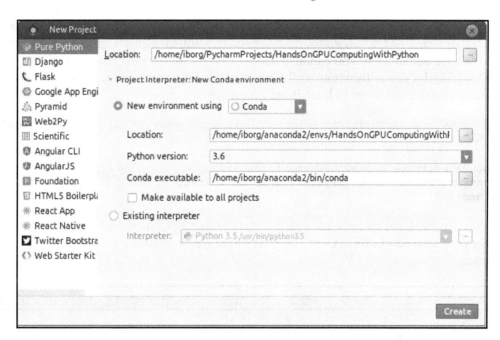

After creating the Conda environment, you will have a ready-to-use PyCUDA development environment.

Now you can import pycuda within your Python programs. As you can see next, PyCharm detects and recommends the pycuda (<built-in>) just as you begin to type import pycuda:

Note that `<built-in>` refers to a Conda-wide `pycuda` package. At this stage, we are done configuring PyCUDA on the IDE.

But as alternate measure (optional), you could also create the virtual environment with a Terminal (as we saw in our Jupyter installation in Chapter 5, *Setting Up Your Environment for GPU Programming*, on IDEs). In the following, we create a new virtual environment with the new name, `HandsOnGPUComputingWithPython`, which has already been created by PyCharm:

```
$ conda create --name HandsOnGPUComputingWithPython2
---
proceed ([y]/n)? y
```

All virtual environments are created in a directory called `envs` in your Anaconda directory (`$HOME/anaconda2` or `$HOME/anaconda3`). Even though we already have `pycuda` within our Conda base installation, you can also choose to activate the new environment and install PyCUDA locally within it as well. This is helpful if you do not want a Conda-wide `pycuda` installation and want to keep it only for a specific project.

Use the following commands from a Terminal to activate your virtual environment and install PyCUDA:

```
$ conda activate HandsOnGPUComputingWithPython
(HandsOnGPUComputingWithPython) $ conda install -c lukepfister pycuda
python=3.6
```

When you use this local `pycuda` configuration, note that PyCharm will show you the complete path instead of `<built-in>` as it now has access to its own local PyCUDA environment:

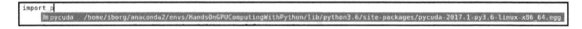

Now let's see how a system-wide installation with `pip` can be done for PyCUDA.

pip-based system-wide environment

To configure a system-wide PyCUDA installation for Python, you can create a new project on PyCharm or change your system interpreter. Follow these steps to configure PyCharm to use the system-wide installation of Python:

1. Create a new project in PyCharm:

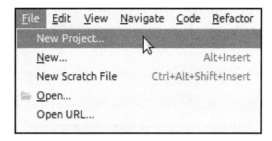

2. Instead of a Conda environment, we will now select the preinstalled system-wide Python installation on Ubuntu:

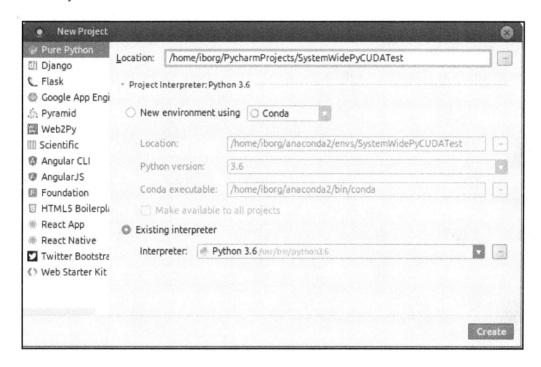

Once this environment has been created, you can now start using the user-specific system-wide PyCUDA installation on PyCharm:

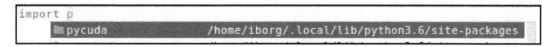

PyCharm will still prefer to use the system-wide configuration if you want to go back to using your Conda-based PyCUDA projects that were set up within the virtual environment. To make PyCharm re-recognize the Conda-based PyCUDA package once again, you'll have to perform the following steps:

1. First, go to **Settings** in the **File** menu:

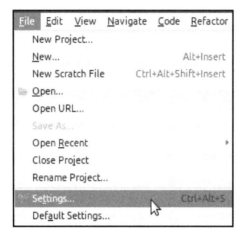

2. Now click on the gear symbol shown on the top-right area of the **Settings** window:

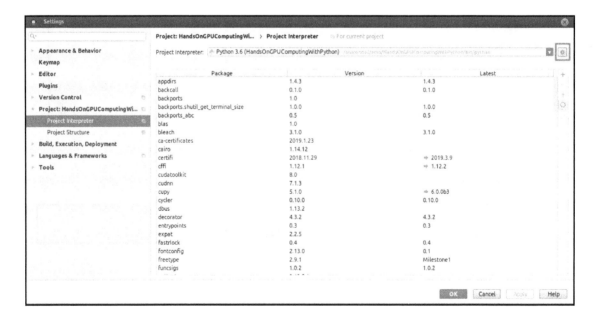

3. Click on **Show All**:

4. Select your project interpreter from the list and click on the icon that says **Show paths for the selected interpreter** when you hover over it using the mouse:

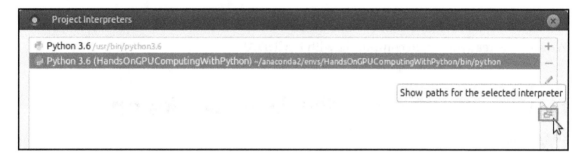

5. Remove the user-specified path that PyCharm sees system-wide. Click **OK**:

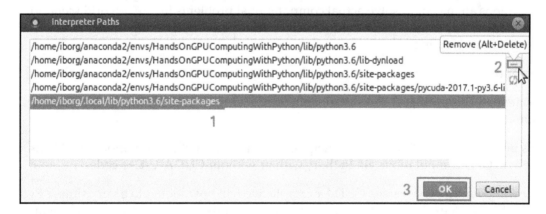

6. Hit **OK** once again in the **Project Interpreters** window. Finally, click on **Apply** in the **Settings** window for the changes to take effect.
7. Now you can start using your Conda-specific local PyCUDA package once again:

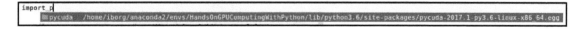

If you wish to switch between the two, all you have to do is toggle between **Python 3.6 /usr/bin/python3.6** and the Conda-based virtual environment in the system interpreter window:

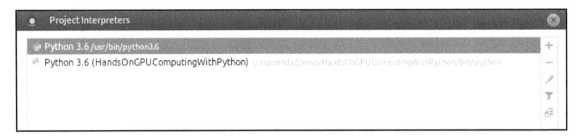

We are now ready to begin computing with PyCUDA!

How computing in PyCUDA works on Python

In our very first chapter, we emphasized that computing is application-specific and is a technique to calculate any measurable entity across multi-disciplinary fields. These calculations are meant to solve actual computational problems in a real-world scenario, which is why our focus is on computational problem solving, catering to the prime objective of computing.

Computing: The answer to every computational problem lies in its computed solution.

Accelerated computing: A computationally intensive problem requires an accelerated solution.

Let's understand how PyCUDA can help us solve a myriad of computational problems based on GPU computations via Python, with or without CUDA-C/C++ code.

Following our first C++ versus CUDA example, we will now look into a very simple Python versus PyCUDA example with a similar approach, hands-on with PyCharm. Following this, we'll shift our focus toward actual GPU-accelerated computations to solve specific computational problems with PyCUDA.

Perform the following steps to create a simple program in Python that will initialize two arrays with values and then calculate a third array whose values will the the product of corresponding elements in the two arrays, using the PyCharm IDE:

1. Launch PyCharm as illustrated earlier and create a new empty Python file:

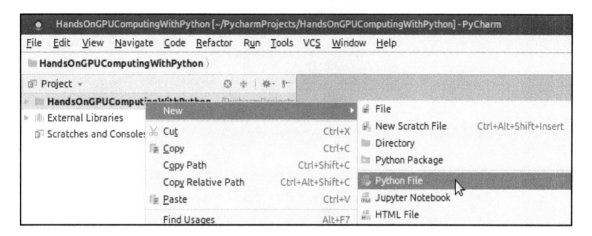

2. Now use the following code. We again try to use 500 million elements with double precision:

```python
import numpy as np
from timeit import default_timer as timer

N = 500000000 #500 Million Elements

# CPU Function to multiply two array elements and also update the
results on the second array
def multiply(p_cpu, q_cpu):
    for i in range(N):
        q_cpu[i] = p_cpu[i] * q_cpu[i]

def main():
    #Initialize the two arrays of double data type all with 0.0
values upto N
    p = np.zeros(N, dtype=np.double)
    q = np.zeros(N, dtype=np.double)
    #Update all the elements in the two arrays with 23.0 and 12.0
respectively
    p.fill(23.0)
    q.fill(12.0)
```

`default_timer` is used to compute the CPU computation time:

```
#Time the CPU Function
begin = timer()
multiply(p, q)
numpy_cpu_time = timer() - begin

#Report CPU Computation Time
print("CPU function took %f seconds." % numpy_cpu_time)
#Choose a random integer index value between 0 to N
random = np.random.randint(0, N)
#Verify all values to be 276.0 for second array by random
selection
print("New value of second array element with random index",
random, "is", q[random])

if __name__ == "__main__":
    main()
```

3. Right-click over the code and select **Run 'conventional_python_...'**:

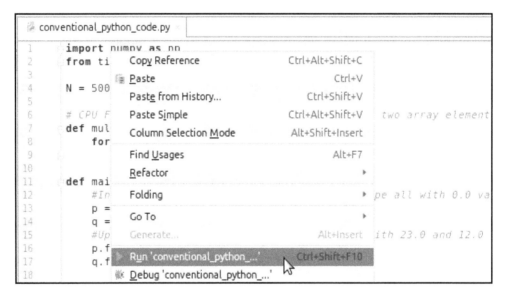

Python does not have built-in array support and that is why we import the `numpy` library for this. This time, we find that the CPU computation time is many times higher than we previously saw on C++ in the first section of this chapter. It took `114.381630` seconds:

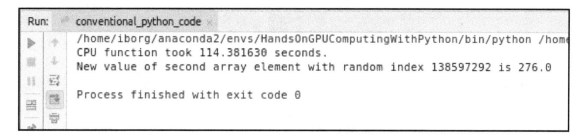

cProfile is a command-line-based Python profiler similar to nvprof in CUDA. With the following command, you can profile your complete Python code inclusive of GPU-based allocations and look up the CPU+GPU computation time:

```
python -m cProfile -s cumulative your_program.py | less
```

To exit from the interface, press *Q*.

For our PyCUDA version of the same code we used in the preceding code, we choose a version that includes minimal C code:

```
import pycuda.autoinit
import pycuda.driver as cudadrv
import numpy
import pycuda.gpuarray as gpuarray
from pycuda.elementwise import ElementwiseKernel

# Here, we multiply the two values and update all the elements of the
second array with the new product

# Note that we pass C syntax into the ElementwiseKernel
multiply = ElementwiseKernel (
        "double *a_gpu, double *b_gpu",
        "b_gpu[i] = a_gpu[i] * b_gpu[i]",
        "multiply")

N = 500000000 # 500 Million Elements

a_gpu = gpuarray.to_gpu(numpy.zeros(N).astype(numpy.double))
b_gpu = gpuarray.to_gpu(numpy.zeros(N).astype(numpy.double))
```

The following code snippet assigns values to all the elements of the two arrays, calculates and stores their product using the multiply function, and then prints the results and time taken:

```
a_gpu.fill(23.0)
b_gpu.fill(12.0)
begin = cudadrv.Event()
```

```
end = cudadrv.Event()

# Time the GPU function
begin.record()
multiply(a_gpu, b_gpu)
end.record()
end.synchronize()
gpu_multiply_time = begin.time_till(end)
random = numpy.random.randint(0,N)

# Randomly choose index from second array to confirm changes to second
array
print("New value of second array element with random index", random, "is",
b_gpu[random])

# Report GPU Function time
print("GPU function took %f milliseconds." % gpu_multiply_time)
```

The GPU function now computes the same operation in 62.38826 milliseconds:

First, we import `autoinit` from PyCUDA, which automatically performs all the steps necessary to get CUDA ready to submit the NVIDIA GPU compute kernels. The `driver` module is imported from PyCUDA to calculate the GPU computation time. PyCUDA's own `gpuarray` module is imported to initialize the arrays with the GPU. As per the official PyCUDA documentation, evaluating involved expressions on GPUArray instances can be somewhat inefficient, because a new temporary variable is created for each intermediate result. So, we import the `elementwise` module from PyCUDA, which contains tools to help generate kernels to evaluate multi-stage expressions on one or several operands in a single pass.

To understand this a bit better, let's remove the `elementwise` kernel and try a similar operation but with the `gpuarray` module:

```
import pycuda.autoinit
import pycuda.gpuarray as gpuarray
import numpy as np
import pycuda.driver as cudrv
```

```
N = 500000000

begin = cudrv.Event()
end = cudrv.Event()
begin.record()
a_gpu = gpuarray.to_gpu(np.zeros(N).astype(np.double))
a_gpu.fill(23.0)
b_gpu=a_gpu*12.0
end.record()
end.synchronize()
pycuda_gpu_time = begin.time_till(end)
random = np.random.randint(0,N)
```

We now check our new multiplication product value by randomly choosing an index and also reporting the computation time:

```
print("Choosing second array element with index", random, "at random:",
b_gpu[random])
print("\nGPU took %f milliseconds." % pycuda_gpu_time)
```

The result gets computed in around 2.5 seconds on the GPU:

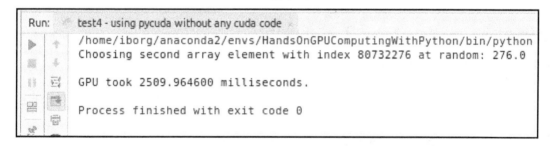

Even though this code appears to be just like a conventional Python program, it took more than two seconds to complete. So, now we know the significance of using the `elementwise` kernel.

Now let's come back to addressing the core concept of computing: how can this approach be utilized to solve a computational problem? Let's choose a problem scenario, say in the field of biostatistics, which relates to the statistical study of biological data. Suppose we want to correlate one series of such biological big data with another. With PyCUDA and other GPU-accelerated Python modules, we can compute values to understand the relationship between two biological data arrays by using a statistical formula. After we illustrate our first PyCUDA program, we'll further explore this approach later in this chapter through a real-world example.

Comparing PyCUDA to CUDA – an introductory perspective on reduction

Let's compare PyCUDA to CUDA in terms of simplicity in parallelization before we write our first PyCUDA program on PyCharm.

In the following table, we can explore the scope of PyCUDA with respect to CUDA so as to understand scenarios when PyCUDA could be advantageous to CUDA:

CUDA	PyCUDA
Based on C/C++ programming language	Based on the Python programming language
Uses C/C++ combined with specialized code to accelerate computations	Uses Python for GPUs to interface CUDA and accelerate computations
Reduction is a key feature in CUDA that is extremely important to maximize parallelization and efficiently harness threads.	Reduction in PyCUDA is much simpler to use than CUDA, considering the significance of reduction.

What is reduction?

Reduction is an optimization strategy that is an expansion of the global kernel. With reduction, you can use multiple thread blocks and decompose a computation into multiple kernel invocations. So, reduction maximizes parallelization and lowers computation times by a huge extent.

To achieve reduction in CUDA-C/C++, you need to expand the __global__ kernel with multiple lines of code.

With PyCUDA, you can perform reduction in a single line by importing the reduction module. It is known as ReductionKernel and can be implemented with GPUArrays. You also have the option to use actual CUDA C/C++ reduction within the __global__ kernel itself, on PyCUDA.

We will revisit this perspective again in the next chapter when we compare PyOpenCL to CUDA and ROCm.

Writing your first PyCUDA programs to compute a general-purpose solution

Let's continue our exciting journey forward. Now is the right time to get our hands dirty and write our first PyCUDA program that will compute a general-purpose solution. Follow the next steps to get started:

1. First, open a new file in PyCharm:

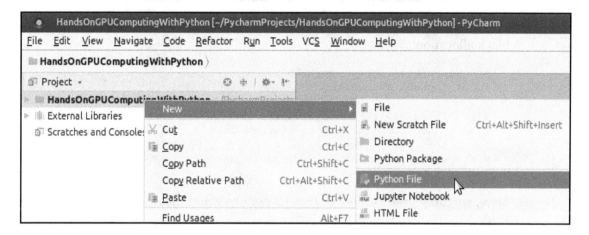

2. Now use the following code to print `Hello World from NVIDIA GPU!` from the GPU device itself! This is a regular and basic format in PyCUDA:

```
# Auto initialization for CUDA (can be done manually as well)
import pycuda.autoinit

# Importing SourceModule from the PyCUDA Compiler module
from pycuda.compiler import SourceModule

# Printing from the GPU device itself!
mod = SourceModule("""
__global__ void hello_from_nvidia_gpu()
{
printf("Hello World from NVIDIA GPU!");
}
""")

#Referencing the function for the GPU kernel
hello = mod.get_function("hello_from_nvidia_gpu")
```

```
#Invoking the NVIDIA GPU Kernel on a single thread in a single
block
hello(block=(1, 1, 1), grid=(1, 1))
```

The following is the output of this program:

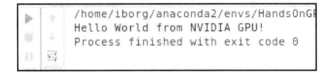

3. We can also modify the same program to a customizable format for thread and block allocation:

```
# Auto initialization for CUDA
import pycuda.autoinit

# Importing SourceModule from the PyCUDA Compiler module
from pycuda.compiler import SourceModule

# For a single thread on a single block
N=1
```

4. Here, we can set the number of threads per block and the number of blocks per grid:

```
# Setting threads per block. Here, it is set to 1
Threads_per_block = (int(1))

# Setting blocks per grid, also calculated as 1.
Blocks_per_grid = (int((N + Threads_per_block - 1) /
Threads_per_block))

# Printing from the GPU device itself!
mod = SourceModule("""
__global__ void hello_from_nvidia_gpu()
{
printf("Hello World from NVIDIA GPU!");
}
""")

# Return the Function name in the get_function module
hello_from_nvidia_gpu = mod.get_function("hello_from_nvidia_gpu")

# Invoking the NVIDIA GPU Kernel
hello_from_nvidia_gpu(block=(Threads_per_block, 1, 1),
grid=(Blocks_per_grid, 1))
```

The output will be similar to the following screenshot:

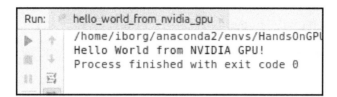

Now that we can start writing and testing our own PyCUDA program, let's see how we can use PyCUDA to solve a problem computationally, since we focus on a computing approach.

Previously, we explored an example using the `ElementwiseKernel`. Let's now modify it and create a new array containing all values based on a new mathematical equation:

```
import pycuda.autoinit
import numpy
import pycuda.gpuarray as gpuarray
import pycuda.driver as drv
from pycuda.elementwise import ElementwiseKernel

# Here, we compute a mathematical formula
# Note that we pass C/C++ syntax into the ElementwiseKernel
compute = ElementwiseKernel(
        "double *a_gpu, double *b_gpu, double *c_gpu",
        "c_gpu[i] = (cos(a_gpu[i])*cos(a_gpu[i])) * (b_gpu[i]*
b_gpu[i])+sin(a_gpu[i]*b_gpu[i])",
        "compute")
```

You can find the actual formula at the end of this section:

```
N = 500000000

# Threads_per_block = (int(1024))
# Blocks_per_grid = (int((N + Threads_per_block - 1) / Threads_per_block))
a_gpu = gpuarray.to_gpu(numpy.zeros(N).astype(numpy.double))
b_gpu = gpuarray.to_gpu(numpy.zeros(N).astype(numpy.double))
c_gpu = gpuarray.to_gpu(numpy.zeros(N).astype(numpy.double))
a_gpu.fill(24.0)
b_gpu.fill(12.0)
start = drv.Event()
end = drv.Event()

# Time the GPU function
start.record()
compute(a_gpu, b_gpu, c_gpu)
```

```
    end.record()
    end.synchronize()
```

`time_till()` is based on the `pycuda.driver` module:

```
    gpu_compute_time = start.time_till(end)
    random = numpy.random.randint(0,N)

    # Randomly choose index from second array to confirm changes to second
    array
    print("New value of second array element with random index ", random, "is
    ", c_gpu[random])

    # Report times
    print("GPU function took %f milliseconds." % gpu_compute_time)
```

When we use the assigned values, the answer will be displayed as follows:

```
Run:    mathematical_formula

        /home/iborg/anaconda2/envs/HandsOnGPUComputingWithPython/bin/python /home/iborg/Pycha
        New value of second array element with random index  75685459 is  25.054103187466794
        GPU function took 245.692581 milliseconds.

        Process finished with exit code 0
```

Note that our original formula was simply this:

$$y = x \times y$$

This was done to update an array of elements with the product of itself and another. The more complex the formula gets, the more intensive the computation becomes. For our most recent program, the mathematical formula would be as follows:

$$q = y^2 \cos^2 x \ + \ sin \ xy$$

Useful exercise on computational problem solving

Mathematical equations are only useful when you can apply them to solve a social problem or, in other words, serve society through computing. We do this through the convergence of multiple interdisciplinary fields.

Before you try to computationally solve a problem, always consider breaking it down into a series of categorized steps:

1. **Problem outline:** Finding the nature of the problem and choosing the most effective way of solving it and displaying the result
2. **Problem solution:** Choosing the most effective mathematical formula to solve the problem
3. **Program code:** Programming the underlying solution to the problem
4. **Solution testing:** Applying the previous methodologies to solve a computational problem with Python code to provide an effectively programmed solution

For example, tobacco is linked to many diseases, including cancer. To understand this better, we can try to correlate tobacco consumers to different cases of those diseases. So, our first dataset (array) in that case would be the tobacco consumer population in different regions. Our second dataset would be disease cases in the same respective regions.

Exercise

With PyCUDA, correlate tobacco with two diseases: cancer and infertility. Use Karl Pearson's correlation coefficient.

Karl Pearson's correlation coefficient is a measure of the strength of a linear association between two variables. It is denoted by r and varies from -1 to +1. A value toward -1 is a negative correlation and a value toward +1 is a positive correlation. 0 indicates no correlation.

Pearson's correlation coefficient is represented by the following formula:

$$r = \frac{n\sum xy - \sum x \sum y}{\sqrt{(n\sum x^2 - (\sum x)^2)(n\sum y^2 - (\sum y)^2)}}$$

The variables in the formula are defined as:

- n is the number of pairs of values in the datasets
- x and y are the given pair of values
- $\sum xy$ is the sum of the products of the paired scores
- $\sum x$ is the sum of scores of the first dataset

- $\sum y$ is the sum of scores of the second dataset
- $\sum x^2$ is the sum of the squares of the first dataset scores
- $\sum y^2$ is the sum of the squares of the second dataset scores

Note that the most intensive part of your computational code would be $\sum x$, $\sum y$, $\sum xy$, $\sum x^2$, and $\sum y^2$.

Program the underlying solution to the problem:

1. Correlate a tobacco dataset to a cancer dataset within the same region, city-wise
2. Correlate a tobacco dataset to an infertility dataset within the same region, city-wise

Use random values to generate your samples. If you can, also try to use real-world data available from open source databases.

Summary

In this chapter, the general syntax of CUDA code was explained with a comparative example. Syntax-wise, the concept of threads and blocks was introduced. The steps to install PyCUDA with or without Anaconda were illustrated within an existing CUDA environment. How to set up PyCUDA was explained step by step. Then, we learned how computing works in Python, and the significance of computational problem-solving was highlighted. With a comparison of PyCUDA and CUDA, the concept of parallel reduction was introduced.

At this stage, you should now be able to test your own CUDA program. As you have already learned how to install CUDA previously in this book, you can also install and configure PyCUDA within an existing CUDA environment. You should now have some understanding of the concept of computational problem solving as an essential and primary approach to computing. You can now start experimenting with applying your own equations to leverage GPUs with PyCUDA. It is highly recommended that you now carry out the exercise on Karl Pearson's correlation coefficient as illustrated in the final section of this chapter. You can now adopt different approaches to computing the correlation coefficient.

In the next chapter, we delve into an open source world! We will learn about ROCm's Heterogeneous Computing and Portability APIs for open source GPU computing inclusive of OpenCL. We'll also learn how to convert a CUDA program into a cross-platform format (HIP) via HIPify, usable on both NVIDIA and AMD GPUs. We will learn about the difference between computing on NVIDIA GPUs and computing on AMD GPUs. An in-depth Python programming approach will follow: PyOpenCL.

Further reading

You can use the following links and articles to learn more about the topics discussed in this chapter:

- *PlinkGPU: A Framework for GPU Acceleration of Whole Genome Data Analysis*, J Poznanovic *(2010)*, Master of Science, School of Informatics, University of Edinburgh, `http://www.inf.ed.ac.uk/publications/thesis/online/IM100799.pdf`
- CUDA-based GPU implementation of the Pearson correlation: `https://github.com/TravisCG/CudaCorr`.
- **gpuCor**: Calculate various correlation coefficients with a GPU. This can be found at `https://rdrr.io/cran/gputools/man/gpuCor.html`.
- *GPU-PCC: A GPU Based Technique to Compute Pairwise Pearson's Correlation Coefficients for Big fMRI Data*, T Eslami, F Saeed (2018), (online) 7(2), p.11. Available at: `https://scholarworks.wmich.edu/cgi/viewcontent.cgi?article=1008context=pcds_reports`.
- *Smoking-Related Knowledge, Attitudes, Behaviors, Smoking Cessation Idea, and Education Level among Young Adult Male Smokers in Chongqing, China*, X Xu, L Liu, M Sharma, Y Zhao *(2015)*. International Journal of Environmental Research and Public Health, (online) 12(2), pages 2,135-2,149. Available at: `https://www.mdpi.com/1660-4601/12/2/2135/pdf`.
- *Tobacco chewing and male infertility*, R Kumar, G Gautam, Indian J Urol (serial online), 2006, 22:161-2. Available from: `http://www.indianjurol.com/text.asp?2006/22/2/161/26581`
- *18 places to find data sets for data science projects*, V Paruchuri *(2016)*, Dataquest (online). Available at: `https://www.dataquest.io/blog/free-datasets-for-projects/`.

- To maximize CUDA-C/C++ CPU-GPU optimization, the following links are extremely useful:
    - CUDA syntax – a very useful resource for quick reference from a single webpage: `https://www.icl.utk.edu/~mgates3/docs/cuda.html`
    - CUDA-C best practices guide: `https://docs.nvidia.com/cuda/cuda-c-best-practices-guide/`
    - Unified memory for CUDA beginners: `https://devblogs.nvidia.com/unified-memory-cuda-beginners/`
    - Using shared memory in CUDA C/C++: `https://devblogs.nvidia.com/using-shared-memory-cuda-cc/`
    - CUDA dynamic parallelism API and principles: `https://devblogs.nvidia.com/cuda-dynamic-parallelism-api-principles/`
    - Optimizing parallel reduction in CUDA – extremely helpful when working with huge amounts of data: `https://developer.download.nvidia.com/assets/cuda/files/reduction.pdf`
    - *Parallel Reduction in CUDA*: `http://www.techdarting.com/2014/06/parallel-reduction-in-cuda.html`
    - *IMPLEMENTING PARALLEL REDUCTION IN CUDA*: `http://www.elemarjr.com/en/2018/03/parallel-reduction-in-cuda/`
    - Reduction in PyCUDA: `https://documen.tician.de/pycuda/array.html#module-pycuda.reduction`

7
Working with ROCm and PyOpenCL

In this chapter, we will continue with our hands-on experience with PyOpenCL. We will follow our CUDA program example that we discussed in the previous chapter and will try to make it a cross-platform venture with ROCm's HIP. In order to do this, we will use the `hipify` tool that we learned to build in `Chapter 4`, *Fundamentals of GPU Programming*. With `hipify`, we will try to create `.cpp` files from `.cu` files. With a practical approach, we will see the entire process of converting CUDA code into HIP code.

C programming enthusiasts will be encouraged to invoke AMD and NVIDIA GPUs within their program code with HIP, while Python programming enthusiasts will be motivated to use PyOpenCL to invoke AMD and NVIDIA GPUs within their program code. We will first start with the understanding of how a ROCm HIP-C program works. The fundamental concepts behind an OpenCL program and its components will be discussed with some basic examples that will help you transition toward a PyOpenCL CUDA environment. PyOpenCL will be explained with a practical approach and will be compared to OpenCL. We will focus on the applicability preference of PyOpenCL over OpenCL, again pertaining to the simplicity and power of Python syntax.

This chapter contains the following topics:

- Understanding how ROCm-C/C++ works with `hipify`, HIP, and OpenCL
- Installing PyOpenCL for Python (AMD and NVIDIA)
- Configuring PyOpenCL on your Python IDE
- How computing in PyOpenCL works on Python
- Comparing PyOpenCL to HIP and OpenCL – revisiting the reduction perspective
- Writing your first PyOpenCL programs to compute a general-purpose solution
- Useful exercise on computational problem solving

Technical requirements

Check out the following video to see the Code in Action:

```
http://bit.ly/2Hfrays
```

Understanding how ROCm-C/C++ works with hipify, HIP, and OpenCL

In this section, we will learn how CUDA code is converted into cross-platform HIP code and how to use the HIP compiler to compile the ported code. Finally, we will explore an OpenCL example by comparing it to CUDA through its documentation, so as to understand the open computing language in an easier manner.

Converting CUDA code into cross-platform HIP code with hipify

As we begin understanding ROCm for both AMD and NVIDIA GPUs, what can be more practical than a hands-on approach to converting our first CUDA program in this book into an ROCm HIP version? Follow these steps to achieve that:

1. Make sure you have the Terminal open at the location where you have the `gpu_multiply.cu` file created for understanding CUDA.
2. Assuming you have `hipify` installed, as described previously in Chapter 4, *Fundamentals of GPU Programming*, let's use the following command to port the `.cu` program into a more familiar `.cpp` program extension:

   ```
   $ hipify gpu_multiply.cu -o gpu_multiply_ported_to_hip.cpp
   ```

   We have now HIPified CUDA! Note the replacement of `cuda` prefixes to `hip` in the converted code.

3. The following is the HIPified program (`gpu_multiply_ported_to_hip.cpp`):

   ```
   #include <hip/hip_runtime.h>
   #include <iostream>

   #define N 500000000 //500 Million Elements
   #define THREADS_PER_BLOCK 1024
   ```

```
// GPU kernel function to multiply two array elements and also
update the results on the second array
__global__ void multiply(double *p, double *q, unsigned long n) {
  int index = threadIdx.x + blockIdx.x * blockDim.x;
  if (index < n) q[index] = p[index] * q[index];
}

int main(void) {
  double *p, *q; // host copies of p, q
  double *gpu_p, *gpu_q; // device copies of p, q
  unsigned long size = N * sizeof(unsigned long); // we need space
for N unsigned long integers
  unsigned long i;
```

hipMalloc is similar to cudaMalloc in that it allocates memory using variables on the GPU device:

```
// Allocate GPU/device copies of gpu_p, gpu_q
hipMalloc((void**)&gpu_p, size);
hipMalloc((void**)&gpu_q, size);

// Allocate CPU/host copies of p, q
p = (double *)malloc(size);
q = (double *)malloc(size);

// Setup input values
for (i = 0; i < N - 1; ++i) {
  p[i] = 24.0;
  q[i] = 12.0;
}

// Copy inputs to device
hipMemcpy(gpu_p, p, size, hipMemcpyHostToDevice);
hipMemcpy(gpu_q, q, size, hipMemcpyHostToDevice);
```

Note that only the following comment has been modified manually for HIP:

```
//INITIALIZE HIP EVENTS
hipEvent_t start, stop;
float elapsedTime;
//CREATING EVENTS
hipEventCreate(&start);
hipEventCreate(&stop);
hipEventRecord(start, 0);

//HIP KERNEL STUFF HERE...
// Launch multiply() kernel on GPU with N threads
hipLaunchKernelGGL(multiply, dim3((N + THREADS_PER_BLOCK - 1) /
```

```
    THREADS_PER_BLOCK), dim3(THREADS_PER_BLOCK), 0, 0, gpu_p, gpu_q,
    N);

      //FINISH RECORDING
      hipEventRecord(stop, 0);
      hipEventSynchronize(stop);
```

4. `hipEventElapsedTime` stores the computation time through `elapsedTime` in the following code:

```
      //CALCULATE ELAPSED TIME
      hipEventElapsedTime(&elapsedTime, start, stop);

      //DISPLAY COMPUTATION TIME
      hipDeviceProp_t prop;
      int count;
      hipGetDeviceCount(&count);
      for (int igtx = 0; igtx < count; igtx++) {
        hipGetDeviceProperties(&prop, igtx);
        printf("\nGPU Device used for computation: %s\n", prop.name);
        printf("\nMultiplication on GPU computed in: %f milliseconds",
    elapsedTime);
      }

      // Copy device result back to host copy of q
      hipMemcpy(q, gpu_q, size, hipMemcpyDeviceToHost);
```

5. The next step is verifying whether the multiplication done through the GPU is correct:

```
      // Verifying all values to be 288.0
      // fabs(q[i]-288) (absolute value) should be 0
      double maxError = 0.0;
      for (int i = 0; i < N-1; ++i) maxError = fmax(maxError,
    fabs(q[i]-288.0));
      std::cout << "\nMax error: " << maxError << std::endl;

      // Clean CPU memory allocations
      free(p); free(q);
      // Clean GPU memory allocations
      hipFree(gpu_p);
      hipFree(gpu_q);
      return 0;
    }
```

After this, let's check how ROCm-C/C++ works with HIP by executing the same example.

Understanding how ROCm-C/C++ works with HIP

Now that we have readily available code ported from CUDA, let's understand how HIP works. To get the executable output, we will use the C++11 standard when compiling the program with `hipcc`, as follows:

```
$ hipcc -std=c++11 gpu_multiply_ported_to_hip.cpp -o
gpu_multiply_ported_to_hip
```

Now, we execute the program using the following command:

```
$ ./gpu_multiply_ported_to_hip
```

Output on an NVIDIA platform

The following output is obtained by using a HIP compiler to create the executable, as shown in the preceding section:

```
GPU Device used for computation: GeForce GTX TITAN X

Multiplication on GPU computed in: 51.659714 milliseconds
Max error: 0
```

As we can see, the execution time for the multiply function with HIP on the Maxwell architecture-based NVIDIA Titan X GPU is `51.659714` milliseconds.

Output on an AMD platform

Now let's compile and test the same code on the all-new Vega 20 architecture-based AMD Radeon VII GPU! This new system also has ROCm installed, as illustrated previously in `Chapter 4`, *Fundamentals of GPU Programming*. We get the following output:

```
GPU Device used for computation: Vega 20

Multiplication on GPU computed in: 31.587000 milliseconds
Max error: 0
```

The same code gets executed on the Radeon VII (reported as Vega 20) in `31.587000` milliseconds. The configurations for both systems are as shown here:

Hardware Configuration 1	Hardware Configuration 2
Intel Core i7 4770K processor at 3.5 Ghz	AMD Ryzen 7 2700X processor at 3.7 Ghz
NVIDIA Titan X 12 GB DDR5 GPU (Maxwell architecture)	AMD Radeon VII 16 GB HBM2 GPU (Vega 20 architecture)
32 GB GSkill DDR3 RAM	32 GB Corsair DDR4 RAM
256 GB Adata SSD	500 GB WD M2 SSD
2 TB Western Digital HDD Green	4 TB Western Digital HDD Red

In the previous chapter, we discussed the concept of threads, blocks, and grids in the CUDA section. Now let's see how the `hipify` tool made changes to our previous CUDA code in order to make a cross-compatible `.cpp` program inclusive of GPU code similar to CUDA.

In the very first line, we notice the inclusion of a new header file called `hip_runtime.h`:

```
#include <hip/hip_runtime.h>
```

So, starting with the index on the GPU `global` function, we find that the syntax remains unchanged and is no different than the CUDA version (`threadIdx.x`, `blockIdx.x`, and `blockDim.x`).

The next change we notice is that `cudaMalloc` gets changed to `hipMalloc`. `cudaMemcpy` and `cudaMemcpyHostToDevice` have changed to `hipMemcpy` and `hipMemcpyHostToDevice`, respectively.

Let's look at all the changes in our new HIP program with the help of a comparative table:

CUDA program	HIPified program
`gpu_multiply.cu`	`gpu_multiply_ported_to_hip.cpp`
N/A	`#include <hip/hip_runtime.h>`
`cudaMalloc`	`hipMalloc`
`cudaMemcpy`	`hipMemcpy`
`cudaMemcpyHostToDevice`	`hipMemcpyHostToDevice`
`cudaMemcpyDeviceToHost`	`hipMemcpyDeviceToHost`
`cudaEvent_t`	`hipEvent_t`
`cudaEventCreate`	`hipEventCreate`
`cudaEventRecord`	`hipEventRecord`

cudaEventSynchronize	hipEventSynchronize
cudaEventElapsedTime	hipEventElapsedTime
cudaDeviceProp	hipDeviceProp_t
cudaGetDeviceCount	hipGetDeviceCount
cudaGetDeviceProperties	hipGetDeviceProperties
cudaFree	hipFree
multiply <<<>>> (kernel invocation)	hipLaunchKernelGGL(multiply) (kernel invocation)

In CUDA, our kernel invocation was as follows:

```
multiply <<<(N + THREADS_PER_BLOCK - 1) / THREADS_PER_BLOCK,
THREADS_PER_BLOCK >>>(gpu_p, gpu_q, N);
```

Now, in the HIP program, we find the most noticeable change to be the following:

```
hipLaunchKernelGGL(multiply, dim3((N + THREADS_PER_BLOCK - 1) /
THREADS_PER_BLOCK), dim3(THREADS_PER_BLOCK), 0, 0, gpu_p, gpu_q, N);
```

hipLaunchKernelGGL launches the GPU kernel for executing the kernel function on the GPU. We can note the use of dim3 integer vector data types for specifying the number of threads and blocks.

In the HIP program, we notice that hipMalloc specifically allocates memory for GPU-only variables. In that case, like CUDA, we would have to specify transferring the variables from the CPU to the GPU and bring the computed results back to the CPU again. To enable access to variables from both the CPU or the GPU, HIP does not support the use of unified memory allocation (hipMallocManaged and hipMemPrefetchAsync) yet.

To confirm this, we will use hipify again:

```
$ hipify gpu_multiply_revised.cu -o gpu_multiply_revised_ported_to_hip.cpp
/tmp/gpu_multiply_revised.cu-f8183e.hip:33:3: warning: CUDA identifier is
unsupported in HIP.
    cudaMallocManaged((void**)&p, size);
    ^
/tmp/gpu_multiply_revised.cu-f8183e.hip:34:4: warning: CUDA identifier is
unsupported in HIP.
    cudaMallocManaged((void**)&q, size);
    ^
/tmp/gpu_multiply_revised.cu-f8183e.hip:58:2: warning: CUDA identifier is
unsupported in HIP.
    cudaMemPrefetchAsync(p, N * sizeof(double), 0);
    ^
```

```
/tmp/gpu_multiply_revised.cu-f8183e.hip:59:2: warning: CUDA identifier is
unsupported in HIP.
    cudaMemPrefetchAsync(q, N * sizeof(double), 0);
    ^
4 warnings generated when compiling for host.
```

The code is converted but with the exception of `cudaMallocManaged` and `cudaMemPrefetchAsync`. Note that the commented sections within the code are ignored:

```
#include <hip/hip_runtime.h>
#include <iostream>

#define N 500000000 //500 Million Elements
#define THREADS_PER_BLOCK 1024

// GPU kernel function to multiply two array elements and also update the
results on the second array
__global__ void multiply(double *p, double *q, unsigned long n) {
  int index = threadIdx.x + blockIdx.x * blockDim.x;
  if (index < n) q[index] = p[index] * q[index];
}

int main(void) {
  double *p, *q; // host copies of p, q
  //double *gpu_p, *gpu_q; // device copies of p, q
  unsigned long size = N * sizeof(unsigned long); // we need space for N
unsigned long integers
  unsigned long i;
```

`cudaMalloc` allocations are commented out in the code to test **Unified Memory Allocation (UMA)**:

```
/*
// Allocate GPU/device copies of gpu_p, gpu_q
cudaMalloc((void**)&gpu_p, size);
cudaMalloc((void**)&gpu_q, size);
// Allocate CPU/host copies of p, q
p = (double *)malloc(size);
q = (double *)malloc(size);
*/
```

Here, `cudaMallocManaged` for UMA is unchanged and just like in the previous chapter, HIP does not support UMA currently:

```
//Unified Memory Allocation for CPU and GPU
cudaMallocManaged((void**)&p, size);
cudaMallocManaged((void**)&q, size);
// Setup input values
```

```
for (i = 0; i < N - 1; ++i) {
  p[i] = 24.0;
  q[i] = 12.0;
}
```

cudaMemcpy allocations are commented out, as UMA does not require them:

```
/*
// Copy inputs to device
cudaMemcpy(gpu_p, p, size, cudaMemcpyHostToDevice);
cudaMemcpy(gpu_q, q, size, cudaMemcpyHostToDevice);
*/

//INITIALIZE CUDA EVENTS
hipEvent_t start, stop;
float elapsedTime;
//CREATING EVENTS
hipEventCreate(&start);
hipEventCreate(&stop);
hipEventRecord(start, 0);
cudaMemPrefetchAsync(p, N * sizeof(double), 0);
cudaMemPrefetchAsync(q, N * sizeof(double), 0);
hipDeviceSynchronize();
```

The most noticeable change in the converted CUDA code is the GPU kernel invocation:

```
//HIP KERNEL STUFF HERE...
// Launch multiply() kernel on GPU with N threads
hipLaunchKernelGGL(multiply, dim3((N + THREADS_PER_BLOCK - 1) /
THREADS_PER_BLOCK), dim3(THREADS_PER_BLOCK), 0, 0, p, q, N);
//FINISH RECORDING
hipEventRecord(stop, 0);
hipDeviceSynchronize();
hipEventSynchronize(stop);
//CALCULATE ELAPSED TIME
hipEventElapsedTime(&elapsedTime, start, stop);
//DISPLAY COMPUTATION TIME
hipDeviceProp_t prop;
int count;
hipGetDeviceCount(&count);
for (int igtx = 0; igtx < count; igtx++) {
  hipGetDeviceProperties(&prop, igtx);
```

The following code section verifies the results and computation time:

```
printf("\nGPU Device used for computation: %s\n", prop.name);
printf("\nMultiplication on GPU computed in: %f milliseconds",
elapsedTime);
```

```
    }
    /*
    // Copy device result back to host copy of q
    cudaMemcpy(q, gpu_q, size, cudaMemcpyDeviceToHost);
    */
    // Verifying all values to be 288.0
    // fabs(q[i]-288) (absolute value) should be 0
    double maxError = 0.0;
    for (int i = 0; i < N-1; ++i) maxError = fmax(maxError,
fabs(q[i]-288.0));
    std::cout << "\nMax error: " << maxError << std::endl;
```

hipFree is just the HIP alternative to cudaFree in order to clear memory allocations in the end after using them through the code:

```
    // Finally, we notice an alternative to cudaFree as hipFree.
    // Clean unified memory allocations
    hipFree(p);
    hipFree(q);
    return 0;
}
```

There were warnings but no errors during compilation, so let's try to execute the program:

```
$ hipcc -std=c++11 gpu_multiply_revised_ported_to_hip.cpp -o
gpu_multiply_revised_ported_to_hip

$ ./gpu_multiply_revised_ported_to_hip
GPU Device used for computation: GeForce GTX TITAN X
Multiplication on GPU computed in: 720.770325 milliseconds
Max error: 0
```

We can get a familiar output to what we saw in the *Understanding how CUDA-C/C++ works via a simple example* section in the previous chapter. So, this program is using both NVCC and HIP code in parts. Hopefully, hipMallocManaged and hipMemPrefetchAsync will be supported in the future.

Understanding how OpenCL works

Now let's look at how OpenCL works. Note that OpenCL is independent of ROCm, but is also provided when the latter is installed.

OpenCL is a cross-platform language and relatively more complex than CUDA, but not difficult to learn. In order to understand OpenCL easily, let's compare its syntax with that of CUDA's through the following OpenCL program. It computes a similar operation as to the one we did on CUDA in the previous chapter.

The first thing to note is that an OpenCL kernel code is to be written inside a separate kernel file with a .cl extension. Contrary to a CUDA .cu file, an OpenCL .cl file contains only kernel code, which is equivalent to the global function we write on CUDA, along with the main code. In OpenCL, the main code is written in a conventional format as a .c or .cpp file, where the .cl file is read and used for computation on the OpenCL device. In this example, we use a .cpp extension.

This time, we set a limit of 15 million elements and also store the results on a third array instead of updating the second array.

An advantageous point is that our kernel code always stays separate. In that way, we can organize and focus on our general code syntax and parallel code syntax separately, which makes code management more convenient.

First, let's take a look at our OpenCL kernel file (gpu_multiply_kernel.cl):

```
// GPU kernel function to multiply two array elements and also update the
results on a third array
__kernel void multiply(__global double *p, __global double *q, __global
double *r) {
  // Indexing the current element to process - equivalent to int index =
threadIdx.x + blockIdx.x * blockDim.x in CUDA
  int index = get_global_id(0);

  // Simultaneous multiplication within this OpenCL kernel
  r[index] = p[index] * q[index];
}
```

Note that instead of __global__ as on CUDA, the syntax used here is __kernel for defining the function.

Instead of using threadIdx.x + blockIdx.x * blockDim.x for the index, we use get_global_id(0).

For the main program, we use the following syntax in contrast to CUDA. It is highly recommended to go through each of the comments in-between the lines of the code to understand OpenCL by comparing it to CUDA.

`main.cpp` contains generic C/C++ code, as shown in the following code block:

```
#include <stdio.h>
#include <stdlib.h>
#include <CL/cl.h>
#include <math.h>
#include <iostream>

using namespace std;

#define N (0x15000000) //15 Million Elements

int main(void) {
  // Creating two input arrays with two values on each
  double *p = (double*)malloc(sizeof(double)*N);
  double *q = (double*)malloc(sizeof(double)*N);
  for(int i = 0; i < N-1; ++i) {
    p[i] = 23;
    q[i] = 12;
  }
```

Here, we use `gpu_multiply_kernel.cl` in our main program:

```
  // Loading source code from .cl file into the array cl_source
  FILE *opencl_file;
  char *cl_source;
  size_t source_size;
  opencl_file = fopen("gpu_multiply_kernel.cl", "r");
  if (!opencl_file) {
    fprintf(stderr, "Failed to load opencl_kernel.\n");
    exit(1);
  }
  cl_source = (char*)malloc(N);
  source_size = fread( cl_source, 1, N, opencl_file);
  fclose( opencl_file );
```

Now, we fetch platform and device IDs:

```
  // Fetching platform and device information
  cl_platform_id platform_id = NULL;
  cl_device_id device_id = NULL;
  cl_uint get_num_devices;
  cl_uint get_num_platforms;
  cl_int for_kernel = clGetPlatformIDs(1, &platform_id,
&get_num_platforms);
  for_kernel = clGetDeviceIDs( platform_id, CL_DEVICE_TYPE_DEFAULT, 1,
&device_id, &get_num_devices);
  // Creating an OpenCL context
```

```
   cl_context opencl_context = clCreateContext( NULL, 1, &device_id, NULL,
NULL, &for_kernel);
   // Creating a command queue and enabling profiling to find computation
time
   cl_command_queue_properties profiling_on[] {CL_QUEUE_PROPERTIES,
CL_QUEUE_PROFILING_ENABLE, 0};
   cl_command_queue command_queue =
clCreateCommandQueueWithProperties(opencl_context, device_id, profiling_on,
&for_kernel);
```

clCreateBuffer **and** clEnqueueWriteBuffer **are similar to** cudaMalloc **and**
cudaMemcpyHostToDevice, **respectively, which are used in CUDA:**

```
   // Creating memory buffers on the device for each array - similar to
cudaMalloc on CUDA
   cl_mem p_gpu = clCreateBuffer(opencl_context, CL_MEM_READ_ONLY, N *
sizeof(double), NULL, &for_kernel);
   cl_mem q_gpu = clCreateBuffer(opencl_context, CL_MEM_READ_ONLY, N *
sizeof(double), NULL, &for_kernel);
   cl_mem r_gpu = clCreateBuffer(opencl_context, CL_MEM_WRITE_ONLY, N *
sizeof(double), NULL, &for_kernel);
  // Transferring p and q to their respective memory buffers on the device
for multiplication - similar to cudaMemcpyHostToDevice on CUDA
   for_kernel = clEnqueueWriteBuffer(command_queue, p_gpu, CL_TRUE, 0, N *
sizeof(double), p, 0, NULL, NULL);
   for_kernel = clEnqueueWriteBuffer(command_queue, q_gpu, CL_TRUE, 0, N *
sizeof(double), q, 0, NULL, NULL);
```

Now, we create and build the OpenCL program and kernel. We also pass kernel
arguments:

```
    // Creating an OpenCL program from the opencl_kernel source
   cl_program opencl_program = clCreateProgramWithSource(opencl_context, 1,
(const char **)&cl_source, (const size_t *)&source_size, &for_kernel);
   // Building the OpenCL program
   for_kernel = clBuildProgram(opencl_program, 1, &device_id, NULL, NULL,
NULL);
   // Creating the OpenCL kernel
   cl_kernel opencl_kernel = clCreateKernel(opencl_program, "multiply",
&for_kernel);
   // Arguments of the OpenCL kernel for the device
   for_kernel = clSetKernelArg(opencl_kernel, 0, sizeof(cl_mem), (void
*)&p_gpu);
   for_kernel = clSetKernelArg(opencl_kernel, 1, sizeof(cl_mem), (void
*)&q_gpu);
   for_kernel = clSetKernelArg(opencl_kernel, 2, sizeof(cl_mem), (void
*)&r_gpu);
```

Here, we allocate work items and groups for the OpenCL kernel. To relate better in terms of familiarity, note that work items correspond to threads, and groups correspond to blocks, respectively, in CUDA:

```
  // Allocation of work items and groups - work items are similar to
threads and groups are similar to blocks as on CUDA.
  size_t global_item_size = N; // Setting the global item size - similar to
maximum number of threads' usage
  size_t local_item_size = 1024; // Dividing work items into groups of 1024

  // C++ and OpenCL allocations for displaying device name
  int pf_index, dev_index;
  char* device_name;
  size_t nameSize;
  cl_uint platform_count;
  cl_platform_id* platforms;
  cl_uint device_count;
  cl_device_id* devices;
```

The following code is used to fetch all OpenCL devices:

```
  // Fetching all platforms to display device name
  clGetPlatformIDs(0, NULL, &platform_count);
  platforms = (cl_platform_id*) malloc(sizeof(cl_platform_id) *
platform_count);
  clGetPlatformIDs(platform_count, platforms, NULL);
  for (pf_index = 0; pf_index < platform_count; pf_index++) {
    // Fetching all OpenCL supported devices in the system
    clGetDeviceIDs(platforms[pf_index], CL_DEVICE_TYPE_ALL, 0, NULL,
&device_count);
    devices = (cl_device_id*) malloc(sizeof(cl_device_id) * device_count);
    clGetDeviceIDs(platforms[pf_index], CL_DEVICE_TYPE_ALL, device_count,
devices, NULL);
```

Now it's time to display the device (GPU) name:

```
  // Display critical attributes for each device (just one here in our
case)
    for (dev_index = 0; dev_index < device_count; dev_index++) {
      // Display the device name
      clGetDeviceInfo(devices[dev_index], CL_DEVICE_NAME, 0, NULL,
&nameSize);
      device_name = (char*) malloc(nameSize);
      clGetDeviceInfo(devices[dev_index], CL_DEVICE_NAME, nameSize,
device_name, NULL);
      printf("Device used for computation: %s\n", device_name);
      free(device_name);
    }
```

```
    free(devices);
  }
  free(platforms);
  cl_event event; // Creating an event variable for timing
  for_kernel = clEnqueueNDRangeKernel(command_queue, opencl_kernel, 1,
NULL, &global_item_size, &local_item_size, 0, NULL, &event);
```

The following code snippet will make the script wait for the event to finish:

```
  clWaitForEvents (1, &event); // Waiting for the event
  clFinish(command_queue); //Waiting until all commands have completed
```

To record computation time using OpenCL profiling, we use `clGetEventProfilingInfo`. Note that in contrast to CUDA, which computes this time in milliseconds, OpenCL does the same in nanoseconds instead:

```
  // Obtaining the start and end time for the event
  cl_ulong begin;
  cl_ulong end;

  clGetEventProfilingInfo(event, CL_PROFILING_COMMAND_START, sizeof(begin),
&begin, NULL);
  clGetEventProfilingInfo(event, CL_PROFILING_COMMAND_END, sizeof(end),
&end, NULL);

  double duration = end - begin;

  // Printing the device computation time - note that on OpenCL, the
default unit is nanoseconds in contrast to milliseconds on CUDA.
  printf("Multiplication on device computed in: %lf nanoseconds = %lf
milliseconds\n", duration, duration/1000000);
```

`clEnqueueReadBuffer` is similar to `cudaMemcpyDeviceToHost` as on CUDA:

```
  // Transferring r_gpu to its respective memory buffer on the host -
similar to cudaMemcpyDeviceToHost on CUDA
  double *r = (double*)malloc(sizeof(double)*N);
  for_kernel = clEnqueueReadBuffer(command_queue, r_gpu, CL_TRUE, 0, N *
sizeof(double), r, 0, NULL, NULL);

  // Verifying all values to be 276.0
  // fabs(q[i]-288) (absolute value) should be 0
  double maxError = 0.0;
  for (int i = 0; i < N-1; ++i) maxError = fmax(maxError,
fabs(r[i]-276.0));
  std::cout<<"\nMax error: "<<maxError<<std::endl;
```

For clearing memory allocations, `clReleaseMemObject` is similar to `cudaFree` is on CUDA:

```
// Cleaning up memory allocations
for_kernel = clFlush(command_queue);
for_kernel = clFinish(command_queue);
for_kernel = clReleaseKernel(opencl_kernel);
for_kernel = clReleaseProgram(opencl_program);
for_kernel = clReleaseCommandQueue(command_queue);
for_kernel = clReleaseContext(opencl_context);
// clReleaseMemObject on OpenCL is similar to cudaFree on CUDA.
for_kernel = clReleaseMemObject(p_gpu);
for_kernel = clReleaseMemObject(q_gpu);
for_kernel = clReleaseMemObject(r_gpu);
free(p);
free(q);
free(r);
return 0;
}
```

Use the following to compile and execute this program:

```
$ g++ main.cpp -l OpenCL -o gpu_multiply_opencl
$ ./gpu_multiply_opencl
Device used for computation: GeForce GTX TITAN X
Multiplication on device computed in: 33358656.000000 nanoseconds =
33.358656 milliseconds

Max error: 0
```

For 15 million elements, the identical multiplication values stored on the third array are all computed on the OpenCL device in 33.358656 milliseconds.

In the next section, we will start exploring how to make use of OpenCL with the simplicity of Python code, which is now even more important considering the complex syntax of OpenCL in contrast to CUDA. When we begin computing with PyOpenCL, we'll explore the scope of the functionalities and parallelism features we cited previously, specifically in Python. While PyCUDA allows you to use both OpenCL and Python code, our focus will once again be on making the most of a Python programming approach toward AMD and NVIDIA GPUs.

From this point onward, we will gradually transition toward a Python-only programming environment after covering PyOpenCL. But, before we do that, it is important that we summarize the three computing languages based on C/C++ for GPU computing by comparing their syntactic differences based on the official ROCm documentation: namely for CUDA, HIP, and OpenCL. This is extremely useful to recapitulate our coverage on the three computing languages we've explored so far:

Term	CUDA	HIP	OpenCL
Device	`int deviceId`	`int deviceId`	`cl_device`
Queue	`cudaStream_t`	`hipStream_t`	`cl_command_queue`
Event	`cudaEvent_t`	`hipEvent_t`	`cl_event`
Memory	`void *`	`void *`	`cl_mem`
	grid	grid	NDRange
	block	block	work-group
	thread	thread	work-item
	warp	warp	sub-group
Thread-index	`threadIdx.x`	`hipThreadIdx_x`	`get_local_id(0)`
Block-index	`blockIdx.x`	`hipBlockIdx_x`	`get_group_id(0)`
Block-dim	`blockDim.x`	`hipBlockDim_x`	`get_local_size(0)`
Grid-dim	`gridDim.x`	`hipGridDim_x`	`get_global_size(0)`
Device Kernel	`__global__`	`__global__`	`__kernel`
Device Function	`__device__`	`__device__`	Implied in device compilation
Host Function	`__host_` (default)	`__host_` (default)	Implied in host compilation.
Host + Device Function	`__host__` `__device__`	`__host__` `__device__`	No equivalent
Kernel Launch	`<<< >>>`	`hipLaunchKernelGGL`	`clEnqueueNDRangeKernel`
Term	CUDA	HIP	OpenCL
Global Memory	`__global__`	`__global__`	`__global`
Group Memory	`__shared__`	`__shared__`	`__local`

Constant	__constant__	__constant__	__constant
	__syncthreads	__syncthreads	barrier(CLK_LOCAL_MEMFENCE)
Atomic Builtins	atomicAdd	atomicAdd	atomic_add
Term	CUDA	HIP	OpenCL
Precise Math	cos(f)	cos(f)	cos(f)
Fast Math	__cos(f)	__cos(f)	native_cos(f)
Vector	float4	float4	float4

In our HIPified program, the terms hipThreadIdx_x, hipBlockIdx_x, and hipBlockDim_x were not found in place of threadIdx.x, blockIdx.x, and blockDim.x, respectively. Instead, the syntax was unchanged and identical to that of CUDA's. But you can also try replacing the terms as shown in the preceding table. Both versions perform very similarly.

Installing PyOpenCL for Python (AMD and NVIDIA)

Through our documented source code on OpenCL, we now know the basic ways of OpenCL implementation compared to CUDA syntax. So, let's get started with our PyOpenCL installation procedure for Python. Once again, note that you need not install Python, as it is already available (both 2.x and 3.x) with a freshly installed version of an Ubuntu 18.04 Linux operating system.

Setting up PyOpenCL will enable implementing OpenCL kernels within your existing Python setup of choice and then compute them on your AMD or NVIDIA GPU.

Once again, we will re-examine our two primary ways of installation, as we illustrated previously for PyCUDA. Note that these steps are independent of the previous chapter and can be used as a standalone reference for installing PyOpenCL.

Anaconda-based installation of PyOpenCL

This is the recommended way to get started with PyOpenCL for a productivity environment to ensure risk-free experimentation. To set up PyOpenCL within Anaconda, first, let's install `pyopencl` with `conda` with the following commands on a Terminal. Proceed by entering `y`. The first command will be necessary, depending on the updated state of the Anaconda installation:

```
$ conda update -n base conda -c anaconda
Collecting package metadata: done
Solving environment: done
---
proceed ([y]/n)? y
---
$ conda install -c conda-forge pyopencl
Collecting package metadata: done
Solving environment: done
The following NEW packages will be INSTALLED:
pyopencl conda-forge/linux-64::pyopencl-2018.2.5-py36h8619c78_0
---
proceed ([y]/n)? y
```

Here is an important reference for Conda-based PyOpenCL: `https://documen.tician.de/pyopencl/misc.html`.

pip – system-wide Python base installation of PyOpenCL

For a system-wide installation of PyOpenCL that would be tied to your existing Python base, we would first have to install `pip`, which is a tool for installing Python packages.

To install `pip` for Python 3.x, use the following command:

```
sudo apt install python3-pip
```

`pip` for Python 2.x can be installed via the following command:

```
sudo apt install python-pip
```

This is an important note from the developers of `pip`:

```
Python 2.7 will reach the end of its life on January 1st, 2020. Please
upgrade your Python as Python 2.7 won't be maintained after that date. A
future version of pip will drop support for Python 2.7.
```

Hence, it is recommended to use/transition to Python 3.x to work on Python-based packages or develop new Python software to ensure future-proof GPU support.

Coming back to our system-wide PyOpenCL installation, the Python 3.x version can be installed with the following commands on a terminal:

```
$ pip3 install --upgrade pip
$ pip3 install --user pyopencl
```

Note that `pip install --user pyopencl` also performs the same operation as `pip3 install --user pyopencl`.

The alternative command for installing PyOpenCL for Python 2.x would be as follows:

```
$ pip2 install --upgrade pip
$ pip2 install --user pyopencl
```

Now, you have a user-specified configuration ready to use system-wide on your Ubuntu Linux system. In the next section, we'll learn how to configure both the Conda-based and the user-specified system-wide configurations on the PyCharm IDE.

Note for AMD GPU users
For a ROCm-based PyOpenCL installation, you might have to create a symbolic link as `/usr/lib/libOpenCL.so` from your ROCm's OpenCL installation and also make sure that the `opencl-headers` package is installed before using PyOpenCL:
```
$ sudo ln -s /opt/rocm/opencl/lib/x86_64/libOpenCL.so.1
/usr/lib/libOpenCL.so && sudo apt install opencl-headers
```

Configuring PyOpenCL on your Python IDE

To configure PyOpenCL with PyCharm, we again have to follow up the two ways of installation we discussed in the previous section. The following steps are independent of the previous chapter and can be used as a standalone reference guide for getting started with PyOpenCL directly.

Conda-based virtual environment

Now, let's create a virtual environment with Conda as a new PyCharm pure Python project:

1. Launch **PyCharm Professional Edition**:

2. Choose **New Project** from the PyCharm main menu. Skip this step if you've already created a project:

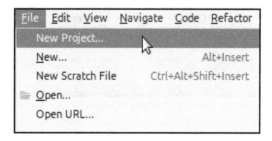

3. Create a new virtual environment with Conda if not already present:

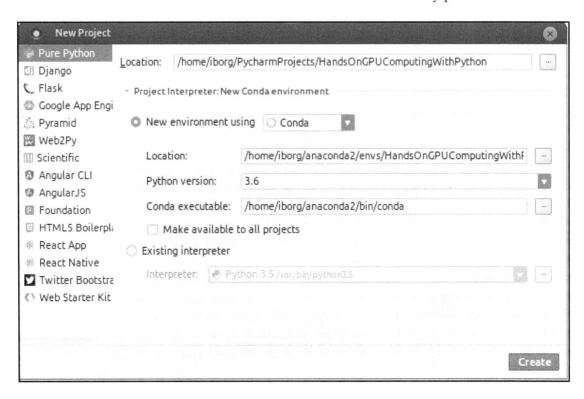

4. Wait while the Conda environment gets created:

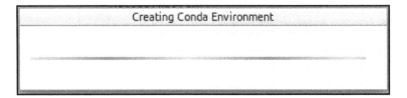

After creating the Conda environment, you will have a ready-to-use PyOpenCL development environment:

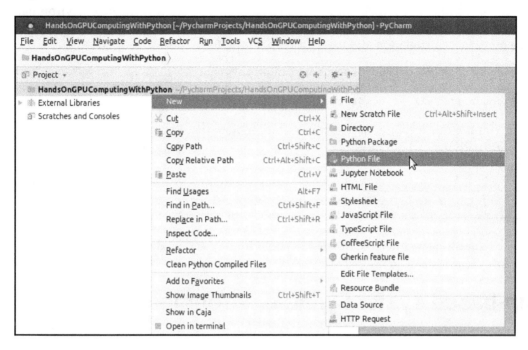

5. Now, you can import `pyopencl` within your Python programs. As you can see, PyCharm detects and recommends the same, just as you begin to type import `pyopencl`:

Note that `<built-in>` refers to a Conda-wide `pyopencl` package. At this stage, we are done configuring PyOpenCL on the IDE.

As an alternate measure (optional), you could also create the virtual environment with a Terminal (as we saw in our Jupyter installation in Chapter 6, *Working with CUDA and PyCUDA*). Here, we create a new virtual environment with a new name. The `HandsOnGPUComputingWithPython` and `HandsOnGPUComputingWithPython2` virtual environments have already been created:

```
$ conda create --name HandsOnGPUComputingWithPython3
---
proceed ([y]/n)? y
```

All virtual environments are created in a directory called `envs` in your Anaconda directory (`$HOME/anaconda2` or `$HOME/anaconda3`). Even though we already have `pyopencl` within our Conda base installation, you can also choose to activate the new environment and install PyOpenCL locally within it as well. This is helpful if you do not want a Conda-wide `pyopencl` installation and want to keep it only for a specific project:

```
$ conda activate HandsOnGPUComputingWithPython
(HandsOnGPUComputingWithPython)
$ conda install -c conda-forge pyopencl python=3.6
```

When you use this local `pyopencl` configuration, note that PyCharm will show you the complete path instead of `<built-in>` as it now has access to its own local PyOpenCL environment:

Now, let's see how a system-wide installation with `pip` can be done for PyOpenCL.

pip-based system-wide environment

To configure a system-wide PyOpenCL installation for Python, you can create a new project on PyCharm or change your system interpreter:

1. For a new project, proceed as follows:

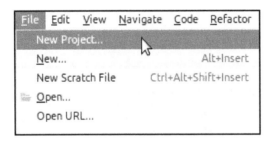

2. Instead of a Conda environment, we will now select the pre-installed system-wide Python installation on Ubuntu:

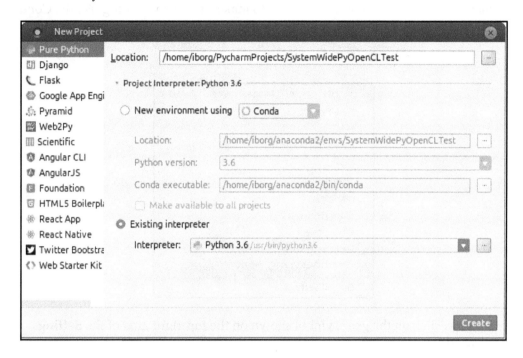

3. Once this environment has been created, you can now start using the user-specific system-wide PyOpenCL installation on PyCharm:

PyCharm may still prefer to use the system-wide configuration if you want to go back to using your Conda-based PyOpenCL projects that were set up within the virtual environment. In such a case, you would have to make PyCharm re-recognize the Conda-based PyOpenCL package in the manually created virtual environment once again:

1. First, go to settings from the **File** menu:

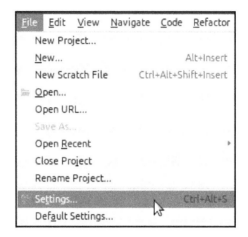

2. Now, click on the gear symbol shown on the top-right area of the **Settings** window:

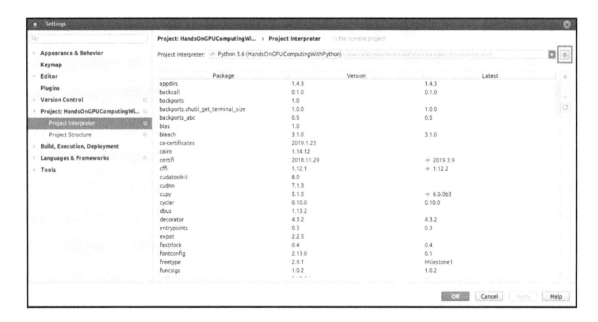

3. Click on **Show All**:

4. Select your project interpreter from the list and click on the icon that says **Show paths for the selected interpreter** when you hover over it with the mouse pointer:

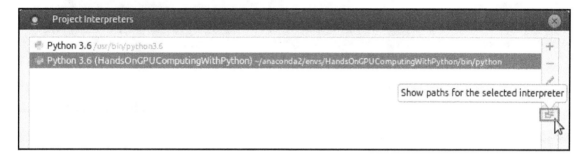

5. Remove the user-specified path that PyCharm sees system-wide and click **OK**:

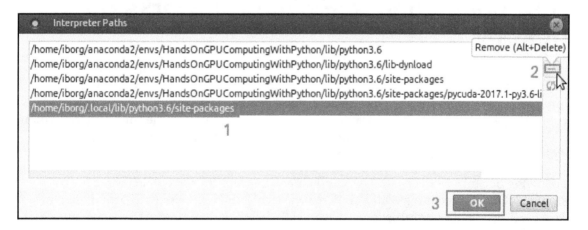

6. Hit **OK** once again in the **Project Interpreters** window. Finally, click on **Apply** in the **Settings** window for the changes to take effect.

7. Now, you can start using your Conda-specific local PyOpenCL package once again:

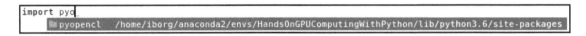

```
import pyo
    pyopencl   /home/iborg/anaconda2/envs/HandsOnGPUComputingWithPython/lib/python3.6/site-packages
```

If you wish to switch between the two, all you have to do is toggle between **Python 3.6 /usr/bin/python3.6** and the Conda-based virtual environment in the system interpreter window:

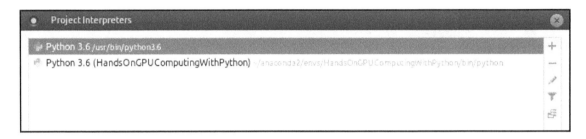

We are now ready to begin computing with PyOpenCL!

How computing in PyOpenCL works on Python

Like PyCUDA, PyOpenCL can help us solve a number of computational problems based on GPU computations via Python, with or without OpenCL-C/C++ code. PyOpenCL is important in regards to OpenCL because it significantly minimizes the latter's code complexity and makes it much easier and user-friendly—thanks to the simplicity of Python code. We will try to understand this through an example in this section. All PyOpenCL code in this chapter has been tested on a new AMD Radeon VII GPU.

Following our first C++ versus CUDA and OpenCL examples, we will look into a very simple PyOpenCL example with a similar approach, hands-on with PyCharm. Following this, we'll again shift our focus toward actual GPU-accelerated computations for solving specific computational problems with PyOpenCL.

We will now write a PyOpenCL program to initialize two array elements with two values for each and then update all the elements in a third array as a product of the two values.

Launch PyCharm, as illustrated earlier, and create a new, empty Python file:

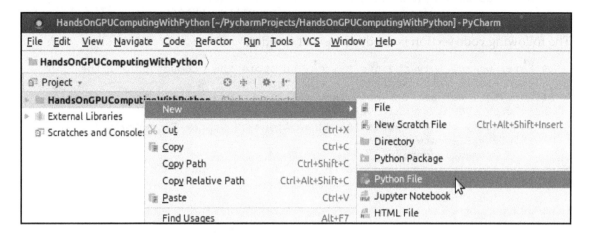

Now, we will use a PyOpenCL Python program that follows our OpenCL C++ example from the *Understanding how OpenCL works* section of this chapter. We will again try to use 500 million elements with double precision, as we did previously for PyCUDA. Note how the program code is much easier and simpler to understand with Python and PyOpenCL than PyOpenCL C++ itself. Multiple lines of C++ code can be replaced with just a line of Python code.

ElementwiseKernel is also present in PyOpenCL, just like PyCUDA, for minimal use of OpenCL code. But there is a minor difference. Before you pass your arguments into the ElementwiseKernel, you'll have to initialize a context first and then instantiate a command queue.

Please follow the comments in the following code for line-by-line interpretation:

```
import pyopencl as cl
import numpy as np
import pyopencl.array as clarray
from time import time
from pyopencl.elementwise import ElementwiseKernel

N = 500000000 #500 Million Elements

gpu_start_time = time() # Noting GPU start time

# In contrast to PyCUDA, note that in PyOpenCL, we have to initialize a
Context first.
pyopencl_context = cl.create_some_context()
# Now we instantiate a Command Queue with the PyOpenCL Context and also
```

```
enable profiling to report computation time.
command_queue = cl.CommandQueue(pyopencl_context,
properties=cl.command_queue_properties.PROFILING_ENABLE)
```

The following code section is used for context creation:

```
# Here, we multiply the two values and store the product on all the
elements of a third array
# Note that we pass C syntax into the ElementwiseKernel. The difference
here with PyCUDA is that we have
# to specify the Context first as an argument to the ElementWiseKernel
multiply = ElementwiseKernel(
        pyopencl_context,
        "double *a_gpu, double *b_gpu, double *c_gpu",
        "c_gpu[i] = a_gpu[i] * b_gpu[i]",
        "multiply")

# Initialize three PyOpenCL arrays all with zeroes
a_gpu = clarray.to_device(command_queue, np.zeros(N).astype(np.double))
b_gpu = clarray.to_device(command_queue, np.zeros(N).astype(np.double))
c_gpu = clarray.to_device(command_queue, np.zeros(N).astype(np.double))

# Update the first two arrays with values 23 and 12 respectively
a_gpu.fill(23.0)
b_gpu.fill(12.0)
```

The following code section invokes the kernel and displays results:

```
event = multiply(a_gpu, b_gpu, c_gpu)
event.wait() # Waiting until the event completes
elapsed = 1e-6 * (event.profile.end - event.profile.start)

# Calculating execution time (Multiplying by 10^6 to get value in
milliseconds from nanoseconds)
print("GPU Kernel Function took {0} milliseconds".format(elapsed)) #
Reporting kernel execution time
gpu_end_time = time() # Get the GPU end time
print("GPU Time(Inclusive of memory transfer between host and device
(GPU)): {0} seconds".format(gpu_end_time - gpu_start_time))

# Reporting GPU execution time, including memory transfers between host and
device
random = np.random.randint(0,N)
# Randomly choose index from second array to confirm changes to the third
array
print("New value of third array element with random index", random, "is",
c_gpu[random])
```

Right-click over the code and select **Run**:

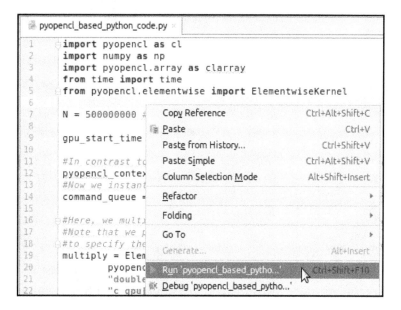

Python does not have built-in array support and so we again import the numpy library to provide array support, like we did for PyCUDA. Note that the GPU kernel function executed in around 23 milliseconds:

```
Run:    pyopencl_based_python_code
     GPU Kernel Function took 22.959746 milliseconds
     GPU Time(Inclusive of memory transfer between host and device (GPU)): 6.434994697570801 seconds
     New value of third array element with random index 340795000 is 276.0

     Process finished with exit code 0
```

For our second PyOpenCL code, let's also try to repeat the same process as we did for our earlier PyCUDA Python program that used two arrays:

```python
import pyopencl as cl
import numpy as np
import pyopencl.array as clarray
from time import time
from pyopencl.elementwise import ElementwiseKernel

N = 500000000 #500 Million Elements

gpu_start_time = time() # Noting GPU start time
```

Next, we initialize a context for OpenCL:

```
# In contrast to PyCUDA, note that in PyOpenCL, we have to initialize a
Context first.
pyopencl_context = cl.create_some_context()
# Now we instantiate a Command Queue with the PyOpenCL Context and also
enable profiling to report computation time.
command_queue = cl.CommandQueue(pyopencl_context,
properties=cl.command_queue_properties.PROFILING_ENABLE)

# Here, we multiply the two values and store the product on all the
elements of a third array
# Note that we pass C syntax into the ElementwiseKernel. The difference
here with PyCUDA is that we have to specify the Context first as an
argument to the ElementWiseKernel
multiply = ElementwiseKernel(
        pyopencl_context,
        "double *a_gpu, double *b_gpu",
        "b_gpu[i] = a_gpu[i] * b_gpu[i]",
        "multiply")
```

Next, we initialize the arrays to zeros then and update them with new values:

```
# Initialize two PyOpenCL arrays all with zeroes
a_gpu = clarray.to_device(command_queue, np.zeros(N).astype(np.double))
b_gpu = clarray.to_device(command_queue, np.zeros(N).astype(np.double))

# Update the first two arrays with values 23 and 12 respectively
a_gpu.fill(23.0)
b_gpu.fill(12.0)

event = multiply(a_gpu, b_gpu)

event.wait() # Waiting until the event completes
```

In OpenCL, the default time unit when profiling is measured in nanoseconds, in contrast to milliseconds in CUDA:

```
elapsed = 1e-6 * (event.profile.end - event.profile.start) # Calculating
execution time (Multiplying by 10^6 to get value in milliseconds from
nanoseconds)

print("GPU Kernel Function took {0} milliseconds".format(elapsed)) #
Reporting kernel execution time

gpu_end_time = time() # Get the GPU end time

print("GPU Time(Inclusive of memory transfer between host and device
```

```
(GPU)): {0} seconds".format(gpu_end_time - gpu_start_time)) # Reporting GPU
execution time, including memory transfers between host and device

random = np.random.randint(0,N)

#Randomly choose index from second array to confirm its updated changes
print("New value of third array element with random index", random, "is",
b_gpu[random])
```

The GPU function now computes the same operation in 17.676814 milliseconds. The total
GPU time is now lessened by around 1.45 times:

```
Run:    pyopencl_version_of_pycuda_exam... ×
        GPU Kernel Function took 17.676814 milliseconds
        GPU Time(Inclusive of memory transfer between host and device (GPU)): 4.429342031478882 seconds
        New value of third array element with random index 287997311 is 276.0

        Process finished with exit code 0
```

First, we import the main `pyopencl` module, which is essential for creating the PyOpenCL
context and also instantiating the command queue. PyOpenCL's own `array` module is
imported to initialize the arrays with the GPU. Just like PyCUDA, as per the official
documentation of PyOpenCL, evaluating involved expressions on `array` instances can be
somewhat inefficient, because a new temporary is created for each intermediate result. So,
we import the `elementwise` module from PyOpenCL that contains tools to help generate
kernels to evaluate multi-stage expressions on one or several operands in a single pass.

To understand this a bit better, let's once again remove the `elementwise` kernel and try a
similar operation, this time only with the `array` module in PyOpenCL:

```
import pyopencl as cl
import pyopencl.array as clarray
from time import time
import numpy as np

N = 500000000 #500 Million Elements

begin1 = time()

# In contrast to PyCUDA, note that in PyOpenCL, we have to initialize a
Context first.
pyopencl_context = cl.create_some_context()
# Now we instantiate a Command Queue with the PyOpenCL Context
command_queue = cl.CommandQueue(pyopencl_context)
```

Note we are not using any C syntax here:

```
a_gpu = clarray.to_device(command_queue, np.zeros(N).astype(np.double))
a_gpu.fill(23.0)
begin2 = time()
b_gpu=a_gpu*12.0
end = time()

pyopencl_gpu_time = (end-begin2)/1e-3

total_gpu_time = end-begin1

random = np.random.randint(0,N)

print("\nGPU multiplication of array took %f milliseconds." %
pyopencl_gpu_time)

print("\nGPU Time including dependent code %f seconds." % total_gpu_time)

print("\nChoosing second array element with index", random, "at random:",
b_gpu[random])
```

We test the pure Python code once again with PyOpenCL without any C/C++ code:

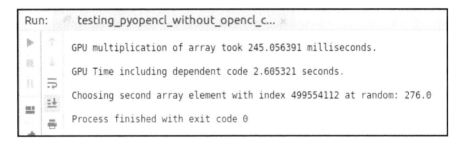

Even though this code appears to look like a conventional Python program, the total execution time took more than two seconds to complete, as we saw for PyCUDA.

Coming back to the core concept of computing toward solving a computational problem, let's choose a problem scenario, where we want to reset a huge number of elements to identical values. With simultaneous operations, as we saw for updating the second array, we can apply the same concept toward solving such a problem. For example, consider a large database that requires resetting a particular column with the same values simultaneously at periodic intervals. With automated GPU acceleration, we can carry out the same task easily.

Comparing PyOpenCL to HIP and OpenCL – revisiting the reduction perspective

As in the previous chapter, let's compare PyOpenCL to HIP and OpenCL in terms of simplicity in parallelization before we write our first PyCUDA programs on PyCharm.

In the following table, we are exploring the scope of PyOpenCL with respect to HIP and OpenCL to note when to prefer PyOpenCL over OpenCL:

HIP	OpenCL	PyOpenCL
Based on C/C++ programming language.	Based on C/C++ programming language.	Based on Python programming language.
Includes both device and host code in a single `.c` or `.cpp` file.	Requires creation of a separate `.cl` file for device code along with a `.c` or `.cpp` file that calls the same code from the host for parallelization.	Includes both device and host code in a single `.py` file.
Uses C/C++ combined with specialized code to accelerate computations.	Uses C/C++ combined with specialized code (called as the `.cl` file) to accelerate computations.	Uses Python for GPUs to interface OpenCL and accelerate computations.
Easy to use, like CUDA.	Uses much more complex syntax than CUDA or HIP.	Makes OpenCL much easier to implement by simplifying its complex code usage via Python.
Like CUDA, reduction is a key feature in HIP that is extremely important to maximize parallelization and efficiently harness threads.	In OpenCL, reduction is also a key feature in HIP that is extremely important to maximize parallelization and efficiently harness work items.	Similar to CUDA and PyCUDA, reduction in PyOpenCL is much simpler to use than OpenCL, considering the significance of reduction.

Reduction with HIP, OpenCL, and PyOpenCL

With reduction on HIP, you can use multiple thread blocks and decompose a computation into multiple kernel invocations, similar to CUDA, by maximizing parallelization and significantly lowering computation times.

To achieve reduction in HIP-C/C++, you need to expand the HIP __global__ kernel with multiple lines of code, just like CUDA.

To achieve reduction in OpenCL-C/C++, similarly, you need to expand the OpenCL __kernel function with multiple lines of code in the .cl file.

With PyOpenCL, you can perform reduction in a single line by importing the reduction module, just like in PyCUDA. It is also known as ReductionKernel, and you have the option to use actual OpenCL-C/C++ reduction code within the __kernel itself, on PyOpenCL.

Writing your first PyOpenCL programs to compute a general-purpose solution

As we discussed in the previous section, PyOpenCL has a clear advantage with respect to code length over OpenCL and HIP as the former is Python-based. Now, let's get our hands dirty and write our first PyOpenCL code. Follow these steps to get started:

1. First, open a new file on PyCharm:

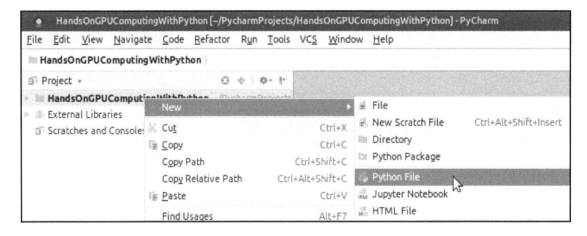

2. Now, let's use the following code to implement OpenCL code within a single .py Python file. This is a regular and basic format in PyOpenCL:

```
import pyopencl as cl # Importing the OpenCL API
import numpy # Import Numpy for using numbers
from time import time # Import access to the current time
```

```
N = 500000000 # 500 Million Elements

a = numpy.zeros(N).astype(numpy.double) # Create a numpy array with
all zeroes
b = numpy.zeros(N).astype(numpy.double) # Create a second numpy
array with all zeroes

a.fill(23.0) # set all values as 23
b.fill(12.0) # set all values as 12

opencl_context = cl.create_some_context() # Initialize the Context

command_queue = cl.CommandQueue(opencl_context,
properties=cl.command_queue_properties.PROFILING_ENABLE) #
Instantiate a Queue and enable profiling to report computation time
```

Note that two variables are to be read and the third one to be written with a computed result:

```
a_buffer = cl.Buffer(opencl_context, cl.mem_flags.READ_ONLY |
cl.mem_flags.COPY_HOST_PTR, hostbuf=a)

b_buffer = cl.Buffer(opencl_context, cl.mem_flags.READ_ONLY |
cl.mem_flags.COPY_HOST_PTR, hostbuf=b)

c_buffer = cl.Buffer(opencl_context, cl.mem_flags.WRITE_ONLY,
b.nbytes) # Creating three memory buffers on the device (GPU)

opencl_kernel = """
// GPU kernel function to multiply two array elements and also
update the results on a third array

__kernel void multiply(__global double *p, __global double *q,
__global double *r)
{
    // Indexing the current element to process - equivalent to int
index = threadIdx.x + blockIdx.x * blockDim.x in CUDA

    int index = get_global_id(0);
```

3. Now, we will carry out the parallel operation through the OpenCL kernel:

```
    // Simultaneous multiplication within this OpenCL kernel
    r[index] = p[index] * q[index];
}""" # OpenCL Kernel Creation: Note these are the exact same
contents as we saw on our .cl file

opencl_program = cl.Program(opencl_context, opencl_kernel).build()
```

```
gpu_start_time = time() # Get the GPU start time

event = opencl_program.multiply(command_queue, a.shape, None,
a_buffer, b_buffer, c_buffer) # Enqueue the multiply program on the
GPU device

event.wait() # Waiting until event completion

elapsed = 1e-6 * (event.profile.end - event.profile.start) #
Calculating execution time (Multiplying by 10^6 to get value in
milliseconds from nanoseconds)
```

4. The following code section will report the computation time, fetching results and displaying them:

```
print("GPU Kernel Function took: {0} milliseconds".format(elapsed))
# Reporting kernel execution time

c_gpu = numpy.empty_like(a) # Creating an empty array the same size
as array a to receive computed results from the GPU device

cl.enqueue_copy(command_queue, c_gpu, c_buffer).wait() # Get back
the data from GPU device memory into array c_gpu

gpu_end_time = time() # Stores time point at the end of GPU
computation

print("GPU Time(Inclusive of memory transfer between host and
device (GPU)): {0} seconds".format(gpu_end_time - gpu_start_time))
# Reporting GPU execution time, including memory transfers between
host and device

random = numpy.random.randint(0, N)

# Randomly choose index from second array to confirm changes to
second array
print("New value of third array element with random index", random,
"is", c_gpu[random])
```

The output after compilation looks like the following screenshot:

```
Run:    pyopencl_simplified_opencl_with_p...
        GPU Kernel Function took: 15.799202 milliseconds
        GPU Time(Inclusive of memory transfer between host and device (GPU)): 1.1336390972137451 seconds
        New value of third array element with random index 21645289 is 276.0

        Process finished with exit code 0
```

We can also modify the same program to pass the kernel content directly. Follow these steps:

1. Here, we skip defining the kernel separately and pass the OpenCL instructions directly to the following line of code:

```
opencl_program = cl.Program(opencl_context, opencl_kernel).build()
```

2. In the following program, the `opencl_kernel` argument is replaced with the kernel content itself:

```
import pyopencl as cl # Importing the OpenCL API
import numpy # Import tools to work with numbers
from time import time # Import access to the current time

N = 500000000 # 500 Million Elements

a = numpy.zeros(N).astype(numpy.double) # Create a numpy array with
all zeroes
b = numpy.zeros(N).astype(numpy.double) # Create a second numpy
array with all zeroes
c_gpu = numpy.empty_like(a) # Creating an empty array the same size
as array a to receive computed results from the GPU device
a.fill(23.0) # set all values as 23
b.fill(12.0) # set all values as 12

opencl_context = cl.create_some_context() # Initialize the Context
command_queue = cl.CommandQueue(opencl_context,
properties=cl.command_queue_properties.PROFILING_ENABLE) #
Instantiate a Queue and enable profiling to report computation time
```

3. Next, we define the kernel within the `opencl_program` variable itself instead of using a separate line, like we did on the earlier program:

```
a_buffer = cl.Buffer(opencl_context, cl.mem_flags.READ_ONLY |
cl.mem_flags.COPY_HOST_PTR, hostbuf=a)
b_buffer = cl.Buffer(opencl_context, cl.mem_flags.READ_ONLY |
cl.mem_flags.COPY_HOST_PTR, hostbuf=b)
c_buffer = cl.Buffer(opencl_context, cl.mem_flags.WRITE_ONLY,
b.nbytes) # Creating three memory buffers on the device (GPU)
opencl_program = cl.Program(opencl_context, """

// GPU kernel function to multiply two array elements and also
update the results on a third array
__kernel void multiply(__global double *p, __global double *q,
__global double *r)
{
```

```
    // Indexing the current element to process - equivalent to int
index = threadIdx.x + blockIdx.x * blockDim.x in CUDA
    int index = get_global_id(0);
    // Simultaneous multiplication within this OpenCL kernel
    r[index] = p[index] * q[index];
}""").build() # Compiling the device program by directly defining
kernel content.

gpu_start_time = time() # Get the GPU start time
```

4. After invoking the kernel with the necessary arguments, we wait for the event to complete and specify event.wait():

```
event = opencl_program.multiply(command_queue, a.shape, None,
a_buffer, b_buffer, c_buffer)
event.wait() # Waiting until event completion
elapsed = 1e-6 * (event.profile.end - event.profile.start) #
Calculating execution time (Multiplying by 10^6 to get value in
milliseconds from nanoseconds)

print("GPU Kernel Function took: {0} seconds".format(elapsed)) #
Reporting kernel execution time
cl.enqueue_copy(command_queue, c_gpu, c_buffer).wait() # Get back
the data from GPU device memory into array c_gpu
gpu_end_time = time() # Stores time point at the end of GPU
computation
print("GPU Time(Inclusive of memory transfer between host and
device (GPU)): {0} seconds".format(gpu_end_time - gpu_start_time))
# Reporting GPU execution time, including memory transfers between
host and device

random = numpy.random.randint(0, N)
# Randomly choose index from second array to confirm changes to
second array
print("New value of third array element with random index", random,
"is", c_gpu[random])
```

Now, we execute the program and get the following output:

```
Run:    pyopencl_shortened_kernel_with_p... ×
  GPU Kernel Function took: 15.762132 milliseconds
  GPU Time(Inclusive of memory transfer between host and device (GPU)): 1.0502707958221436 seconds
  New value of third array element with random index 212970759 is 276.0

  Process finished with exit code 0
```

Now, you can use OpenCL syntax within Python code in a much simpler way through PyOpenCL. Though you can compile the device program in a single line, defining the kernel separately makes it a bit more convenient to understand.

Previously, we saw an example of using the `ElementwiseKernel` to compute a random trigonometric equation and store the same value on all the elements of an array simultaneously. This time, let's store random numbers on the two arrays. We will treat the first array values as numerators and the second array values as denominators. Follow these steps:

1. Here, the quotient will be computed with the GPU device and stored in a third array, as shown in the following code:

```
import pyopencl as cl
import numpy as np
import pyopencl.array as clarray
from time import time
from pyopencl.elementwise import ElementwiseKernel

N = 500000000 #500 Million Elements

gpu_start_time = time() # Noting GPU start time

# In contrast to PyCUDA, note that in PyOpenCL, we have to
initialize a Context first.
pyopencl_context = cl.create_some_context()
# Now we instantiate a Command Queue with the PyOpenCL Context and
also enable profiling to report computation time.
command_queue = cl.CommandQueue(pyopencl_context,
properties=cl.command_queue_properties.PROFILING_ENABLE)

# Here, we multiply the two values and store the product on all the
elements of a third array
# Note that we pass C syntax into the ElementwiseKernel. The
difference here with PyCUDA is that we have to specify the Context
first as an argument to the ElementWiseKernel
```

2. Here, we simply replaced the multiplication operator with division within the OpenCL kernel:

```
multiply = ElementwiseKernel(
        pyopencl_context,
        "double *a_gpu, double *b_gpu, double *c_gpu",
        "c_gpu[i] = a_gpu[i] / b_gpu[i]",
        "multiply")

# Initialize the first two arrays with random values and the third
```

```
as zeroes
a_gpu = clarray.to_device(command_queue,
np.random.rand(N).astype(np.double))
b_gpu = clarray.to_device(command_queue,
np.random.rand(N).astype(np.double))
c_gpu = clarray.to_device(command_queue,
np.zeros(N).astype(np.double))
event = multiply(a_gpu, b_gpu, c_gpu)
event.wait() # Waiting until the event completes
elapsed = 1e-6 * (event.profile.end - event.profile.start) #
Calculating execution time (Multiplying by 10^6 to get value in
milliseconds from nanoseconds)

print("GPU Kernel Function took {0} milliseconds".format(elapsed))
# Reporting kernel execution time
gpu_end_time = time() # Get the GPU end time
```

3. The next step is verifying computation time and results:

```
print("GPU Time(Inclusive of memory transfer between host and
device (GPU)): {0} seconds".format(gpu_end_time - gpu_start_time))
# Reporting GPU execution time, including memory transfers between
host and device
random = np.random.randint(0,N)
# Randomly choose index from second array to confirm changes to the
third array
print("New value of third array element with random index", random,
"is", c_gpu[random])
```

When we use randomly assigned values, the answer will be displayed as follows:

```
Run:     simultaneous_division ×
    GPU Kernel Function took 23.553461 milliseconds
    GPU Time(Inclusive of memory transfer between host and device (GPU)): 14.137887716293335 seconds
    New value of third array element with random index 427580637 is 1.5279051344784071

    Process finished with exit code 0
```

How can we apply the use of the simultaneous division of 500 million elements toward solving a computational problem? Let's ponder this in our next section on computational problem solving.

Useful exercise on computational problem solving

You must have heard about the **Body Mass Index** (**BMI**). It is very useful for monitoring a person's health, especially in the cases of obesity and diabetes. You might have already undergone a process to determine your BMI during a routine medical checkup. BMI can also be quite significant in understanding other medical conditions. It is calculated as follows:

$$BMI = \frac{Person's\ weight\ in\ Kg}{(Person's\ height\ in\ m)^2}$$

So, we divide the person's weight in kilograms by their squared height (in meters).

Now, suppose we have a database of millions of people with a record of their weights, along with their corresponding heights. Through GPU-accelerated computing, we can conveniently deduce the average BMI in a particular region.

Before you try to computationally solve the problem, remember to follow the four steps we discussed earlier for computing the solution.

So, our first dataset (array) in that case would be the weights of people residing in a particular region. Our second dataset would be their corresponding heights.

With PyOpenCL, use the GPU to compute the BMI corresponding to each of the weight-and-height pairs and store those values in a separate array. Use the formula as stated and follow these steps:

1. Compute the square of the corresponding heights and store the results on a third array.
2. Use the values on the first and the new third array to compute the corresponding BMIs. Store the values on a fourth array through an OpenCL kernel.
3. Finally, deduce the average BMI in the region. You can also try to parallelize the summation of all the BMI values stored on the fourth array before calculating the average BMI.

You can use random values to generate your samples. But, again, also try to use real-world data to establish the significance of the study.

Solution assistance

The following are a list of sources that you can go through to get further assistance. These studies will broaden your horizons and help you visualize the concepts involved and gain first-hand experience with PyOpenCL:

- Conventional Python program to calculate the BMI of a single individual: `https://www.geeksforgeeks.org/program-to-calculate-bmi/`.
- *Evaluation of GPU-Based CT Reconstruction for Morbidly Obese Patients*, R Liu, M K Kalra, H Yu, (2017). JSM Biomedical Imaging Data Papers. (online) 4 (1), Available at `https://www.ncbi.nlm.nih.gov/pmc/articles/PMC5931393/`.
- *The Significance of Body Mass Index in Calculating the Cut-Off Points for Low Muscle Mass in the Elderly: Methodological Issues*, R Krzymińska-Siemaszko, N Czepulis, A Suwalska, L Dworak, A Fryzowicz, B Madej-Dziechciarow, K Wieczorowska-Tobis (2014), BioMed Research International (online) 2014, pp.1-8. Available at `https://www.hindawi.com/journals/bmri/2014/450396/`.
- *DeepFog: Fog Computing-Based Deep Neural Architecture for Prediction of Stress Types, Diabetes and Hypertension Attacks*, R Priyadarshini, R Barik, H Dubey (2018), Computation (online) 6(4), p.62. Available at `https://www.mdpi.com/2079-3197/6/4/62/htm`.

To understand how a BMI can relate to the prediction of stress types and diabetes, you can refer to the final part of the introduction section of the last paper cited and also *Case Study 2—Prediction of Diabetes*.

Summary

In this chapter, the general syntax of HIP and OpenCL code was explained with documented examples. The steps to install PyOpenCL with or without Anaconda were illustrated within an existing NVIDIA or AMD OpenCL environment. The configuration measures to set up PyOpenCL were explained step by step, we learned how computing works in Python, and the significance of computational problem solving was highlighted. With a comparison of PyOpenCL, HIP, and OpenCL, the concept of parallel reduction was revisited.

Now that this chapter is at its end, you should now be able to test your own HIP or OpenCL program. You should also be able to install and configure PyOpenCL within an existing OpenCL environment. Porting your own CUDA code to a cross-platform HIP format that can be run on both NVIDIA and AMD GPUs will also be very convenient from now on. You can now start experimenting by applying your own equations and solving computational problems to leverage both brands of GPUs with PyOpenCL.

In `Chapter 8`, *Working with Anaconda, CuPy, and Numba for GPUs*, we will continue our journey of *Hands-On GPU Computing with Python* but primarily focus purely on a Python programmable syntax (exclusive of any C/C++ code) through Anaconda. We will learn about **CuPy**, which is a GPU implementation of CUDA for Python that was designed specifically to provide an API like NumPy. Then, we will explore the capabilities of **Numba**, previously known as Anaconda Accelerate, which was released under a proprietary licence that was later released under an open source licence through Numba. Numba can be implemented both through CUDA and ROCm and we will explore just that as we begin our next chapter. We will also compare Anaconda, CuPy, and Numba before going through our computational exercise, again in the last section.

Further reading

- *Exploring utilisation of GPU for database applications*, S Walkowiak, K Wawruch, M Nowotka, L Ligowski, W Rudnicki (2010), Procedia Computer Science (online) 1(1), pp.505-513. Available at `https://www.sciencedirect.com/science/article/pii/S1877050910000554/pdf?md5=1db96e3ff6793878ce491d31b8e99354pid=1-s2.0-S1877050910000554-main.pdf`.
- *GPU Acceleration for SQL Queries on Large-Scale Distributed Systems*, L Nguyen, P Hemler (2017). The Journal of Computational Science Education (online) 8(1), pp.20-26. Available at `https://www.shodor.org/media/content//jocse/volume8/issue1/Nguyen_final`.
- *GPU SQL Query Accelerator*, K Yong, H Ong, V Yap (2016), International Journal of Information Technology (online) 22(1). Available at `http://www.intjit.org/journal/download/down.php?file=/22/1/221_3.pdf`

- To maximize OpenCL CPU-GPU optimization, the following links are very much recommended for further reference as we move on to setting up and using Python with OpenCL (PyOpenCL):
    - OpenCL syntax – a very useful resource for quick reference from a single document: `https://www.khronos.org/files/opencl-quick-reference-card.pdf`
    - OpenCL best practices guide: `https://indico.kfki.hu/event/249/contributions/240/attachments/296/663/OpenCLBestPractices.pdf`
    - AMD's unified CPU and GPU processor concept: `http://www.ziti.uni-heidelberg.de/ziti/uploads/ce_group/seminar/2013-Sven-Nobis-presentation.pdf`
    - OpenCL parallel reduction: `https://www.fz-juelich.de/SharedDocs/Downloads/IAS/JSC/EN/slides/opencl/opencl-05-reduction.pdf?__blob=publicationFile` and `https://www.khronos.org/registry/OpenCL/sdk/2.1/docs/man/xhtml/work_group_reduce.html`
    - Using shared memory in OpenCL: `https://www.khronos.org/registry/OpenCL/sdk/2.1/docs/man/xhtml/sharedVirtualMemory.html`
    - Dynamic parallelism in OpenCL 2.0: `https://simpleopencl.blogspot.com/2013/09/dynamic-parallelization-in-opencl-20.html`
    - Reduction on HIP: `https://github.com/ROCm-Developer-Tools/HIP-Examples/tree/master/reduction`
    - Reduction on OpenCL: `https://github.com/sschaetz/nvidia-opencl-examples/tree/master/OpenCL/src/oclReduction`
    - Reduction on PyOpenCL: `https://documen.tician.de/pyopencl/algorithm.html#pyopencl.reduction.ReductionKernel`

8
Working with Anaconda, CuPy, and Numba for GPUs

Continuing with our hands-on experience, we now focus on our most important chapter, about using Python-only code, which essentially simplifies the GPU computing approach. We will revisit Anaconda and after a short reintroduction including Miniconda, we will begin our exploration by looking into it with a GPU computing perspective. In particular, CuPy and Numba will be covered to highlight the significance of Python-only syntax for GPU computing. We will carry out the same by seamlessly restructuring our earlier examples in a much simpler manner through CuPy and Numba.

Python programming enthusiasts will be encouraged to invoke NVIDIA GPUs within their program code with CuPy and CUDA-enabled Numba, while also not excluding AMD GPU users from experimenting with ROCm-enabled Numba. We start with gaining an understanding of how a CuPy program works by recalling our first conventional Python program and then comparing the same program structure with that of CuPy. Following this, we continue the chapter with computing via CUDA and ROCm-enabled Numba on Python.We focus on the applicability preference of CuPy and Numba over traditional NumPy, pertaining to the extremely similar, but more powerful, Python syntax.

The following topics will be covered in the chapter:

- Understanding how Anaconda works with CuPy and Numba
- Installing CuPy and Numba and how to make it recognizable within an existing PyCharm environment with Anaconda
- Implementing CuPy and Numba on PyCharm with customized hands-on examples
- Writing your first CuPy and Numba programs on PyCharm
- GPU-based computational problem-solving with CuPy and Numba
- Understanding the significance of computational problem-solving with Python-only syntax

Technical requirements

Check out the following video to see the Code in Action:

`http://bit.ly/2LzGZ8O`

Understanding how Anaconda works with CuPy and Numba

You must be familiar by now with the free and open source Anaconda distribution, as we have been using it for all our code examples so far. Let's further explore Anaconda and learn more about its features, especially in terms of accelerated computing. Accelerated computing in Anaconda is extremely significant in the deployment for scientific computing with Python.

So far, we covered Python programming implementations inclusive of C/C++ syntax. But from now on, it is important that we focus more on a programming implementation only with pure Python syntax, a perspective that is highly significant for maintaining a seamless programming experience with Python, irrespective of the CPU or GPU platform. Adopting this approach makes it a lot easier for Python programmers to migrate towards a GPU-enabled experience. The more similar the GPU syntax is to CPU syntax on Python, the better the universality in terms of accelerated computing with Python.

In `Chapter 6`, *Working with CUDA and PyCUDA*, and `Chapter 7`, *Working with ROCm and PyOpenCL*, we learned to implement parallel operations in different ways, namely through CUDA, HIP, OpenCL, PyCUDA, and PyOpenCL . In this chapter, we also continue to implement this, as learning to solve a problem in different ways helps a lot in understanding the problem and its solution.

But before we do that, let's first revisit Anaconda in brief and understand its differences to Miniconda. We already know that Anaconda is a package management and deployment distribution. However, it also includes many built-in scientific packages. But if your requirement is very specific for a particular application, you can opt for Miniconda instead, which includes only the repository management system without any extra packages. Let's look more into their differences, as shown in the following table:

Anaconda	Miniconda
Preferable for beginners.	Preferable for experienced users.

Consists of the repository management system that includes over 150 scientific packages.	Consists of only the repository management system without any extra packages.
Focused on a multi-purpose experience.	Focused on a more customized experience.
Requires access to a minimum of 3 GB disk space.	Requires only 400 MB of disk space.
An Anaconda installer is around 650 MB.	A Miniconda installer is only around 65 MB.
Individual package installation not required.	Requires installation of specific individual packages.

Both Anaconda and Miniconda provide usage of Conda, which we will learn about in brief now.

The Anaconda team builds, reviews, and maintains thousands of packages at `https://repo.continuum.io/pkgs/`. To install and manage all of these packages, you can make use of Conda in its default Anaconda or Miniconda configurations.

On April 4, 2019, the availability of a new version of PyCharm with enhanced Anaconda support was announced at AnacondaCON. It is known as PyCharm for Anaconda and can be obtained from `https://www.jetbrains.com/pycharm/promo/anaconda/`.

Conda

Like Anaconda, Conda is an open source package and environment management system that quickly installs, runs, and updates packages and their dependencies while also facilitating creating, saving, loading, and also switching between local virtual environments on your computer. We have already learned these via hands-on experience in our previous chapters. Conda was first created for Python programs, but it can package and distribute software for any language, including R, Ruby, Lua, Scala, Java, JavaScript, C/ C++, and FORTRAN.

CuPy

CuPy is an open source interface that is highly compatible with NumPy, which is the fundamental package for scientific computing with Python. As it follows the same NumPy model, just for CUDA GPUs, it can be used as a drop-in replacement for NumPy in most cases. All you need to do is just simply replace `numpy` with `cupy` in your Python code. We will look into a comparative example later in this chapter.

CuPy also uses NVIDIA's CUDA-related libraries, such as cuBLAS, cuDNN, cuSolver, cuSPARSE, cuFFT, cuRand, and NCCL, to harness the CUDA GPU architecture.

Like NumPy's `numpy.ndarray`, CuPy also consists of a similar implementation through `cupy.ndarray`. We will learn setting up CuPy in the next section.

Numba

Numba is also an open source **just-in-time** (**JIT**) compiler for Python that can efficiently work on code that uses NumPy arrays, functions, and loops. It translates a subset of Python and NumPy code into fast machine code. It uses a collection of decorators that can be applied to your Python functions for Numba compilation. When a call is made to a Numba decorated function, it is compiled to machine code JIT for execution and your code can subsequently run at native machine code speed (CPU or GPU).

A JIT compiler runs after a program starts and compiles bytecode (compiled from source code into low-level code). In this manner, JIT has access to dynamic runtime information, thus enabling better tuning of code. In the case of a traditional compiler, this isn't possible, because it compiles the entire code into machine language before the program can be executed.

GPU-accelerated Numba on Python

Numba can be implemented on both NVIDIA CUDA and AMD ROCm GPUs, though the latter is still under experimentation:

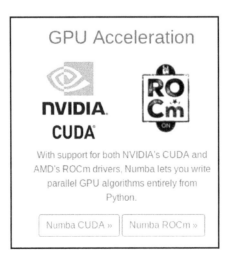

Let's understand them in brief before we move on to the installation process in the next section:

- **Numba CUDA**: NVIDIA CUDA GPU computing with Numba can be implemented by directly compiling a restricted subset of Python code into CUDA kernels and device functions. The **Compute Unified Device Architecture** (**CUDA**) execution model is the foundation of Numba CUDA.
- **Numba ROCm**: AMD ROC GPU computing with Numba can be implemented by directly compiling a restricted subset of Python code into HSA kernels and device functions. The **Heterogeneous System Architecture** (**HSA**) execution model is the foundation of Numba ROCm.

Numba kernels appear to have direct access to NumPy arrays that can automatically be transferred between the CPU and the GPU.

Installing CuPy and Numba for Python within an existing Anaconda environment

Here, we will learn how to integrate CuPy and Numba into our code development environment so that we can communicate with GPU devices in a simpler way than we saw for PyCUDA and PyOpenCL.

Coupling Python with CuPy

Since we have already learned about CUDA's installation and implementation, it will now be easier for us to get started with our CuPy installation procedure for Python, as it was originally developed to implement CUDA. As we have also learned about Anaconda and its setup, we can make use of Python 2.x or 3.x, which are readily available with an existing Anaconda configuration. Setting up CuPy will enable implementing CUDA kernels within your existing Python setup of choice and then compute with it on your NVIDIA GPU.

The NVIDIA driver version installed system-wide should always be greater than, or at least be the same as, the toolkit (Conda package) version. If a system has CUDA 9.0 (both the driver and toolkit installed system-wide), but is compiled against an earlier version of CUDA, say 7.5 (Conda package), CUDA 9.0 would automatically let the CUDA 7.5 Conda package installation work with the older toolkit. But if it's the other way round, then that would not compile, because the 9.0 (Conda package) toolkit isn't compatible with the 7.5 system-wide driver.

To use `conda` during your installations and get line-by-line reports during the process in verbose mode, use the `--debug flag` when you install packages with Conda. Consider the following, for example: **conda install <package-name> --debug**. This way you won't have to wait for the `Collecting package metadata` and `Solving environment` messages and you can log the entire process throughout the installation.

Conda-based installation of CuPy

This is the recommended way to get started with CuPy for a production environment. By using a virtual environment, you can safely experiment with your programming skills without affecting the system-wide Python setup.

To set up CuPy within Anaconda, follow these instructions:

First, let's install `cupy` with `conda` with the following commands on a Terminal. Proceed by entering `y`. The first command would be necessary depending upon the updated state of the Anaconda installation. Here, we additionally choose the `cudatoolkit conda` package specifically for CUDA 9.0 (installed system-wide):

```
$ conda update -n base conda -c anaconda
Collecting package metadata: done
Solving environment: done


---
proceed ([y]/n)? y
---
$ conda install -c anaconda cupy cudatoolkit=9.0
Collecting package metadata: done
Solving environment: done
The following NEW packages will be INSTALLED:
---
cudatoolkit anaconda/linux-64::cudatoolkit-9.0-h13b8566_0
cupy anaconda/linux-64::cupy-5.1.0-py37h686fdb1_0
---
proceed ([y]/n)? y
```

pip-based installation of CuPy

After going through the Conda-based installation of CuPy, let's explore another method that also can be used. You can use `pip` to install CuPy with the local environment. The following code demonstrates how you can do this:

```
$ pip3 install --upgrade pip
$ pip3 install --user cupy-cuda90
```

Note that `pip install --user cupy-cuda90` performs the same operation as `pip3 install --user cupy-cuda90`. The command for CUDA 10.0 is `pip3 install cupy-cuda100`.

The alternative command for installing CuPy for Python 2.x would be the following:

```
$ pip2 install --upgrade pip
$ pip2 install --user cupy-cuda90
```

Note that the preceding command is specific for CUDA 9.0. CuPy also supports versions 8.0, 9.1, 9.2, and 10.0.

Using just `cupy` instead of `cupy-9-0` would install it from source. So now, you have a user-specified configuration ready to use CuPy system-wide on your Ubuntu Linux system.

Coupling Python with Numba for CUDA and ROCm

Since we have already learned about CUDA's installation and implementation, it will now be easier for us to get started with our Numba installation procedure for Python. You do not need to install Python, as it is already available (both 2.x and 3.x) with a freshly installed version of an Ubuntu 18.04 Linux operating system.

Installing Numba with Conda for NVIDIA CUDA GPUs

This is the recommended way to get started with accelerated Numba for a production environment.

To set up Numba for CUDA within Anaconda, follow these instructions:

First, let's install numba with the following conda commands on a Terminal. Proceed by entering y. The first command will be necessary depending upon the updated state of the Anaconda installation. Also here, we choose the cudatoolkit Conda package specifically for CUDA 9.0 (installed system-wide):

```
$ conda update -n base conda -c anaconda
Collecting package metadata: done
Solving environment: done


---
proceed ([y]/n)? y
---
$ conda install -c anaconda numba cudatoolkit=9.0
Collecting package metadata: done
Solving environment: done
The following NEW packages will be INSTALLED:
---

numba anaconda/linux-64::numba-0.43.1-py37h962f231_0
---
proceed ([y]/n)? y
```

Installing Numba with Conda for AMD ROC GPUs

To set up Numba for ROCm within Anaconda, follow these steps:

1. First, let's install numba with conda with the following commands on a Terminal. Proceed by entering y. The first command would be necessary depending upon the updated state of the Anaconda installation:

   ```
   $ conda update -n base conda -c anaconda
   Collecting package metadata: done
   Solving environment: done
   ---
   proceed ([y]/n)? y
   ---
   $ conda install -c anaconda numba
   Collecting package metadata: done
   Solving environment: done
   The following NEW packages will be INSTALLED:
   ---
   numba anaconda/linux-64::numba-0.43.1-py37h962f231_0
   ---
   proceed ([y]/n)? y
   ```

2. Now that you have a Conda configuration ready to use Numba with the experimental version of ROC tools package on your Ubuntu Linux system, use the following command to install this:

```
$ conda install -c numba roctools
```

System-wide installation of Numba with pip (optional)

Note that `pip` can also be used to install Numba both system-wide, or even on your local Conda installation (provided that `pip` is installed locally, with `conda install pip`) with the following command:

```
$ pip install numba
```

In the next section, we'll learn how to configure both the Conda-based and the user-specified system-wide configurations on the PyCharm IDE.

Configuring CuPy on your Python IDE

The following steps are specific to the PyCharm IDE. But if you prefer a different IDE, you can still use these steps as a reference for setting up CuPy, because the procedure is very similar. To configure CuPy with PyCharm, we focus on our Conda-based installation:

1. First, let's create a virtual environment with Conda as a new PyCharm pure Python project. Choose **New Project...** from the PyCharm main menu:

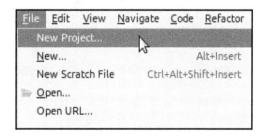

2. Create a **Pure Python** project within a new local Conda environment, as shown in the following screenshot:

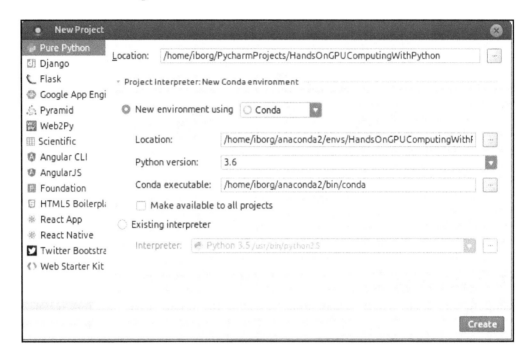

3. Wait for the environment to be created, as shown:

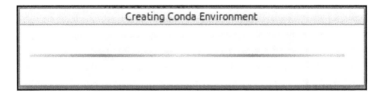

4. After creating the Conda environment, you will have a ready-to-use CuPy development environment, as shown in the following screenshot:

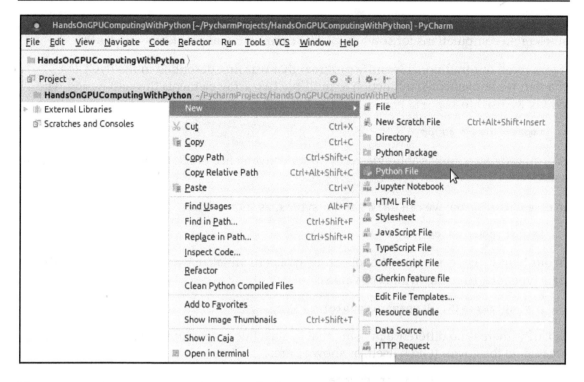

Now you can import `cupy` within your Python programs. As you can see, PyCharm Edu detects and recommends this as you begin to type `import cupy`:

A confirmation of the import of the `cuda` module from `cupy`, as shown in the following screenshot:

At this stage, we are done configuring CuPy on the PyCharm IDE.

How computing in CuPy works on Python

The basics of GPU computing with CuPy can be very easily understood with a side-by-side comparison with the traditional use of NumPy code on Python.

Once we explore the simple terminologies, we will shift our focus towards actual GPU-accelerated computations for solving specific computational problems with CuPy.

If you recall our traditional NumPy program that was first described in the PyCUDA chapter, we implemented a function to multiply two array elements through `numpy`. The syntax we used to `import numpy` was the following:

```
import numpy as np
```

As you can see, `numpy` is abbreviated as `np` for convenience of use throughout the program code.

In case of CuPy, too, we can use a similar syntax, as shown here:

```
import cupy as cp
```

In our NumPy code, we used the following syntax to initialize two arrays of the `double` data type for `N` elements with zero values:

```
p = np.zeros(N, dtype=np.double)
```

In CuPy, there is no difference in using that syntax. But instead of the host (CPU), it gets created on the device (GPU) itself, as shown here:

```
p = cp.zeros(N, dtype=cp.double)
```

To change all the values of each array according to our choice, we used `numpy.ndarray.fill`, as follows:

```
p.fill(23.0)
```

We do not have to change anything in the preceding declaration if we replace a `numpy` `import` with that of `cupy`. It is exactly the same.

We had also used NumPy to set a random integer index value between `0` to `N`, like so:

```
random = np.random.randint(0, N)
```

With CuPy, the declaration is no different. Just replace `np` with `cp` to use the GPU for the random operation, as follows:

```
random = cp.random.randint(0, N)
```

CuPy can also be used to move an array created with NumPy to the GPU device like so:

```
p = np.zeros(N, dtype=np.double)
p_gpu = cp.asarray(p)
```

After using it for carrying out mathematical operations of our choice, we can move the GPU device array back to the host via the following:

```
p = cp.asnumpy(p_gpu)
```

You can also use the following:

```
p = p_gpu.get()
```

You might also remember that the `ElementwiseKernel` was first explored in `Chapter 6`, *Working with CUDA and PyCUDA*, with PyCUDA as shown here:

```
multiply = ElementwiseKernel(
        "double *a_gpu, double *b_gpu",
        "b_gpu[i] = a_gpu[i] * b_gpu[i]",
        "multiply")
```

In a similar manner, you can also use CuPy for the same with a very minor modification like so:

```
multiply = cp.ElementwiseKernel(
        "double *a_gpu, double *b_gpu",
        "b_gpu[i] = a_gpu[i] * b_gpu[i]",
        "multiply")
```

In Numpy, universal functions (also called `ufuncs`) operate on `ndarrays` element-wise, supporting array broadcasting, output type determination, and many other features. They are instances of the `numpy.ufunc` class. As a vectorized wrapper for a function, a `ufunc` takes a fixed number of specific inputs and correspondingly produces a fixed number of specific outputs.

Built-in functions in `ufunc` are mostly implemented in compiled C code. Basic `ufuncs` operate on scalars and sub-arrays, such as vectors and matrices. Custom `ufunc` instances can also be created by using the `frompyfunc` factory function.

Like NumPy, CuPy also allows the use of universal functions to support various elementwise operations. CuPy's `ufunc` supports features similar to that of `ufunc` in NumPy.

CuPy can be used for implementing raw CUDA kernels, as well with `cupy.RawKernel()`.

Implementing multiple GPUs with CuPy

When using more than one GPU on the same system, CuPy can be used to specify the exact GPU device to be worked with. By default, Device(0) is the first GPU.

To specify a second GPU, we can use the following, where the second GPU, Device(1), is being used to initialize p array:

```
cp.cuda.Device(1).use()
p = np.zeros(N, dtype=np.double)
```

By default, all operations are done on Device(0), the first GPU. An array created on Device(1) will not work when used with Device(0).

You can also move an array from GPU 1 to GPU 2 just as from a CPU to a GPU, like so:

```
with cp.cuda.Device(0):
gpu1 = np.zeros(N, dtype=np.double)
with cp.cuda.Device(1):
gpu2 = cp.asarray(gpu1) # Moving array to the second GPU
```

To confirm the GPU device you are working on, you can use the following:

```
print(p.device) # where p is our array used earlier
```

The following output would be displayed on a single GPU setup:

```
<CUDA Device 0>
```

In the next section, we will learn how to configure Numba with CUDA and ROCm on PyCharm.

Configuring Numba on your Python IDE

You can use the following steps as a reference for setting up Numba, because the procedure is very similar. To configure Numba with PyCharm, we again focus on our Conda-based installation:

1. First, let's create a virtual environment with Conda as a new PyCharm pure-Python project. Choose **New Project...** from the PyCharm main menu, as shown in the following screenshot:

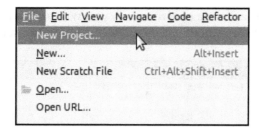

2. Create a **Pure Python** project within a new local Conda environment. Skip this step if you have already created one:

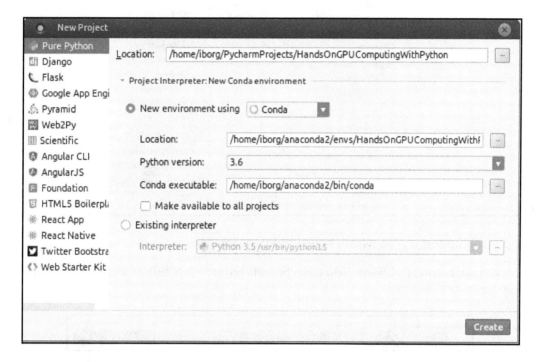

3. Wait for the environment to be created, as shown here:

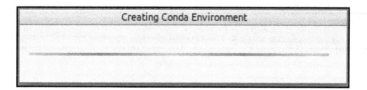

4. After creating the Conda environment, you will have a ready-to-use Numba development environment, as shown in the following screenshot:

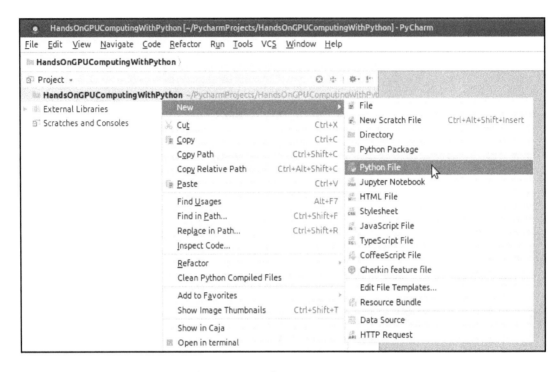

Now you can import numba within your Python programs.

As you can see below, PyCharm Edu detects and recommends this as you begin to type import numba:

The following screenshot shows the confirmation of the import of cuda from numba:

The confirmation of the import of `roc` import from `numba` is shown in this screenshot:

At this stage, we are done configuring Numba on the PyCharm IDE. Let's now explore how computing in Numba works on Python in our next section.

How computing in Numba works on Python

To understand the basics of GPU computing with Numba, it is important that we first learn how a `@jit` decorator works. It is a central feature of Numba. Using this decorator, Numba's JIT compiler can be used to optimize a function.

To `import jit` from Numba, we use the following syntax:

```
from numba import jit
```

In traditional Python, we use the following syntax for defining a function (recall our conventional `multiply` function-based program used earlier):

```
def multiply(p_cpu, q_cpu):
    for i in range(N):
        q_cpu[i] = p_cpu[i] * q_cpu[i]
```

To use JIT with Numba, we only have to add the following just before defining the function:

```
@jit
def multiply(p_cpu, q_cpu):
    for i in range(N):
        q_cpu[i] = p_cpu[i] * q_cpu[i]
```

The preceding change will allow the JIT compiler to take over the `multiply` function and translate it into fast machine code at execution time.

To make Numba report an error whenever the code is not optimized, you can use `@njit` instead, which is a short replacement for `@jit(nopython=True)`.

Using Numba, we can also use other decorators such as `@vectorize`, `@guvectorize`, `@stencil`, `@jitclass`, `@cfunc`, and `@overload`.

For our GPU computing objective, let's focus on the `@vectorize` decorator to implement CUDA and ROCm.

When discussing CuPy earlier, we talked about NumPy `ufuncs` in brief. Numba's `vectorize` allows Python functions to take scalar input arguments to be used as NumPy `ufuncs`. Creating a traditional NumPy `ufunc` involves writing C code. Numba makes `ufuncs` easy by the use of the `vectorize()` decorator. With `vectorize`, Numba can compile a pure Python function into a `ufunc` that operates over NumPy arrays at speeds that are equally comparable to traditional `ufuncs` written in C.

Using vectorize

To use the `vectorize` decorator, we can use the same syntax as we saw for the JIT decorator. The following code shows the multiple functions implemented with `vectorize` as a dynamic universal function (DUFunc):

```
@vectorize
def multiply(p, q):
    q = p * q
```

We call it a dynamic universal function because there are no signatures passed into the `@vectorize` decorator.

When passing signatures, the code would be modified as follows:

```
@vectorize(["float32(float32, float32)"])
def multiply(p, q):
    q = p * q
```

Now, let's see how a GPU implementation for NVIDIA CUDA GPUs is followed:

```
@vectorize(["float32(float32, float32)"], target='cuda')
def multiply(p, q):
    q = p * q
```

In the case of ROCm (experimental), the following syntax would use AMD ROCm GPUs for HSA:

```
@vectorize(["float32(float32, float32)"], target='roc')
def multiply(p, q):
    q = p * q
```

Explicit kernels

You can also use Numba to write kernels explicitly in NVIDIA CUDA or AMD ROCm (HSA).

In CUDA, we use syntax that we are already familiar with:

```
@cuda.jit
def multiply(p, q):
    # Thread id in a 1D block
    tx = cuda.threadIdx.x
    # Block id in a 1D grid
    ty = cuda.blockIdx.x
    # Block width, i.e. number of threads per block
    bw = cuda.blockDim.x
    # Computing flattened index inside the array
    index = tx + ty * bw
    if index < N: # Check array size limit
        q[index]=p[index]*q[index]
```

In ROCm, we use the following OpenCL syntax:

```
@roc.jit
def multiply(p, q):
    # workitem id in a 1D workgroup
    tx = roc.get_local_id(0)
    # workgroup id in a 1D grid
    ty = roc.get_group_id(0)
    # workgroup size, i.e. number of workitems per workgroup
    bw = roc.get_local_size(0)
    # Computing flattened index inside the array
    index = tx + ty * bw
    # The above is equivalent to pos = roc.get_global_id(0)
    if index < N: # Check array size limit
        q[index]=p[index]*q[index]
```

In the next section, we will learn writing our first CuPy and Numba programs on PyCharm.

Writing your first CuPy and Numba enabled accelerated programs to compute GPGPU solutions

Beginning first with CuPy, we will apply the implementations that we learned about CuPy so far, with our first CuPy program. Note that it does not use NumPy to generate the random number as well. In fact, it's a pure CuPy program. The NumPy module is not imported at all.

1. First, open a new file on PyCharm, as shown here in the screenshot:

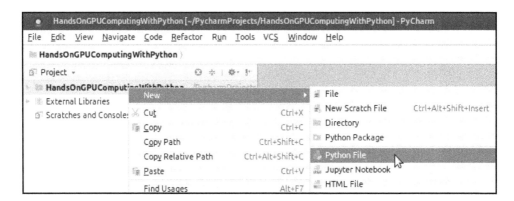

2. Now use the following code that simply replaces NumPy syntax with CuPy. This is a regular and basic format in CuPy that looks exactly like NumPy, apart from the importing of the latter module:

```python
import cupy as cp #Importing CuPy
from timeit import default_timer as timer #To record computation
time

N = 500000000 #500 million elements

# Starting timer to record GPU computation time
start = timer()
# Setting two arrays all with zero values
a_cp = cp.zeros(N).astype(cp.double)
b_cp = cp.zeros(N).astype(cp.double)

# Initializing two values for each array
a_cp.fill(23.0)
b_cp.fill(12.0)
```

```
#Updating second array as a product of both arrays
b_cp = a_cp * b_cp
```

Note that we also use CuPy instead of NumPy to generate a random number, as shown here:

```
# Choosing a random index
random = cp.random.randint(0,N)
# Displaying random element
print("Choosing array element %d at random:" % random)
print("Random array element value is %lf" % b_cp[random])
# Displaying current GPU device
print(b_cp.device)
# GPU computation time
cupy_gpu_time = timer() - start
#Displaying GPU computation time
print("CuPy on GPU took %f seconds." % cupy_gpu_time)
```

The output is shown as follows:

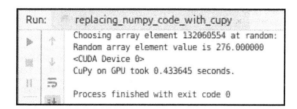

We can also use CuPy to write a raw CUDA kernel. The raw CUDA kernel needs to be properly structured to get the necessary output. So, make sure to indent the code properly before execution like so:

```
import cupy as cp #Importing CuPy
# Defining the CUDA kernel
multiply = cp.RawKernel(r'''
extern "C" __global__
void multiply(const int* p, const int* q, int* z) {
 int tid = blockDim.x * blockIdx.x + threadIdx.x;
 z[tid] = p[tid] * q[tid];
}
''', 'multiply')
```

As with NumPy, we can also use CuPy for managing arrays, as shown in the following code:

```
# First two arrays are set as 0,1,2,3....upto 300
p = cp.arange(300, dtype=cp.int)
q = cp.arange(300, dtype=cp.int)
```

```
# Setting a new array with zeros to pass to kernel for computation
z = cp.zeros(300, dtype=cp.int)

# Invoking the kernel with a grid of 250 blocks, each consisting of 1024
threads
multiply((250,1), (1024,1), (p, q, z)) # grid, block and arguments

# Displaying the output computed on the kernel
print(z)
```

The output is as follows:

```
Run:       raw_cuda_kernel_on_cupy

    [    0     1     4     9    16    25    36    49    64    81   100   121
       144   169   196   225   256   289   324   361   400   441   484   529
       576   625   676   729   784   841   900   961  1024  1089  1156  1225
      1296  1369  1444  1521  1600  1681  1764  1849  1936  2025  2116  2209
      2304  2401  2500  2601  2704  2809  2916  3025  3136  3249  3364  3481
      3600  3721  3844  3969  4096  4225  4356  4489  4624  4761  4900  5041
      5184  5329  5476  5625  5776  5929  6084  6241  6400  6561  6724  6889
      7056  7225  7396  7569  7744  7921  8100  8281  8464  8649  8836  9025
      9216  9409  9604  9801 10000 10201 10404 10609 10816 11025 11236 11449
     11664 11881 12100 12321 12544 12769 12996 13225 13456 13689 13924 14161
     14400 14641 14884 15129 15376 15625 15876 16129 16384 16641 16900 17161
     17424 17689 17956 18225 18496 18769 19044 19321 19600 19881 20164 20449
     20736 21025 21316 21609 21904 22201 22500 22801 23104 23409 23716 24025
     24336 24649 24964 25281 25600 25921 26244 26569 26896 27225 27556 27889
     28224 28561 28900 29241 29584 29929 30276 30625 30976 31329 31684 32041
     32400 32761 33124 33489 33856 34225 34596 34969 35344 35721 36100 36481
     36864 37249 37636 38025 38416 38809 39204 39601 40000 40401 40804 41209
     41616 42025 42436 42849 43264 43681 44100 44521 44944 45369 45796 46225
     46656 47089 47524 47961 48400 48841 49284 49729 50176 50625 51076 51529
     51984 52441 52900 53361 53824 54289 54756 55225 55696 56169 56644 57121
     57600 58081 58564 59049 59536 60025 60516 61009 61504 62001 62500 63001
     63504 64009 64516 65025 65536 66049 66564 67081 67600 68121 68644 69169
     69696 70225 70756 71289 71824 72361 72900 73441 73984 74529 75076 75625
     76176 76729 77284 77841 78400 78961 79524 80089 80656 81225 81796 82369
     82944 83521 84100 84681 85264 85849 86436 87025 87616 88209 88804 89401]

    Process finished with exit code 0
```

In the preceding program, we have multiplied two array elements within the raw CUDA kernel.

Let's now focus on our first Numba program. Using JIT, we revise our conventional numpy Python program (first example in the *How computing in PyCUDA works on Python* section of Chapter 6, *Working with CUDA and PyCUDA*) as follows:

```
import numpy as np # Importing NumPy
from numba import njit # Importing njit module from Numba
from timeit import default_timer as timer # To record computation time
```

```
N = 500000000 # 500 Million Elements

# Function to multiply two array elements and also update the results on
the second array
@njit #Equivalent to @jit(nopython=True)
def multiply(p_cpu, q_cpu):
    for i in range(N):
        q_cpu[i] = p_cpu[i] * q_cpu[i]

def main():
    #Initialize the two arrays of double data type all with 0.0 values upto
N
    p = np.zeros(N, dtype=np.double)
    q = np.zeros(N, dtype=np.double)
```

We are currently using NumPy here. But we'll also see later how we can use both CuPy (replacing NumPy) and Numba in the same program to enable interoperability:

```
    # Update all the elements in the two arrays with 23.0 and 12.0
respectively
    p.fill(23.0)
    q.fill(12.0)
    # Time the Function
    begin = timer()
    multiply(p, q)
    numpy_cpu_time = timer() - begin
    # Report Computation Time
    print("Function took %f seconds." % numpy_cpu_time)
    # Choose a random integer index value between 0 to N
    random = np.random.randint(0, N)
    # Verify all values to be 276.0 for second array by random selection
    print("New value of second array element with random index", random,
"is", q[random])
    return 0
```

Finally, we set our main Python function to launch the complete code, as shown here:

```
if __name__ == "__main__":
    main()
```

The output is as follows:

```
Run:    using_jit_with_numba
    Function took 0.651918 seconds.
    New value of second array element with random index 238747054 is 276.0

    Process finished with exit code 0
```

For our next program, we try to use the `vectorize` decorator based on Numba and also specify a CUDA target:

```
import numpy as np # Importing NumPy
from timeit import default_timer as timer # To record computation time
from numba import vectorize #Importing vectorize module from Numba

N = 500000000 #500 million elements

#The @vectorize decorator turns the function into a GPU-based vectorized
function.
@vectorize(["double(double, double)"], target='cuda')
def vector_multiply_gpu(a, b):
    return a * b

def main():
    #Initialize the two arrays of double data type all with 0.0 values upto
N
    p = np.zeros(N, dtype=np.double)
    q = np.zeros(N, dtype=np.double)
    # Update all the elements in the two arrays with 23.0 and 12.0
respectively
    p.fill(23.0)
    q.fill(12.0)
```

Setting a timer to compute the computation time for our `vectorized` function, is shown in the following code:

```
    # Time the GPU function
    start = timer()
    # Display computed array
    print(vector_multiply_gpu(p, q))
    vector_multiply_gpu_time = timer() - start
    # Report Computation Time
    print("GPU function took %f seconds." % vector_multiply_gpu_time)
    return 0

if __name__ == "__main__":
    main()
```

The output is as follows:

```
Run:    using_numba_with_vectorized_cuda_t...
        [276. 276. 276. ... 276. 276. 276.]
        GPU function took 2.627332 seconds.

        Process finished with exit code 0
```

We discussed the way CUDA and ROCm kernels are written in Numba. The following program is specific for CUDA. Note that defining the kernel is a lot simpler and easier without any C/C++ code, though it is extremely similar and familiar:

```
from numba import cuda # Importing cuda module from Numba
import numpy as np # Importing NumPy
from timeit import default_timer as timer #To record computation time

N = 500000000 # 500 million elements

@cuda.jit
def multiply(p, q):
    # Thread id in a 1D block
    tx = cuda.threadIdx.x
    # Block id in a 1D grid
    ty = cuda.blockIdx.x
    # Number of threads per block
    bw = cuda.blockDim.x
    # Computing flattened index inside the array
    index = tx + ty * bw
```

Note that the preceding line is similar to CUDA syntax—`index = cuda.threadIdx.x + cuda.blockIdx.x * cuda.blockDim.x`:

```
    if index < N: # Check array size limit
        q[index]=p[index]*q[index]

def main():
    #Initialize the two arrays of double data type all with 0.0 values upto
N
    a_source = np.zeros(N, dtype=np.double)
    b_source = np.zeros(N, dtype=np.double)
    a_source.fill(23)
    b_source.fill(12)
    threadsperblock = 1024
    blockspergrid = (N + (threadsperblock - 1)) // threadsperblock
    # Time the GPU function
    start = timer()
    multiply[blockspergrid, threadsperblock](a_source,b_source)
    vector_multiply_gpu_time = timer() - start
```

Reporting computation time and generating a random index for the value is shown in the following code:

```
    # Report GPU Computation time
    print("GPU function took %f seconds." % vector_multiply_gpu_time)
    random = np.random.randint(0,N)
```

```
    print("Choosing array element %d at random:" % random)
    print("Random array element value is %lf" % b_source[random])

if __name__ == "__main__":
    main()
```

The output is as follows:

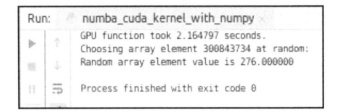

How would the preceding Numba program work if we replace the NumPy import with CuPy? Let's find out in the next section.

Interoperability between CuPy and Numba within a single Python program

In this section, we try to test the interoperability between two different modules within the same Python program, namely, CuPy and Numba. So, we import the cuda module from numba and cupy, as well:

```
from numba import cuda #Using Numba
import cupy as cp #Using CuPy
from timeit import default_timer as timer

N = 500000000

@cuda.jit
def multiply(p, q):
    # Thread id in a 1D block
    tx = cuda.threadIdx.x
    # Block id in a 1D grid
    ty = cuda.blockIdx.x
    # Number of threads per block
    bw = cuda.blockDim.x
    # Compute flattened index inside the array
    index = tx + ty * bw
```

Like on our previous program, we compute the product based on a condition, as shown in the following code:

```
if index < N: # Check array size limit
    q[index]=p[index]*q[index]

def main():
    a_source = cp.zeros(N, dtype=cp.double)
    b_source = cp.zeros(N, dtype=cp.double)
    a_source.fill(23)
    b_source.fill(12)
```

Here we set the maximum number of threads per block for a NVIDIA Titan X GPU, which is 1024 and use our earlier method to calculate the grid size, as well:

```
threadsperblock = 1024
blockspergrid = (N + (threadsperblock - 1)) // threadsperblock
# Time the GPU function
start = timer()
multiply[blockspergrid, threadsperblock](a_source,b_source)
vector_multiply_gpu_time = timer() - start
# Report times
print("GPU function took %f seconds." % vector_multiply_gpu_time)
random = cp.random.randint(0,N)
print("Choosing array element %d at random:" % random)
print("Random array element value is %lf" % b_source[random])

if __name__ == "__main__":
    main()
```

The output is as follows:

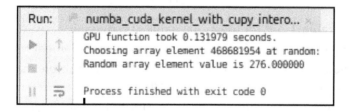

Now, we can confirm that replacing NumPy code with CuPy inside an existing Numba program (*Writing your first CuPy and Numba enabled accelerated programs to compute GPGPU solutions* section in `Chapter 8`, *Working with Anaconda, CuPy, and Numba for GPUs*) accelerates the program by more than 16 times!

Comparing CuPy to NumPy and CUDA

Let's compare CuPy to NumPy and CUDA in terms of simplicity in parallelization. In the following table, we explore the scope of CuPy with respect to NumPy and CUDA so as to understand the scenarios when CuPy could be advantageous to both. Here are some of the differences:

CUDA	NumPy	CuPy
Based on C/C++ programming language.	Based on Python programming language.	Based on Python programming language.
Uses C/C++ combined with specialized code to accelerate computations.	Fundamental package for scientific computing with Python on conventional CPUs.	Uses NumPy syntax but can be used for GPUs.
Casting behaviors from float to integer are defined in CUDA specification.	Casting behaviors from float to integer are defined in C++ specification.	Casting behaviors from float to integer are not defined in C++ specification.
cuRAND is available in CUDA C/C++ for random value generation.	Random value generator does not support dtype option and always returns a float32 value.	It supports any type of float values because of using cuRAND in CuPy.
CUDA handles out-of-bounds integer array indexing by raising an error.	NumPy handles out-of-bounds integer array indexing by raising an error.	CuPy handles out-of-bounds indices differently by wrapping around them.

To achieve reduction in CuPy, you can perform reduction in a manner that is very similar to implementing an `ElementwiseKernel`. As per the official documentation, it is also known as `ReductionKernel` (as in PyCUDA and PyOpenCL) and can be implemented by defining the following four parts of the kernel code:

1. **Identity value**: Used for the initial value of reduction.
2. **Mapping expression**: Used for preprocessing each element for reduction.
3. **Reduction expression**: An operator to reduce the multiple mapped values. Special variables, a and b are used for its operands.
4. **Post mapping expression**: Used to transform the resulting reduced values. The special variable *a*, is used as its input. The output should be written to the output parameter.

Comparing Numba to NumPy, ROCm, and CUDA

Let's now compare Numba to NumPy, ROCm, and CUDA in terms of simplicity in parallelization. In the following table, we explore the scope of Numba with respect to NumPy, ROCm, and CUDA to understand the scenarios when Numba could be advantageous to both. Some of the differences are as follows:

CUDA	ROCm	NumPy	Numba
Based on C/C++ programming language.	Based on C/C++ programming language.	Based on Python programming language.	Based on Python programming language.
Uses C/C++ combined with specialized code to accelerate computations.	Uses C/C++ combined with specialized code to accelerate computations for HCC and HIP.	Fundamental package for scientific computing with Python on conventional CPUs.	Natively understands NumPy arrays, shapes, and dtypes and can index a NumPy array without relying on Python (close to C efficiency).
Universal functions can be implemented CUDA ufuncs in Numba.	Universal functions can be implemented ROCm ufuncs (experimental) in Numba.	Universal functions (ufuncs) are much more prevalent in NumPy and allows mapping of scalar operations.	ufuncs are typically built using Numpy's C API. Numba provides the vectorize decorator to build ufunc.
cuRAND is available in CUDA C/C++ for random value generation.	rocRAND is available in HIP and hcRNG is available in HCC for random value generation.	Random value generator does not support dtype option and always returns a float32 value.	It supports any type of float values because of using cuRAND in CuPy.

			In Numba, range checking is not performed to allow generating code that performs better. Code needs to carefully examined as any indexing that goes out of range can cause a bad-access or a memory overwrite, and crash the interpreter process.
CUDA handles out-of-bounds integer array indexing by raising an error.	HCC/HIP also handles out-of-bounds integer array indexing by raising an error.	NumPy handles out-of-bounds integer array indexing by raising an error.	

To achieve GPU reduction in Numba, you can use the `@reduce` decorator with CUDA, which is an instance of the `Reduce` class.

Useful exercise on computational problem solving

Using the `ElementwiseKernel` Python program example in `Chapter 6`, *Working with CUDA and PyCUDA*, (6.4) and the discussion in the *How computing in CuPy works on Python* section, develop a CuPy version of the same program.

With or without an `ElementwiseKernel`, use Numba and CuPy to compute the following formula given based on our earlier Numba examples:

$$PollutionIndex = \frac{Pollutant\ Concentration}{Pollutant\ Standard\ Level} \times 100$$

The **Pollution Index** or **Pollution Standard Index** (**PSI**) is used to check pollution levels in a certain city, region, or country. It considers six air pollutants: **sulphur dioxide (SO2)**, **particulate matter (PM10)**, **fine particulate matter (PM2.5)**, **nitrogen dioxide (NO2)**, **carbon monoxide (CO)**, and **ozone (O3)**. It is scaled between 0–500 and can be classified into the following five levels:

PSI	Descriptor	General health effects
0–50	Good	None.
51–100	Moderate	Few or none for the general population.

101–200	Unhealthy	Everyone may begin to experience health effects; members of sensitive groups may experience more serious health effects. Stay indoors.
201-300	Very unhealthy	Health warnings of emergency conditions. The entire population is more likely to be affected.
301+	Hazardous	Health alert: everyone may experience more serious health effects.

On an hourly basis, a pollution standard level can be considered as 80 µg/m3. On a daily basis, it is 50 µg/m3.

Design your own version of a GPU accelerated pollution monitor based on random values. At the end of your experimentation, also try to use real-world data.

Assistance in coming up with your solution can be found at the following links:

- Molnár, F., Szakály, T., Mészáros, R. and Lagzi, I. (2010). *Air pollution modelling using a Graphics Processing Unit with CUDA*. Computer Physics Communications, [online] 181(1), pp.105-112. Available at `https://arxiv.org/pdf/0912.3223.pdf`.
- Calculating a station air quality index. Available at `https://www.epa.vic.gov.au/your-environment/air/air-pollution/air-quality-index/calculating-a-station-air-quality-index`.
- EPA AirWatch | Environment Protection Authority Victoria | EPA Victoria. Available at `https://www.epa.vic.gov.au/our-work/monitoring-the-environment/epa-airwatch`.
- Pollutant Standards Index. Available at `https://en.wikipedia.org/wiki/Pollutant_Standards_Index`.
- Air pollutant concentrations at station level (statistics). Datasets available at `https://www.eea.europa.eu/data-and-maps/data/air-pollutant-concentrations-at-station`.
- GUI on Python — Tkinter — Python interface to Tcl/Tk. Available at `https://docs.python.org/2/library/tkinter.html`.
- Tkinter — Python Wiki. Available at `https://wiki.python.org/moin/Tkinter`.

Summary

In this chapter, the general syntax of CuPy code was explained using the comparative example of NumPy. The steps to install CuPy and Numba within an existing Anaconda environment were described. The configuration settings to set up CuPy and Numba were explained step by step. We also learned how computing works in both CuPy and Numba. CuPy was compared to NumPy and CUDA, whereas Numba was compared to NumPy, ROCm, and CUDA. Reduction was also explored for both CuPy and Numba.

At this stage, you should now be able to test your own CuPy and Numba programs. Based on the CUDA installation steps discussed previously in this book, you can also install and configure CuPy within an existing CUDA environment. Additionally, you should be able to install and configure Numba, based on both our CUDA and ROCm installation procedures.

Now, you should be thoughtful about the ways to maximize performance out of CuPy and Numba based on pure Python GPU programming. These options will help you solve computing problems in a much simpler manner. You can now start experimenting with applying your own equations to leverage GPUs with CuPy and Numba. It is highly recommended to work on the final exercise on pollution indexing, described in the final section of this chapter. You can now adopt different approaches toward creating your own version of a pollution control monitor.

In the next chapter, we move on towards the containerization arena. We will learn about the different ready-to-deploy, programmable environments for GPUs and their advantages of use. Alongside this, we will compare open-ended, system-wide environments with closed environments.

Further reading

- Overview—CuPy 5.3.0 documentation. [online] Available at: `https://docs-cupy.chainer.org/en/stable/overview.html`.
- Numba documentation. [online] Available at: `http://numba.pydata.org/numba-doc/latest/index.html`.
- Numba for NVIDIA CUDA GPUs. [online] Available at: `https://numba.pydata.org/numba-doc/dev/cuda/index.html`.
- Numba for AMD ROC GPUs. [online] Available at: `https://numba.pydata.org/numba-doc/dev/roc/index.html`.

- Universal functions (`ufunc`)—NumPy v1.16 Manual. [online] Available at: `https://docs.scipy.org/doc/numpy/reference/ufuncs.html`.
- Universal Functions (`ufunc`)—CuPy 5.3.0 documentation. [online] Available at: `https://docs-cupy.chainer.org/en/stable/reference/ufunc.html`.
- CUDA Math API :: CUDA Toolkit Documentation. [online] Available at: `https://docs.nvidia.com/cuda/cuda-math-api/group__CUDA__MATH__INTRINSIC__CAST.html`.
- HIP MATH APIs Documentation. [online] Available at: `https://rocm-documentation.readthedocs.io/en/latest/ROCm_API_References/HIP-MATH.html`.
- CuPy Support on AMD GPU via HIP (ROCm2.0.0+) by okuta · Pull Request #1094 · cupy/cupy. [online] Available at: `https://github.com/cupy/cupy/pull/1094`.
- `numpy.ufunc.reduce`—NumPy v1.16 Manual. [online] Available at: `https://docs.scipy.org/doc/numpy/reference/generated/numpy.ufunc.reduce.html`.
- Difference between CuPy and NumPy—CuPy 5.3.0 documentation. [online] Available at: `https://docs-cupy.chainer.org/en/stable/reference/difference.html`.
- NumPy and numba—numba 0.12.0 documentation. [online] Available at: `http://numba.pydata.org/numba-doc/0.12/tutorial_numpy_and_numba.html`.
- Reduction Kernels—CuPy 5.3.0 documentation. [online] Available at: `https://docs-cupy.chainer.org/en/stable/tutorial/kernel.html#reduction-kernels`.
- GPU Reduction—Numba. [online] Available at: `https://numba.pydata.org/numba-doc/dev/cuda/reduction.html`.

Section 3: Containerization and Machine Learning with GPU-Powered Python

By going through this section, you will gain a comprehensive idea about GPU-enabled machine learning libraries and how containers work with a comparison between open and closed environments.

The following chapters are included in this section:

- Chapter 9, *Containerization on GPU-Enabled Platforms*
- Chapter 10, *Accelerated Machine Learning on GPUs*
- Chapter 11, *GPU Acceleration for Scientific Applications Using DeepChem*

Containerization on GPU- Enabled Platforms

9

In this new chapter, we will continue our exploration with GPUs while specifically focusing on user accessibility. You will learn about different environments to choose from when setting up a GPU-based programmable platform. These environments will be compared and discussed to help you decide on the most suitable one pertaining to usability and different situations or conditions. Following this, system-wide and virtual environments will be explained. Their advantages and disadvantages will also be explored.

Virtualenv, which is similar to Conda, will be discussed as an example of a closed environment separate from the base system. We will also look at a scenario where both system-wide and Virtualenv packages can co-exist and work together when accessed from a virtual environment.

Exploring further, containers such as **Docker** and **Kubernetes** will be introduced. Local and cloud-based containers will be discussed and compared. Both Docker and Kubernetes will be studied, both as local and cloud containers. The installation process for both will be elaborated step by step. **NVIDIA** Docker and **ROCm** Docker will be discussed with hands-on examples. As a great example of a Jupyter Notebook-style cloud container, **Google Colabolatory** will be discussed in detail in the cloud containers' section.

This chapter will take you through the following topics:

- Programmable environments
- Open-ended environments
- Closed environments
- Local containers
- Cloud containers

Programmable environments

So far in our last three chapters, we have learned about using **Conda** to implement different Python-based programming modules for GPU computing. We also learned about system-wide installations for this. As you might already know, Conda can be used system-wide, but it is not primarily meant to be used so in practice. Rather, it is focused toward creating and managing virtual local environments invisible to the remaining outer part of the OS. In this section, we explore both system-wide and virtual ways of accessibility through the exploration of different programmable environments.

Programmable environments – system-wide and virtual

A **system-wide programmable environment** is one that has packages installed at a global level in the OS. Such packages are set in the system path and hence is visible and accessible from any location within the OS. For example, when you use the `pip` command from the Terminal to install a Python package, it can be implemented from anywhere within the system.

A virtual programmable environment is one that is limited for access only to a certain location within the OS. This location is specific to the user's preference and the packages installed within it are only accessible in that particular directory. For example, when you use the `pip` command from the Terminal to install a Python package in an environment created with Conda, it can be implemented only within the virtual directory and leaves the remaining OS unaffected.

Specific situations of usage

Using a Python module can differ in terms of usability in light of different situations or conditions. To understand this better, let's look at the two scenarios of preference.

Preferring virtual over system-wide

Closed virtual environments can be preferable when carrying out untested source code implementations that could otherwise disrupt the entire OS if installed system-wide. A virtual environment allows the user to safely test code before actually compiling and building them for release. This is very helpful, especially during the alpha and beta testing stages of a software under development.

Preferring system-wide over virtual

Open system-wide environments can be preferable when testing stable releases. It can also be helpful for alpha and beta releases as well, when backup procedures have already been undertaken in fresh OS installations in a physical computer system.

That being said, it is also possible to use both as a hybrid preference. We will see an example later in this chapter.

System-wide (open) environments

It is obvious that a system-wide environment, in general, is the base accessible system of an OS. Whatever packages are installed, compiled, or built are affected on the main system path. In a Linux system, there are two locations in general where an application installer can set its path and configuration for visibility within the OS.

$HOME directory

In this location (`/home/directory/`), you can find one particular file called `.bashrc` that stores paths specific to the user. In addition, there is also a directory named `.config`. Many applications install system-wide, store configuration information in the form of a `.conf` file in this directory and paths in the `.bashrc` file. These applications access the configuration files from this location while under execution, based on the paths set in `.bashrc`. We can say that the `$HOME` location is a user-specific system-wide environment.

System directories

System directories are not user-specific and are effective throughout multiple users. The `/etc/` location specifically stores a lot of system-specific information including path and configuration. `/etc/` consists of a file named `environment` that stores the default system path. Shell files (`.sh`) stored in the `/etc/profile.d/` directory can also be used to export path or configuration specifications.

Advantages of open environments

Open environments are extremely useful to assess application performance at a system level in real time. The reason for this the presence of the system-wide environment installed on physical computer hardware. Problems and errors can be encountered during the deployment and testing of alpha, beta, and final versions of software. Logging these problems and errors in real time helps eliminate issues to ensure stability of software products at the end-user level. Physical hardware with system-wide environments are most ideal and suitable for carrying out computational tasks with large amounts of data.

Disadvantages of open environments

Setting up open environments and upgrading them will always be dependent on physical hardware. Due to the mandatory necessity of physical devices and components, cost and space are two very important constraints that cannot be compromised. Maintenance of physical hardware with system-wide environments can significantly affect the up-time of data centers and servers operating in real-time deployment scenarios. Portability is also another important factor to consider because of the resources required to handle physical hardware.

Virtual (closed) environments

In a virtual environment, the base accessible system is contained within itself. Whichever packages are installed, compiled, or built are affected in the local virtual directory, leaving the outer OS configuration untouched. In a Linux system with a virtual package manager, there are also two locations in general where an application installer can set its path for visibility within the OS. Let's see how it differs for virtual environments.

$HOME directory

Virtual package managers such as Conda also use this location (`/home/directory/`) to enable path and configuration access. The path to the Conda executable is stored in the `.bashrc` file. Many applications, installed locally, store configuration information by default at `$HOME/anaconda3/envs/virtual-directory`. These applications work based on modules installed in the same location. So, we can say that the location is an application-specific local environment.

Virtual system directories

System directories, in this case, are specific to the local virtual directory. The `/etc/` location specifically stores many system specific information including path and configuration.

Advantages of closed environments

Setting up closed environments and upgrading them is a process independent of any physical hardware, which makes the entire process a lot more convenient. The costs involved are significantly lower and there are no space requirements. Maintenance of virtualized environments can be relatively easier due to no involvement of actual hardware, and that significantly increases the up-time of data centers and servers operating in virtual deployment scenarios. Portability is also extremely convenient and easy. Virtualization is most ideal and suitable when deploying and implementing a system across multiple users on a large scale.

Disadvantages of closed environments

Though **closed environments** make it a lot easier to test deployments through virtualization, assessing the performance level will never be the same as on real hardware. The reason for this is the use of virtualized hardware instead of physical hardware. Problems and errors encountered during deployment and testing will always require a real-time physical hardware test in order to ensure complete stability. This is because logging these problems and errors in real time isn't equally feasible as with actual hardware. High-performance computing with huge amounts of data is also not feasible due to the lack of real hardware.

Virtualization

Now that we know about the basic differences between open and closed environments, along with their advantages and disadvantages, let's proceed further into the virtualization concept. This is essential before we move on to our primary discussion—containerization, which is the main theme of this chapter.

As you might be well aware now, virtualization is a way to run applications and operating systems in an isolated location, allocated on a physical hard disk and RAM. Physical hard disk space and RAM can be use to allocate resources and create multiple virtual environments. The physical space allocation is referred to as the **host**, whereas the virtual space allocations are referred to as **guests**.

In the earlier chapters, we discussed installation and configuration steps for different Python modules with Conda. All of those steps were in fact, ways to virtualize application development.

Virtualenv

Virtualenv is yet another example that can be used to create isolated Python environments. It is also focused on developing and testing individual applications separated from the outer OS space and environment.

Installing virtualenv on Ubuntu Linux system

To install `virtualenv`, first let's update our Ubuntu Linux system. If you recall the ROCm installation, this was the first step there, as well:

```
sudo apt update
```

Now let's upgrade the system:

```
sudo apt upgrade
```

Using `dist-upgrade` intelligently manages dependencies and removes older packages when performing the upgrade, whereas using only `upgrade` keeps older packages while upgrading to the newest available ones.

If you do not have `pip` already installed, run the following:

```
sudo apt install python3-pip
```

After installing `pip`, use it to finally install `virtualenv`:

```
pip install virtualenv
```

`pip` will then install `virtualenv` as shown in the following code:

```
Collecting virtualenv

 Downloading
https://files.pythonhosted.org/packages/33/5d/314c760d4204f64e4a968275182b7
751bd5c3249094757b39ba987dcfb5a/virtualenv-16.4.3-py2.py3-none-any.whl
(2.0MB)

    100% |████████████████████████████████| 2.0MB
14.5MB/s

Installing collected packages: virtualenv

Successfully installed virtualenv-16.4.3
```

The preceding Terminal output is based on a cloud container called Google Colaboratory. Hence, that amazing speed we see (`14.5MB/s`) is on the server side. We will read about it in the final section of our chapter.

Using Virtualenv to create and manage a virtual environment

In this section, we will explore how to use Virtualenv to create, as well as manage, a virtual environment. You will now discover the usefulness of our Virtualenv installation that we just learned. This will further enhance our knowledge about virtualization from the context of GPU programming. Follow these steps to get started:

1. Launch a new Terminal. Create a new empty directory in the `$HOME` location (`/home/user-directory/`). Here, we name it `env`:

    ```
    sudo mkdir env
    ```

2. After creating the directory, let's now use `virtualenv` to place the new environment on it:

    ```
    virtualenv env
    ```

3. The preceding command will yield an output similar to the following result on your screen:

    ```
    Using base prefix '/usr'

    New python executable in /home/avimanyu/env/bin/python3
    ```

```
Also creating executable in /home/avimanyu/env/bin/python

Installing setuptools, pip, wheel...

done.
```

4. Now the virtual environment has been created in our newly creating directory. You can verify the new contents with the `ls` command:

```
ls env
```

The new contents are inclusive of three directories: `bin`, `include`, and `lib`:

```
bin/ include/ lib/
```

5. Let's now check the contents of each of these three directories in our new virtual environment:

```
ls ~/env/bin
```

The contents of $HOME/env/bin are revealed:

```
activate          activate_this.py    pip*        python3*
activate.csh      activate.xsh        pip3*       python3.6@
activate.fish     easy_install*       pip3.6*     python-config*
activate.ps1      easy_install-3.6*   python@     wheel*
```

6. Similarly, we can also find out the contents of the other two directories:

```
ls ~/env/include
```

This will give us the following output:

```
python3.6m@
```

Here, `m` signifies a configuration done with the `--with-pymalloc` flag. It is a faster implementation than `malloc`.

7. Now we check the contents of the last directory in our virtual environment directory:

```
ls ~/env/lib
python3.6/

ls ~/env/lib/python3.6
```

The last command will give the following output:

```
abc.py@                          heapq.py@                        re.py@
base64.py@                       hmac.py@                         rlcompleter.py@
bisect.py@                       importlib@                       shutil.py@
_bootlocale.py@                  imp.py@                          site-packages/
codecs.py@                       io.py@                           site.py
collections@                     keyword.py@                      sre_compile.py@
_collections_abc.py@             lib-dynload@                     sre_constants.py@
config-3.6m-x86_64-linux-gnu@    LICENSE.txt@                     sre_parse.py@
copy.py@                         linecache.py@                    stat.py@
copyreg.py@                      locale.py@                       struct.py@
distutils/                       no-global-site-packages.txt      tarfile.py@
_dummy_thread.py@                ntpath.py@                       tempfile.py@
encodings@                       operator.py@                     tokenize.py@
enum.py@                         orig-prefix.txt                  token.py@
fnmatch.py@                      os.py@                           types.py@
functools.py@                    posixpath.py@                    warnings.py@
__future__.py@                   __pycache__/                     weakref.py@
genericpath.py@                  random.py@                       _weakrefset.py@
hashlib.py@                      reprlib.py@
```

Here, we again find three directories: distutils, __pycache__, and site-packages.

8. Let's explore their contents as well. We do this to gain a brief idea on every part of the entire environment structure:

```
ls ~/env/lib/python3.6/distutils
distutils.cfg   __init__.py __pycache__/

ls ~/env/lib/python3.6/distutils/pycache
__init__.cpython-36.pyc
```

.pyc files are compiled bytecode files in Python. They enable faster access when importing libraries. Using bytecode makes the process more convenient:

```
ls ~/env/lib/python3.6/__pycache__
```

This command will give the following output:

```
abc.cpython-36.pyc                    os.cpython-36.pyc
base64.cpython-36.pyc                 posixpath.cpython-36.pyc
bisect.cpython-36.pyc                 random.cpython-36.pyc
_bootlocale.cpython-36.pyc            re.cpython-36.pyc
codecs.cpython-36.pyc                 reprlib.cpython-36.pyc
_collections_abc.cpython-36.pyc       shutil.cpython-36.pyc
copy.cpython-36.pyc                   site.cpython-36.pyc
copyreg.cpython-36.pyc                sre_compile.cpython-36.pyc
enum.cpython-36.pyc                   sre_constants.cpython-36.pyc
fnmatch.cpython-36.pyc                sre_parse.cpython-36.pyc
functools.cpython-36.pyc              stat.cpython-36.pyc
__future__.cpython-36.pyc             struct.cpython-36.pyc
genericpath.cpython-36.pyc            tarfile.cpython-36.pyc
hashlib.cpython-36.pyc                tempfile.cpython-36.pyc
heapq.cpython-36.pyc                  token.cpython-36.pyc
hmac.cpython-36.pyc                   tokenize.cpython-36.pyc
io.cpython-36.pyc                     types.cpython-36.pyc
keyword.cpython-36.pyc                warnings.cpython-36.pyc
linecache.cpython-36.pyc              weakref.cpython-36.pyc
locale.cpython-36.pyc                 _weakrefset.cpython-36.pyc
operator.cpython-36.pyc
```

9. Finally, we find that there are many sub-directories present in `site-packages`. It also contains its own `pip` package manager that is isolated to our virtual environment only:

```
ls ~/env/lib/python3.6/site-packages
```

The command will give the following output:

```
easy_install.py          pkg_resources/     setuptools-41.0.0.dist-info/
pip/                     __pycache__/       wheel/
pip-19.0.3.dist-info/    setuptools/        wheel-0.33.1.dist-info/
```

Let's stop our navigation at this stage. Now we have a brief outlook on how a newly created virtualenv environment is structured.

Now, let's activate the virtual environment:

```
$ source ~/env/bin/activate

(env) $ which python
/home/avimanyu/env/bin/python

(env) $ deactivate
```

We can confirm from the preceding code that our virtual environment is indeed using the local `python` executable and not the system-wide version. It is isolated from the outer system:

```
$ which python
/usr/local/bin/python
```

Now that we are out of the virtual environment after deactivating it, the system-wide `python` executable is back in charge.

Key benefits of using Virtualenv

After learning how to install Virtualenv, let's have a look at some the key features that sets it apart from the rest:

- Virtualenv isolates your workspace for developing applications individually without using system Python
- It facilitates installation of local packages unseen from the system-wide `python` executable
- It can execute Python programs by using the `python` executable available in a virtual environment
- It eliminates conflicts across multiple applications with different dependencies

It also possible to use both the system-wide and Virtualenv packages and make them work together when accessed from Virtualenv.

By using the `--system-site-packages` flag, we can create a virtual environment to make the environment use the global `site-packages` modules instead of the built-in modules as demonstrated:

```
virtualenv --system-site-packages env2
```

Another way around it is to create a symbolic link of the system directory in the local directory:

```
sudo ln -s /usr/lib/python3.6/dist-packages/cupy ~/env/lib/python3.6/site-packages
```

In a system where CuPy is installed system-wide, a virtual environment can also make good use of it through the newly created symbolic link.

 A few alternatives to Virtualenv for creating and managing isolated virtual environments are `pipenv` and `pyenv`.

VirtualBox

VirtualBox is another GUI-based example that can be used to install and run multiple (guest) operating systems. It is focused on developing and testing applications within these isolated OS environments.

Installing VirtualBox

After learning how to work through Virtualenv, let's look at another GUI-based VM named VirtualBox. Follow the next steps to install VirtualBox:

1. Let's begin by updating and upgrading the system. Follow the code instructions as demonstrated:

   ```
   sudo apt update
   sudo apt upgrade
   ```

2. Install VirtualBox along with the extensions pack that will allow you to use additional features when using the guest operating systems:

   ```
   sudo apt install virtualbox virtualbox-ext-pack
   ```

3. After the installation completes, you can run VirtualBox with the `virtualbox` command. After a reboot, it should be added to the menu as well.

4. A typical **VirtualBox Manager** looks like this:

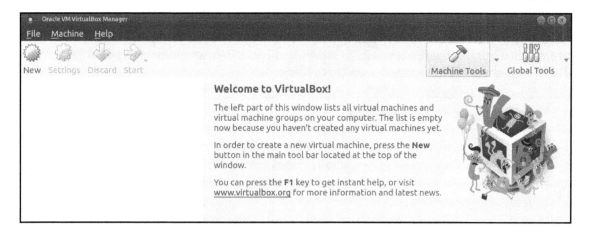

Here, the environment isolation is many times more, because the Python-based applications that you want to develop and test would be running on a guest operating system, completely aloof from your host OS. It is necessary to enable virtualization from the motherboard's BIOS in order to install and use the guest OS.

GPU passthrough

When you install your guest OS, VirtualBox will still use a virtual video driver for the display and so GPU hardware recognition is disabled. **GPU passthrough** is a method to transfer the ownership of the GPU device directly to the guest OS. In this manner, you can avail all the core features of your GPU on the guest OS in VirtualBox. The feature is experimental on VirtualBox and is actually called PCI passthrough. **PCIe** is how you connect your graphics card to your system's motherboard.

Virtual Machine ware (**VMware**) and **Quick EMUlator** (**QEMU**) are other examples similar to VirtualBox when guest OSes are concerned.

Local containers

Containerization is a concept that takes the idea of virtualization many steps further. It is the process of providing readily deployable applications and their dependencies, preinstalled and preconfigured within individual containers at operating system level. These containers are all isolated user space instances:

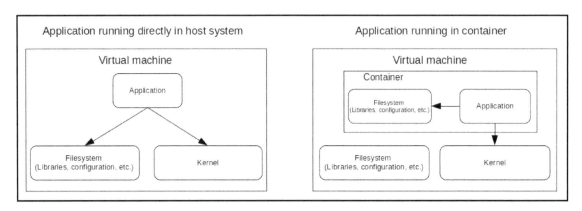

By Natlibfi-arlehiko - Own work, CC BY-SA 4.0, https://commons.wikimedia.org/w/index.php?curid=69328769

With containerization, you no longer require even setting up a virtualized environment, as all of those measures are already taken care of. You can quickly get started with a production-ready interface. Hence we can conclude that containerization boosts productivity by a huge margin.

When we set up containers in a locally accessible system, it is referred to as **local containerization**. In this section, we are going to continue our discussion on local containers with special focus on GPUs.

Two good examples of containerization are Docker and Kubernetes.

Docker

Docker is a software program that enables usage of applications through virtualization at operating-system level. It is available both as **Enterprise** and **Community** editions.

Installing Docker Community Edition (CE) on Ubuntu 18.04

On a fresh Ubuntu installation, the following steps will get you an operational version of Docker CE on your system:

1. Update your packages:

   ```
   sudo apt update
   ```

2. Enable installation via HTTPS:

   ```
   sudo apt-get install apt-transport-https ca-certificates curl
   gnupg-agent software-properties-common
   ```

3. Add the official GPG key of Docker with `curl`:

   ```
   curl -fsSL https://download.docker.com/linux/ubuntu/gpg | sudo apt-
   key add -
   ```

4. Docker recommends verifying the key. The following command does that:

   ```
   $ sudo apt-key fingerprint 0EBFCD88
   pub rsa4096 2017-02-22 [SCEA]
   9DC8 5822 9FC7 DD38 854A E2D8 8D81 803C 0EBF CD88
   uid [ unknown] Docker Release (CE deb) <docker@docker.com>
   sub rsa4096 2017-02-22 [S]
   ```

5. Let's now add the repository so that we can install Docker:

   ```
   sudo add-apt-repository "deb [arch=amd64]
   https://download.docker.com/linux/ubuntu \
   $(lsb_release -cs) \
   stable"
   ```

   You will see an output similar to the following:

   ```
   Get:1 https://download.docker.com/linux/ubuntu bionic InRelease
   [64.4 kB]
   Ign:2
   https://developer.download.nvidia.com/compute/cuda/repos/ubuntu1804
   /x86_64 InRelease
   Hit:3 http://ppa.launchpad.net/graphics-drivers/ppa/ubuntu bionic
   InRelease
   Hit:4 http://security.ubuntu.com/ubuntu bionic-security InRelease
   Hit:5 http://archive.ubuntu.com/ubuntu bionic InRelease
   Ign:6
   ```

```
https://developer.download.nvidia.com/compute/machine-learning/repo
s/ubuntu1804/x86_64 InRelease
Hit:7
https://developer.download.nvidia.com/compute/cuda/repos/ubuntu1804
/x86_64 Release
Hit:8
https://developer.download.nvidia.com/compute/machine-learning/repo
s/ubuntu1804/x86_64 Release
Get:9 https://download.docker.com/linux/ubuntu bionic/stable amd64
Packages [5,970 B]
Hit:10 http://archive.ubuntu.com/ubuntu bionic-updates InRelease
Hit:11 https://cloud.r-project.org/bin/linux/ubuntu bionic-cran35/
InRelease
Hit:12 http://ppa.launchpad.net/marutter/c2d4u3.5/ubuntu bionic
InRelease
Hit:13 http://archive.ubuntu.com/ubuntu bionic-backports InRelease
Fetched 70.4 kB in 1s (53.3 kB/s)
Reading package lists... Done
```

Note that the Docker repository changes have been highlighted in bold.

6. Install Docker after updating the packages:

```
sudo apt update
sudo apt-get install docker-ce docker-ce-cli containerd.io
```

7. Now you have Docker installed, you can confirm it by downloading and running
the hello-world image:

```
docker run hello-world
```

The output will be similar to the following:

```
Unable to find image 'hello-world:latest' locally
latest: Pulling from library/hello-world
78445dd45222: Pull complete
Digest:
sha256:c5515758d4c5e1e838e9cd307f6c6a0d620b5e07e6f927b07d05f6d12a1a
c8d7
Status: Downloaded newer image for hello-world:latest
Hello from Docker!
This message shows that your installation appears to be working
correctly.
To generate this message, Docker took the following steps:

1. The Docker client contacted the Docker daemon.

2. The Docker daemon pulled the "hello-world" image from the Docker
```

```
Hub.

3. The Docker daemon created a new container from that image which
runs the executable that produces the output you are currently
reading.

4. The Docker daemon streamed that output to the Docker client,
which sent it to your terminal.
Share images, automate workflows, and more with a free Docker ID:
https://cloud.docker.com/
For more examples and ideas, visit:
https://docs.docker.com/engine/userguide/
```

In contrast to Anaconda, Docker creates a single object, containing an application with its dependencies. These Docker containers are portable across multiple Docker-enabled machines and therefore, the application within the container executes in environments that are identical. This ensures better quality assurance when testing applications. So, Docker is heavily customized for applications.

NVIDIA Docker

Now that have learned how to install Docker, let's also cover how to proceed with an NVIDIA Docker installation on Ubuntu 18.04:

Use the following commands for adding the repositories:

```
curl -s -L https://nvidia.github.io/nvidia-docker/gpgkey | \
sudo apt-key add -

curl -s -L
https://nvidia.github.io/nvidia-docker/ubuntu18.04/nvidia-docker.list | \
sudo tee /etc/apt/sources.list.d/nvidia-docker.list

sudo apt-get update
```

Installing NVIDIA Docker

Follow these steps to install NVIDIA Docker:

1. Install NVIDIA Docker on your environment by using the following command:

```
sudo apt install nvidia-docker2
```

2. Reload the Docker daemon configuration to reflect changes:

```
sudo pkill -SIGHUP dockerd
```

3. You can check the `nvidia-smi` command from the CUDA image with the following command:

```
docker run --runtime=nvidia --rm nvidia/cuda:9.0-base nvidia-smi
```

4. You can also check the `nvcc` version via the following:

```
sudo docker run --rm --runtime=nvidia nvidia/cuda:9.0-devel nvcc --version
```

ROCm Docker

Like NVIDIA, AMD also provides Docker usage. It can be installed through four simple steps:

1. Clone the `ROCm-docker` repository from GitHub (assuming `git` is installed):

```
git clone https://github.com/RadeonOpenCompute/ROCm-docker
```

2. Change the current directory to the newly downloaded `ROCm-docker` directory:

```
cd ROCm-docker
```

3. Next, build `rocm-terminal`:

```
sudo docker build -t rocm/rocm-terminal rocm-terminal
```

4. Finally, add it to the `video` group:

```
sudo docker run -it --device=/dev/kfd --device=/dev/dri --group-add video rocm/rocm-terminal
```

A Docker configuration can also be very easily set up on the PyCharm Professional Edition IDE.

Kubernetes

Kubernetes is a containerization system for automating deployment, scaling, and management of containerized applications. It is open source.

The primary difference between Docker and Kubernetes is that the latter is an orchestration system that enables coordination and scheduling among containers. So, Kubernetes cannot be directly compared to Docker, but to Docker Swarm instead. Docker Swarm is also an orchestration system like Kubernetes.

To be able to use Kubernetes locally, we can use the following steps for installation:

1. First off, update and enable HTTPS:

   ```
   sudo apt update
   sudo apt install apt-transport-https
   ```

   You can omit the preceding command if you already have it installed as per our Docker installation.

2. Add the repository configuration:

   ```
   curl -s https://packages.cloud.google.com/apt/doc/apt-key.gpg |
   sudo apt-key add -

   echo "deb https://apt.kubernetes.io/ kubernetes-xenial main" | sudo
   tee -a /etc/apt/sources.list.d/kubernetes.list
   ```

3. Next, install `kubectl` to interact with the Kubernetes cluster:

   ```
   sudo apt-get update
   sudo apt-get install kubectl
   ```

4. Now we install `minicube`, which is a tool to run a single-node Kubernetes cluster in a virtual machine (we have already learned how to set up VirtualBox):

   ```
   curl -Lo minikube
   https://storage.googleapis.com/minikube/releases/latest/minikube-li
   nux-amd64

   chmod +x minikube

   mv minikube /usr/local/bin
   ```

/usr/local/bin is already in the system path. So, the system can now access the minikube executable directly.

5. Launch minikube (assuming VirtualBox and Docker are both installed and configured):

```
minikube start
```

Let's also have a brief look at the experimental support for GPUs on Kubernetes.

For enabling NVIDIA GPUs on Kubernetes, two plugins are available. One is official, while the other is available via Google Cloud.

The official plugins require the following prerequisites:

- Kubernetes nodes have to be pre-installed with NVIDIA drivers
- Kubernetes nodes have to be pre-installed with nvidia-docker 2.0
- nvidia-container-runtime must be configured as the default runtime for Docker, instead of runc
- NVIDIA drivers ~= 361.93

The Google Cloud plugin doesn't require using nvidia-docker and should work with any container runtime compatible with the Kubernetes **Container Runtime Interface** (**CRI**).

For AMD GPUs, Kubernetes nodes have to be pre-installed with the AMD GPU Linux driver before installing their plugin.

On PyCharm, Kubernetes is available as a plugin for editing resource files.

Cloud containers

Unlike local containers, **cloud containers** are available on the server side that can be remotely accessed from anywhere. Physical maintenance costs are heavily reduced in such scenarios.

One great example of cloud based containerization is Google **Colaboratory** (**Colab**) that allows execution of Linux Terminal commands, in addition to Python-based development and testing on Jupyter notebooks. For a brief overview on Jupyter Notebook and Jupyter Lab, please refer to Chapter 5, *Setting Up Your Environment for GPU Programming*.

The GitHub page for Colab's backend container can be found at https://github.com/googlecolab/backend-container.

Our primary focus in this section is Google Colab on the cloud, specifically because, since April 2019, it offers free access to an NVIDIA Tesla T4 Tensor Core GPU for AI inference! It is actually a card that belongs to the Turing architecture. Earlier, Colab provided a Tesla K80 belonging to the Maxwell architecture. The specifications for NVIDIA T4 Tensor Core GPU are as follows:

NVIDIA Turing tensor cores	320
NVIDIA CUDA cores	2,560
Single-precision	8.1 TFLOPS
Mixed-precision (FP16/FP32)	65 TFLOPS
Double-precision (FP64)	254.4 GFLOPS
INT8	130 TOPS
INT4	260 TOPS
GPU memory	16 GB GDDR6, 300 GB/sec
ECC	Yes
Interconnect bandwidth	32 GB/sec
System interface	x16 PCIe Gen3
Form factor	Low-profile PCIe
Thermal solution	Passive
Compute APIs	CUDA, NVIDIA TensorRT™, ONNX

The following screenshot shows the specifications of the device displayed using the `tensorflow.python.client` module:

```
from tensorflow.python.client import device_lib
device_lib.list_local_devices()

[name: "/device:CPU:0"
device_type: "CPU"
memory_limit: 268435456
locality {
}
incarnation: 8097481313537670403, name: "/device:XLA_CPU:0"
device_type: "XLA_CPU"
memory_limit: 17179869184
locality {
}
incarnation: 3509578143695564125
physical_device_desc: "device: XLA_CPU device", name: "/device:XLA_GPU:0"
device_type: "XLA_GPU"
memory_limit: 17179869184
locality {
}
incarnation: 8079698124687756107
physical_device_desc: "device: XLA_GPU device", name: "/device:GPU:0"
device_type: "GPU"
memory_limit: 14800692839
locality {
  bus_id: 1
  links {
  }
}
incarnation: 1379948111412660623
physical_device_desc: "device: 0, name: Tesla T4, pci bus id: 0000:00:04.0, compute capability: 7.5"]
```

Each session for using the Tesla T4 on Google Colab can be as long as 12 hours, after which you can even move on to another VM, making it a brilliant option for developers and researchers, especially when with limited resources. All you need is a free Google account.

An overview on GPU computing with Google Colab

Step by step, let's see how to install the different Python-based modules that we have learned about so far on Google Colab. We will explore with CUDA and PyCUDA in particular. Please refer to Chapter 6, *Working with CUDA and PyCUDA*, for easy access to the commands and code. This time, we are going to revisit them, but on the GPU cloud!

Here are the steps for installation:

1. Assuming you already have a Google account, visit `https://colab.research.google.com` on your browser (Firefox or Chrome). The following interface will appear:

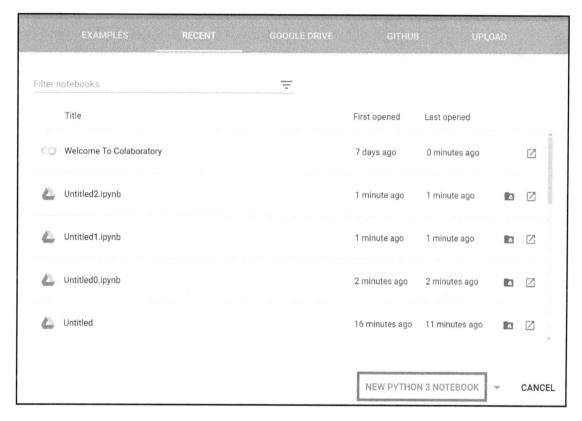

As marked in red, select **NEW PYTHON 3 NOTEBOOK**.

2. Now, you have access to a pre-configured and readily available Python programming interface:

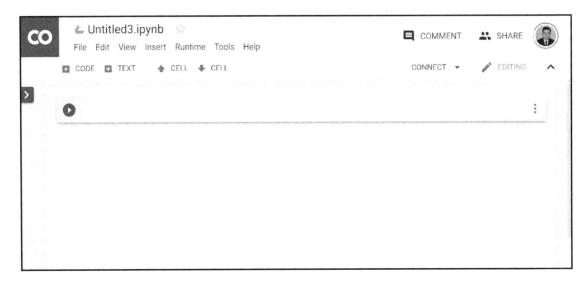

3. At this stage, our environment runtime does not have the GPU enabled by default. So, let's change that setting to enable the GPU:

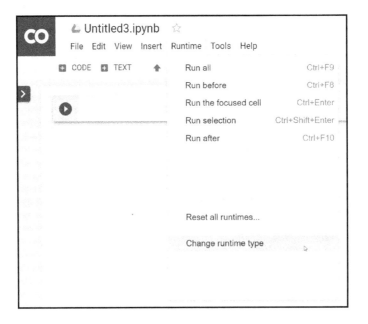

4. As we can see, by default, no hardware accelerator is enabled. So, we change it as follows:

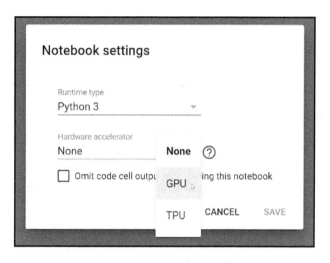

Note that Colab also offers you the option to choose a **Tensor Processing Unit** (TPU)!

Each cell in the Notebook can be used in two essential ways:

- **Python code**:

You can execute this line by clicking on the play symbol or using the keyboard shortcut *Shift + Enter*:

- **Terminal commands**: To differentiate between Python code and Terminal commands, the latter has to prefixed with an exclamation symbol:

```
[4]  !ls

 ⟶   sample_data
```

So, we can see the contents of the current directory in the Colab session.

Now let's begin our CUDA (10.1) installation on Google Colab. Use the following commands sequentially, cell by cell:

1. Download the official CUDA 10.1 package (a .deb Debian-based file) for Ubuntu 18.04 with the wget tool:

   ```
   !wget
   https://developer.nvidia.com/compute/cuda/10.1/Prod/local_installer
   s/cuda-repo-ubuntu1804-10-1-local-10.1.105-418.39_1.0-1_amd64.deb
   ```

2. dpkg prepares the installation (-i):

   ```
   !dpkg -i cuda-repo-ubuntu1804-10-1-
   local-10.1.105-418.39_1.0-1_amd64.deb
   ```

3. Add the apt-key to configure your local repository:

   ```
   !apt-key add /var/cuda-repo-10-1-local-10.1.105-418.39/7fa2af80.pub
   ```

4. Update your Colab's Ubuntu Linux system:

   ```
   !apt-get update
   ```

5. Finally, we install the cuda meta-package:

   ```
   !apt-get install cuda
   ```

6. Verify your new CUDA installation on the cloud:

```
[10]  !nvcc -V

 ⟶   nvcc: NVIDIA (R) Cuda compiler driver
      Copyright (c) 2005-2019 NVIDIA Corporation
      Built on Fri Feb  8 19:08:17 PST 2019
      Cuda compilation tools, release 10.1, V10.1.105
```

7. To install PyCUDA, let's use `pip`:

```
!pip install pycuda
```

This command will give the following output:

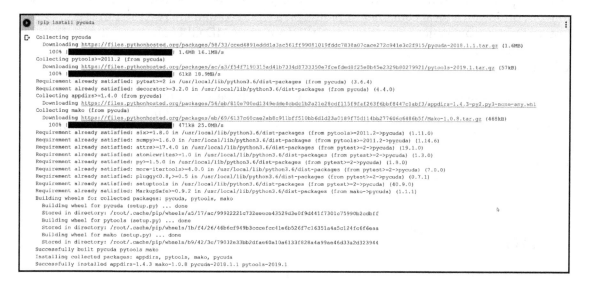

Now you can start developing and testing your own Python programs. You can use each cell to include the entire source code and then execute it.

Summary

In this chapter, programmable environments were discussed with a perspective on system-wide and virtual environments. Scenarios where a particular option is preferred were discussed. The directory structures of both system-wide and virtual environments were explored, in addition to their advantages and disadvantages. The containerization concept was introduced as an evolution from virtualization. Finally, local and cloud containers were explored in detail with a hands-on approach.

You are now familiar with the different environments to choose from in order to set up and use a development platform with GPUs. With Virtualenv and VirtualBox, you can now set up your own isolated development environments. The benefits of using Virtualenv will help prepare you to customize future preferences when setting up a closed programmable environment. Depending upon your usability requirements and situations, you can choose to work offline on a local container or online on a cloud container. You can now start testing Docker applications on either an NVIDIA or an AMD GPU platform. If you do not own a GPU, you can still make use of the freely accessible Tesla T4 GPU and develop your GPU-based Python code.

In the next chapter, we move on to a new section purely based on machine learning. In `Chapter 10`, *Accelerated Machine Learning on GPUs*, we will learn about the significance of GPU-enabled Python in **Artificial Intelligence** (**AI**) and science. We will look into how deep learning evolved from AI through machine learning. An introduction to machine learning frameworks such as Tensorflow and Theano will follow, particularly their GPU-focused modules via Python.

Further reading

- *pyenv/pyenv, Simple Python version management*: `https://github.com/pyenv/pyenv`
- *Pipenv, Python Dev Workflow for Humans*—pipenv 2018.11.27.dev0 documentation: `https://pipenv.readthedocs.io/en/latest/`
- Oracle VM VirtualBox: `https://www.virtualbox.org`
- *PCI Passthrough* (experimental): `https://www.virtualbox.org/manual/ch09.html#pcipassthrough`
- *NVIDIA/nvidia-docker, Build and run Docker containers leveraging NVIDIA GPUs*: `https://github.com/NVIDIA/nvidia-docker`
- *RadeonOpenCompute/ROCm-docker, Dockerfiles for the various software layers defined in the Radeon Open Compute Platform*: `https://github.com/RadeonOpenCompute/ROCm-docker`
- *Kubernetes versus Docker, What Does It Really Mean?*: `https://www.sumologic.com/blog/kubernetes-vs-docker/`
- Play with Docker: `https://labs.play-with-docker.com/`
- Play with Kubernetes: `https://labs.play-with-k8s.com/`

- *Schedule GPUs - Kubernetes*: `https://kubernetes.io/docs/tasks/manage-gpus/scheduling-gpus/`
- *Kubernetes on NVIDIA GPUs Installation Guide: Data Center Documentation*: `https://docs.nvidia.com/datacenter/kubernetes/kubernetes-install-guide/index.html`
- *NVIDIA/k8s-device-plugin, NVIDIA device plugin for Kubernetes*: `https://github.com/NVIDIA/k8s-device-plugin`
- *RadeonOpenCompute/k8s-device-plugin, Kubernetes (k8s) device plugin to enable registration of AMD GPU to a container cluster*: `https://github.com/RadeonOpenCompute/k8s-device-plugin`
- *NVIDIA Tesla K80 GPU Accelerator for High Performance Computing | NVIDIA*: `https://www.nvidia.in/object/tesla-k80-dual-gpu-accelerator-oct-14-2014-in.html`
- Google Colaboratory: GPU availability: `https://research.google.com/colaboratory/faq.html#gpu-availability`

Accelerated Machine Learning on GPUs

10

In this chapter, we begin a new discussion with machine learning through GPU-enabled Python. The end objective of these chapters is to encourage the user to develop applications to benefit the scientific AI community. The fundamental steps to write a machine learning-based program will be illustrated via use cases.

With the help of the use cases, we will establish how GPU-enabled Python and machine learning can work in tandem to facilitate processing and analysis of large datasets. We will look at the significance of big data management, deep learning, and other crucial concepts. Additionally, computational exercises will be revisited but with a machine learning approach. The solution assistance section will help you devise your own techniques to implement machine learning on the three unique problems discussed previously through chapters 6, 7, and 8. The chapter is divided into two parts—an initial introduction to machine learning, and a hands-on walkthrough for machine learning.

Keeping all the discussion pointers in mind, the chapter is divided into the following sections to make learning seamless:

- The significance of the dual advantage – an AI perspective
- The evolution of artificial intelligence
- The emergence of machine learning
- Introducing machine learning frameworks
- Introducing TensorFlow
- Introducing PyTorch
- Installing TensorFlow and PyTorch for GPUs
- Configuring TensorFlow on PyCharm and Google Colab
- Configuring PyTorch on PyCharm and Google Colab

- Machine learning with TensorFlow and PyTorch
- Writing your first GPU-accelerated machine learning programs
- Revisiting our computational exercises with a machine learning approach

Technical requirements

Check out the following video to see the Code in Action:

```
http://bit.ly/2VYNMws
```

The significance of Python in AI – the dual advantage

In the scenarios delineated in `Appendix A`, GPUs are shown to be ideal for big data management, whereas Python is shown to be ideal for data science. But in fact, it is also true the other way around. Hence, Python and GPUs are equally important in both data science and big data, which can be clearly be stated as a dual advantage.

If you look closely at the research papers cited in Appendix A, you will observe that Python and GPUs complement each other very well in terms of AI computing. This fact has led to the creation of machine learning modules in existing frameworks written in Python specifically for GPUs. Before we look into them, we must understand the significance of the dual advantage.

The need for big data management

To illustrate a large dataset, let's consider the example of cancer research data. The number of patients suffering from this deadly disease are only growing every year. A lot of cancer research is still underway and from the machine learning standpoint, the amount of data being generated for one cancer type on a global scale alone is enormous. Now if we were to expand that to all the other types of cancer, the amount of data would only increase exponentially; this will increase even further as we move from all cancer types to all disease types. So now, we are looking at nothing but big data, because the data being handled is to be processed, analyzed, and stored on an incredibly large scale.

This is where AI comes to the rescue with its incredible processing abilities, and working in tandem with Python, the big data processing becomes easier. In AI, machine learning algorithms can be the most effective when training on enormous datasets and inferred effectively. The higher the quality and quantity of the datasets, the better the effectiveness of training. Only then, will intelligent systems evolve better. The thousands of cores available in today's GPUs make them a perfect choice for training large datasets.

Using Python for machine learning

Big data management and machine learning share a strong correlation. This is because both use algorithms that are data-driven and involve filtering out patterns to reveal important outcomes when assessing an analytic prediction. Because of a diverse community of practitioners from backgrounds not just pertaining to computer science, Python is the perfect choice to develop such data-driven programs due to its simple syntax. The availability of a huge number of pre-existing libraries in scientific computing such as NumPy, SciPy, TensorFlow, Theano, and many others makes one very easily adapt towards embracing AI development through Python.

Exploring machine learning training modules

Machine learning emerged as a technique by which a computer can learn from data, without using a complex set of different rules. This approach is mainly based on training a model from datasets. The better the quality of the datasets, the better the accuracy of the machine learning model:

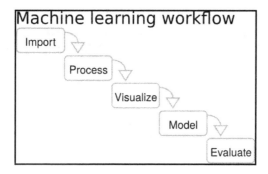

By Brylie Christopher Oxley - Own work, Wikimedia, CC0

A basic machine learning workflow involves all the steps illustrated in the preceding diagram. Also, the following flowchart describes the role of a machine learning algorithm in the practice of machine learning techniques. Both training and test data greatly influence a hypothesis, which can be further improved through performance-driven feedback to the same machine learning algorithm. The end result further strengthens the hypothesis:

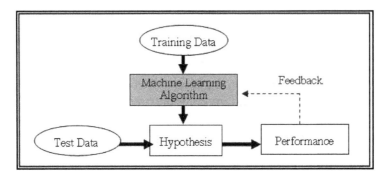

By Jinapattanah - Own work, CC BY-SA 3.0, https://commons.wikimedia.org/w/index.php?curid=18005985

Primarily, there are three forms of machine learning: supervised learning, unsupervised learning, and reinforcement learning. While supervised learning involves training on labeled datasets, unsupervised learning is done via unlabeled datasets. In reinforcement learning, an algorithm is rewarded for every correct response.

An amalgamation of all these learning models is called deep learning, which mimics the functioning of human brain. We will look at deep learning in the following section.

The advent of deep learning

Deep learning as we know today is a machine learning-based algorithm that mimics the functioning of human brain. The actual foundation of deep learning was laid in the mid-1960s when Alexey Ivakhnenko and his associate, Valentin Grigor'evich Lapa, used multiple layers of nonlinear features with polynomial activation functions. This was an approach similar to today's deep learning techniques. It followed by the use of manually weighted neural networks and an application of back-propagation of errors to train deep models that could yield useful distributed representation. **Convolutional Neural Networks (CNNs)** were introduced in the 1990s specifically for image recognition problems.

For further information, you can refer to the research paper cited in `Appendix A`.

At that time, the potential of deep learning remained unrealized and unexplored due to:

- Lack of very large datasets
- Lack of computing power
- Lack of relevant algorithmic techniques

But as the age of big data, GPUs, and efficient algorithms arrived, these issues started to get resolved in the mid-2000s and through the decade, the *deep learning* term evolved to be used as frequently as AI due to its rapid adaptation to this day.

The fundamental tenet of deep learning is entwined in mimicking the neuron network of a human brain. This is done to create various neural network that can be utilized to make self-learning machines. It basically consists of inputs and outputs with hidden layers in between. These concepts are the foundation of current approaches in deep learning today. To get a holistic view, follow the following URL that provides a pictorial representation of neural network: `https://www.needpix.com/photo/1315699/neural-network-networks-neuron`.

Every artificial neural network model that we see in the image (in the preceding URL) are based on the artificial neuron derived from the biological model.

If we closely observe, we can infer that machine learning has always been a subset of AI, whereas deep learning is a subset of machine learning.

We can conclude that the recent advancements in AI have eliminated the need for manual creation of features to run machine learning algorithms. These recent advancements have evolved as representation learning collectively through the latest machine learning and deep learning techniques. It allows a system to automatically discover the representations needed for feature detection or classification from raw data with combined training and inference.

In our next section, we will learn about different machine learning frameworks in Python for GPUs.

Introducing machine learning frameworks

Now as we are acquainted with the fundamentals of machine learning, let's look into some interesting machine learning frameworks and libraries that we can use in Python. In this book, we are going to discuss two specific open source machine learning frameworks, namely TensorFlow and PyTorch.

Basically, a machine learning framework can be a tool, a library or even serve as an interface to get you started with building your machine learning models.

Tensors by example

You might have come across this term many times, primarily because of the popular TensorFlow frameworks and TPU. Before understanding what a tensor is, it is important to recall our high school understanding of scalar and vector. Scalars have only magnitude but no direction, whereas vectors have both.

An example of a scalar would be temperature. The temperature has only magnitude that can be represented with a Celsius/Fahreinheit/kelvin unit with no directional attribute at all. Such a scalar can be called as tensor of rank 0.

An example of a vector would be velocity. Velocity has both magnitude and direction that can be represented with a distance unit with respect to time. Such a vector can be called as tensor of rank 1.

An example of a tensor of rank 2 would be stress. Stress can be represented as an effective force per unit area. But it can be experienced in multiple directions.

Let's illustrate this with the example. In the following diagram, force exerted on various surface of a cube is demonstrated. Force on each side of the visible surfaces is defined by 3 unit vectors. On each of these 3 surfaces, 1 force is the usual normal force, whereas 2 others are sideway forces. Opposing forces and torques on the opposite 6 sides ensure mechanical equilibrium. So, the remaining 6 surfaces need not be considered. This state of stress can be decomposed into 9 (3x3) components, as demonstrated:

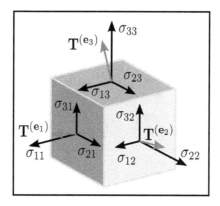

So, the properties of tensors can transform according to certain rules under a change of coordinates.

Introducing TensorFlow

TensorFlow is an open source framework for **dataflow** and **differentiable programming** in diverse areas. Based on Theano (another machine learning framework), it is a symbolic math library, used mostly for deep learning applications. It was originally developed by the Google Brain team for internal purposes but later released under the Apache 2.0 license on 9th November, 2015.

Dataflow programming

In mathematical graph theory, a directed graph is a graph of vertices connected by edges, where each edge has a direction associated with itself, as shown in the following diagram:

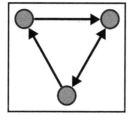

Wikimedia Public Domain Image

There can also be two way edges, as shown in the following diagram:

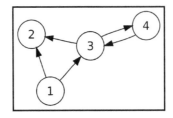

Wikimedia Public Domain Image

A programming model that is fundamentally based on the concept of a directed graph for data flowing between operations to enforce datastream principles is known as dataflow programming. It is also referred to as datastream programming.

Differentiable programming

A set of techniques to numerically evaluate the derivative of a mathematical function specified by a computer program is known as automatic differentiation. Also referred to as algorithmic or computational differentiation, it applies the chain rule repeatedly to a sequence of arithmetic operations and functions in a program and an arbitrary order derivative is computed automatically. The end result is accurately of working precision. The following diagram demonstrates the functionality of automatic differentiation:

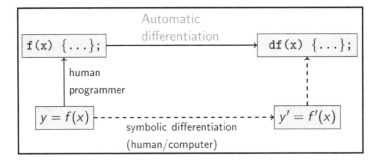

Wikimedia Public Domain Image

A programming model in which entire programs are differentiated through automatic differentiation is known as differentiable programming. So, these are the two fundamental programming concepts that can be implemented with TensorFlow. The name is derived from the operations that neural networks perform on multidimensional data arrays, which are referred to as tensors (recall our stress cube example from the previous section).

TensorFlow on GPUs

The default `pip` installation package for TensorFlow is built for CPUs and is known as `tensorflow`, whereas the variant built for GPUs is known as the `tensorflow-gpu` package.

Devices in the TensorFlow system are represented as strings. For example, a single GPU device is represented as `/device:GPU:0`.

Introducing PyTorch

PyTorch is an open-source machine learning framework for Python, based on Torch (a deprecated machine learning library, scientific computing framework, and scripting language). It has a wide variety of applications, including natural language processing, object detection and classification, social media algorithms, photorealistic video-to-video translation, and recommender systems, such as on Netflix. PyTorch was primarily developed by Facebook.

On 2nd April, 2019, Facebook open sourced its PyTorch-BigGraph (PBG) tool that makes it much faster and easier to produce graph embeddings for extremely large graphs.

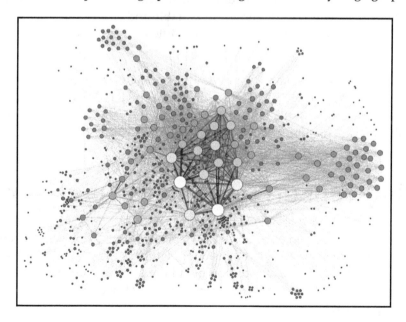

By Martin Grandjean - Grandjean, Martin (2014). "La connaissance est un réseau". Les Cahiers du Numérique 10 (3): 37-54. DOI:10.3166/LCN.10.3.37-54., CC BY-SA 3.0, https://commons.wikimedia.org/w/index.php?curid=29364647

In our previous section, we saw a very simple example of a graph with 4 vertices. The preceding visualization is a similar example of gigantic graph network, based on a social network analysis visualization.

Let's now look at the two primary features of PyTorch in the next section.

The two primary features of PyTorch

Now that we've got an overview of PyTorch, let's explore further and discuss its nitty-gritty. The two primary features of PyTorch are as follows:

- It assists in tensor computation (like NumPy) with strong GPU acceleration (similar to CuPy, as discussed in `Chapter 8`, *Working with Anaconda, CuPy, and Numba for GPUs*).
- PyTorch is essential for deep neural networks built on a tape-based automatic differentiation (as discussed in the previous section) system.

An **epoch** is one complete training cycle on a training dataset. Once every sample in the set is seen, the second epoch begins. The AutoGrad module in PyTorch implements automatic differentiation. It is helpful in building neural networks and can save time on one epoch by calculating differentiation of the parameters at the forward pass itself. The `nn` module in PyTorch can be helpful when AutoGrad is not suitable and sufficiently low level for defining complex neural networks. The `optim` module implements various optimization algorithms used for building neural networks.

The default `pip` installation packages for both CPUs and GPUs is known as `pytorch`. Through the `cuda` module in `torch`, you can check the availability of an NVIDIA GPU device. So, for an existing NVIDIA GPU, `torch.cuda.is_available()` returns `True`. PyTorch is still experimental on AMD GPUs.

Installing TensorFlow and PyTorch for GPUs

Since we have already learned about CUDA's installation and implementation, it will now be easier for us to get started on our TensorFlow and PyTorch installation procedure. Additionally, we also need **cuDNN** to be installed, which is the predefined deep neural network library for CUDA. To be able to download the library, you have to fill in a free registration at `https://developer.nvidia.com/`, which is the official web portal for the NVIDIA Developer program.

Installing cuDNN

In this section, we are going to install cuDNN 7.4.2 for both TensorFlow and PyTorch. Follow these steps to get started:

1. Download the corresponding archive from the cuDNN repository:

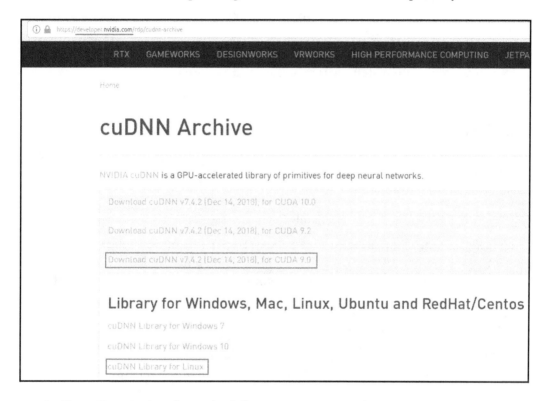

2. Use a Terminal and run the following commands from your Downloads directory:

```
cd Downloads
tar -xvzf cudnn-9.0-linux-x64-v7.4.2.24.tgz
sudo cp cuda/include/cudnn.h /usr/local/cuda-9.0/include
sudo cp -P cuda/lib64/libcudnn* /usr/local/cuda-9.0/lib64/
```

The -P flag ensures the symbolic links are copied just as they are, instead of as actual files.

3. Provide read access system-wide to the cuDNN library in the Linux system:

```
sudo chmod a+r /usr/local/cuda-9.0/lib64/libcudnn*
```

Now cuDNN has been configured with the existing CUDA 9.0 installation.

4. Before proceeding with installing TensorFlow and PyTorch for Conda, make sure you activate your virtual environment first:

```
conda activate HandsOnGPUComputingWithPython
```

Now we can proceed with installing TensorFlow and PyTorch.

Coupling Python with TensorFlow for GPUs

Assuming that Anaconda or `pip` is already configured, setting up TensorFlow will enable us to make use of the GPU-supported version that we are going to install. Additionally, we will also install Matplotlib for plotting graphs.

There are primarily two methods of installation.

The first is a **Conda-based installation of TensorFlow**: This is the recommended way in this book to get started with TensorFlow for a production environment. By using a virtual environment, you can safely experiment with your programming skills without affecting the system-wide Python setup.

To set up TensorFlow within Anaconda, follow these steps.

First, let's install the `tensorflow-gpu` package with Conda on a Terminal. Proceed by entering `Y`. The first command will be necessary depending upon the updated state of the Anaconda installation:

```
$ conda update -n base conda -c anaconda
Collecting package metadata: done
Solving environment: done
---
proceed ([y]/n)? y
---
$ conda install tensorflow-gpu matplotlib
Collecting package metadata: done
Solving environment: done
The following NEW packages will be INSTALLED:
---
tensorboard        pkgs/main/linux-64::tensorboard-1.13.1-py36hf484d3e_0
tensorflow         pkgs/main/linux-64::tensorflow-1.13.1-gpu_py36h26cf82e_0
```

```
tensorflow-base        pkgs/main/linux-64::tensorflow-base-1.13.1-
gpu_py36h8f37b9b_0
tensorflow-estima~ pkgs/main/noarch::tensorflow-estimator-1.13.0-py_0
tensorflow-gpu         pkgs/main/linux-64::tensorflow-gpu-1.13.1-h0d30ee6_0
matplotlib             pkgs/main/linux-64::matplotlib-3.0.3-py36h5429711_0
---
proceed ([y]/n)? y
```

Pip-based installation of TensorFlow: Alternatively, you can also use `pip` to install TensorFlow within the local environment:

```
$ pip3 install --upgrade pip
$ pip3 install --user tensorflow-gpu matplotlib
```

 Note that `pip install --user tensorflow-gpu` also performs the same operation as `pip3 install --user tensorflow-gpu`.

An alternative command for installing TensorFlow for Python 2.x is as follows:

```
$ pip2 install --upgrade pip
$ pip2 install --user tensorflow-gpu matplotlib
```

So, now you have a user-specified configuration, ready to use with TensorFlow and system-wide on your Ubuntu Linux system. Next, we will take a look at coupling Python with PyTorch for GPUs.

Coupling Python with PyTorch for GPUs

There are basically two ways to get started with PyTorch for GPUs on your local system. The first one is to utilize a closed environment, such as Conda, that will keep your virtual environment concealed from the outer OS. The second way, with `pip`, is less preferable on a local system but can be useful for Google Colab (beginning the `pip` command with a ! prefix on the Colab Jupyter notebook).

Conda-based installation of PyTorch: As discussed in the previous section, this is the recommended way. To set up PyTorch within Anaconda, follow these steps.

First, let's install the `pytorch`, `torchvision`, and `cudatoolkit=9.0` packages with Conda on a Terminal. Note that we used the same CUDA package for CuPy as well. Proceed by entering `Y`. The first command will be necessary depending upon the updated state of the Anaconda installation:

```
$ conda update -n base conda -c anaconda
Collecting package metadata: done
Solving environment: done
---
proceed ([y]/n)? y
---
$ conda install pytorch torchvision cudatoolkit=9.0 -c pytorch
Collecting package metadata: done
Solving environment: done
The following NEW packages will be INSTALLED:
---
pytorch pytorch/linux-64::pytorch-1.0.1-py3.6_cuda9.0.176_cudnn7.4.2_2
torchvision pytorch/noarch::torchvision-0.2.2-py_3
---
proceed ([y]/n)? y
```

Pip-based installation of TensorFlow: Alternatively, you can also use `pip` to `install tensorflow` with the local environment:

```
$ pip3 install --upgrade pip
$ pip3 install --user
https://download.pytorch.org/whl/cu90/torch-1.0.1-cp36-cp36m-win_amd64.whl
$ pip3 install --user torchvision
```

 Note that `pip install` also performs the same operation as `pip3 install`.

So, now you have a user-specified configuration ready to use PyTorch system-wide on your Ubuntu Linux system.

For **Miniconda**, the first command regarding the updates before the installations would be this one:

```
$ conda update -n base conda
```

In the next section, we'll learn how to configure both the Conda-based and the user-specified system-wide configurations on the PyCharm IDE.

Configuring TensorFlow on PyCharm and Google Colab

As you may already know by now, TensorFlow and PyTorch can be implemented on either your local IDE or on the cloud. Let's see how.

Using TensorFlow on PyCharm

The next steps are specific to the PyCharm IDE. If you prefer a different IDE, you can still use these steps as a reference for setting up TensorFlow. To configure TensorFlow with PyCharm, we focus on our Conda-based installation:

1. If you haven't done it already, create a virtual environment with Conda as a new PyCharm **Pure Python** project. Choose **New Project...** from the PyCharm main menu:

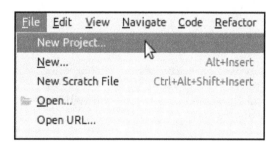

2. Create a **Pure Python** project within a new local **Conda** environment:

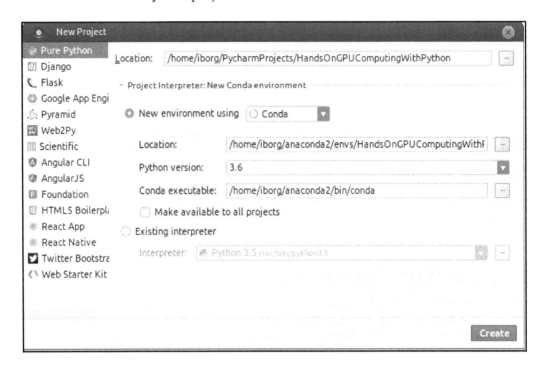

3. Wait for the environment to be created:

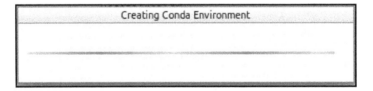

4. After creating the **Conda** environment, you will have a ready-to-use TensorFlow development environment:

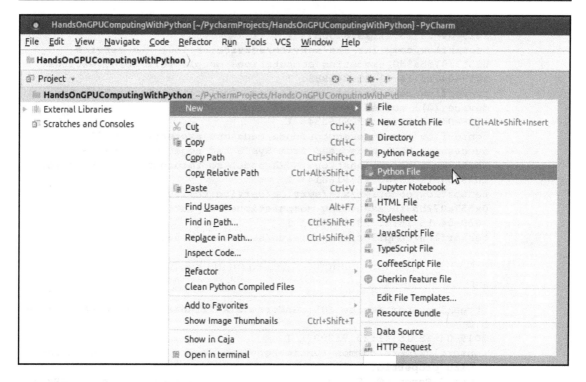

5. Now you can import TensorFlow within your Python programs. As you can see, PyCharm Edu detects and recommends this as you begin to type `import tensorflow`:

6. When you run the following code in PyCharm, TensorFlow will detect the CPU and GPU properties:

```
from tensorflow.python.client import device_lib
device_lib.list_local_devices()
```

7. An output similar to the following will be displayed:

```
2019-04-15 15:41:23.815279: I
tensorflow/core/platform/cpu_feature_guard.cc:141] Your CPU
supports instructions that this TensorFlow binary was not compiled
to use: SSE4.1 SSE4.2 AVX AVX2 FMA
2019-04-15 15:41:23.845610: I
tensorflow/core/platform/profile_utils/cpu_utils.cc:94] CPU
```

```
Frequency: 3499100000 Hz
2019-04-15 15:41:23.845967: I
tensorflow/compiler/xla/service/service.cc:150] XLA service
0x557a075ba9d0 executing computations on platform Host. Devices:
2019-04-15 15:41:23.845982: I
tensorflow/compiler/xla/service/service.cc:158] StreamExecutor
device (0): <undefined>, <undefined>
2019-04-15 15:41:23.916334: I
tensorflow/stream_executor/cuda/cuda_gpu_executor.cc:998]
successful NUMA node read from SysFS had negative value (-1), but
there must be at least one NUMA node, so returning NUMA node zero
2019-04-15 15:41:23.916814: I
tensorflow/compiler/xla/service/service.cc:150] XLA service
0x557a072b53f0 executing computations on platform CUDA. Devices:
2019-04-15 15:41:23.916829: I
tensorflow/compiler/xla/service/service.cc:158]
```

Here, NVIDIA GPU information is revealed on the PyCharm console with TensorFlow:

```
StreamExecutor device (0): GeForce GTX TITAN X, Compute Capability
5.2
2019-04-15 15:41:23.917097: I
tensorflow/core/common_runtime/gpu/gpu_device.cc:1433] Found device
0 with properties:
name: GeForce GTX TITAN X major: 5 minor: 2 memoryClockRate(GHz):
1.076
pciBusID: 0000:01:00.0
totalMemory: 11.92GiB freeMemory: 11.45GiB
2019-04-15 15:41:23.917108: I
tensorflow/core/common_runtime/gpu/gpu_device.cc:1512] Adding
visible gpu devices: 0
2019-04-15 15:41:23.918234: I
tensorflow/core/common_runtime/gpu/gpu_device.cc:984] Device
interconnect StreamExecutor with strength 1 edge matrix:
2019-04-15 15:41:23.918248: I
tensorflow/core/common_runtime/gpu/gpu_device.cc:990] 0
2019-04-15 15:41:23.918255: I
tensorflow/core/common_runtime/gpu/gpu_device.cc:1003] 0: N
2019-04-15 15:41:23.918453: I
tensorflow/core/common_runtime/gpu/gpu_device.cc:1115] Created
TensorFlow device (/device:GPU:0 with 11142 MB memory) -> physical
GPU (device: 0, name: GeForce GTX TITAN X, pci bus id:
0000:01:00.0, compute capability: 5.2)
Process finished with exit code 0
```

At this stage, we are done configuring TensorFlow on the PyCharm IDE. Let's move on to the next section, where we will explore how to use TensorFlow on **Google Colab**.

Using TensorFlow on Google Colab

Follow the next set of steps to get started with using TensorFlow on Google Colab. Note that these steps are specific to Google Colab only, where TensorFlow already comes preinstalled:

1. First, visit the Google Colab URL, at `https://colab.research.google.com`.
2. Create a new Python 3 Jupyter notebook:

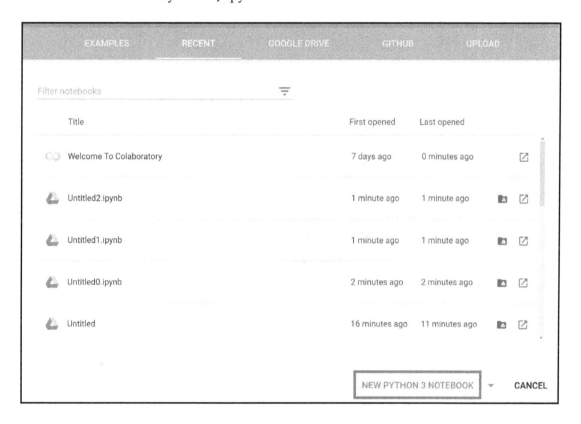

3. Change the runtime to the GPU as discussed previously in `Chapter 9`, *Containerization on GPU-Enabled Platforms* (cloud containers):

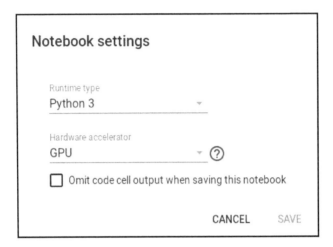

4. Confirm the changes by listing all the devices to get the GPU information with the following code in a notebook cell:

```
from tensorflow.python.client import device_lib
device_lib.list_local_devices()
```

Now you should see the GPU (note that the Tesla K80 was later replaced with the Tesla T4):

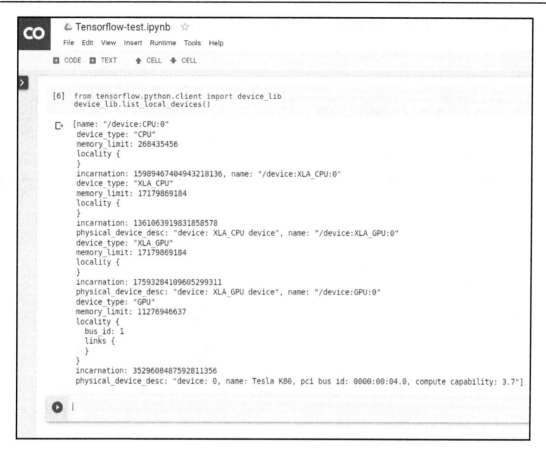

5. You can also do the same for checking the **Tensor Processing Units** (**TPUs**) as well. But make sure you change the runtime to **TPU**:

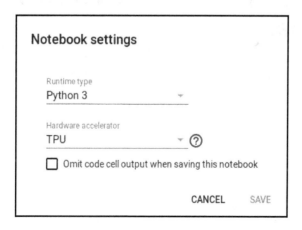

6. Now use the following code to list the `TPU Devices`:

```
import tensorflow as tf
import os
tpu_path = 'grpc://' + os.environ['COLAB_TPU_ADDR']
print ('TPU Address:', tpu_path)
print ('TPU Devices:')
tf.Session(tpu_path).list_devices()
```

Eight TPU devices are listed:

We are now done, and know how to configure TensorFlow for both GPUs and TPUs on Google Colab!

Configuring PyTorch on PyCharm and Google Colab

In this section, we will learn how to configure PyTorch on PyCharm and Google Colab. We will look at all the steps and commands involved in a sequential manner. Let's read on.

Using PyTorch on PyCharm

The next steps are specific to the PyCharm IDE. But if you prefer a different IDE, you can still use these steps as a reference for setting up PyTorch because the procedure is very similar. To configure PyTorch with PyCharm, we again focus on our Conda-based installation:

1. Create a **Pure Python** project within a new local **Conda** environment (skip this step if you've already done this):

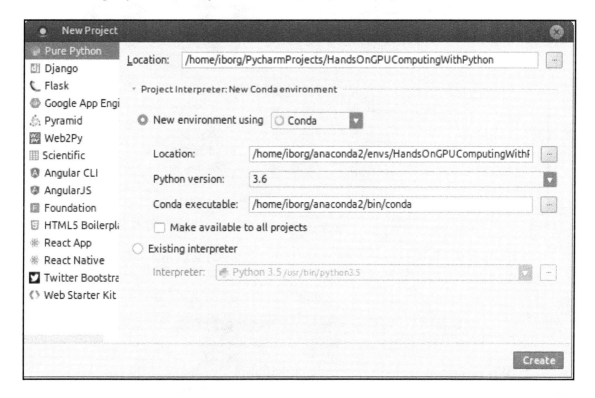

2. Wait for the environment to be created:

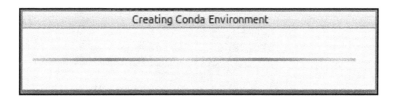

3. After creating the **Conda** environment, you will have a ready-to-use PyTorch development environment:

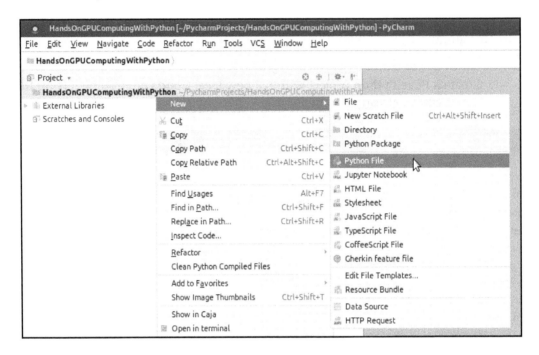

4. Now you can `import torch` within your Python programs. As you can see, PyCharm Edu detects and recommends this as you begin to type `import torch`:

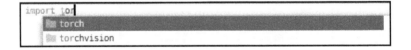

5. When you run the following code in PyCharm, PyTorch will the current device properties:

```
import torch
device=torch.cuda.current_device()
print(device)
print(torch.cuda.device_count())
print(torch.cuda.get_device_name(device))
print(torch.cuda.get_device_capability(device))
```

The following output will be displayed for a Maxwell Titan X with CUDA Capability 5.2. The current device (0) count is 1:

```
0
1
GeForce GTX TITAN X
(5, 2)

Process finished with exit code 0
```

At this stage, we are done configuring PyTorch on the PyCharm IDE.

Using PyTorch on Google Colab

The following steps demonstrate how to use PyTorch on Google Colab. Note that the steps are specific to Google Colab only, where PyTorch is also pre-installed:

1. First, visit the Google Colab URL at `https://colab.research.google.com`.
2. Create a new Python 3 Jupyter notebook:

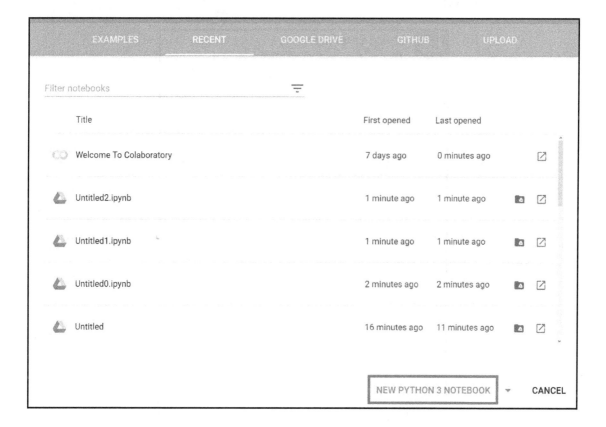

3. Change the runtime to **GPU**, as discussed previously:

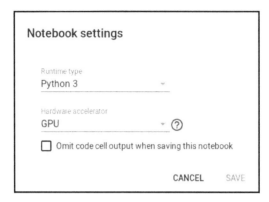

4. Now let's get the GPU information with the following lines of code each on notebook cell:

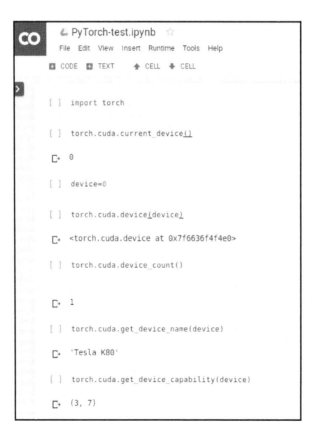

Working with a TPU is under active development in Google Colab. But it can be implemented with **Accelerated Linear Algebra (XLA)**: https://github.com/pytorch/xla.

After changing the runtime, you can still get the address of the TPU to implement with XLA on the cloud:

```
import os

tpu_path = 'grpc://' + os.environ['COLAB_TPU_ADDR']
print ('TPU Address:', tpu_path)
```

```
TPU Address: grpc://10.28.7.170:8470
```

At this stage, we are done configuring PyTorch on Google Colab.

Machine learning with TensorFlow and PyTorch

Now that we have learned how to install configure TensorFlow and PyTorch, it's time to begin our hands-on experience. Before we do that, let's learn a little about the datasets we be downloading, consider another interesting piece of information.

MNIST

MNIST is a database of a large number of handwritten digits. The classic MNIST dataset is preferred by many enthusiasts when getting started with or testing machine learning systems. MNIST is very useful to develop intelligent image-processing systems. MNIST datasets are based on the MNIST database.

Fashion-MNIST

The official TensorFlow documentation suggests using the **Fashion-MNIST** dataset, as it is a bit more of a challenging computational problem than the classic version. Instead of handwritten digits, these datasets include images of different types of clothing and related objects such as shoes or bags.

CIFAR-10

CIFAR-10 datasets are based on the **Canadian Institute for Advanced Research (CIFAR)** database. The suffix 10 denotes 10 different classes, representing `plane`, `car`, `bird`, `cat`, `deer`, `dog`, `frog`, `horse`, `ship`, and `truck`.

Keras

Keras is an open source neural network library that can run on top of TensorFlow and many other machine learning frameworks. Like Python, it uses very simple syntax.

Dataset downloads

Let's do one last thing before our hands-on experience. Let's first learn the mechanism by which TensorFlow and PyTorch download datasets through Python code and where they actually store themselves in our systems after retrieval. You will eventually note that the default locations for both TensorFlow and PyTorch are very different.

Downloading Fashion-MNIST with Keras

First, let's look at how look at how this works in Keras. In the following code, we import it as a module from the `tensorflow` library:

```
from tensorflow import keras
fashion_mnist = keras.datasets.fashion_mnist
(train_images, train_labels), (test_images, test_labels) =
fashion_mnist.load_data()
```

The third line from the preceding code will download the datasets:

```
Downloading data from
https://storage.googleapis.com/tensorflow/tf-keras-datasets/train-labels-id
x1-ubyte.gz
32768/29515 [==============================] - 0s 1us/step
Downloading data from
https://storage.googleapis.com/tensorflow/tf-keras-datasets/train-images-id
x3-ubyte.gz
26427392/26421880 [==============================] - 3s 0us/step
Downloading data from
https://storage.googleapis.com/tensorflow/tf-keras-datasets/t10k-labels-idx
1-ubyte.gz
8192/5148 [===========================================] - 0s 1us/step
```

```
Downloading data from
https://storage.googleapis.com/tensorflow/tf-keras-datasets/t10k-images-idx
3-ubyte.gz
4423680/4422102 [==============================] - 1s 0us/step
Process finished with exit code 0
```

You will be able to view the `.keras` directory after doing this additional step:

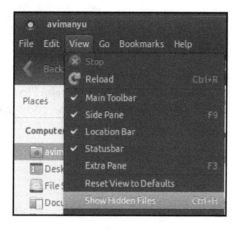

You will now be able to find the Fashion-MNIST datasets downloaded with Keras stored in your `$HOME (~)` directory as follows:

~/.keras/datasets/fashion-mnist

This is how it looks on Ubuntu's default file manager (**Caja**):

Note that there are two series of files. Two include images, while the other two include labels. Recall again that supervised learning uses **labeled datasets**. The files with the `train` prefix are used for inference, while the other two with the `t10k` prefix are tested against them for training.

Note that this is a hidden directory and you must always reveal it, as shown in the first screenshot in this subsection.

Downloading CIFAR-10 with PyTorch

For our first PyTorch program, we are going to test downloading CIFAR-10 according to the official PyTorch documentation. As we did with TensorFlow, we again download both the training and test datasets. Here is a related part of the code that we are going to use in the next section:

```
import torch
import torchvision
import torchvision.transforms as transforms
normalize = transforms.Compose(
    [transforms.ToTensor(), transforms.Normalize((0.5, 0.5, 0.5), (0.5,
0.5, 0.5))]
)
trainset = torchvision.datasets.CIFAR10(root='./pytorch', train=True,
download=True, transform=normalize)
```

The new dataset files will be downloaded to the same location where you ran the preceding code. `root='./pytorch'` is how you can customize the download. In this case, a directory named `pytorch` will be created:

```
Downloading https://www.cs.toronto.edu/~kriz/cifar-10-python.tar.gz to
./pytorch/cifar-10-python.tar.gz
100.0%Files already downloaded and verified
Process finished with exit code 0
```

As we saw in the case of the Fashion-MNIST dataset, the local download location of the dataset files is your PyCharm project folder itself. Here, our PyCharm project subfolder is `PyTorch`, which has our `pytorch` dataset files:

~/PyCharmProjects/HandsOnGPUComputingWithPython/PyTorch/pytorch

It will be immediately reflected when you download the CIFAR-10 datasets for the first time with PyTorch:

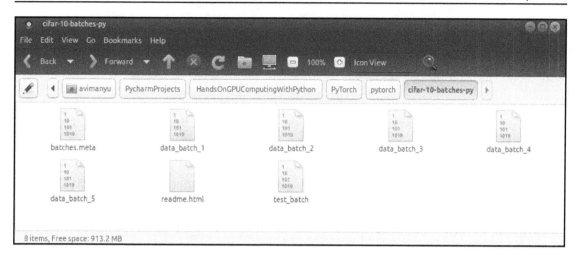

Now, let's dive into our first GPU-accelerated machine learning experience!

Writing your first GPU-accelerated machine learning programs

For our first GPU-accelerated program, let's run the following code for training based on five important steps.

To ensure best accuracy for inference from the training datasets, these important steps that are required to be performed sequentially are as follows:

1. Building the model
2. Compiling the model
3. Training the model
4. Evaluating accuracy
5. Making predictions

Instead of describing the preceding steps theoretically, let's use a hands-on approach based on code execution in order to understand them better. We will now see an example of how they are implemented.

Fashion-MNIST prediction with TensorFlow

Through our first Keras-based TensorFlow program, we will perform machine learning with a GPU to train MNIST datasets.

The following program has been modified to use a hundred training cycles or epochs to learn from training datasets. It is based on a demonstration by François Chollet, hosted on the official TensorFlow repositories and based on an MIT license:

```
#@title MIT License
 # Copyright (c) 2019 François Chollet
 # Permission is hereby granted, free of charge, to any person obtaining a
 # copy of this software and associated documentation files (the
"Software"),
 # to deal in the Software without restriction, including without
limitation
 # the rights to use, copy, modify, merge, publish, distribute, sublicense,
 # and/or sell copies of the Software, and to permit persons to whom the
 # Software is furnished to do so, subject to the following conditions:
 # The above copyright notice and this permission notice shall be included
in
 # all copies or substantial portions of the Software.
 # THE SOFTWARE IS PROVIDED "AS IS", WITHOUT WARRANTY OF ANY KIND, EXPRESS
OR
 # IMPLIED, INCLUDING BUT NOT LIMITED TO THE WARRANTIES OF MERCHANTABILITY,
 # FITNESS FOR A PARTICULAR PURPOSE AND NONINFRINGEMENT. IN NO EVENT SHALL
 # THE AUTHORS OR COPYRIGHT HOLDERS BE LIABLE FOR ANY CLAIM, DAMAGES OR
OTHER
 # LIABILITY, WHETHER IN AN ACTION OF CONTRACT, TORT OR OTHERWISE, ARISING
 # FROM, OUT OF OR IN CONNECTION WITH THE SOFTWARE OR THE USE OR OTHER
 # DEALINGS IN THE SOFTWARE.
```

For more information, please see `https://www.tensorflow.org/tutorials/keras/basic_classification`.

First, we import the required modules. `matplotlib.pyplot` is required for predicting our model (the fashion objects and graphs):

```
from __future__ import absolute_import, division, print_function
import tensorflow as tf
from tensorflow import keras
import numpy as np
import matplotlib.pyplot as plot
```

Download Fashion-MNIST data, define the apparel names, and inspect the first image in our training set:

```
fashion_mnist = keras.datasets.fashion_mnist
(train_images, train_labels), (test_images, test_labels) =
fashion_mnist.load_data()
class_names = ['T-shirt/top', 'Trouser', 'Pullover', 'Dress', 'Coat',
              'Sandal', 'Shirt', 'Sneaker', 'Bag', 'Ankle boot']
plot.figure()
plot.imshow(train_images[0])
plot.colorbar()
plot.grid(False)
plot.show()
```

We can see in this plot that the pixel values are in a range from **0** to **255**:

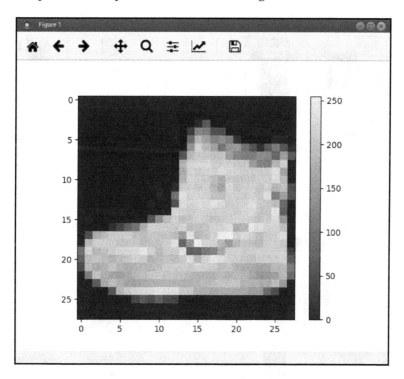

Before feeding the neural network, the images are scaled to a range of 0 to 1. We do this for both the training set and the test set, as we can see in the first two lines of this code block:

```
train_images = train_images / 255.0
test_images = test_images / 255.0
plot.figure(figsize=(10,10))
```

```
for i in range(25):
    plot.subplot(5,5,i+1)
    plot.xticks([])
    plot.yticks([])
    plot.grid(False)
    plot.imshow(train_images[i], cmap=plot.cm.binary)
    plot.xlabel(class_names[train_labels[i]])
plot.show()
```

Now, we will find different clothing-related items from the training set:

Note that there are different types of ankle boots, sneakers, and sandals.

Now we start building the model, which is the first step:

```
model = keras.Sequential([
    keras.layers.Flatten(input_shape=(28, 28)),
    keras.layers.Dense(128, activation=tf.nn.relu),
    keras.layers.Dense(10, activation=tf.nn.softmax)
])
```

Now we compile the model, which is the second step:

```
model.compile(optimizer='adam',
              loss='sparse_categorical_crossentropy',
              metrics=['accuracy'])
```

The first two steps, building (`model`) and compiling (`model.compile`) the model, are extremely important. In TensorFlow in particular, training the model without building and compiling it first can reduce the accuracy by as much as 85%.

Now, we test training via a single epoch. We set it as `epochs=1` to quickly see how the process works for one training cycle. Note that training is the third step in our machine learning program:

```
model.fit(train_images, train_labels, epochs=1)
```

Evaluating or testing the accuracy is the fourth step, as we saw at the beginning of this section:

```
test_loss, test_acc = model.evaluate(test_images, test_labels)
print('Test accuracy:', test_acc)
```

Making `predictions` from test images of objects is our final step:

```
predictions = model.predict(test_images)
print(predictions[0])
print(np.argmax(predictions[0]))
print(test_labels[0])

def plot_image(i, predictions_array, true_label, img):
    predictions_array, true_label, img = predictions_array[i],
true_label[i], img[i]
    plot.grid(False)
```

```
    plot.xticks([])
    plot.yticks([])
    plot.imshow(img, cmap=plot.cm.binary)
```

Correct predictions are marked in `blue`, while incorrect ones are marked in `red`:

```
predicted_label = np.argmax(predictions_array)
if predicted_label == true_label:
    color = 'blue'
else:
    color = 'red'
```

Note that `predicted_label` is defined by `predictions_array`:

```
 plot.xlabel("{} {:2.0f}% ({})".format(class_names[predicted_label],
                            100*np.max(predictions_array),
                            class_names[true_label]),
                            color=color)

def plot_value_array(i, predictions_array, true_label):
    predictions_array, true_label = predictions_array[i], true_label[i]
    plot.grid(False)
    plot.xticks([])
    plot.yticks([])
    thisplot = plot.bar(range(10), predictions_array, color="#777777")
    plot.ylim([0, 1])
    predicted_label = np.argmax(predictions_array)
    thisplot[predicted_label].set_color('red')
    thisplot[true_label].set_color('blue')
```

Now let's look at the `predictions`:

```
i = 0
plot.figure(figsize=(6,3))
plot.subplot(1,2,1)
plot_image(i, predictions, test_labels, test_images)
plot.subplot(1,2,2)
plot_value_array(i, predictions, test_labels)
plot.show()
```

The true descriptor is shown in brackets during the prediction. Here we see it recognizes the ankle boot correctly!

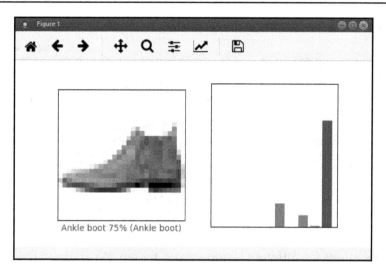

Let's look at the next prediction:

```
i = 12
plot.figure(figsize=(6,3))
plot.subplot(1,2,1)
plot_image(i, predictions, test_labels, test_images)
plot.subplot(1,2,2)
plot_value_array(i, predictions, test_labels)
plot.show()
```

Oops! It got it wrong! It recognizes a sneaker as a sandal! Note that it can be wrong even when confident (even when showing a 59% prediction percentage):

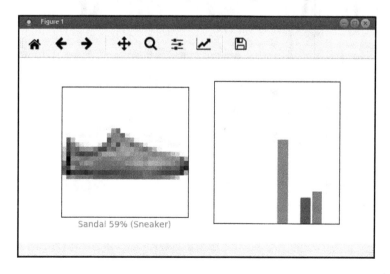

Instead of just one, let's try plotting several clothing items and related objects with their predictions:

```
# Plot the first X test images, their predicted label, and the true label
# Color correct predictions in blue, incorrect predictions in red
num_rows = 5
num_cols = 3
num_images = num_rows*num_cols
plot.figure(figsize=(2*2*num_cols, 2*num_rows))
for i in range(num_images):
    plot.subplot(num_rows, 2*num_cols, 2*i+1)
    plot_image(i, predictions, test_labels, test_images)
    plot.subplot(num_rows, 2*num_cols, 2*i+2)
    plot_value_array(i, predictions, test_labels)
plot.show()
```

There are 15 predictions for different fashion types shown. What's with the sandal?:

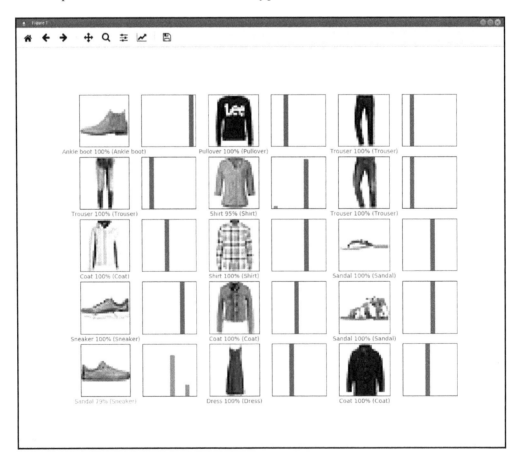

Next, we make a prediction for a single object. So, here, `test_images[0]` is an ankle boot:

```
# Grab an image from the test dataset
img = test_images[0]
print(img.shape)
# Add the image to a batch where it's the only member.
img = (np.expand_dims(img,0))
print(img.shape)
predictions_single = model.predict(img)
print(predictions_single)
plot_value_array(0, predictions_single, test_labels)
_ = plot.xticks(range(10), class_names, rotation=45)
plot.show()
print(np.argmax(predictions_single[0]))
```

This is the output for a single object (ankle boot via `test_images[0]`):

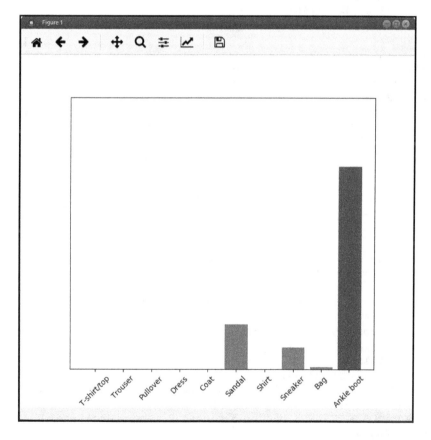

Now, let's see the output on the PyCharm console.

TensorFlow output on the PyCharm console

While we were busy watching our predictions, the PyCharm console was also producing its respective output while generating the image predictions:

```
WARNING:tensorflow:From
/home/avimanyu/miniconda3/envs/HandsOnGPUComputingWithPython/lib/python3.6/
site-packages/tensorflow/python/ops/resource_variable_ops.py:435:
colocate_with (from tensorflow.python.framework.ops) is deprecated and will
be removed in a future version.
Instructions for updating:
Colocations handled automatically by placer.
2019-04-15 23:47:42.474784: I
tensorflow/core/platform/cpu_feature_guard.cc:141] Your CPU supports
instructions that this TensorFlow binary was not compiled to use: SSE4.1
SSE4.2 AVX AVX2 FMA
2019-04-15 23:47:42.497612: I
tensorflow/core/platform/profile_utils/cpu_utils.cc:94] CPU Frequency:
3499100000 Hz
2019-04-15 23:47:42.497975: I
tensorflow/compiler/xla/service/service.cc:150] XLA service 0x7fe9cc0076d0
executing computations on platform Host. Devices:
2019-04-15 23:47:42.497993: I
tensorflow/compiler/xla/service/service.cc:158] StreamExecutor device (0):
<undefined>, <undefined>
2019-04-15 23:47:42.591876: I
tensorflow/stream_executor/cuda/cuda_gpu_executor.cc:998] successful NUMA
node read from SysFS had negative value (-1), but there must be at least
```

From this output, we can confirm that the GPU is indeed being used for the training, as it clearly says it is `executing computations on platform CUDA` devices, with the respective GPU device information as well:

```
one NUMA node, so returning NUMA node zero
2019-04-15 23:47:42.592354: I
tensorflow/compiler/xla/service/service.cc:150] XLA service 0x55b6cecc0c60
executing computations on platform CUDA. Devices:
2019-04-15 23:47:42.592366: I
tensorflow/compiler/xla/service/service.cc:158] StreamExecutor device (0):
GeForce GTX TITAN X,
Compute Capability 5.2
2019-04-15 23:47:42.592645: I
tensorflow/core/common_runtime/gpu/gpu_device.cc:1433] Found device 0 with
properties:
name: GeForce GTX TITAN X major: 5 minor: 2 memoryClockRate(GHz): 1.076
pciBusID: 0000:01:00.0
totalMemory: 11.92GiB freeMemory: 11.38GiB
```

```
2019-04-15 23:47:42.592656: I
tensorflow/core/common_runtime/gpu/gpu_device.cc:1512] Adding visible gpu
devices: 0
2019-04-15 23:47:42.593243: I
tensorflow/core/common_runtime/gpu/gpu_device.cc:984] Device interconnect
StreamExecutor with strength 1 edge matrix:
```

Here, we have a test accuracy of 0.843:

```
2019-04-15 23:47:42.593253: I
tensorflow/core/common_runtime/gpu/gpu_device.cc:990] 0
2019-04-15 23:47:42.593257: I
tensorflow/core/common_runtime/gpu/gpu_device.cc:1003] 0: N
2019-04-15 23:47:42.593446: I
tensorflow/core/common_runtime/gpu/gpu_device.cc:1115] Created TensorFlow
device (/job:localhost/replica:0/task:0/device:GPU:0 with 11073 MB memory)
-> physical GPU (device: 0, name: GeForce GTX TITAN X, pci bus id:
0000:01:00.0, compute capability: 5.2)
2019-04-15 23:47:43.194903: I tensorflow/stream_executor/dso_loader.cc:152]
successfully opened CUDA library libcublas.so.9.0 locally
60000/60000 [==============================] - 4s 59us/sample - loss:
0.5001 - acc: 0.8249
10000/10000 [==============================] - 0s 31us/sample - loss:
0.4420 - acc: 0.8430

Test accuracy: 0.843
[4.12563641e-05 6.64358367e-06 1.17065661e-04 4.64575423e-05
 1.29905544e-04 1.65009499e-01 1.03111066e-04 8.08488578e-02
 7.55999703e-03 7.46137142e-01]
```

Two consecutive 9 values confirm that the prediction is correct. The first one is the correct value and the second is the prediction. The model is confident that the fashion object is an ankle boot:

```
9
9
(28, 28)
(1, 28, 28)
[[[4.12563240e-05 6.64358367e-06 1.17065661e-04 4.64575423e-05
   1.29905544e-04 1.65009543e-01 1.03111066e-04 8.08488354e-02
   7.55999284e-03 7.46137142e-01]]
9

Next, let's have a look at how to train
```

Training Fashion-MNIST for 100 epochs

To use 100 training cycles, we again to do a small change to the code:

```
model.fit(train_images, train_labels, epochs=100)
```

The same process will happen, but for 100 epochs, so it will take some time:

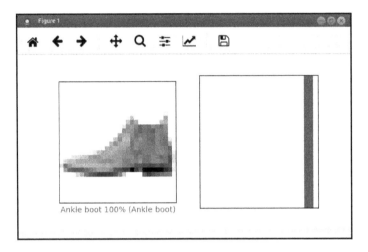

There's that sandal again! We see a prediction percentage improvement by 20%. Remember that, still, it is not the deciding factor. It is the red color that shows it's wrong. We humans can easily infer this. But there are far more complex objects that can be used instead of fashion objects, where even we humans require careful precision (we will explore that in the next chapter):

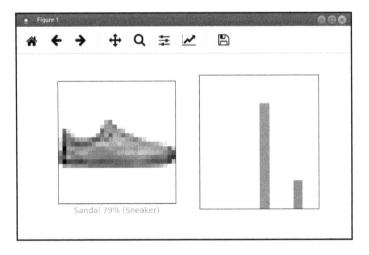

Here are multiple predictions of fashion objects:

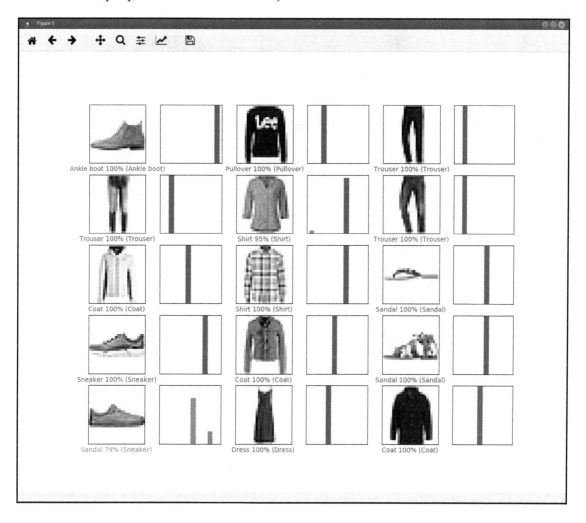

The following screenshot contains a graph that shows the **Ankle boot** predictions out of a range of fashion objects:

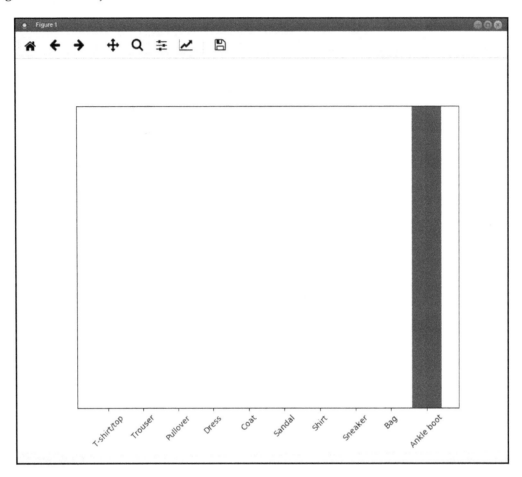

Here, the test accuracy is 0.8847:

```
Test accuracy: 0.8847
[7.4342118e-29 4.1356295e-30 4.7422809e-23 0.0000000e+00 0.0000000e+00
 1.0638165e-15 4.0747047e-34 8.4883472e-12 6.1694383e-28 1.0000000e+00]
9
9
(28, 28)
(1, 28, 28)
[[7.4342118e-29 4.1356927e-30 4.7422809e-23 0.0000000e+00 0.0000000e+00
  1.0638165e-15 4.0747364e-34 8.4883472e-12 6.1694614e-28 1.0000000e+00]]
9
```

So, we have just experienced a hands-on prediction of different fashion objects based on the Fashion-MNIST dataset with TensorFlow.

CIFAR-10 prediction with PyTorch

Let's explore the CIFAR-10 dataset, but with PyTorch. We are going to use a program that is based on the official PyTorch documentation for CPUs. I've extensively modified this program for GPUs for both training and prediction.

But, first, we must include a copy of the PyTorch license from GitHub. Through a series code blocks, we can now take a look at the GitHub license:

```
From PyTorch:

Copyright (c) 2016-     Facebook, Inc          (Adam Paszke)
Copyright (c) 2014-     Facebook, Inc          (Soumith Chintala)
Copyright (c) 2011-2014 Idiap Research Institute (Ronan Collobert)
Copyright (c) 2012-2014 Deepmind Technologies   (Koray Kavukcuoglu)
Copyright (c) 2011-2012 NEC Laboratories America (Koray Kavukcuoglu)
Copyright (c) 2011-2013 NYU                     (Clement Farabet)
Copyright (c) 2006-2010 NEC Laboratories America (Ronan Collobert, Leon
Bottou, Iain Melvin, Jason Weston)
Copyright (c) 2006      Idiap Research Institute (Samy Bengio)
Copyright (c) 2001-2004 Idiap Research Institute (Ronan Collobert, Samy
Bengio, Johnny Mariethoz)
```

Here are some contributions from organisations and Yangqing Jia:

```
From Caffe2:

Copyright (c) 2016-present, Facebook Inc. All rights reserved.

All contributions by Facebook:
Copyright (c) 2016 Facebook Inc.

All contributions by Google:
Copyright (c) 2015 Google Inc.
All rights reserved.

All contributions by Yangqing Jia:
Copyright (c) 2015 Yangqing Jia
All rights reserved.
```

This block includes further information on contribution rights:

```
All contributions from Caffe:
Copyright(c) 2013, 2014, 2015, the respective contributors
All rights reserved.

All other contributions:
Copyright(c) 2015, 2016 the respective contributors
All rights reserved.

Caffe2 uses a copyright model similar to Caffe: each contributor holds
copyright over their contributions to Caffe2. The project versioning
records
all such contribution and copyright details. If a contributor wants to
further
mark their specific copyright on a particular contribution, they should
indicate their copyright solely in the commit message of the change when it
is
committed.
All rights reserved.
```

Now we can see all the conditions for redistributing the PyTorch code:

```
Redistribution and use in source and binary forms, with or without
modification, are permitted provided that the following conditions are met:

1. Redistributions of source code must retain the above copyright
   notice, this list of conditions and the following disclaimer.

2. Redistributions in binary form must reproduce the above copyright
   notice, this list of conditions and the following disclaimer in the
   documentation and/or other materials provided with the distribution.

3. Neither the names of Facebook, Deepmind Technologies, NYU, NEC
Laboratories America
   and IDIAP Research Institute nor the names of its contributors may be
   used to endorse or promote products derived from this software without
   specific prior written permission.
```

Finally, we see some warranty-related discussion:

```
THIS SOFTWARE IS PROVIDED BY THE COPYRIGHT HOLDERS AND CONTRIBUTORS "AS IS"
AND ANY EXPRESS OR IMPLIED WARRANTIES, INCLUDING, BUT NOT LIMITED TO, THE
IMPLIED WARRANTIES OF MERCHANTABILITY AND FITNESS FOR A PARTICULAR PURPOSE
ARE DISCLAIMED. IN NO EVENT SHALL THE COPYRIGHT OWNER OR CONTRIBUTORS BE
LIABLE FOR ANY DIRECT, INDIRECT, INCIDENTAL, SPECIAL, EXEMPLARY, OR
CONSEQUENTIAL DAMAGES (INCLUDING, BUT NOT LIMITED TO, PROCUREMENT OF
SUBSTITUTE GOODS OR SERVICES; LOSS OF USE, DATA, OR PROFITS; OR BUSINESS
```

Now let's hop into our heavily modified PyTorch program created for using a GPU device:

 The original CPU device-specific code can be found here: `https://pytorch.org/tutorials/beginner/blitz/cifar10_tutorial.html`.

```
import torch
import torchvision
import torchvision.transforms as transforms
```

`transforms` is used for normalization. Also, we specifically tell PyTorch to use the GPU when available via `torch.device()`, instead of the CPU:

```
device = torch.device("cuda:0" if torch.cuda.is_available() else "cpu")

normalize = transforms.Compose(
  [transforms.ToTensor(),
   transforms.Normalize((0.5, 0.5, 0.5), (0.5, 0.5, 0.5))])
trainset = torchvision.datasets.CIFAR10(root='./pytorch', train=True,
download=True, transform=normalize)
trainloader = torch.utils.data.DataLoader(trainset, batch_size=4,
shuffle=True, num_workers=2)
testset = torchvision.datasets.CIFAR10(root='./pytorch', train=False,
download=True, transform=normalize)
testloader = torch.utils.data.DataLoader(testset, batch_size=4,
shuffle=False, num_workers=2)
classes = ('plane', 'car', 'bird', 'cat',
         'deer', 'dog', 'frog', 'horse', 'ship', 'truck')
```

Now, we import `matplotlib.pyplot` for the plots:

```
import matplotlib.pyplot as plot
import numpy as np

# functions to show an image
def imshow(img):
    img = img / 2 + 0.5 # unnormalize
    npimg = img.numpy()
    plot.imshow(np.transpose(npimg, (1, 2, 0)))
    plot.show()
```

We get some some randomly trained objects (ship, bird 1, frog, and bird 2):

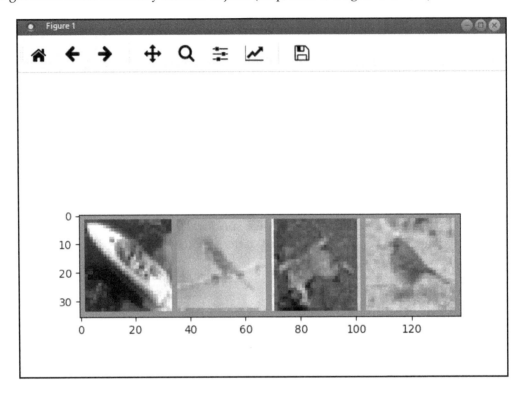

We are now going to predict four such objects that belong to 4 of the 10 CIFAR types. We will do that by cross-validating a trained model with a test model:

```
# get some random training images
dataiter = iter(trainloader)
images, labels = dataiter.next()
# show images
imshow(torchvision.utils.make_grid(images))
# print labels
print(' '.join('%5s' % classes[labels[j]] for j in range(4)))
```

Now we will import `torch.nn` to define a convolutional neural network. From `self.conv1` to `self.fc3`, I've added the suffix `.cuda()` for using the GPU device:

```
import torch.nn as nn
import torch.nn.functional as F
# Define a convolutional neural network to take 3-channel images
class Net(nn.Module):
    def __init__(self):
        super(Net, self).__init__()
        self.conv1 = nn.Conv2d(3, 6, 5).cuda()
        self.pool = nn.MaxPool2d(2, 2).cuda()
        self.conv2 = nn.Conv2d(6, 16, 5).cuda()
        self.fc1 = nn.Linear(16 * 5 * 5, 120).cuda()
        self.fc2 = nn.Linear(120, 84).cuda()
        self.fc3 = nn.Linear(84, 10).cuda()
```

Moving forward, we pass `device`, as defined in the beginning of this program, to x. This makes sure we are using the neural network on the GPU:

```
    def forward(self, x):
        x = x.to(device)
        x = self.pool(F.relu(self.conv1(x)))
        x = self.pool(F.relu(self.conv2(x)))
        x = x.view(-1, 16 * 5 * 5)
        x = F.relu(self.fc1(x))
        x = F.relu(self.fc2(x))
        x = self.fc3(x)
        return x
```

Convert parameters and buffers to CUDA tensors with `net.to(device)`:

```
net = Net()
net.to(device)

# Assuming that we are on a CUDA machine, this should print a CUDA device:
import torch.optim as optim

criterion = nn.CrossEntropyLoss()
optimizer = optim.SGD(net.parameters(), lr=0.001, momentum=0.9)
```

Now we define the training cycle and loop over the dataset multiple times. `inputs` and `labels` are used with a GPU:

```
for epoch in range(2): # loop over the dataset multiple times
    running_loss = 0.0
    for i, (inputs, labels) in enumerate(trainloader, 0):
        # get the inputs
        inputs, labels = inputs.to(device), labels.to(device)

        # zero the parameter gradients
        optimizer.zero_grad()

        # forward + backward + optimize
        outputs = net(inputs)
        loss = criterion(outputs, labels)
        loss.backward()
        optimizer.step()
```

Then we finish training after printing statistics:

```
        # print statistics
        running_loss += loss.item()
        if i % 2000 == 1999: # print every 2000 mini-batches
            print('[%d, %5d] loss: %.3f' % (epoch + 1, i + 1, running_loss
/ 2000))
            running_loss = 0.0

print('Finished Training')
```

`GroundTruth` is for cross-validation with our predicted output:

```
dataiter = iter(testloader)
images, labels = dataiter.next()

# print images
imshow(torchvision.utils.make_grid(images))
print('GroundTruth: ', ' '.join('%5s' % classes[labels[j]] for j in
range(4)))
```

The four images are of a cat, ship 1, ship 2, and a plane. We can just make out two different ship images:

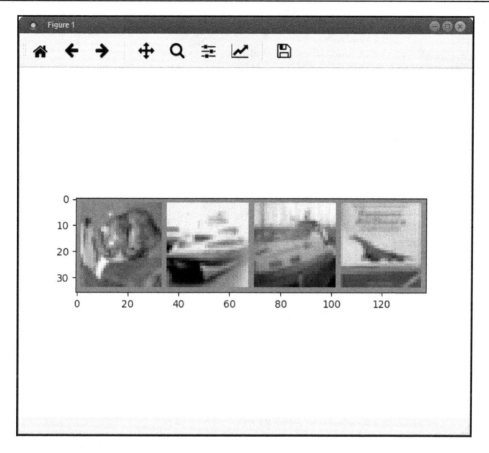

We will find out what it predicted through our next section, reporting all outputs on the PyCharm console:

```
outputs = net(images)

_, predicted = torch.max(outputs, 1)

print('Predicted: ', ' '.join('%5s' % classes[predicted[j]] for j in
range(4)))
```

`images` and `labels` are also used with a GPU:

```
correct = 0
total = 0
with torch.no_grad():
    for (images, labels) in testloader:
        images, labels = images.to(device), labels.to(device)
        outputs = net(images)
```

```
    _, predicted = torch.max(outputs.data, 1)
    total += labels.size(0)
    correct += (predicted == labels).sum().item()

print('Accuracy of the network on the 10000 test images: %d %%' % (100 *
correct / total))
```

In the preceding code, we report the accuracy of the network when trained with 10,000 types of CIFAR-10 images:

```
class_correct = list(0. for i in range(10))
class_total = list(0. for i in range(10))
with torch.no_grad():
    for (images, labels) in testloader:
        images, labels = images.to(device), labels.to(device)

        outputs = net(images)
        _, predicted = torch.max(outputs, 1)
        c = (predicted == labels).squeeze()
        for i in range(4):
            label = labels[i]
            class_correct[label] += c[i].item()
            class_total[label] += 1


for i in range(10):
    print('Accuracy of %5s : %2d %%' % (classes[i], 100 * class_correct[i]
/ class_total[i]))
```

Finally, we predict the accuracy level of each type of CIFAR object in the preceding code.

PyTorch output on a PyCharm console

First, we display the GPU device name:

```
Device used: GeForce GTX TITAN X
Files already downloaded and verified
Files already downloaded and verified
```

As we will see next, we can identify a ship, a bird, a frog, and another bird. These are pre-trained images, so the labels are shown correctly:

```
ship bird frog bird
[1,  2000] loss: 2.161
[1,  4000] loss: 1.832
[1,  6000] loss: 1.663
```

```
[1, 8000] loss: 1.589
[1, 10000] loss: 1.519
[1, 12000] loss: 1.455
[2, 2000] loss: 1.381
[2, 4000] loss: 1.357
[2, 6000] loss: 1.335
[2, 8000] loss: 1.324
[2, 10000] loss: 1.313
[2, 12000] loss: 1.281
Finished Training
```

After training, we first show the correct prediction and cross-validate it with the new prediction. Here, we see that apart from the second object, all the other predictions are correct. So, our results are pretty accurate. Also, the accuracy level of the entire network consisting of 10,000 test images as a whole is shown, as well as accuracy levels for each type of CIFAR object is also reported. Accuracy by chance is 10% (the act of randomly picking 1 object out of 10 objects). So, we can say that our model has, indeed, learned something.

Does the previous paragraph remind you of mathematical concepts such as probability, permutations, and combinations?

```
GroundTruth: cat ship ship plane
Predicted: cat car ship plane
Accuracy of the network on the 10000 test images: 56 %
Accuracy of plane : 63 %
Accuracy of car : 73 %
Accuracy of bird : 42 %
Accuracy of cat : 26 %
Accuracy of deer : 51 %
Accuracy of dog : 48 %
Accuracy of frog : 64 %
Accuracy of horse : 67 %
Accuracy of ship : 60 %
Accuracy of truck : 71 %
Process finished with exit code 0
```

In the next section, we will revisit our earlier computational exercises with a machine learning approach.

Revisiting our computational exercises with a machine learning approach

In this section, let's apply all the knowledge we've acquired so far. Try using a real-world dataset, as discussed in `Chapter 6`, *Working with CUDA and PyCUDA*, and use the *Solution Assistance* section to get started with the following exercises to step up your machine learning game:

1. Use TensorFlow or PyTorch to implement Karl Pearson's correlation coefficient. Based on the computed coefficient, use machine learning to predict the probability of a certain population in a region to be affected with a correlated disease. You can also use image datasets of tobacco and its linked diseases to widen the scope of the study.
2. Create a machine learning model with TensorFlow or PyTorch for the prediction of diabetes. Use real-world data after testing your model.
3. Create a machine learning model with TensorFlow or PyTorch for predicting air pollution levels in a region of your choice. Use real-world data after testing your model.

Solution assistance

- *How Machines Make Predictions: Finding Correlations in Complex Data*: `https://medium.freecodecamp.org/how-machines-make-predictions-finding-correlations-in-complex-data-dfd9f0d87889`
- Pearson Correlation Coefficient using TensorFlow: `https://gist.github.com/lucasvenez/5adf645a30f97517c741c40da30c462c`
- Using machine learning to predict if someone has diabetes: `https://medium.com/@edwardleoni/using-machine-learning-to-predict-if-someone-has-diabetes-21dc52118d8f`
- TensorFlow Regression Example: Diabetes: `https://github.com/fisproject/TensorFlow-Regression-Examples/blob/master/simple-nn-diabetes.py`
- *Air Cognizer: Predicting Air Quality with TensorFlow Lite*: `https://medium.com/tensorflow/air-cognizer-predicting-air-quality-with-tensorflow-lite-942466b3d02e`
- *Using Machine Learning to Predict the Weather*: `https://stackabuse.com/using-machine-learning-to-predict-the-weather-part-1/`
- A collection of datasets ready to use with TensorFlow: `https://www.tensorflow.org/datasets/`

Summary

Throughout this chapter, you have learned the basics of installing, configuring, and using TensorFlow and PyTorch on your Conda environment. You have also learned how to work with both frameworks on Google Colaboratory. You learned five basic steps to implement machine learning on Python. You now know how the dataset structures should look on both TensorFlow and PyTorch, along with with their locations after download.

You can now start working either on PyCharm locally, harnessing a local GPU for machine learning with both TensorFlow and PyCharm, or do the same on Google Colab. Both GPUs and TPUs with TensorFlow can be your portable interface from now on. Also, you are now familiar with the use of PyTorch on Google Colab by default for GPUs as well. You can now revisit the computational exercises discussed earlier to understand their significance with a machine learning approach.

In the final chapter, we are going to learn about **DeepChem**, a Python-based and GPU-enabled machine learning library, developed with TensorFlow for molecular machine learning and drug discovery. We will learn in detail how it works, looking at the fundamental concepts behind it. A hands-on guide to installing DeepChem as both open-ended and closed environments will be included. After this, configuration methods for PyCharm and a live example will be illustrated.

Further reading

- `docs.nvidia.com` (2018), *NVIDIA TensorRT Inference Server*—NVIDIA TensorRT Inference Server 1.0.0 documentation (online). Available at `https://docs.nvidia.com/deeplearning/sdk/tensorrt-inference-server-guide/docs/`.
- NVIDIA. (n.d.), **Artificial Intelligence** (**AI**) containers (online). Available at `https://www.nvidia.com/en-us/gpu-cloud/deep-learning-containers/`.
- NVIDIA. (n.d.), The **NVIDIA GPU Accelerated Cloud** (**NGC**) for Deep Learning (online). Available at `https://www.nvidia.com/en-us/gpu-cloud/deep-learning-containers/`.
- `docs.nvidia.com` (2019), NVIDIA GPU Cloud Documentation (online). Available at `https://docs.nvidia.com/ngc/`.
- AMD (2019), **Machine Learning** (**ML**) | **Deep Learning** (**DL**) (online). Available at `https://www.amd.com/en/technologies/deep-machine-learning`.
- AMD (n.d.), *AMD Radeon Instinct™ MI60: Unleash Discovery on the World's Fastest Double Precision PCIe® Accelerator* | Deep Learning and HPC (online). Available at `https://www.amd.com/en/products/professional-graphics/instinct-mi60`.

11

GPU Acceleration for Scientific Applications Using DeepChem

In this final chapter, we are going to apply all that we have learned throughout this book so far from an application perspective. DeepChem is a perfect example that combines the power of GPUs, Python, and deep learning toward solving computational problems in science.

To understand its usage as simply as possible, we will start with a brief introduction to basic scientific concepts related to the example that will follow. You will learn about molecular machine learning by revisiting some elementary terminologies in science, such as atoms, molecules, proteins, and enzymes.

A hands-on guide to install and configure DeepChem as an open-ended and closed environment will be included before testing the live example for medicinal drug prediction through deep learning. As a final thought, readers will be encouraged to develop their own deep learning frameworks such as DeepChem.

This chapter is divided into the following sections to facilitate the learning process:

- Knowledge of the practical applicability of GPU-enabled deep learning with Python
- Installing and configuring DeepChem through Colab, Anaconda, or Docker
- Validating an existing DeepChem Conda environment on PyCharm for developing deep learning models
- Testing an AI-based scientific library
- Getting started with the development of a new machine learning framework such as DeepChem

Technical requirements

Check out the following video to see the Code in Action:

```
http://bit.ly/2E0dhnb
```

Decoding scientific concepts for DeepChem

Before you learn about **molecular machine learning** and DeepChem, it is essential that we learn some elementary terminologies used in physics, mathematics, biology, and, most importantly, chemistry: the foundation of DeepChem is **cheminformatics**.

Cheminformatics is an interdisciplinary field unifying computer science and chemistry. It is a continuously evolving field that involves developing computational methods and software tools to analyze and interpret chemical or biochemical data.

The concepts that follow from this point onward will help you understand its usage better before you start installing, configuring, and using the tool chain.

Atom

An **atom** is the smallest unit of matter with elemental chemical properties. It consists of electrons, protons, and neutrons. The protons and neutrons reside at the nucleus, while the electrons revolve around it. For example, an average silicon atom has 14 neutrons, 14 protons, and 14 electrons.

Here is a simple diagram of a 3D atom:

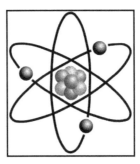

Image via https://www.flickr.com/photos/sn1cks/3631728569, CC 2.0 https://creativecommons.org/licenses/by-sa/2.0/

But what is a molecule? Let's understand the basics.

Molecule

When two or more atoms are held together in a group via chemical bonds that does not have any electrical charge (neutral), it is known to be a molecule. For example, a water molecule has the chemical formula H_2O. It can be represented as a 3D image, as shown in this diagram:

In the preceding diagram, you can see the oxygen atom in red, bonded with two hydrogen atoms shown in white.

Now, let's look at some basic definitions of a number of terms used in elementary chemistry:

Term	Definition
Chemical compound	A chemical substance that comprises many identical molecules composed of atoms from more than one element held together by chemical bonds can be called a **chemical compound**. So, the previous water molecule can also be referred to as a simple form of a chemical compound.
Valency	A measure of the combining capacity of an atom or molecules determined by the number of electrons it can lose, add, or share when reacting with other atoms or groups is known as a **valency**.

Covalency	**Covalency** is a form of valency in which electrons are shared among participating atoms.
Ion	An atom or molecule that is not neutral with an electrical charge is called an **ion**. This charge is obtained by gaining or losing one or more electrons.
Organic compound	Any chemical compound with a carbon atom is known as an **organic compound**.
Organic chemistry	**Organic chemistry** is the branch of chemistry that is all about the study of organic compounds.
Functional group	A group of atoms within a molecule that is collectively responsible for the properties and reactions of the molecule is known as a **functional group**.
Carbonyl group	A functional group composed of a carbon atom double-bonded to an oxygen atom is known as a **carbonyl group**.
Hydroxyl group	A functional group composed of a hydrogen atom covalently bonded to an oxygen atom is known as a **hydroxyl group**.
Carboxyl group	A functional organic compound that is composed of a carbonyl group and a hydroxyl group through a single bond is a **carboxyl group**.
Peptide bonds	A **peptide bond** is a chemical bond formed between two molecules when the carboxyl group of one molecule reacts with the amino group of the other molecule, releasing a molecule of water (H_2O).

Moving on from atoms and molecules, let's now specifically look at what a **protein molecule** is.

Protein molecule

A protein molecule is a large molecule containing chains of amino acids linked by peptide bonds. It is also known as a receptor in the field of drug discovery. Receptors in drug design are mostly proteins.

There are basically three kinds of protein structures: primary, secondary, and tertiary.

Primary structures are the sequence of amino acids in the polypeptide chain and secondary structures:

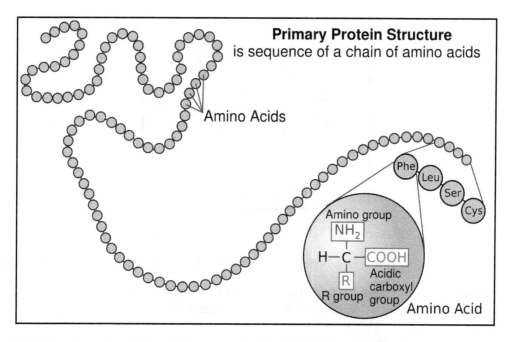

Secondary structures are the local segments of proteins that are commonly of two types: Beta (β) sheets and Alpha (∝) helices:

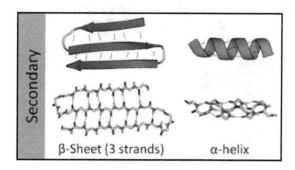

The third type is the complete 3D shape of the entire protein molecule that is known as a tertiary structure of protein, as can be seen in the following image:

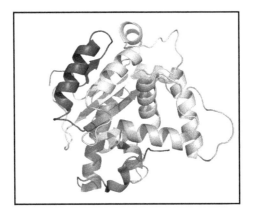

The preceding is an example of a tertiary protein structure. Did you notice the beta sheet?

There is also a fourth type of protein structure. It is known as a **quaternary protein structure**, and is an association of several protein chains or subunits in a closely packed arrangement:

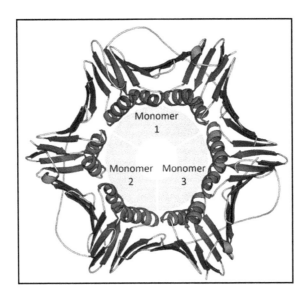

So, we have just discussed what a protein molecule basically is and its four different structure types.

Biological cell

A **cell** is the smallest unit of life as we know it. It is structural, functional, and biological in nature and presents in all known living organisms. The term *cellular* relates to, or consists of, living cells:

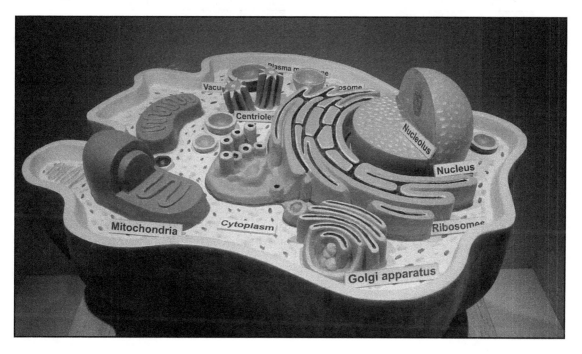

By Royroydeb – own work, CC BY-SA 4.0, https://commons.wikimedia.org/w/index.php?curid=37598972

There can be more than 100 million protein molecules per cell. Prokaryotic cells are bacteria or archaea of a size ranging between 1 and 5 µm, and eukaryotic cells are protists, fungi, plants, and animals of a size between 10 and 100 µm. µm refers to a micrometer that is one millionth of a meter. We humans are eukaryotic organisms.

Let's now look at some more terminologies to be able to understand DeepChem better:

Term	Definition
Catalyst	A **catalyst** is a substance that can accelerate a chemical reaction without being consumed. This process is known as catalysis.
Biochemistry	**Biochemistry**, or biological chemistry, is the study of chemical processes regarding living or biological organisms such as we humans.
Biocatalysis	**Biocatalysis** refers to the use of biological systems or their parts to accelerate biochemical reactions. So, these are essentially biocatalysts.
Enzymes	**Enzymes** are biocatalysts that accelerate biochemical reactions. They are known to catalyze more than 5,000 biochemical reaction types.
Pathogen	An infectious agent that causes a disease is a **pathogen**.
Inhibitor	A substance that decelerates or prevents a chemical reaction or other process, or which reduces the activity of a particular reactant, catalyst, or enzyme, is known as an **inhibitor**.
Binding	The process of how a ligand binds to a particular site within a large molecule is known as **binding**.
Molecular docking	A method that predicts the preferred orientation of one molecule to a second through binding is called **molecular docking**. The end result in its totality is a stable complex.
Enzyme inhibitor	This is a molecule that binds to an enzyme and decreases its activity. Blocking an enzyme's activity can kill a pathogen or fix a metabolic imbalance. If not all, many drugs, can be used as enzyme inhibitors to treat a disease.

All the concepts discussed in the two tables are part of the fundamental concepts behind a broad range of metrics used in DeepChem.

Medicinal drug – a small molecule

A **medicinal drug** is a small molecule that can be used to treat a disease. It is also referred to as a **ligand**. Selective ligands have a tendency to bind to very limited kinds of receptor, whereas non-selective ligands bind to several types of receptors.

A typical ligand in 2D format looks like the following:

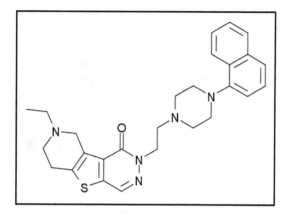

Author: Meodipt on Wikipedia in English – translated from en.wikipedia to Shared Server. Translated by Dcirovic, public property,
https://commons.wikimedia.org/w/index.php?curid=15883107

This is a selective ligand with the code DE19900637A1 and K_i=124 nM. So, what is a K_i? Let's understand that in the next section.

K_i

K_i is a kinetic constant for binding an inhibitor to a receptor. It is independent of enzyme concentration and associated with the binding and unbinding reaction of receptor and ligand molecules.

In this 2D representation of the bypyridine ligand, N stands for *nitrogen*:

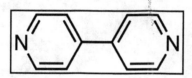

By Su-no-G – selfmade with ChemDraw, public domain, https://commons.wikimedia.org/w/index.php?curid=1371770

The bypyridine ligand in 3D would be as follows:

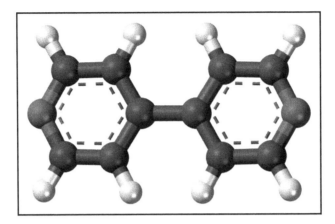

Crystallographic structures

In **crystallography**, a crystal structure is an orderly arrangement of atoms, ions, or molecules in a crystalline material that is a microscopic structure and forms a crystal lattice that extends in all directions:

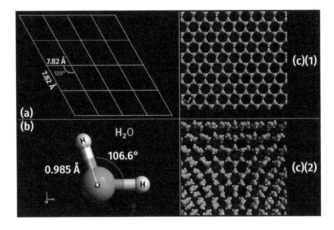

The (3D) crystal structure of H2O ice Ih (c) consists of bases of H2O ice molecules (b) located on lattice (`https://en.wikipedia.org/wiki/Bravais_lattice`) points within the (2D) hexagonal space lattice (a). The values for the H–O–H angle and O–H distance have come from the physics of ice with uncertainties of ± 1.5° and ± 0.005 Å, respectively. The white box in (c) is the unit cell defined by Bernal and Fowler.

Ice as a crystal is a simple example shown in the previous diagram. Structures of complex biological molecules are mostly determined through X-ray crystallography.

Assays

Various receptor molecules of interest arranged in the form of a 2D physical array and tested for qualitative and quantitative inhibition/binding are called **assays**. Each of the mini-circular grids you see in the next photo is for an assay called **96 well plate**, which can be used to test inhibition:

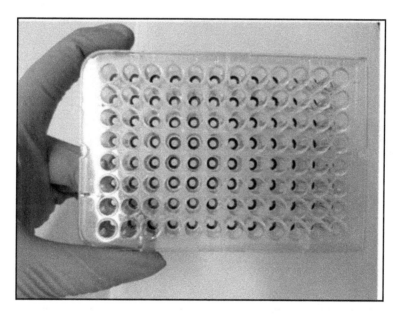

By Oppenheimer.reboot – own work, CC BY-SA 4.0, https://commons.wikimedia.org/w/index.php?curid=73989582

Think of representing this as a dataset.

They are test systems that are created as one of the first steps in drug development and toxicity testing. The effects of chemical compounds on cellular, molecular, or biochemical processes are evaluated on assays.

Histogram

The distribution of numerical data that is accurately represented in a statistical format is called a **histogram**. It is basically a graphical plot, like we saw in our machine learning outputs in `Chapter 10`, *Accelerated Machine Learning on GPUs*. Histograms can be used to assess a number of parameters and estimations across diverse disciplines. Remember Karl Pearson's correlation coefficient? It was he who first introduced this concept:

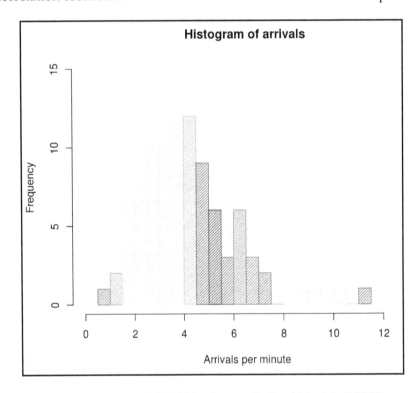

The preceding diagram is an example of a histogram.

Open Source Drug Discovery (OSDD)

Open Source Drug Discovery (OSDD) is an initiative to discover new medicines to fight diseases with an open source approach. Bharath Ramsundar, who initiated the development of a Python library based on deep learning for drug discovery, materials science, quantum chemistry, and biology, called DeepChem, wrote a remarkable article about why drug discovery should be open source. With DeepChem as an example, he has clearly explained the concept, highlighting how great the impact is when scientific software is open source (please find it in the references). Also, crowdsourcing can greatly impact OSDD.

Now, let's understand what **molecular deep learning** means.

Molecular deep learning is the process of using deep learning techniques to build applicable frameworks dedicated to predict properties of molecules. It has the capability of tackling problems such as predicting the toxicity levels of chemical complexes to treat diseases based on the synthesis and design of drug-like molecules.

Molecular deep learning requires you to have a basic understanding of the following concepts that follow until the end of the section.

Convolution

Convolution is an operation of two mathematical functions to produce a third function that expresses how the shape of one is modified by the other. The term *convolution* refers to both the third result function and also the process of computing it. Computing the inverse of a convolution operation is a **deconvolution**.

Ensemble

A group of items observed as a whole, rather than as single entities, is called an **ensemble**. For example, a large group of trees can be collectively referred to as a forest, which is an ensemble:

By Nickrds09 – own work, CC BY-SA 3.0 no, https://commons.wikimedia.org/w/index.php?curid=21789934

The next section explores a bit further into this concept.

Random Forest (RF)

Random Forest (**RF**) is an algorithm based on supervised learning that is one of the types of machine learning. Remember labeled datasets? Forests are basically an ensemble of decision trees. A random forest builds multiple ensembles and merges them collectively to get a machine learning prediction that is more stable and accurate.

Graph convolutional neural networks (GCN)

A **Graph Convolution Network** (**GCN**) is a very powerful neural network architecture for machine learning on graphs. Hence, it can more specifically be referred to as a powerful deep learning technique in graph theory. Please recall our discussion on graphs, including edges and vertices from Chapter 10, *Accelerated Machine Learning on GPUs*.

One-shot learning

One-shot learning can be focused on the challenging problem of the availability of a very low amount of quality drug-related datasets. Most machine learning-based techniques require training on hundreds or thousands of datasets, whereas one-shot learning aims to learn information about object categories from one or just a few training datasets (ligands).

When **Graph Convolutional Neural Networks** (**GCNNs**) are combined with one-shot learning, this significantly improves learning of meaningful distance metrics over small molecules (ligands), thus addressing the challenge faced in a traditional machine learning approach that requires a huge amount of datasets for training.

In DeepChem, molecules can be perceived mathematically within Python code. You can input them as arrays based on the 3D coordinates of a protein and ligand to compute pairwise distances in **Angstroms**. An Angstrom is a metric unit of length equal to one ten billionth of a meter.

Datasets contain many different ways of representing a molecule. One example is the **Kier Benzene-Likeliness Index** (**KBLI**), a **topological index**.

A topological index is a type of molecular descriptor calculated on the basis of the molecular graph of a chemical compound. A molecular graph is a labeled graph whose vertices correspond to the atoms of the compound, and whose edges correspond to chemical bonds.

Through the next few sections, we will focus on an example of drug prediction for Alzheimer's with DeepChem. But before we start using DeepChem for this, it is necessary that we configure and install it first as shown in our previous chapters.

Multiple ways to install DeepChem

In this section, we are going to discuss three ways of installing DeepChem in your system. The recommended way of installation, according to the official documentation, is to use a Conda-based distribution, such as Anaconda or Miniconda.

The three ways that we are sequentially going to show are via the following:

- Google Colab
- Conda on PyCharm
- NVIDIA Docker

Let's first start with Google Colab, hands-on!

Installing Google Colab

This method is highly recommended to get started with DeepChem. Why? At this time of writing, Google has recently replaced Tesla K80 with Tesla T4, which is an AI inference accelerator GPU with tensor cores and 16 GB of memory:

```
from tensorflow.python.client import device_lib
device_lib.list_local_devices()

[name: "/device:CPU:0"
device_type: "CPU"
memory_limit: 268435456
locality {
}
incarnation: 16861077266969563597, name: "/device:XLA_CPU:0"
device_type: "XLA_CPU"
memory_limit: 17179869184
locality {
}
incarnation: 13289663721869503433
physical_device_desc: "device: XLA_CPU device", name: "/device:XLA_GPU:0"
device_type: "XLA_GPU"
memory_limit: 17179869184
locality {
}
incarnation: 15512174984466094799
physical_device_desc: "device: XLA_GPU device", name: "/device:GPU:0"
device_type: "GPU"
memory_limit: 14800692839
locality {
  bus_id: 1
  links {
  }
}
incarnation: 158464110753286612
physical_device_desc: "device: 0, name: Tesla T4, pci bus id: 0000:00:04.0, compute capability: 7.5"]
```

As mentioned in `Chapter 10`, *Accelerated Machine Learning on GPUs*, it remains free to access for anyone with a Google account. An AI accelerator built for inference is intriguing, because that is a very important feature in one-shot learning, as discussed earlier. The Tesla T4 GPU belongs to the Turing architecture.

We are going to use a system-wide strategy but on Colab only. So, you can safely experiment with your deep learning skills in that notebook after checking out DeepChem. It is not installed by default, as you can see here:

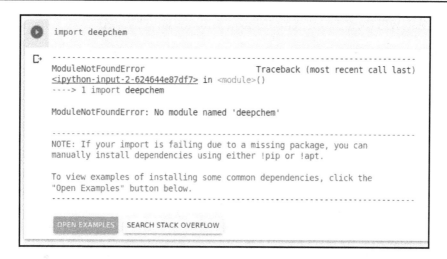

To set up DeepChem within Conda on Colab, follow these steps:

1. Download `miniconda` by using the following command:

   ```
   !wget
   https://repo.continuum.io/miniconda/Miniconda3-latest-Linux-x86_64.
   sh -O miniconda.sh
   ```

   Here, we are using a simplified name for the Miniconda installer, `miniconda.sh`:

```
!wget https://repo.continuum.io/miniconda/Miniconda3-latest-Linux-x86_64.sh -O miniconda.sh

--2019-04-16 13:45:07--  https://repo.continuum.io/miniconda/Miniconda3-latest-Linux-x86_64.sh
Resolving repo.continuum.io (repo.continuum.io)... 104.18.200.79, 104.18.201.79, 2606:4700::6812:c94f, ...
Connecting to repo.continuum.io (repo.continuum.io)|104.18.200.79|:443... connected.
HTTP request sent, awaiting response... 200 OK
Length: 69826864 (67M) [application/x-sh]
Saving to: 'miniconda.sh'

miniconda.sh        100%[===================>]  66.59M  86.2MB/s    in 0.8s

2019-04-16 13:45:08 (86.2 MB/s) - 'miniconda.sh' saved [69826864/69826864]
```

2. Configure Conda and install DeepChem for the GPU system wide, specifically on your Colab virtual machine. The suffix =2.1.0 is for the most recent version of the `deepchem-gpu` package:

   ```
   !chmod +x miniconda.sh
   !bash ./miniconda.sh -b -f -p /usr/local
   !conda install -y --prefix /usr/local -c deepchem -c rdkit -c
   conda-forge -c omnia deepchem-gpu=2.1.0
   ```

3. Colab will then perform all three operations step by step:

```
!chmod +x miniconda.sh
!bash ./miniconda.sh -b -f -p /usr/local
!conda install -y --prefix /usr/local -c deepchem -c rdkit -c conda-forge -c omnia deepchem-gpu=2.1.0

PREFIX=/usr/local
reinstalling: python-3.7.1-h0371630_7 ...
Python 3.7.1
reinstalling: ca-certificates-2018.03.07-0 ...
reinstalling: conda-env-2.6.0-1 ...
reinstalling: libgcc-ng-8.2.0-hdf63c60_1 ...
reinstalling: libstdcxx-ng-8.2.0-hdf63c60_1 ...
reinstalling: libffi-3.2.1-hd88cf55_4 ...
reinstalling: ncurses-6.1-he6710b0_1 ...
reinstalling: openssl-1.1.1a-h7b6447c_0 ...
reinstalling: xz-5.2.4-h14c3975_4 ...
reinstalling: yaml-0.1.7-had09818_2 ...
reinstalling: zlib-1.2.11-h7b6447c_3 ...
reinstalling: libedit-3.1.20170329-h6b74fdf_2 ...
reinstalling: readline-7.0-h7b6447c_5 ...
reinstalling: tk-8.6.8-hbc83047_0 ...
reinstalling: sqlite-3.26.0-h7b6447c_0 ...
reinstalling: asn1crypto-0.24.0-py37_0 ...
reinstalling: certifi-2018.11.29-py37_0 ...
reinstalling: chardet-3.0.4-py37_1 ...
reinstalling: idna-2.8-py37_0 ...
```

4. After it is done, we need to add `/usr/local/lib/python3.6/site-packages/` to this configuration:

```
import sys
sys.path
```

This shows you the existing paths:

```
import sys
sys.path

['',
 '/env/python',
 '/usr/lib/python36.zip',
 '/usr/lib/python3.6',
 '/usr/lib/python3.6/lib-dynload',
 '/usr/local/lib/python3.6/dist-packages',
 '/usr/lib/python3/dist-packages',
 '/usr/local/lib/python3.6/dist-packages/IPython/extensions',
 '/root/.ipython']
```

5. Now, use the following line of code to add it:

```
sys.path.append('/usr/local/lib/python3.6/site-packages/')
```

Executing this line will append a new path:

Confirm the change:

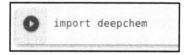

```
sys.path

['',
 '/env/python',
 '/usr/lib/python36.zip',
 '/usr/lib/python3.6',
 '/usr/lib/python3.6/lib-dynload',
 '/usr/local/lib/python3.6/dist-packages',
 '/usr/lib/python3/dist-packages',
 '/usr/local/lib/python3.6/dist-packages/IPython/extensions',
 '/root/.ipython',
 '/usr/local/lib/python3.6/site-packages/']
```

6. Confirm your `deepchem` installation:

```
import deepchem
```

This time, you should not get any error:

```
import deepchem
```

If all goes well, you will not see any Python error, and the outcome of the command will be as shown.

 As this installation affects the backend container system wide, you may want to reset all runtimes on Colab when you want to use a fresh Colab notebook. For more information, check here: https://research.google. com/colaboratory/faq.html.

Now, you're all set to start programming with DeepChem.

Conda on your local PyCharm IDE

Create a new pure Python project with the following configuration. Make sure you create a separate new directory in our existing project directory. Conda will automatically set a new environment in PyCharm, ready for creation. We use DeepChem instead of deepchem to distinguish it as an environment name rather than a package name. You can use any other name of your choice if you want. Remember that naming is case sensitive on Linux:

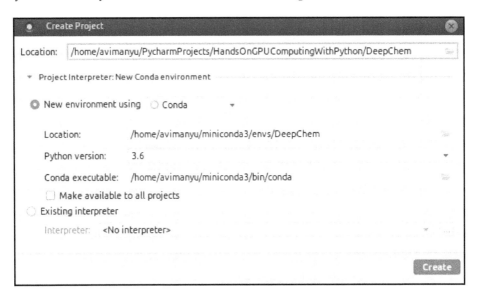

Update conda and run the subsequent command from a Terminal:

```
$ conda activate DeepChem
conda update -n base conda -c anaconda
Collecting package metadata: done
Solving environment: done
---
proceed ([y]/n)? y
---
$ conda install -c deepchem -c rdkit -c conda-forge -c omnia deepchem-
gpu=2.1.0
Collecting package metadata: done
Solving environment: done

The following NEW packages will be INSTALLED:
---
deepchem-gpu    deepchem/linux-64::deepchem-gpu-2.1.0-py36_0
---
proceed ([y]/n)?
```

Further configuration steps will be discussed in the next section. For now, let's focus on another installation method for DeepChem on GPUs.

NVIDIA Docker-based deployment

Assuming you have Docker and NVIDIA Docker already installed, as illustrated in `Chapter 9`, *Containerization on GPU-Enabled Platforms*, download the latest stable `deepchem docker` image and create a container out of it using the following commands:

```
docker pull deepchemio/deepchem
nvidia-docker run -i -t deepchemio/deepchem
```

You are now in a Docker container whose Python has DeepChem installed as a closed environment configuration ready to use on your Ubuntu Linux system.

Configuring DeepChem on PyCharm

The next steps are specific to the PyCharm IDE. To configure DeepChem with PyCharm, we have to focus on our Conda-based installation that we did earlier in the previous section. Assuming the Conda environment is created, you will already have a DeepChem development environment:

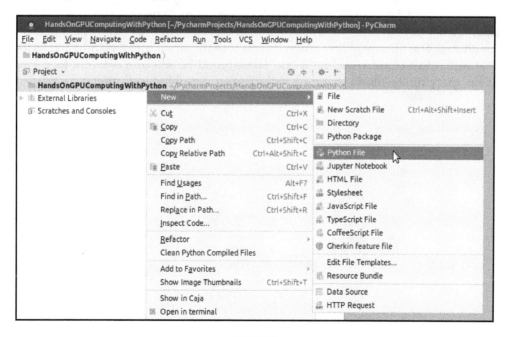

Now, you can import `deepchem` within your Python programs. As you can see, PyCharm Edu detects and recommends this as you begin to type `import deepchem`:

At this stage, we are done configuring DeepChem on the PyCharm IDE for a hands-on molecular deep learning experience with GPUs.

Testing an example from the DeepChem repository

Before testing the example, it is important that you have thoroughly studied the first section of this chapter and the concepts that follow. Without studying these concepts, it will be extremely difficult to understand the complete functionality of DeepChem.

How medicines reach their targets in our body

Some of you might already be aware that ibuprofen is a popular drug as a painkiller (for example, for a headache, backache, or other forms of pain). When you consume this medicine, it reaches your stomach and starts disintegrating in the acidic fluids present there within minutes! The dissolved ibuprofen travels into the small intestine and across its intestinal wall into a blood vessel network. These blood vessels as a network feed into a blood vein, carrying the blood that now includes our dissolved ibuprofen:

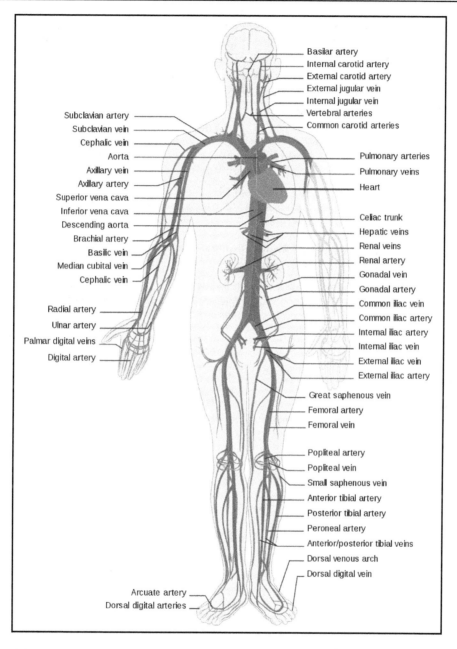

Basilar artery
Internal carotid artery
External carotid artery
External jugular vein
Internal jugular vein
Vertebral arteries
Common carotid arteries

Subclavian artery
Subclavian vein
Cephalic vein
Aorta
Axillary vein
Axillary artery
Superior vena cava
Inferior vena cava
Descending aorta
Brachial artery
Basilic vein
Median cubital vein
Cephalic vein

Radial artery
Ulnar artery
Palmar digital veins
Digital artery

Pulmonary arteries
Pulmonary veins
Heart

Celiac trunk
Hepatic veins
Renal veins
Renal artery
Gonadal vein
Gonadal artery
Common iliac vein
Common iliac artery
Internal iliac artery
Internal iliac vein
External iliac vein
External iliac artery

Great saphenous vein
Femoral artery
Femoral vein

Popliteal artery
Popliteal vein
Small saphenous vein
Anterior tibial artery
Posterior tibial artery
Peroneal artery
Anterior/posterior tibial veins
Dorsal venous arch
Dorsal digital vein

Arcuate artery
Dorsal digital arteries

The blood is then transported into the liver. The blood and the ibuprofen drug molecules travel through the blood vessels in the liver. Most of the ibuprofen makes it through, unaffected, continuing its journey out of the liver, through the blood veins into the circulatory system of the body (see the preceding diagram). This happens after around 30 minutes after you have consumed the tablet. Now, it travels through the circulatory blood stream, passing through every limb and organ, such as the heart, brain, kidneys, and back through the liver.

Our body has a highly sophisticated blood loop. When the ibuprofen molecules present in the blood stream come across a location where the body's pain response is at maximum, they bind to specific target protein molecules that are part of that reaction. By doing so, it blocks the production of compounds that transmit pain signals. So, this is how a painkiller travels through your body to ease your pain.

 You can get detailed information on various drugs, including ibuprofen, through the following web portal that is so beautifully designed and well maintained: drugbank.ca. Here is the link to ibuprofen: drugbank.ca/drugs/DB01050. You will find that there are 10 targets in total.

Alzheimer's disease

Alzheimer's disease is extremely infamous due to its induced progressive loss of brain cells that leads to memory loss and the impairment of other thinking skills. The pathogenesis of Alzheimer's disease is extremely complex. Here is an estimate of how the disease is prevalent among us humans:

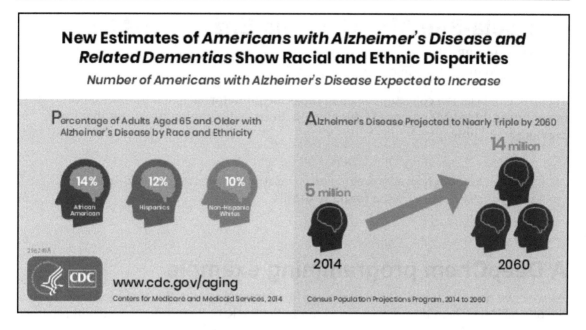

New Estimates of *Americans with Alzheimer's Disease and Related Dementias* Show Racial and Ethnic Disparities

Number of Americans with Alzheimer's Disease Expected to Increase

Image labeled for reuse on Google, via https://www.cdc.gov/aging/data/pdf/american-alzheimers-racial-ethnic-disparities-infographic-508-h.pdf

The previous diagram demonstrates the racial and ethnic disparities of Americans suffering from Alzheimer's Disease and related dementias.

IC50

IC50 is the concentration of an inhibitor where the binding response is reduced by half. This is a metric that can be used to benchmark different small molecules/ligands/drugs. The lower this metric value, the better the suitability of the potential drug.

Our example program uses a dataset that uses pIC50. The proper way to average IC50 values is to take the geometric mean of the IC50 values, which can be easily calculated if pIC50 values are used.

The Beta-Site APP-Cleaving Enzyme (BACE)

The **Beta-Site APP-Cleaving Enzyme** (**BACE**) is a therapeutic target for Alzheimer's disease. It produces Alzheimer's disease peptides.

The BACE dataset is a collection of small molecule inhibitors across a three order of magnitude (nM to µM) range of IC50s along with crystallographic structures that were previously unknown.

 You can take a look at `https://drugdesigndata.org/about/grand-challenge-4/bace` for more details.

A DeepChem programming example

As we have now discussed all the necessary fundamentals so far, here is an example from the official DeepChem repositories, used to predict the K_i of ligands to a protein. It is based on a tutorial at `https://deepchem.io/docs/notebooks/BACE.html`.

Recall that K_i is an important metric for a ligand binding to a protein.

Small changes were required in the code. `MultiTaskClassifier` has been deprecated, so it has been modified to `MultitaskClassifier`. `plt` was replaced with `plot` for clarity.

The following is the GitHub page of DeepChem: `github.com/deepchem/deepchem`.

So, let's now look at the tutorial. You can use PyCharm if you want to see the output step by step and tally it with the code at the same time. The molecule images will be generated in your PyCharm project folder.

DeepChem is licensed under the MIT license. The developers actively support commercial users. Any novel molecular entities found through DeepChem belong entirely to the user and not to DeepChem developers:

```
#Copyright 2019 Pande Lab, Stanford University
#Permission is hereby granted, free of charge, to any person obtaining a
copy of this software and associated documentation files (the "Software"),
# to deal in the Software without restriction, including without limitation
the rights to use, copy, modify, merge, publish, distribute, sublicense,
# and/or sell copies of the Software, and to permit persons to whom the
Software is furnished to do so, subject to the following conditions:
#The above copyright notice and this permission notice shall be included in
```

```
all copies or substantial portions of the Software.
#THE SOFTWARE IS PROVIDED "AS IS", WITHOUT WARRANTY OF ANY KIND, EXPRESS OR
IMPLIED, INCLUDING BUT NOT LIMITED TO THE WARRANTIES OF MERCHANTABILITY,
#FITNESS FOR A PARTICULAR PURPOSE AND NONINFRINGEMENT. IN NO EVENT SHALL
THE AUTHORS OR COPYRIGHT HOLDERS BE LIABLE FOR ANY CLAIM, DAMAGES OR OTHER
LIABILITY,
# WHETHER IN AN ACTION OF CONTRACT, TORT OR OTHERWISE, ARISING FROM, OUT OF
OR IN CONNECTION WITH THE SOFTWARE OR THE USE OR OTHER DEALINGS IN THE
SOFTWARE.
```

The BACE enyzme is analyzed and machine learning models are built for predicting the Ki of ligands to the protein. The DeepChem library loads the relevant data into memory, and splits it into train, test, and validation folds to build and cross-validate models. Finally, it reports statistics based on random forests and deep neural networks:

```
import os
import sys
import deepchem as dc
from deepchem.utils.save import load_from_disk

current_dir = os.path.dirname(os.path.realpath("__file__"))
dc.utils.download_url("https://s3-us-west-1.amazonaws.com/deepchem.io/datas
ets/desc_canvas_aug30.csv",                    current_dir)
```

The dataset to be split is called `desc_canvas_aug30.csv`. It contains a range of small molecules with their respective parametric data. You can view the dataset at `https://github.com/deepchem/deepchem/blob/master/datasets/crystal_desc_canvas_aug30.csv`:

```
dataset_file = "desc_canvas_aug30.csv"
dataset = load_from_disk(dataset_file)
num_display=10
pretty_columns = ("[" + ",".join(["'%s'" % column for column in
dataset.columns.values[:num_display]])  + ",...]")

dc.utils.download_url("https://s3-us-west-1.amazonaws.com/deepchem.io/datas
ets/crystal_desc_canvas_aug30.csv",current_dir)
crystal_dataset_file = "crystal_desc_canvas_aug30.csv"
crystal_dataset = load_from_disk(crystal_dataset_file)

print("Columns of dataset: %s" % pretty_columns)
print("Number of examples in dataset: %s" % str(dataset.shape[0]))
print("Number of examples in crystal dataset: %s" %
str(crystal_dataset.shape[0]))
```

For a visual understanding of compounds in the dataset, RDKit is used. RDKit is a collection of cheminformatics and machine-learning software based on C++ and Python.

Helper functions are defined to get started with the tutorial:

```
import tempfile
from rdkit import Chem
from rdkit.Chem import Draw
from itertools import islice
from IPython.display import Image, display, HTML

def display_images(filenames):
    """Helper to pretty-print images."""
    for filename in filenames:
        display(Image(filename))

def mols_to_pngs(mols, basename="test"):
    """Helper to write RDKit mols to png files."""
    filenames = []
    for i, mol in enumerate(mols):
        filename = "BACE_%s%d.png" % (basename, i)
        Draw.MolToFile(mol, filename)
        filenames.append(filename)
    return filenames
```

Now, we display a compound from the dataset. Note the complex ring structures and polar structures:

```
num_to_display = 12
molecules = []
for _, data in islice(dataset.iterrows(), num_to_display):
    molecules.append(Chem.MolFromSmiles(data["mol"]))
display_images(mols_to_pngs(molecules, basename="dataset"))
```

Now, it's time to picture the compounds in the crystal structure collection. On PyCharm, `display_images(mols_to_pngs())` will generate the corresponding images in the project folder, all in `.png` format:

```
num_to_display = 12
molecules = []
for _, data in islice(crystal_dataset.iterrows(), num_to_display):
    molecules.append(Chem.MolFromSmiles(data["mol"]))
display_images(mols_to_pngs(molecules, basename="crystal_dataset"))
```

Analyzing the distribution of `pIC50` values in the dataset is executed as follows:

```
import matplotlib
import matplotlib.pyplot as plot

import numpy as np
pIC50s = np.array(dataset["pIC50"])
```

```
pIC50s = [pIC50 for pIC50 in pIC50s if pIC50 != '']
n, bins, patches = plot.hist(pIC50s, 50, facecolor='green', alpha=0.75)
plot.xlabel('Measured pIC50')
plot.ylabel('Number of compounds')
plot.title(r'Histogram of pIC50 Values')
plot.grid(True)
plot.show()
```

At this point, a histogram will be displayed for approximately 100 ligands with respect to their measured pIC50 values:

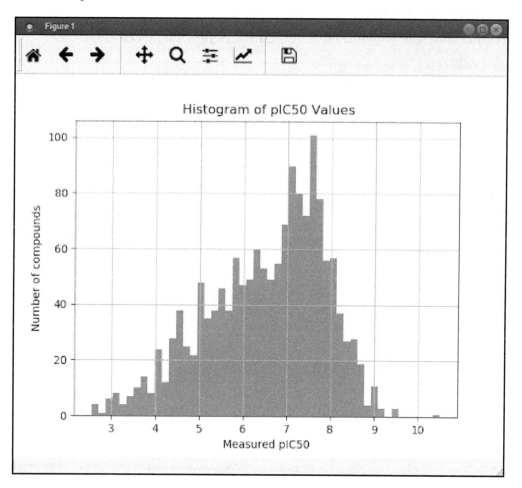

As in the PyCharm-based examples in `Chapter 10`, *Accelerated Machine Learning on GPUs*, unless you close the image window, the program execution will be paused for the DeepChem program. Close it to proceed with executing the pending code (when you run the complete program until RF and DNN outputs are generated as two more image windows).

Featurizing the data using the canvas samples is done by specifying the columns in the data input that correspond to the features. It would be more convenient for you if you use the following data as a file to do that. Note that it's actually a single line, as shown on the official DeepChem website (link given previously).

The data has been split with line breaks for clarity. Here is the first block:

```
user_specified_features =
['MW','AlogP','HBA','HBD','RB','HeavyAtomCount','ChiralCenterCount','Chiral
CenterCountAllPossible','RingCount','PSA','Estate','MR','Polar','sLi_Key','
ssBe_Key','sssssBem_Key','sBH2_Key','ssBH_Key','sssB_Key','ssssBm_Key','sCH3
_Key','dCH2_Key','ssCH2_Key','tCH_Key','dsCH_Key','aaCH_Key','sssCH_Key','d
dC_Key','tsC_Key','dssC_Key','aasC_Key','aaaC_Key','ssssC_Key','sNH3_Key','
sNH2_Key','ssNH2_Key','dNH_Key','ssNH_Key','aaNH_Key','tN_Key','sssNH_Key',
'dsN_Key','aaN_Key','sssN_Key','ddsN_Key','aasN_Key','ssssN_Key','daaN_Key'
,'sOH_Key','dO_Key','ssO_Key','aaO_Key','aOm_Key','sOm_Key','sF_Key','sSiH3
_Key','ssSiH2_Key','sssSiH_Key','ssssSi_Key','sPH2_Key','ssPH_Key','sssP_Ke
y','dsssP_Key','ddsP_Key','sssssP_Key','sSH_Key','dS_Key','ssS_Key','aaS_Ke
y','dssS_Key','ddssS_Key','ssssssS_Key','Sm_Key','sCl_Key','sGeH3_Key','ssG
eH2_Key','sssGeH_Key','ssssGe_Key','sAsH2_Key','ssAsH_Key','sssAs_Key','dss
sAs_Key','ddsAs_Key','sssssAs_Key','sSeH_Key','dSe_Key','ssSe_Key','aaSe_Ke
y','dssSe_Key','ssssssSe_Key','ddssSe_Key','sBr_Key','sSnH3_Key','ssSnH2_Ke
y','sssSnH_Key','ssssSn_Key','sI_Key','sPbH3_Key','ssPbH2_Key','sssPbH_Key'
,'ssssPb_Key','sLi_Cnt','ssBe_Cnt','ssssBem_Cnt','sBH2_Cnt','ssBH_Cnt','sss
B_Cnt','ssssBm_Cnt','sCH3_Cnt','dCH2_Cnt','ssCH2_Cnt','tCH_C
```

And here is the second block:

```
nt','dsCH_Cnt','aaCH_Cnt','sssCH_Cnt','ddC_Cnt','tsC_Cnt','dssC_Cnt','aasC_
Cnt','aaaC_Cnt','ssssC_Cnt','sNH3_Cnt','sNH2_Cnt','ssNH2_Cnt','dNH_Cnt','ss
NH_Cnt','aaNH_Cnt','tN_Cnt','sssNH_Cnt','dsN_Cnt','aaN_Cnt','sssN_Cnt','dds
N_Cnt','aasN_Cnt','ssssN_Cnt','daaN_Cnt','sOH_Cnt','dO_Cnt','ssO_Cnt','aaO_
Cnt','aOm_Cnt','sOm_Cnt','sF_Cnt','sSiH3_Cnt','ssSiH2_Cnt','sssSiH_Cnt','ss
ssSi_Cnt','sPH2_Cnt','ssPH_Cnt','sssP_Cnt','dsssP_Cnt','ddsP_Cnt','sssssP_C
nt','sSH_Cnt','dS_Cnt','ssS_Cnt','aaS_Cnt','dssS_Cnt','ddssS_Cnt','ssssssS_
Cnt','Sm_Cnt','sCl_Cnt','sGeH3_Cnt','ssGeH2_Cnt','sssGeH_Cnt','ssssGe_Cnt',
'sAsH2_Cnt','ssAsH_Cnt','sssAs_Cnt','dsssAs_Cnt','ddsAs_Cnt','sssssAs_Cnt',
'sSeH_Cnt','dSe_Cnt','ssSe_Cnt','aaSe_Cnt','dssSe_Cnt','ssssssSe_Cnt','ddss
Se_Cnt','sBr_Cnt','sSnH3_Cnt','ssSnH2_Cnt','sssSnH_Cnt','ssssSn_Cnt','sI_Cn
t','sPbH3_Cnt','ssPbH2_Cnt','sssPbH_Cnt','ssssPb_Cnt','sLi_Sum','ssBe_Sum',
'sssssBem_Sum','sBH2_Sum','ssBH_Sum','sssB_Sum','ssssBm_Sum','sCH3_Sum','dCH
```

2_Sum','ssCH2_Sum','tCH_Sum','dsCH_Sum','aaCH_Sum','sssCH_Sum','ddC_Sum','t
sC_Sum','dssC_Sum','aasC_Sum','aaaC_Sum','ssssC_Sum','sNH3_Sum','sNH2_Sum',
'ssNH2_Sum','dNH_Sum','ssNH_Sum','aaNH_Sum','tN_Sum','sssNH_Sum','dsN_Sum',
'aaN_Sum','sssN_Sum','ddsN_Sum','aasN_Sum','ssssN_Sum','daaN_Sum','sOH_Sum'
,'dO_Sum','ssO_Sum','aaO_Sum','aOm_Sum','sOm_Sum','sF_Sum','sSiH3_Sum','ssS

Here is the third block:

iH2_Sum','sssSiH_Sum','ssssSi_Sum','sPH2_Sum','ssPH_Sum','sssP_Sum','dsssP_
Sum','ddsP_Sum','sssssP_Sum','sSH_Sum','dS_Sum','ssS_Sum','aaS_Sum','dssS_S
um','ddssS_Sum','ssssssS_Sum','Sm_Sum','sCl_Sum','sGeH3_Sum','ssGeH2_Sum','
sssGeH_Sum','ssssGe_Sum','sAsH2_Sum','ssAsH_Sum','sssAs_Sum','dsssAs_Sum','
ddsAs_Sum','sssssAs_Sum','sSeH_Sum','dSe_Sum','ssSe_Sum','aaSe_Sum','dssSe_
Sum','ssssssSe_Sum','ddssSe_Sum','sBr_Sum','sSnH3_Sum','ssSnH2_Sum','sssSnH
_Sum','ssssSn_Sum','sI_Sum','sPbH3_Sum','ssPbH2_Sum','sssPbH_Sum','ssssPb_S
um','sLi_Avg','ssBe_Avg','ssssBem_Avg','sBH2_Avg','ssBH_Avg','sssB_Avg','ss
ssBm_Avg','sCH3_Avg','dCH2_Avg','ssCH2_Avg','tCH_Avg','dsCH_Avg','aaCH_Avg'
,'sssCH_Avg','ddC_Avg','tsC_Avg','dssC_Avg','aasC_Avg','aaaC_Avg','ssssC_Av
g','sNH3_Avg','sNH2_Avg','ssNH2_Avg','dNH_Avg','ssNH_Avg','aaNH_Avg','tN_Av
g','sssNH_Avg','dsN_Avg','aaN_Avg','sssN_Avg','ddsN_Avg','aasN_Avg','ssssN_
Avg','daaN_Avg','sOH_Avg','dO_Avg','ssO_Avg','aaO_Avg','aOm_Avg','sOm_Avg',
'sF_Avg','sSiH3_Avg','ssSiH2_Avg','sssSiH_Avg','ssssSi_Avg','sPH2_Avg','ssP
H_Avg','sssP_Avg','dsssP_Avg','ddsP_Avg','sssssP_Avg','sSH_Avg','dS_Avg','s
sS_Avg','aaS_Avg','dssS_Avg','ddssS_Avg','ssssssS_Avg','Sm_Avg','sCl_Avg','
sGeH3_Avg','ssGeH2_Avg','sssGeH_Avg','ssssGe_Avg','sAsH2_Avg','ssAsH_Avg','
sssAs_Avg','dsssAs_Avg','ddsAs_Avg','sssssAs_Avg','sSeH_Avg','dSe_Avg','ssS

And here is the fourth block:

e_Avg','aaSe_Avg','dssSe_Avg','ssssssSe_Avg','ddssSe_Avg','sBr_Avg','sSnH3_
Avg','ssSnH2_Avg','sssSnH_Avg','ssssSn_Avg','sI_Avg','sPbH3_Avg','ssPbH2_Av
g','sssPbH_Avg','ssssPb_Avg','First Zagreb (ZM1)','First Zagreb index by
valence vertex degrees (ZM1V)','Second Zagreb (ZM2)','Second Zagreb index
by valence vertex degrees (ZM2V)','Polarity (Pol)','Narumi Simple
Topological (NST)','Narumi Harmonic Topological (NHT)','Narumi Geometric
Topological (NGT)','Total structure connectivity (TSC)','Wiener (W)','Mean
Wiener (MW)','Xu (Xu)','Quadratic (QIndex)','Radial centric (RC)','Mean
Square Distance Balaban (MSDB)','Superpendentic (SP)','Harary (Har)','Log
of product of row sums (LPRS)','Pogliani (Pog)','Schultz Molecular
Topological (SMT)','Schultz Molecular Topological by valence vertex degrees
(SMTV)','Mean Distance Degree Deviation (MDDD)','Ramification
(Ram)','Gutman Molecular Topological (GMT)','Gutman MTI by valence vertex
degrees (GMTV)','Average vertex distance degree (AVDD)','Unipolarity
(UP)','Centralization (CENT)','Variation (VAR)','Molecular
electrotopological variation (MEV)','Maximal electrotopological positive
variation (MEPV)','Maximal electrotopological negative variation
(MENV)','Eccentric connectivity (ECCc)','Eccentricity (ECC)','Average

Here is the fifth block:

```
eccentricity (AECC)','Eccentric (DECC)','Valence connectivity index chi-0
(vX0)','Valence connectivity index chi-1 (vX1)','Valence connectivity index
chi-2 (vX2)','Valence connectivity index chi-3 (vX3)','Valence connectivity
index chi-4 (vX4)','Valence connectivity index chi-5 (vX5)','Average
valence connectivity index chi-0 (AvX0)','Average valence connectivity
index chi-1 (AvX1)','Average valence connectivity index chi-2
(AvX2)','Average valence connectivity index chi-3 (AvX3)','Average valence
connectivity index chi-4 (AvX4)','Average valence connectivity index chi-5
(AvX5)','Quasi Wiener (QW)','First Mohar (FM)','Second Mohar
(SM)','Spanning tree number (STN)','Kier benzene-likeliness index
(KBLI)','Topological charge index of order 1 (TCI1)','Topological charge
index of order 2 (TCI2)','Topological charge index of order 3
(TCI3)','Topological charge index of order 4 (TCI4)','Topological charge
index of order 5 (TCI5)','Topological charge index of order 6
(TCI6)','Topological charge index of order 7 (TCI7)','Topological charge
index of order 8 (TCI8)','Topological charge index of order 9
(TCI9)','Topological charge index of order 10 (TCI10)','Mean topological
charge index of order 1 (MTCI1)','Mean topological charge index of order 2
(MTCI2)','Mean topological charge index of order 3
```

And here is the sixth block:

```
(MTCI3)','Mean topological charge index of order 4 (MTCI4)','Mean
topological charge index of order 5 (MTCI5)','Mean topological charge index
of order 6 (MTCI6)','Mean topological charge index of order 7
(MTCI7)','Mean topological charge index of order 8 (MTCI8)','Mean
topological charge index of order 9 (MTCI9)','Mean topological charge index
of order 10 (MTCI10)','Global topological charge (GTC)','Hyper-distance-
path index (HDPI)','Reciprocal hyper-distance-path index (RHDPI)','Square
reciprocal distance sum (SRDS)','Modified Randic connectivity
(MRC)','Balaban centric (BC)','Lopping centric (LC)','Kier Hall
electronegativity (KHE)','Sum of topological distances between N..N (STD(N
N))','Sum of topological distances between N..O (STD(N O))','Sum of
topological distances between N..S (STD(N S))','Sum of topological
distances between N..P (STD(N P))','Sum of topological distances between
N..F (STD(N F))','Sum of topological distances between N..Cl (STD(N
Cl))','Sum of topological distances between N..Br (STD(N Br))','Sum of
topological distances between N..I (STD(N I))','Sum of topological
distances between O..O (STD(O O))','Sum of topological distances between
O..S (STD(O S))','Sum of topological distances between O..P (STD(O
P))','Sum of topological distances between O..F (STD(O F))','Sum of
```

Here is the seventh block:

```
topological distances between O..Cl (STD(O Cl))','Sum of topological
distances between O..Br (STD(O Br))','Sum of topological distances between
O..I (STD(O I))','Sum of topological distances between S..S (STD(S
S))','Sum of topological distances between S..P (STD(S P))','Sum of
topological distances between S..F (STD(S F))','Sum of topological
distances between S..Cl (STD(S Cl))','Sum of topological distances between
S..Br (STD(S Br))','Sum of topological distances between S..I (STD(S
I))','Sum of topological distances between P..P (STD(P P))','Sum of
topological distances between P..F (STD(P F))','Sum of topological
distances between P..Cl (STD(P Cl))','Sum of topological distances between
P..Br (STD(P Br))','Sum of topological distances between P..I (STD(P
I))','Sum of topological distances between F..F (STD(F F))','Sum of
topological distances between F..Cl (STD(F Cl))','Sum of topological
distances between F..Br (STD(F Br))','Sum of topological distances between
F..I (STD(F I))','Sum of topological distances between Cl..Cl (STD(Cl
Cl))','Sum of topological distances between Cl..Br (STD(Cl Br))','Sum of
topological distances between Cl..I (STD(Cl I))','Sum of topological
distances between Br..Br (STD(Br Br))','Sum of topological distances
between Br..I (STD(Br I))','Sum of topological
```

And here is the eighth block:

```
distances between I..I (STD(I I))','Wiener-type index from Z weighted
distance matrix - Barysz matrix (WhetZ)','Wiener-type index from
electronegativity weighted distance matrix (Whete)','Wiener-type index from
mass weighted distance matrix (Whetm)','Wiener-type index from van der
waals weighted distance matrix (Whetv)','Wiener-type index from
polarizability weighted distance matrix (Whetp)','Balaban-type index from Z
weighted distance matrix - Barysz matrix (JhetZ)','Balaban-type index from
electronegativity weighted distance matrix (Jhete)','Balaban-type index
from mass weighted distance matrix (Jhetm)','Balaban-type index from van
der waals weighted distance matrix (Jhetv)','Balaban-type index from
polarizability weighted distance matrix (Jhetp)','Topological diameter
(TD)','Topological radius (TR)','Petitjean 2D shape (PJ2DS)','Balaban
distance connectivity index (J)','Solvation connectivity index chi-0
(SCIX0)','Solvation connectivity index chi-1 (SCIX1)','Solvation
connectivity index chi-2 (SCIX2)','Solvation connectivity index chi-3
(SCIX3)','Solvation connectivity index chi-4 (SCIX4)','Solvation
connectivity index chi-5 (SCIX5)','Connectivity index chi-0
(CIX0)','Connectivity chi-1 [Randic connectivity] (CIX1)','Connectivity
index chi-2
```

Here is the ninth block:

```
(CIX2)','Connectivity index chi-3 (CIX3)','Connectivity index chi-4
(CIX4)','Connectivity index chi-5 (CIX5)','Average connectivity index chi-0
(ACIX0)','Average connectivity index chi-1 (ACIX1)','Average connectivity
index chi-2 (ACIX2)','Average connectivity index chi-3 (ACIX3)','Average
connectivity index chi-4 (ACIX4)','Average connectivity index chi-5
(ACIX5)','reciprocal distance Randic-type index (RDR)','reciprocal distance
square Randic-type index (RDSR)','1-path Kier alpha-modified shape index
(KAMS1)','2-path Kier alpha-modified shape index (KAMS2)','3-path Kier
alpha-modified shape index (KAMS3)','Kier flexibility (KF)','path/walk 2 -
Randic shape index (RSIpw2)','path/walk 3 - Randic shape index
(RSIpw3)','path/walk 4 - Randic shape index (RSIpw4)','path/walk 5 - Randic
shape index (RSIpw5)','E-state topological parameter (ETP)','Ring Count 3
(RNGCNT3)','Ring Count 4 (RNGCNT4)','Ring Count 5 (RNGCNT5)','Ring Count 6
(RNGCNT6)','Ring Count 7 (RNGCNT7)','Ring Count 8 (RNGCNT8)','Ring Count 9
(RNGCNT9)','Ring Count 10 (RNGCNT10)','Ring Count 11 (RNGCNT11)','Ring
Count 12 (RNGCNT12)','Ring Count 13 (RNGCNT13)','Ring Count 14
(RNGCNT14)','Ring Count 15 (RNGCNT15)','Ring Count 16 (RNGCNT16)','Ring
Count 17 (RNGCNT17)','Ring Count 18 (RNGCNT18)','Ring Count 19
```

And here is the tenth and final block:

```
(RNGCNT19)','Ring Count 20 (RNGCNT20)','Atom Count (ATMCNT)','Bond Count
(BNDCNT)','Atoms in Ring System (ATMRNGCNT)','Bonds in Ring System
(BNDRNGCNT)','Cyclomatic number (CYCLONUM)','Number of ring systems
(NRS)','Normalized number of ring systems (NNRS)','Ring Fusion degree
(RFD)','Ring perimeter (RNGPERM)','Ring bridge count (RNGBDGE)','Molecule
cyclized degree (MCD)','Ring Fusion density (RFDELTA)','Ring complexity
index (RCI)','Van der Waals surface area (VSA)','MR1 (MR1)','MR2
(MR2)','MR3 (MR3)','MR4 (MR4)','MR5 (MR5)','MR6 (MR6)','MR7 (MR7)','MR8
(MR8)','ALOGP1 (ALOGP1)','ALOGP2 (ALOGP2)','ALOGP3 (ALOGP3)','ALOGP4
(ALOGP4)','ALOGP5 (ALOGP5)','ALOGP6 (ALOGP6)','ALOGP7 (ALOGP7)','ALOGP8
(ALOGP8)','ALOGP9 (ALOGP9)','ALOGP10 (ALOGP10)','PEOE1 (PEOE1)','PEOE2
(PEOE2)','PEOE3 (PEOE3)','PEOE4 (PEOE4)','PEOE5 (PEOE5)','PEOE6
(PEOE6)','PEOE7 (PEOE7)','PEOE8 (PEOE8)','PEOE9 (PEOE9)','PEOE10
(PEOE10)','PEOE11 (PEOE11)','PEOE12 (PEOE12)','PEOE13 (PEOE13)','PEOE14
(PEOE14)']
```

Now, we need to featurize the data:

```
import shutil
featurizer = dc.feat.UserDefinedFeaturizer(user_specified_features)
loader = dc.data.UserCSVLoader(
    tasks=["Class"], smiles_field="mol", id_field="mol",
    featurizer=featurizer)
dataset = loader.featurize(dataset_file)
crystal_dataset = loader.featurize(crystal_dataset_file)
```

This data is already split into three subsets. `train` and `test` sets contain 20% and 80%, respectively, of the total data from the BACE enzyme. There is also a `validation` set that contains data from a separate (but related assay). (Note that these names are really misnomers. The `test` set would be called a `validation` set in standard machine learning practice, and the `validation` set would typically be called an `external` test set). Hence, the datasets are renamed after loading them:

```
splitter = dc.splits.SpecifiedSplitter(dataset_file, "Model")
train_dataset, valid_dataset, test_dataset =
splitter.train_valid_test_split(dataset)
```

At this point, `valid_dataset` is to be validated as an external test set to test druggability or, more simply, the suitability of a yet-to-be recognized drug. `test_dataset` contains 80% of known and established drug data against Alzheimer's:

```
#NOTE THE RENAMING:
valid_dataset, test_dataset = test_dataset, valid_dataset
```

So now, `valid_dataset` is loaded with the 80% BACE data from `test_set` containing small molecules that are already known to be therapeutic toward treating Alzheimer's. Also, `test_set` is further reloaded with new data from another related assay data (external) to predict its suitability as a potential ligand/drug. Note that we discussed assays earlier in the first section.

You can take a look at a compound in the validation set. (The compound displayed earlier was drawn from the train set). They will again be generated in your PyCharm project folder:

```
print(valid_dataset.ids)
valid_mols = [Chem.MolFromSmiles(compound)
              for compound in islice(valid_dataset.ids, num_to_display)]
display_images(mols_to_pngs(valid_mols, basename="valid_set"))
```

Let's now write these datasets to disk:

```
print("Number of compounds in train set")
print(len(train_dataset))
print("Number of compounds in validation set")
print(len(valid_dataset))
print("Number of compounds in test set")
print(len(test_dataset))
print("Number of compounds in crystal set")
print(len(crystal_dataset))
```

The performance of common machine learning algorithms can be very sensitive to the preprocessing of the data. One common transformation applied to data is to normalize it to have zero mean and unit standard deviation. We will apply this transformation to the pIC50 values (as seen previously, the pIC50s range from 2 to 11):

```
transformers = [
  dc.trans.NormalizationTransformer(transform_X=True,
dataset=train_dataset),
  dc.trans.ClippingTransformer(transform_X=True, dataset=train_dataset)]

datasets = [train_dataset, valid_dataset, test_dataset, crystal_dataset]
for i, dataset in enumerate(datasets):
  for transformer in transformers:
    datasets[i] = transformer.transform(dataset)
train_dataset, valid_dataset, test_dataset, crystal_dataset = datasets
```

We now fit simple random forest models to our datasets:

```
# Using Ensemble from Scikit learn
from sklearn.ensemble import RandomForestClassifier

def rf_model_builder(model_params, model_dir):
  sklearn_model = RandomForestClassifier(**model_params)
  return dc.models.SklearnModel(sklearn_model, model_dir)
params_dict = {
  "n_estimators": [10, 100],
  "max_features": ["auto", "sqrt", "log2", None],
}

metric = dc.metrics.Metric(dc.metrics.roc_auc_score)
optimizer = dc.hyper.HyperparamOpt(rf_model_builder)
best_rf, best_rf_hyperparams, all_rf_results = optimizer.hyperparam_search(
  params_dict, train_dataset, valid_dataset, transformers,
  metric=metric)
```

Here, we imported the `RandomForestClassifier` from scikit-learn, a free and open source software machine learning library. Test scores will be reported on your PyCharm console:

```
params_dict = {"learning_rate": np.power(10., np.random.uniform(-5, -3,
size=1)), "weight_decay_penalty": np.power(10, np.random.uniform(-6, -4,
size=1)), "nb_epoch": [40] }
n_features = train_dataset.get_data_shape()[0]
def model_builder(model_params, model_dir):
  model = dc.models.MultitaskClassifier( 1, n_features, layer_sizes [1000],
dropouts=.25, batch_size=50, **model_params)
  return model
```

```
optimizer = dc.hyper.HyperparamOpt(model_builder)
best_dnn, best_dnn_hyperparams, all_dnn_results =
optimizer.hyperparam_search(params_dict, train_dataset, valid_dataset,
transformers, metric=metric)
```

Now, let's evaluate the best model on the validation and test sets and save the results to a new .csv dataset. The Regressor train set undergoes evaluation and the model's performance is computed to fetch the RF training score after normalization:

```
from deepchem.utils.evaluate import Evaluator

rf_train_csv_out = "rf_train_regressor.csv"
rf_train_stats_out = "rf_train_stats_regressor.txt"
rf_train_evaluator = Evaluator(best_rf, train_dataset, transformers)
rf_train_score = rf_train_evaluator.compute_model_performance( [metric],
rf_train_csv_out, rf_train_stats_out)
print("RF Train set AUC %f" % (rf_train_score["roc_auc_score"]))

rf_valid_csv_out = "rf_valid_regressor.csv"
rf_valid_stats_out = "rf_valid_stats_regressor.txt"
rf_valid_evaluator = Evaluator(best_rf, valid_dataset, transformers)
rf_valid_score = rf_valid_evaluator.compute_model_performance(
   [metric], rf_valid_csv_out, rf_valid_stats_out)
print("RF Valid set AUC %f" % (rf_valid_score["roc_auc_score"]))

rf_test_csv_out = "rf_test_regressor.csv"
rf_test_stats_out = "rf_test_stats_regressor.txt"
```

These .csv and .txt files will also be created and stored on your PyCharm project folder:

```
rf_test_evaluator = Evaluator(best_rf, test_dataset, transformers)
rf_test_score = rf_test_evaluator.compute_model_performance(
   [metric], rf_test_csv_out, rf_test_stats_out)
print("RF Test set AUC %f" % (rf_test_score["roc_auc_score"]))

rf_crystal_csv_out = "rf_crystal_regressor.csv"
rf_crystal_stats_out = "rf_crystal_stats_regressor.txt"
rf_crystal_evaluator = Evaluator(best_rf, crystal_dataset, transformers)
rf_crystal_score = rf_crystal_evaluator.compute_model_performance(
   [metric], rf_crystal_csv_out, rf_crystal_stats_out)
print("RF Crystal set R^2 %f" % (rf_crystal_score["roc_auc_score"]))

dnn_train_csv_out = "dnn_train_classifier.csv"
dnn_train_stats_out = "dnn_train_classifier_stats.txt"
dnn_train_evaluator = Evaluator(best_dnn, train_dataset, transformers)
dnn_train_score = dnn_train_evaluator.compute_model_performance(
   [metric], dnn_train_csv_out, dnn_train_stats_out)
```

Area Under the Curve (**AUC**) is the definite integral in a plot of drug concentration in blood plasma versus time.

Here, we have another **Receiver Operating Characteristic** (**ROC**). ROC illustrates the diagnostic ability of a binary classifier system based on a discrimination threshold. An ROC curve is created by plotting the **True Positive Rate** (**TPR**) against the **False Positive Rate** (**FPR**) at various thresholds:

```
print("DNN Train set AUC %f" % (dnn_train_score["roc_auc_score"]))

dnn_valid_csv_out = "dnn_valid_classifier.csv"
dnn_valid_stats_out = "dnn_valid_classifier_stats.txt"
dnn_valid_evaluator = Evaluator(best_dnn, valid_dataset, transformers)
dnn_valid_score = dnn_valid_evaluator.compute_model_performance(
  [metric], dnn_valid_csv_out, dnn_valid_stats_out)
print("DNN Valid set AUC %f" % (dnn_valid_score["roc_auc_score"]))

dnn_test_csv_out = "dnn_test_classifier.csv"
dnn_test_stats_out = "dnn_test_classifier_stats.txt"
dnn_test_evaluator = Evaluator(best_dnn, test_dataset, transformers)
dnn_test_score = dnn_test_evaluator.compute_model_performance(
  [metric], dnn_test_csv_out, dnn_test_stats_out)
print("DNN Test set AUC %f" % (dnn_test_score["roc_auc_score"]))

dnn_crystal_csv_out = "dnn_crystal_classifier.csv"
dnn_crystal_stats_out = "dnn_crystal_stats_classifier.txt"
```

Finally, the DNN train set, validation set, and test set AUC scores are displayed:

```
dnn_crystal_evaluator = Evaluator(best_dnn, crystal_dataset, transformers)
dnn_crystal_score = dnn_crystal_evaluator.compute_model_performance(
  [metric], dnn_crystal_csv_out, dnn_crystal_stats_out)
print("DNN Crystal set AUC %f" % (dnn_crystal_score["roc_auc_score"]))
```

We use the following to make directories store the raw and featurized datasets:

```
featurizer = dc.feat.UserDefinedFeaturizer(user_specified_features)
loader = dc.data.UserCSVLoader(
  tasks=["pIC50"], smiles_field="mol", id_field="CID",
  featurizer=featurizer)
dataset = loader.featurize(dataset_file)
crystal_dataset = loader.featurize(crystal_dataset_file)

splitter = dc.splits.SpecifiedSplitter(dataset_file, "Model")
train_dataset, valid_dataset, test_dataset =
splitter.train_valid_test_split(dataset)
#NOTE THE RENAMING:
valid_dataset, test_dataset = test_dataset, valid_dataset
```

In the preceding code block, we once again re-initialized and loaded our datasets:

```
print("Number of compounds in train set")
print(len(train_dataset))
print("Number of compounds in validation set")
print(len(valid_dataset))
print("Number of compounds in test set")
print(len(test_dataset))
print("Number of compounds in crystal set")
print(len(crystal_dataset))

transformers = [
  dc.trans.NormalizationTransformer(transform_X=True,
dataset=train_dataset),
  dc.trans.ClippingTransformer(transform_X=True, dataset=train_dataset)]

datasets = [train_dataset, valid_dataset, test_dataset, crystal_dataset]
for i, dataset in enumerate(datasets):
  for transformer in transformers:
    datasets[i] = transformer.transform(dataset)
train_dataset, valid_dataset, test_dataset, crystal_dataset = datasets
```

Import `RandomForestRegressor` from scikit-learn:

```
from sklearn.ensemble import RandomForestRegressor

def rf_model_builder(model_params, model_dir):
  sklearn_model = RandomForestRegressor(**model_params)
  return dc.models.SklearnModel(sklearn_model, model_dir)
params_dict = {
  "n_estimators": [10, 100],
  "max_features": ["auto", "sqrt", "log2", None],
}

metric = dc.metrics.Metric(dc.metrics.r2_score)
optimizer = dc.hyper.HyperparamOpt(rf_model_builder)
best_rf, best_rf_hyperparams, all_rf_results = optimizer.hyperparam_search(
  params_dict, train_dataset, valid_dataset, transformers,
  metric=metric)

params_dict = {"learning_rate": np.power(10., np.random.uniform(-5, -3,
size=2)), "weight_decay_penalty": np.power(10, np.random.uniform(-6, -4,
size=2)), "nb_epoch": [20] }
```

Note the `learning_rate` parameter.

Display the RF training set scores:

```
n_features = train_dataset.get_data_shape()[0]
def model_builder(model_params, model_dir):
  model = dc.models.MultitaskRegressor(
  1, n_features, layer_sizes=[1000], dropouts=[.25], batch_size=50,
**model_params)
  return model
optimizer = dc.hyper.HyperparamOpt(model_builder)
best_dnn, best_dnn_hyperparams, all_dnn_results =
optimizer.hyperparam_search(params_dict, train_dataset, valid_dataset,
transformers, metric=metric)

rf_train_csv_out = "rf_train_regressor.csv"
rf_train_stats_out = "rf_train_stats_regressor.txt"
rf_train_evaluator = Evaluator(best_rf, train_dataset, transformers)
rf_train_score = rf_train_evaluator.compute_model_performance(
  [metric], rf_train_csv_out, rf_train_stats_out)
print("RF Train set R^2 %f" % (rf_train_score["r2_score"]))
```

Display the RF validation set score:

```
rf_valid_csv_out = "rf_valid_regressor.csv"
rf_valid_stats_out = "rf_valid_stats_regressor.txt"
rf_valid_evaluator = Evaluator(best_rf, valid_dataset, transformers)
rf_valid_score = rf_valid_evaluator.compute_model_performance(
  [metric], rf_valid_csv_out, rf_valid_stats_out)
print("RF Valid set R^2 %f" % (rf_valid_score["r2_score"]))
```

Display the RF test set and crystal set scores:

```
rf_test_csv_out = "rf_test_regressor.csv"
rf_test_stats_out = "rf_test_stats_regressor.txt"
rf_test_evaluator = Evaluator(best_rf, test_dataset, transformers)
rf_test_score = rf_test_evaluator.compute_model_performance(
  [metric], rf_test_csv_out, rf_test_stats_out)
print("RF Test set R^2 %f" % (rf_test_score["r2_score"]))
Random forest crystal structures' set score:

rf_crystal_csv_out = "rf_crystal_regressor.csv"
rf_crystal_stats_out = "rf_crystal_stats_regressor.txt"
rf_crystal_evaluator = Evaluator(best_rf, crystal_dataset, transformers)
rf_crystal_score = rf_crystal_evaluator.compute_model_performance(
  [metric], rf_crystal_csv_out, rf_crystal_stats_out)
print("RF Crystal set R^2 %f" % (rf_crystal_score["r2_score"]))

dnn_train_csv_out = "dnn_train_regressor.csv"
dnn_train_stats_out = "dnn_train_regressor_stats.txt"
```

Display the DNN training set score:

```
dnn_train_evaluator = Evaluator(best_dnn, train_dataset, transformers)
dnn_train_score = dnn_train_evaluator.compute_model_performance(
    [metric], dnn_train_csv_out, dnn_train_stats_out)
print("DNN Train set R^2 %f" % (dnn_train_score["r2_score"]))
```

Display the DNN validation set score:

```
dnn_valid_csv_out = "dnn_valid_regressor.csv"
dnn_valid_stats_out = "dnn_valid_regressor_stats.txt"
dnn_valid_evaluator = Evaluator(best_dnn, valid_dataset, transformers)
dnn_valid_score = dnn_valid_evaluator.compute_model_performance(
    [metric], dnn_valid_csv_out, dnn_valid_stats_out)
print("DNN Valid set R^2 %f" % (dnn_valid_score["r2_score"]))
```

Display the DNN test set score:

```
dnn_test_csv_out = "dnn_test_regressor.csv"
dnn_test_stats_out = "dnn_test_regressor_stats.txt"
dnn_test_evaluator = Evaluator(best_dnn, test_dataset, transformers)
dnn_test_score = dnn_test_evaluator.compute_model_performance(
    [metric], dnn_test_csv_out, dnn_test_stats_out)
print("DNN Test set R^2 %f" % (dnn_test_score["r2_score"]))
```

Display the DNN crystal set score:

```
dnn_crystal_csv_out = "dnn_crystal_regressor.csv"
dnn_crystal_stats_out = "dnn_crystal_stats_regressor.txt"
dnn_crystal_evaluator = Evaluator(best_dnn, crystal_dataset, transformers)
dnn_crystal_score = dnn_crystal_evaluator.compute_model_performance(
    [metric], dnn_crystal_csv_out, dnn_crystal_stats_out)
print("DNN Crystal set R^2 %f" % (dnn_crystal_score["r2_score"]))
```

Predicting `IC50` versus `Secondary Assay` based on RFs is executed as follows:

```
task = "pIC50"
rf_predicted_test = best_rf.predict(test_dataset)
rf_true_test = test_dataset.y
plot.scatter(rf_predicted_test, rf_true_test)
plot.xlabel('Predicted pIC50s')
plot.ylabel('Secondary Assay')
plot.title(r'RF predicted IC50 vs. Secondary Assay')
plot.xlim([2, 11])
plot.ylim([2, 11])
plot.plot([2, 11], [2, 11], color='k')
plot.show()
```

This will show the following histogram:

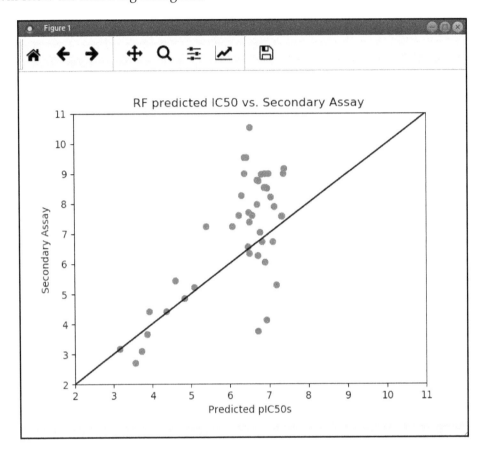

Predicting `IC50` versus `Secondary Assay` based on deep neural networks is executed as follows:

```
dnn_predicted_test = best_dnn.predict(test_dataset, transformers)
dnn_true_test = test_dataset.y
plot.scatter(dnn_predicted_test, dnn_true_test)
plot.xlabel('Predicted pIC50s')
plot.ylabel('Secondary Assay')
plot.title(r'DNN predicted IC50 vs. Secondary Assay')
plot.xlim([2, 11])
plot.ylim([2, 11])
plot.plot([2, 11], [2, 11], color='k')
plot.show()
```

DNN prediction reveals another histogram:

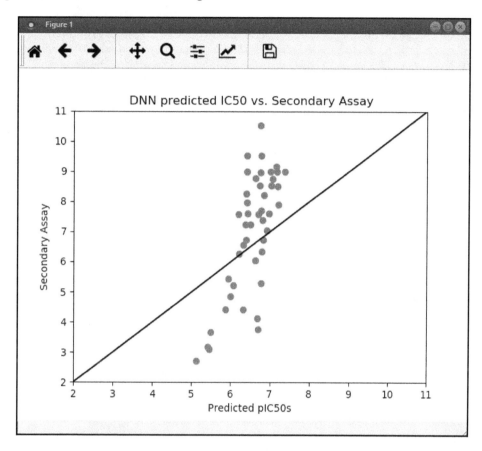

Note that for each of the preceding two histograms, there are a different set of `pIC50` distributions, based on different small molecules from our datasets. The RF prediction is clearly more accurate, showing us a `pIC50` value near 3. Remember, the lesser the value, the better its druggability against the disease.

Output on the PyCharm console

The complete output on the PyCharm execution console for the entire code just shown is collectively as shown hereafter. When running the code on your own computer, you can use it as a reference for tallying.

From this point onward, the output has been split into blocks for clarity.

In the first block, the molecule examples in the dataset number `1522`:

```
/home/avimanyu/miniconda3/envs/DeepChem/lib/python3.6/site-
packages/sklearn/ensemble/weight_boosting.py:29: DeprecationWarning:
numpy.core.umath_tests is an internal NumPy module and should not be
imported. It will be removed in a future NumPy release.
 from numpy.core.umath_tests import inner1d
Columns of dataset:
['mol','CID','Class','Model','pIC50','MW','AlogP','HBA','HBD','RB',...]
Number of examples in dataset: 1522
Number of examples in crystal dataset: 25
<IPython.core.display.Image object>
. . . . . . . . . . . . . . . . . . . . .
```

Whenever the `.png` images will be generated, you'll notice `<IPython.core.display.Image object>` on PyCharm.

Now, let's look at the second block.

Load the CSV file from `crystal_desc_canvas_aug30.csv`:

```
QGtkStyle could not resolve GTK. Make sure you have installed the proper
libraries.XmbTextListToTextProperty result code -2
XmbTextListToTextProperty result code -2
XmbTextListToTextProperty result code -2
Loading raw samples now.
shard_size: 8192
About to start loading CSV from desc_canvas_aug30.csv
Loading shard 1 of size 8192.
TIMING: user specified processing took 0.098 s
TIMING: featurizing shard 0 took 0.124 s
TIMING: dataset construction took 0.326 s
Loading dataset from disk.
Loading raw samples now.
shard_size: 8192
About to start loading CSV from crystal_desc_canvas_aug30.csv
```

Load the dataset from disk and report the construction times:

```
Loading shard 1 of size 8192.
TIMING: user specified processing took 0.090 s
TIMING: featurizing shard 0 took 0.090 s
TIMING: dataset construction took 0.119 s
Loading dataset from disk.
TIMING: dataset construction took 0.033 s
Loading dataset from disk.
```

```
TIMING: dataset construction took 0.024 s
Loading dataset from disk.
TIMING: dataset construction took 0.096 s
Loading dataset from disk.
```

These are molecules represented in Python code:

```
['S(=O)(=O)(N(C)c1cc(cc(c1)C(=O)NC(C(O)CC(OC)C(=O)NC(C(C)C)C(=O)NCc1ccccc1)
COc1cc(F)cc(F)c1)C(=O)NC(C)c1ccccc1)C''O=C(NCCC(C)(C)C)C(Cc1cc2cc(ccc2nc1N)
-
c1ccccc1C)C''Fc1cc(cc(F)c1)CC(NC(=O)C(N1CCC(NC(=O)C)(C(CC)C)C1=O)CCc1ccccc1
)C(O)C1[NH2+]CC(O)C1'...
'Brc1cc(ccc1)C1CC1C=1N=C(N)N(C)C(=O)C=1''O=C1N(C)C(=NC(=C1)C1CC1c1cc(ccc1)-
c1ccccc1)N''Clc1cc2nc(n(c2cc1)CCCC(=O)NCC1CC1)N']
```

Note the preceding representation of molecules in textual format.

There are 1,273 compounds in the validation set:

```
<IPython.core.display.Image object>
. . . . . . . . . . . . . . . .
Number of compounds in train set
204
Number of compounds in validation set
1273
Number of compounds in test set
45
Number of compounds in crystal set
25
/home/avimanyu/miniconda3/envs/DeepChem/lib/python3.6/site-
packages/deepchem/trans/transformers.py:148: RuntimeWarning: invalid value
encountered in true_divide
  X = np.nan_to_num((X - self.X_means) / self.X_stds)
TIMING: dataset construction took 0.019 s
Loading dataset from disk.
```

The timing for dataset construction is shown as follows:

```
TIMING: dataset construction took 0.013 s
Loading dataset from disk.
/home/avimanyu/miniconda3/envs/DeepChem/lib/python3.6/site-
packages/deepchem/trans/transformers.py:148: RuntimeWarning: divide by zero
encountered in true_divide
  X = np.nan_to_num((X - self.X_means) / self.X_stds)
TIMING: dataset construction took 0.132 s
```

```
Loading dataset from disk.
TIMING: dataset construction took 0.061 s
Loading dataset from disk.
TIMING: dataset construction took 0.006 s
Loading dataset from disk.
TIMING: dataset construction took 0.005 s
Loading dataset from disk.
TIMING: dataset construction took 0.005 s
Loading dataset from disk.
TIMING: dataset construction took 0.004 s
Loading dataset from disk.
```

The following snippet shows the output for fitting eight models:

 Note the validation score.

```
Fitting model 1/8
hyperparameters: {'n_estimators': 10, 'max_features': 'auto'}
computed_metrics: [0.7609515059498972]
Model 1/8, Metric roc_auc_score, Validation set 0: 0.760952
    best_validation_score so far: 0.760952
Fitting model 2/8
hyperparameters: {'n_estimators': 10, 'max_features': 'sqrt'}
computed_metrics: [0.723191527869248]
Model 2/8, Metric roc_auc_score, Validation set 1: 0.723192
    best_validation_score so far: 0.760952
Fitting model 3/8
hyperparameters: {'n_estimators': 10, 'max_features': 'log2'}
computed_metrics: [0.731709784778117]
Model 3/8, Metric roc_auc_score, Validation set 2: 0.731710
    best_validation_score so far: 0.760952
```

In this block, we see that the validation score is changing:

```
Fitting model 4/8
hyperparameters: {'n_estimators': 10, 'max_features': None}
computed_metrics: [0.7629197228911423]
Model 4/8, Metric roc_auc_score, Validation set 3: 0.762920
    best_validation_score so far: 0.762920
Fitting model 5/8
hyperparameters: {'n_estimators': 100, 'max_features': 'auto'}
computed_metrics: [0.7813858962048353]
Model 5/8, Metric roc_auc_score, Validation set 4: 0.781386
    best_validation_score so far: 0.781386
Fitting model 6/8
```

```
hyperparameters: {'n_estimators': 100, 'max_features': 'sqrt'}
computed_metrics: [0.7866966884687121]
Model 6/8, Metric roc_auc_score, Validation set 5: 0.786697
    best_validation_score so far: 0.786697
```

The best validation score so far is 0.794502:

```
Fitting model 7/8
hyperparameters: {'n_estimators': 100, 'max_features': 'log2'}
computed_metrics: [0.7945023151057509]
Model 7/8, Metric roc_auc_score, Validation set 6: 0.794502
    best_validation_score so far: 0.794502
Fitting model 8/8
hyperparameters: {'n_estimators': 100, 'max_features': None}
computed_metrics: [0.7728161087119364]
Model 8/8, Metric roc_auc_score, Validation set 7: 0.772816
    best_validation_score so far: 0.794502
computed_metrics: [0.9998077662437523]
Best hyperparameters: (100, 'log2')
train_score: 0.999808
validation_score: 0.794502
Fitting model 1/1
```

CPU information is revealed here, informing us that this version of TensorFlow was not compiled to use:

```
hyperparameters: {'learning_rate': 0.00021151802893473398,
'weight_decay_penalty': 2.722873994359937e-05, 'nb_epoch': 40}
2019-04-17 21:06:56.302642: I
tensorflow/core/platform/cpu_feature_guard.cc:140] Your CPU supports
instructions that this TensorFlow binary was not compiled to use: SSE4.1
SSE4.2 AVX AVX2 FMA
2019-04-17 21:06:56.390492: I
tensorflow/stream_executor/cuda/cuda_gpu_executor.cc:898] successful NUMA
node read from SysFS had negative value (-1), but there must be at least
one NUMA node, so returning NUMA node zero
```

Note
the `tensorflow/stream_executor/cuda/cuda_gpu_executor.cc` in the output.

GPU information is revealed as follow:

```
2019-04-17 21:06:56.390816: I
tensorflow/core/common_runtime/gpu/gpu_device.cc:1212] Found device 0 with
properties:
name: GeForce GTX TITAN X major: 5 minor: 2 memoryClockRate(GHz): 1.076
```

```
pciBusID: 0000:01:00.0
totalMemory: 11.92GiB freeMemory: 11.65GiB
2019-04-17 21:06:56.390828: I
tensorflow/core/common_runtime/gpu/gpu_device.cc:1312]
Adding visible gpu devices: 0
2019-04-17 21:06:57.089654: I
tensorflow/core/common_runtime/gpu/gpu_device.cc:993] Creating TensorFlow
device (/job:localhost/replica:0/task:0/device:GPU:0 with 11280 MB memory)
-> physical GPU (device: 0, name: GeForce GTX TITAN X, pci bus id:
0000:01:00.0, compute capability: 5.2)
```

 Notice that `device:GPU:0` and `compute capability` were also displayed when testing TensorFlow in `Chapter 10`, *Accelerated Machine Learning on GPUs.*

Compute the metrics. These metrics are all based on concepts we learned in the first section of this chapter:

```
computed_metrics: [0.7902491566580029]
Model 1/1, Metric roc_auc_score, Validation set 0: 0.790249
    best_validation_score so far: 0.790249
computed_metrics: [0.9544405997693195]
Best hyperparameters: (0.00021151802893473398, 2.722873994359937e-05, 40)
train_score: 0.954441
validation_score: 0.790249
computed_metrics: [0.9998077662437523]
RF Train set AUC 0.999808
computed_metrics: [0.7945023151057509]
RF Valid set AUC 0.794502
computed_metrics: [0.43181818181818177]
RF Test set AUC 0.431818
/home/avimanyu/miniconda3/envs/DeepChem/lib/python3.6/site-
packages/deepchem/metrics/__init__.py:312: UserWarning: Error calculating
metric roc_auc_score: Only one class present in
```

The scores for different sets are shown as follows:

```
 y_true. ROC AUC score is not defined in that case.
 warnings.warn("Error calculating metric %s: %s" % (self.name, e))
computed_metrics: [nan]
RF Crystal set R^2 nan
computed_metrics: [0.9544405997693195]
DNN Train set AUC 0.954441
computed_metrics: [0.7902491566580029]
DNN Valid set AUC 0.790249
computed_metrics: [0.4545454545454546]
DNN Test set AUC 0.454545
```

```
computed_metrics: [nan]
DNN Crystal set AUC nan
Loading raw samples now.
shard_size: 8192
About to start loading CSV from desc_canvas_aug30.csv
```

Shards are related to horizontal partitioning of data. For more information, click here: https://www.deepchem.io/deepchem.data.html:

```
Loading shard 1 of size 8192.
TIMING: user specified processing took 0.102 s
TIMING: featurizing shard 0 took 0.125 s
TIMING: dataset construction took 0.314 s
Loading dataset from disk.
Loading raw samples now.
shard_size: 8192
About to start loading CSV from crystal_desc_canvas_aug30.csv
Loading shard 1 of size 8192.
TIMING: user specified processing took 0.088 s
TIMING: featurizing shard 0 took 0.088 s
TIMING: dataset construction took 0.118 s
Loading dataset from disk.
TIMING: dataset construction took 0.032 s
Loading dataset from disk.
```

Through the previous code blocks and the ones that follow, we can see the `dataset` construction times:

```
TIMING: dataset construction took 0.023 s
Loading dataset from disk.
TIMING: dataset construction took 0.093 s
Loading dataset from disk.
Number of compounds in train set
204
Number of compounds in validation set
1273
Number of compounds in test set
45
Number of compounds in crystal set
25
/home/avimanyu/miniconda3/envs/DeepChem/lib/python3.6/site-
packages/deepchem/trans/transformers.py:148: RuntimeWarning: invalid value
encountered in true_divide
  X = np.nan_to_num((X - self.X_means) / self.X_stds)
```

Load the dataset from disk:

```
TIMING: dataset construction took 0.022 s
Loading dataset from disk.
TIMING: dataset construction took 0.017 s
Loading dataset from disk.
/home/avimanyu/miniconda3/envs/DeepChem/lib/python3.6/site-
packages/deepchem/trans/transformers.py:148: RuntimeWarning: divide by zero
encountered in true_divide
 X = np.nan_to_num((X - self.X_means) / self.X_stds)
TIMING: dataset construction took 0.097 s
Loading dataset from disk.
TIMING: dataset construction took 0.059 s
Loading dataset from disk.
TIMING: dataset construction took 0.006 s
Loading dataset from disk.
TIMING: dataset construction took 0.005 s
Loading dataset from disk.
```

Remember `model.fit` when we trained our model in TensorFlow? We saw that in `Chapter 11`, *Machine Learning on GPUs – Use Cases*:

```
TIMING: dataset construction took 0.005 s
Loading dataset from disk.
TIMING: dataset construction took 0.004 s
Loading dataset from disk.
Fitting model 1/8
hyperparameters: {'n_estimators': 10, 'max_features': 'auto'}
computed_metrics: [0.18190629948129922]
Model 1/8, Metric r2_score, Validation set 0: 0.181906
   best_validation_score so far: 0.181906
Fitting model 2/8
hyperparameters: {'n_estimators': 10, 'max_features': 'sqrt'}
computed_metrics: [0.3172373086204624]
Model 2/8, Metric r2_score, Validation set 1: 0.317237
   best_validation_score so far: 0.317237
Fitting model 3/8
```

The training continues as follows:

```
hyperparameters: {'n_estimators': 10, 'max_features': 'log2'}
computed_metrics: [0.17452242986326394]
Model 3/8, Metric r2_score, Validation set 2: 0.174522
   best_validation_score so far: 0.317237
Fitting model 4/8
hyperparameters: {'n_estimators': 10, 'max_features': None}
computed_metrics: [0.1925922016731414]
Model 4/8, Metric r2_score, Validation set 3: 0.192592
```

```
    best_validation_score so far: 0.317237
Fitting model 5/8
hyperparameters: {'n_estimators': 100, 'max_features': 'auto'}
computed_metrics: [0.23304574500025754]
Model 5/8, Metric r2_score, Validation set 4: 0.233046
    best_validation_score so far: 0.317237
Fitting model 6/8
```

Finally, the last model is trained:

```
hyperparameters: {'n_estimators': 100, 'max_features': 'sqrt'}
computed_metrics: [0.265387435002302]
Model 6/8, Metric r2_score, Validation set 5: 0.265387
    best_validation_score so far: 0.317237
Fitting model 7/8
hyperparameters: {'n_estimators': 100, 'max_features': 'log2'}
computed_metrics: [0.26943373102232004]
Model 7/8, Metric r2_score, Validation set 6: 0.269434
    best_validation_score so far: 0.317237
Fitting model 8/8
hyperparameters: {'n_estimators': 100, 'max_features': None}
computed_metrics: [0.23785223914232112]
Model 8/8, Metric r2_score, Validation set 7: 0.237852
    best_validation_score so far: 0.317237
computed_metrics: [0.9278750714230614]
```

The training score here is 0.927875:

```
Best hyperparameters: (10, 'sqrt')
train_score: 0.927875
validation_score: 0.317237
Fitting model 1/4
hyperparameters: {'learning_rate': 1.5180799845512146e-05,
'weight_decay_penalty': 3.2526787704215426e-05, 'nb_epoch': 20}
2019-04-17 21:07:02.292824: I
tensorflow/core/common_runtime/gpu/gpu_device.cc:1312] Adding visible gpu
devices: 0
```

 Note that for every step to fit models, there are memory allocations specified for the GPU. In this case, it uses 340 MB. Also, we see the `learning_rate` parameter that we saw in the example source code.

Four models are again being trained here:

```
2019-04-17 21:07:02.292974: I
tensorflow/core/common_runtime/gpu/gpu_device.cc:993] Creating TensorFlow
device (/job:localhost/replica:0/task:0/device:GPU:0 with 340 MB memory) ->
```

```
physical GPU (device: 0, name: GeForce GTX TITAN X, pci bus id:
0000:01:00.0, compute capability: 5.2)
computed_metrics: [0.14680678119321078]
Model 1/4, Metric r2_score, Validation set 0: 0.146807
   best_validation_score so far: 0.146807
Fitting model 2/4
hyperparameters: {'learning_rate': 1.5180799845512146e-05,
'weight_decay_penalty': 7.435273746031895e-06, 'nb_epoch': 20}
2019-04-17 21:07:02.847296: I
tensorflow/core/common_runtime/gpu/gpu_device.cc:1312] Adding visible gpu
devices: 0
2019-04-17 21:07:02.847414: I
tensorflow/core/common_runtime/gpu/gpu_device.cc:993] Creating TensorFlow
device (/job:localhost/replica:0/task:0/device:GPU:0 with 340 MB memory) ->
physical GPU (device: 0, name: GeForce GTX TITAN X, pci bus id:
0000:01:00.0, compute capability: 5.2)
```

The last model is about to be trained:

```
computed_metrics: [0.10237317204510943]
Model 2/4, Metric r2_score, Validation set 1: 0.102373
   best_validation_score so far: 0.146807
Fitting model 3/4
hyperparameters: {'learning_rate': 1.6601776101089376e-05,
'weight_decay_penalty': 3.2526787704215426e-05, 'nb_epoch': 20}
2019-04-17 21:07:03.420227: I
tensorflow/core/common_runtime/gpu/gpu_device.cc:1312]
Adding visible gpu devices: 0
2019-04-17 21:07:03.420337: I
tensorflow/core/common_runtime/gpu/gpu_device.cc:993] Creating TensorFlow
device (/job:localhost/replica:0/task:0/device:GPU:0 with 340 MB memory) ->
physical GPU (device: 0, name: GeForce GTX TITAN X, pci bus id:
0000:01:00.0, compute capability: 5.2)
computed_metrics: [0.09755739017724163]
Model 3/4, Metric r2_score, Validation set 2: 0.097557
   best_validation_score so far: 0.146807
Fitting model 4/4
```

Here, we have the training score, validation score, and computed metrics:

```
hyperparameters: {'learning_rate': 1.6601776101089376e-05,
'weight_decay_penalty': 7.435273746031895e-06, 'nb_epoch': 20}
2019-04-17 21:07:03.927586: I
tensorflow/core/common_runtime/gpu/gpu_device.cc:1312]
Adding visible gpu devices: 0
2019-04-17 21:07:03.927696: I
tensorflow/core/common_runtime/gpu/gpu_device.cc:993] Creating TensorFlow
device (/job:localhost/replica:0/task:0/device:GPU:0 with 340 MB memory) ->
```

```
physical GPU (device: 0, name: GeForce GTX TITAN X, pci bus id:
0000:01:00.0, compute capability: 5.2)
computed_metrics: [0.11598117391019092]
Model 4/4, Metric r2_score, Validation set 3: 0.115981
    best_validation_score so far: 0.146807
computed_metrics: [0.3611376894962157]
Best hyperparameters: (1.5180799845512146e-05, 3.2526787704215426e-05, 20)
train_score: 0.361138
validation_score: 0.146807
computed_metrics: [0.9278750714230614]
```

Here are the RF-based scores and metrics:

```
RF Train set R^2 0.927875
computed_metrics: [0.3172373086204624]
RF Valid set R^2 0.317237
computed_metrics: [0.3297184230952477]
RF Test set R^2 0.329718
computed_metrics: [nan]
RF Crystal set R^2 nan
computed_metrics: [0.3611376894962157]
```

Here are the deep neural network-based scores and metrics:

```
DNN Train set R^2 0.361138
computed_metrics: [0.14680678119321078]
DNN Valid set R^2 0.146807
computed_metrics: [0.24909248602299117]
DNN Test set R^2 0.249092
computed_metrics: [nan]
DNN Crystal set R^2 nan
XmbTextListToTextProperty result code -2
.....
```

Finally, we can confirm that the program executed successfully on the same PyCharm console:

```
Process finished with exit code 0
```

An exit code 0 refers to a clean exit after program execution without problems. An exit code 1 indicates an issue or problem that can make the program exit without completely executing the program.

Now, let's look into how we can replicate such a vast framework and develop one of our own, for applied computing with deep learning.

Developing your own deep learning framework like DeepChem – a brief outlook

Developing your own machine learning or deep learning framework requires perseverance, patience, and hard work. To get started with such an exciting new journey, you can start with a simple hands-on approach.

All developmental files for DeepChem installed with Conda are located at `/home/user/miniconda3/envs/DeepChem/lib/python3.6/site-packages/deepchem`:

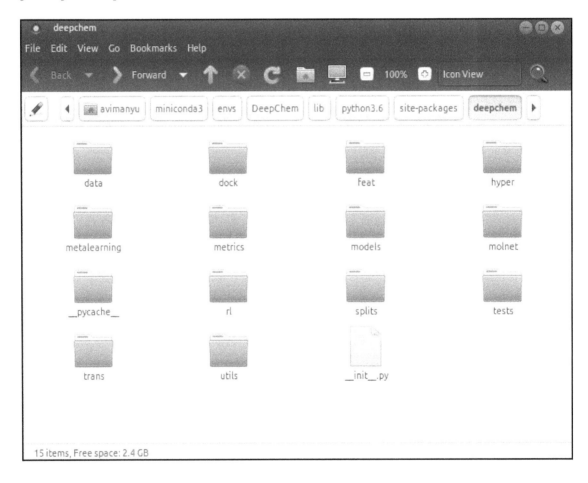

Let's open and see the contents of __init__.py on PyCharm:

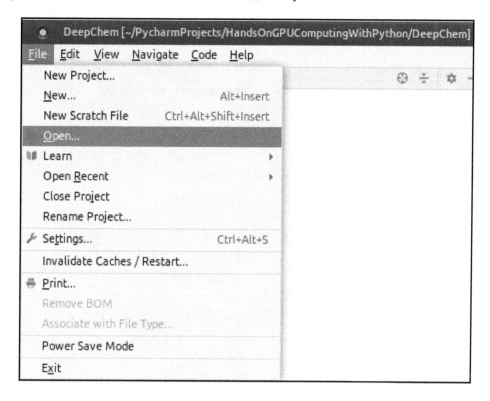

Open `__init__.py`:

So, here are the various modules of DeepChem:

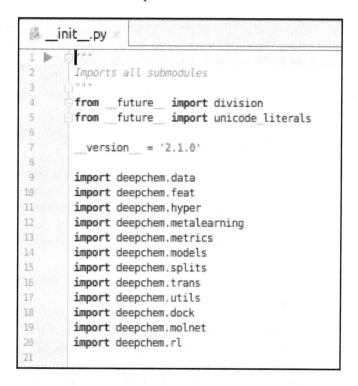

As you can see here, this is only one file. Each of the directories that we see (the first screenshot in this section) contains code on every submodule. You can start checking all of these submodules (directories) and get started with the development of a DeepChem-based framework. A thorough study of each and every documented code among these submodules is very important for replicating such a vast directory structure and building on it to create a version of your own. Please look into the reference papers at the end of this chapter to learn how to get started.

Summary

In our final chapter, we discussed all the necessary concepts required for you to get started with molecular deep learning through DeepChem. We also saw multiple ways of installing and configuring DeepChem locally or on the cloud on a tensor core-based GPU. You learned the basic steps to set up your PyCharm environment. Finally, you read about a simple hands-on approach to get started with developing your own deep learning framework.

From now on, you can practically apply GPU-enabled deep learning with Python for helping society in several scientific ways. You can now learn, work, and develop your own models with DeepChem through Colab, Anaconda, or Docker, and also locally validate an existing DeepChem Conda environment on PyCharm to develop learning models. You now know how drug prediction works as a combination of graph convolutional neural networks and one-shot learning. Also, you can now independently begin the development of a new machine learning framework such as DeepChem.

Final thoughts

I hope you found the book interesting and helpful. Please go ahead and start getting involved with the computing and deep learning community, especially with an open source approach. Please remember that, the application of GPU computing, deep learning, or any other technology is most effective only when applied in the right manner and in the right situation. So, the application of technology becomes more important than the technology itself. I really hope this book brings computer scientists much closer toward application scientists for better collaboration. I wish you all the best in your academic and learning endeavors!

Let's conclude with the following quote from Edgar Dijkstra, the creator of the famous *Dijkstra Algorithm*:

> *"Computer science is no more about computers than astronomy is about telescopes, biology is about microscopes, or chemistry is about beakers and test tubes. Science is not about tools. It is about how we use them, and what we find out when we do."*

References

The following articles serve as references to this chapter and can be used to learn more about the topics discussed in this chapter:

- *Deep Learning for the Life Sciences*, B Ramsundar, P Eastman, P Walters, V Pande, K Leswing, and Z Wu (2019). O'Reilly Media (online). Available at `https://www.amazon.com/Deep-Learning-Life-Sciences-Microscopy/dp/1492039837`.

- *Introduction to Computer Science using Python: A Computational Problem-Solving Focus*, 1st ed, C Dierbach (2015), Wiley (online). Available at `https://www.amazon.in/gp/product/8126556013/`

- *How does your body process medicine?*, Valéry, C. (2017). (online) TED-Ed. Available at `https://ed.ted.com/lessons/how-does-your-body-process-medicine-celine-valery`.

- *Molecular Modeling and Drug Design*, K A Solomon (2008), MJP Publishers (online). Available at `https://www.amazon.in/Molecular-Modelling-Design-Anand-Solomon/dp/8180940608/`.

- *MoleculeNet: a Benchmark for Molecular Machine Learning*, Z Wu, B Ramsundar, E Feinberg, J Gomes, C Geniesse, A Pappu, K Leswing, V Pande (2018), *Chemical Science*, 9(2), pp. 513-530 (online). Available at `https://pubs.rsc.org/en/content/articlehtml/2018/sc/c7sc02664a`.

- *Is Multitask Deep Learning Practical for Pharma?*, B Ramsundar, B Liu, Z Wu, A Verras, M Tudor, R Sheridan, V Pande (2017), Journal of Chemical Information and Modeling, 57(8), pp. 2,068-2,076 (online). Available at `https://pubs.acs.org/doi/abs/10.1021/acs.jcim.7b00146`.

- *One-Shot Learning with Siamese Networks using Keras*, H Lamba (2019) (online) *Towards Data Science*. Available at `https://towardsdatascience.com/one-shot-learning-with-siamese-networks-using-keras-17f34e75bb3d`.

- *Low Data Drug Discovery with One-Shot Learning*, H Altae-Tran, B Ramsundar, A Pappu, V Pande (2017), *ACS Central Science*, 3(4), pp. 283-293 (online). Available at `https://pubs.acs.org/doi/full/10.1021/acscentsci.6b00367`.

- *Computational Modeling of β-Secretase 1 (BACE-1) Inhibitors Using Ligand Based Approaches*, G Subramanian, B Ramsundar, V Pande, R Denny (2016), *Journal of Chemical Information and Modeling*, 56(10), pp. 1,936-1,949 (online). Available at `https://pubs.acs.org/doi/abs/10.1021/acs.jcim.6b00290`.

- *Exploitation of Massively Parallel Architectures for Drug Discovery*, H Pérez Sánchez (2013), *Drug Designing: Open Access*, 02(01). (online). Available at `doi.org/10.4172/2169-0138.1000e108`.

- *Why Should Drug Discovery Be Open Source?*, B Ramsundar (2017) (online) `rbharath.github.io`. Available at `https://rbharath.github.io/why-should-drug-discovery-be-open-source/`.

- *Understanding Disease with Tabula Muris – The Open Source Database via Chan Zuckerberg Biohub*, A Bandyopadhyay (2018) (online), *It's FOSS*. Available at `https://itsfoss.com/understanding-disease-with-tabula-muris/`

- *How Netflix Deploys Open Source AI to Reveal Your Favorites*, A Bandyopadhyay (2018) (online), *It's FOSS*. Available at `https://itsfoss.com/netflix-open-source-ai/`.

- *How Open Source Approach is Impacting Science*, A Bandyopadhyay (2018) (online), *It's FOSS*. Available at `https://itsfoss.com/open-source-impact-on-science/`.

- *Working with GPUs for Accelerated Computing: An Open Source Approach*, A Bandyopadhyay (2019) (online) GizmoQuest Computing Lab. Available at `https://www.gizmoquest.com/2019/04/Computing-Everywhere.html`.

Appendix A

It is interesting to note that neither **NVIDIA** or **AMD** identify itself as a GPU manufacturing company. In fact, NVIDIA identifies itself as an AI computing company, whereas AMD calls itself a semiconductor company. In the first chapter, we looked at various examples in diverse research areas to understand how GPUs empower science and AI. Let's revisit that perspective in terms of GPU-accelerated Python for AI computing. Through three specific examples in AI research, we'll explore different endeavors to perform computational problem solving by deploying AI.

GPU-accelerated machine learning in Python – benchmark research

A study in Boston optimized a set of machine learning algorithms on a GPU. It revealed the performance of two popular GPU integration tools developed in Python, namely, **Cython** and **PyCUDA**. Utilizing the GPU's parallel performance advantages, speedups of 20 times - 200 times over the multi-threaded Scikit Learn (a machine learning library for the Python) CPU-based implementations were highlighted. It also specifically addresses the need for GPUs due to the growing sizes of emerging datasets:

Image by Tumisu (https://pixabay.com/users/tumisu-148124/) from Pixabay.com

For more information, you can refer to the research paper given here:

Accelerating Machine Learning Algorithms in Python. Boston Area Architecture Workshop, P Reilly, L Yu, L, D Kaeli (2017):
www1.coe.neu.edu/~ylm/Files/ml_pycuda_barc2017.pdf.

GPU-accelerated machine learning with Python applied to cancer research

Cancer is gradually claiming more lives in the world than any other disease. There are many types of cancer that affects a human body such as lung, stomach, throat, and liver. In today's scientific age, cancer research has made major technological breakthroughs in the areas of molecular sequencing, molecular and cellular imaging, and high-throughput screening techniques. Such techniques have resulted in the creation of an enormous number of datasets. The analysis of these datasets can be now possible with the help of automated machine learning to understand the disease better.

You can further refer to the following research paper and gain better understanding. This paper talks about the use of Python and GPUs toward the implementation of a workflow framework named **CANDLE**/Supervisor for machine learning and apply it toward cancer research:

CANDLE/Supervisor: a workflow framework for machine learning applied to cancer research, J Wozniak, R Jain, P Balaprakash, J Ozik, N Collier, J Bauer, F Xia, T Brettin, R Stevens, J Mohd-Yusof, C Cardona, B Essen, M Baughman (2018), *BMC Bioinformatics*, 19(S18). doi.org/10.1186/s12859-018-2508-4.

Deep Learning with GPU-accelerated Python for applied computer vision – Pavement Distress

Let's now talk about applications in computer vision for image detection. Note the following photo of a pavement. It is cracked and damaged:

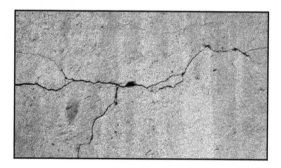

Image via pxhere.com, CC0

Here is another one, it is cracked but in a different manner.

Image via pxhere.com, CC0

There can be many more such images collectively referred to as **datasets**. You can find more here: pxhere.com/en/photo/690701.

The previous pavement photos were captured with a Sony Cybershot DSC-RX100M4 20.1 Megapixel digital camera on 03/09/2017. Python can make use of GPUs to accelerate deep learning and classify/identify such images. It is one of the many applications in computer vision.

The following paper is a review on pavement distress detection. It talks about computer vision-based automated pavement distress detection with deep learning. In the review paper, table 3 enlists the performance of different detection techniques with Python-based deep learning frameworks such as Tensorflow, Theano and many others on various NVIDIA GPUs. The review concludes by highlighting the potential avenues of deep learning to not only detect, but also characterize the type, extent, and severity of distresses from 2D and 3D pavement images. This statement specifically distinguishes between the training and inference concept, and that is very important to understand deep learning. We will explore it further later in this chapter.

Here's the citation for the research paper:

Deep Learning in Data-Driven Pavement Image Analysis and Automated Distress Detection: A Review, K Gopalakrishnan (2018). *Data, 3(3), p.28. doi.org/10.3390/data3030028*

Other Books You May Enjoy

If you enjoyed this book, you may be interested in these other books by Packt:

Hands-On GPU-Accelerated Computer Vision with OpenCV and CUDA
Bhaumik Vaidya

ISBN: 9781789348293

- Understand how to access GPU device properties and capabilities from CUDA programs
- Learn how to accelerate searching and sorting algorithms
- Detect shapes such as lines and circles in images
- Explore object tracking and detection with algorithms
- Process videos using different video analysis techniques in Jetson TX1
- Access GPU device properties from the PyCUDA program
- Understand how kernel execution works

Learn OpenCV 4 By Building Projects - Second Edition
David Millán Escrivá, Vinícius G. Mendonça, Prateek Joshi

ISBN: 9781789341225

- Install OpenCV 4 on your operating system
- Create CMake scripts to compile your C++ application
- Understand basic image matrix formats and filters
- Explore segmentation and feature extraction techniques
- Remove backgrounds from static scenes to identify moving objects for surveillance
- Employ various techniques to track objects in a live video
- Work with new OpenCV functions for text detection and recognition with Tesseract
- Get acquainted with important deep learning tools for image classification

Leave a review - let other readers know what you think

Please share your thoughts on this book with others by leaving a review on the site that you bought it from. If you purchased the book from Amazon, please leave us an honest review on this book's Amazon page. This is vital so that other potential readers can see and use your unbiased opinion to make purchasing decisions, we can understand what our customers think about our products, and our authors can see your feedback on the title that they have worked with Packt to create. It will only take a few minutes of your time, but is valuable to other potential customers, our authors, and Packt. Thank you!

Index

grids 113
guests 276

H

HairWorks 19
hard disk drive (HDD) 59
Hardware Accelerated Cosmology Code (HACC)
   121
HCC
   reference link 118
Heterogeneous System Architecture (HSA) 81,
   239
high airflow 55
high performance computing (HPC) 25, 43
high static pressure 55
high-end budget 67
HIP
   reduction with 223
histogram 368
host 276
host code 113
hydroxyl group 360

I

IC50 381
InfiniBand adapters 80
Information Technology eXtended (ITX) 39
inhibitor 364
Integrated Circuits (ICs) 11
Integrated Development Environment (IDE),
      features
   automated refactoring 132
   integrated debugger 132
   intelligent editor 132
   version control integration 132
Integrated Development Environment (IDE), with
      Python
   Eric 136
   Jupyter Lab 135
   Jupyter Notebook 135
   PyCharm 133
   PyDev 134
   Python IDE, for Eclipse 134
Integrated Development Environment (IDE)
   about 131

   for Python 149
   selecting, for Python code 132
Integrated graphics 13
inter-chip Global Memory Interconnect (xGMI) 85
IronPython 134

J

Jetson Nano 49
Jupyter Lab
   installing 153
Jupyter Notebook
   installing 153
just-in-time (JIT) 238

K

Kepler architecture 44
Keras 17, 328
kernel code
   identity value 262
   mapping expression 262
   post mapping expression 262
   reduction expression 262
kernels explicitly
   writing 253
Kier Benzene-Likeliness Index (KBLI) 371
Kubernetes 271, 289, 290

L

labeled datasets 330
LiClipse 149
   URL, for downloading 151
ligand 364
liquid cooling
   about 45, 48, 49
   aftermarket coolers 47
   airflow management 46
   conventional air cooling 47
   custom coolers 47
   overclocking 47
   specific heat capacity, of cooling agents 48
   stock coolers 47
   temperature factor 46
   thermal paste 46
Llano 76
local containerization 284

local containers 284

M

N

O